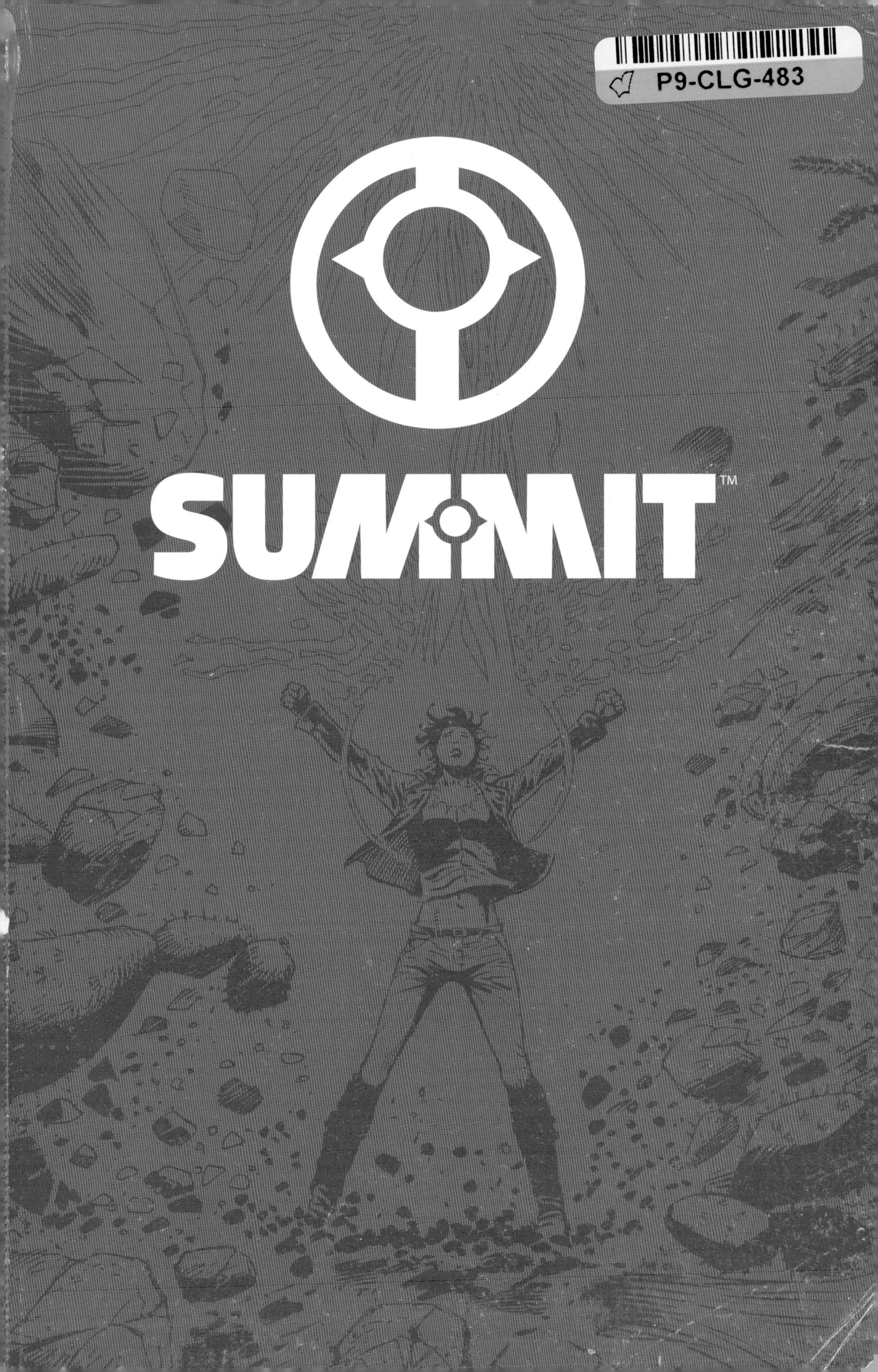
SUMMIT™

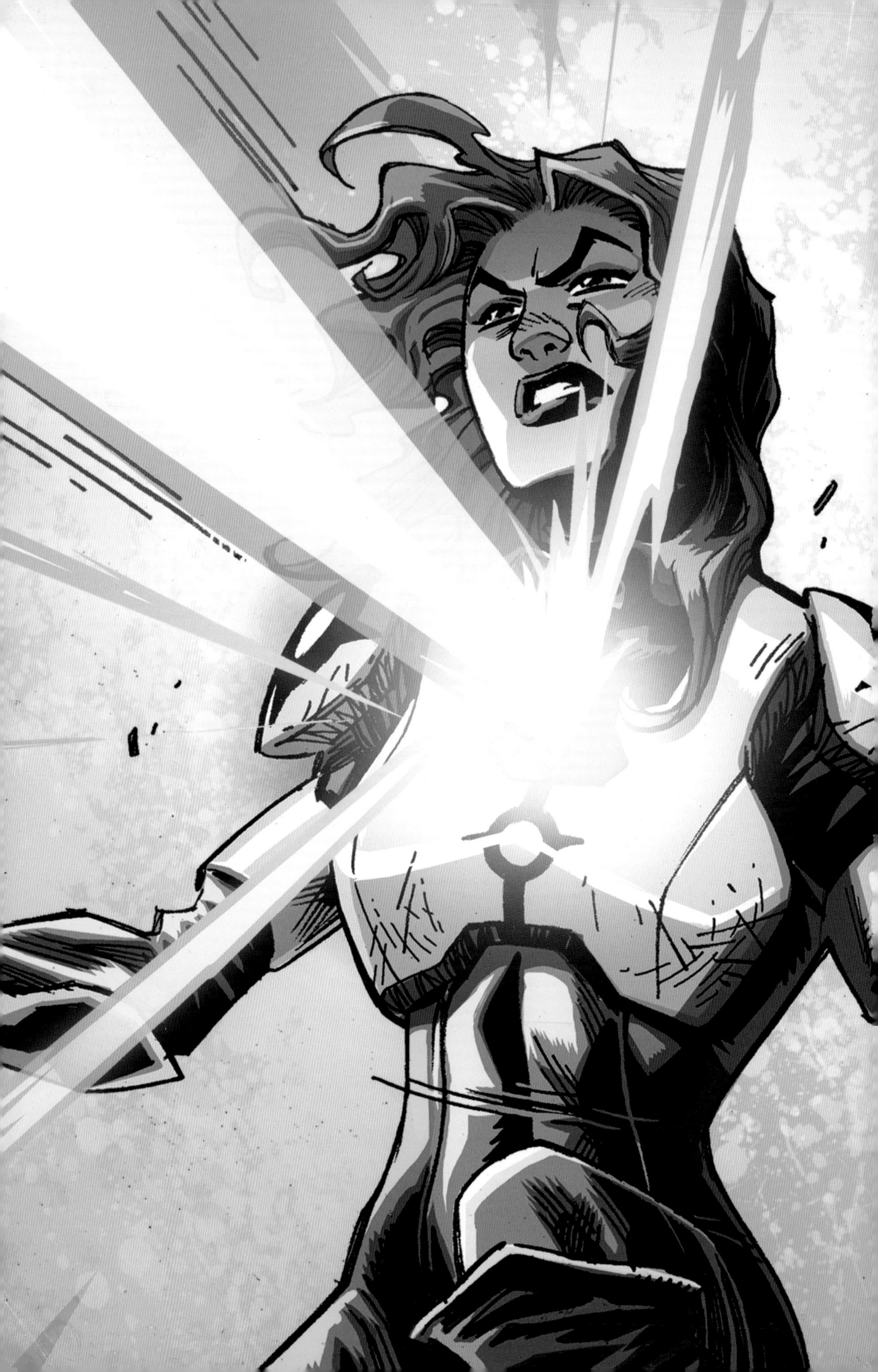

SUMMIT™

THE LONG WAY HOME

written by **AMY CHU**
illustrated by **JAN DUURSEMA**
lettered by **DERON BENNETT** and **AW'S TOM NAPOLITANO**
colored by **PAUL MOUNTS** and **KELLY FITZPATRICK**

JOSEPH ILLIDGE · senior editor
DESIREE RODRIGUEZ · editorial assistant
cover by **JAN DUURSEMA** and **PAUL MOUNTS**

ISBN: 978-1-941302-68-2

Library of Congress Control Number: 2018931324

Summit Vol. 1, published 2018, by The Lion Forge, LLC. Copyright 2018 The Lion Forge, LLC. Portions of this book were previously published in Summit Vol. 1, Issues 1-4 and FCBD 2017 Catalyst Prime: The Event copyright 2017 The Lion Forge, LLC. All Rights Reserved. SUMMIT™, LION FORGE™, CATALYST PRIME™, and their associated distinctive designs, as well as all characters featured in this book and the distinctive names and likenesses thereof, and all related indicia, are trademarks of The Lion Forge, LLC. No similarity between any of the names, characters, persons, or institutions in this issue with those of any living or dead person or institution is intended, and any such similarity which may exist is purely coincidental. Printed in Korea.

10 9 8 7 6 5 4 3 2 1

CHAPTER ONE

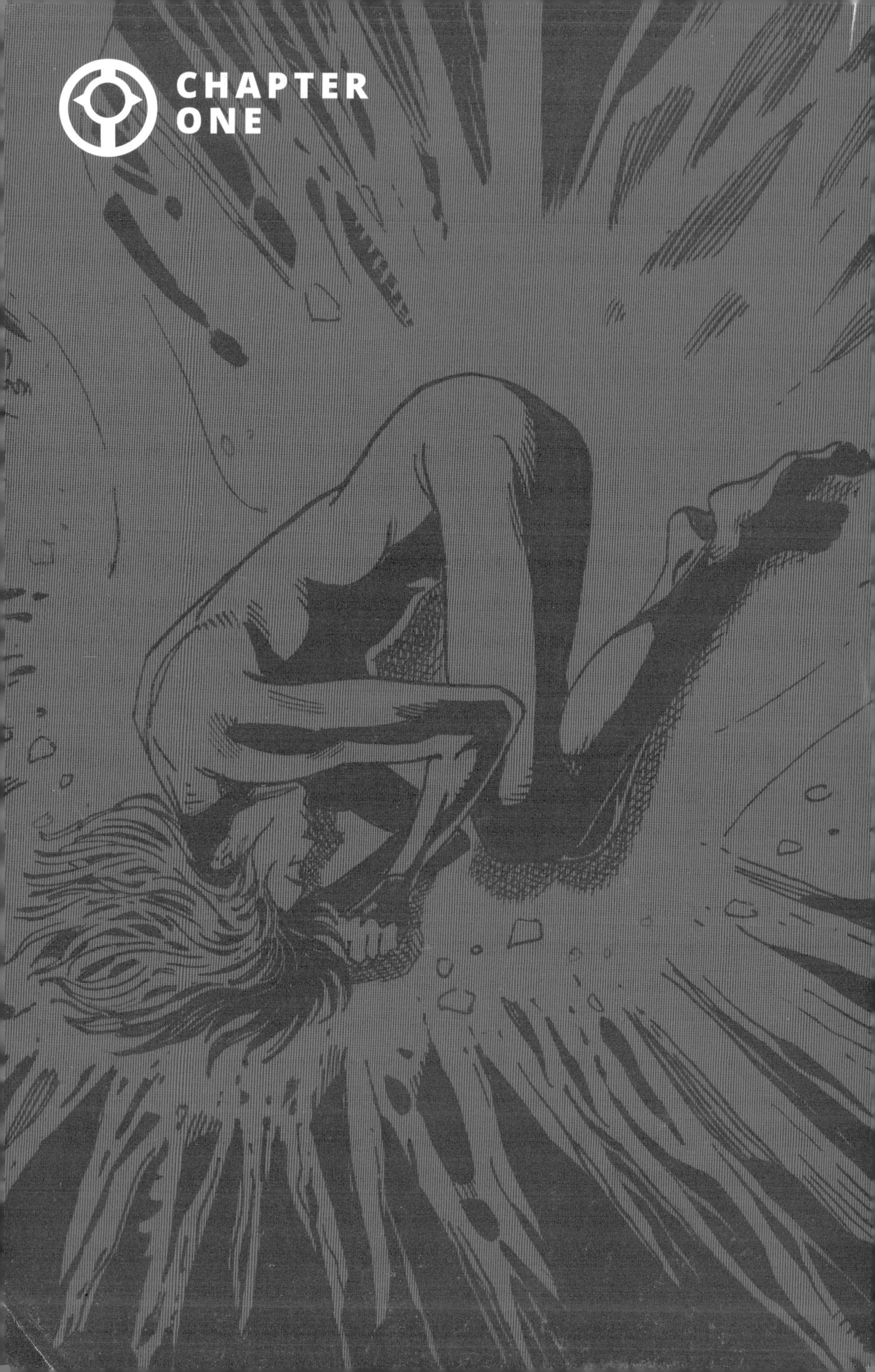

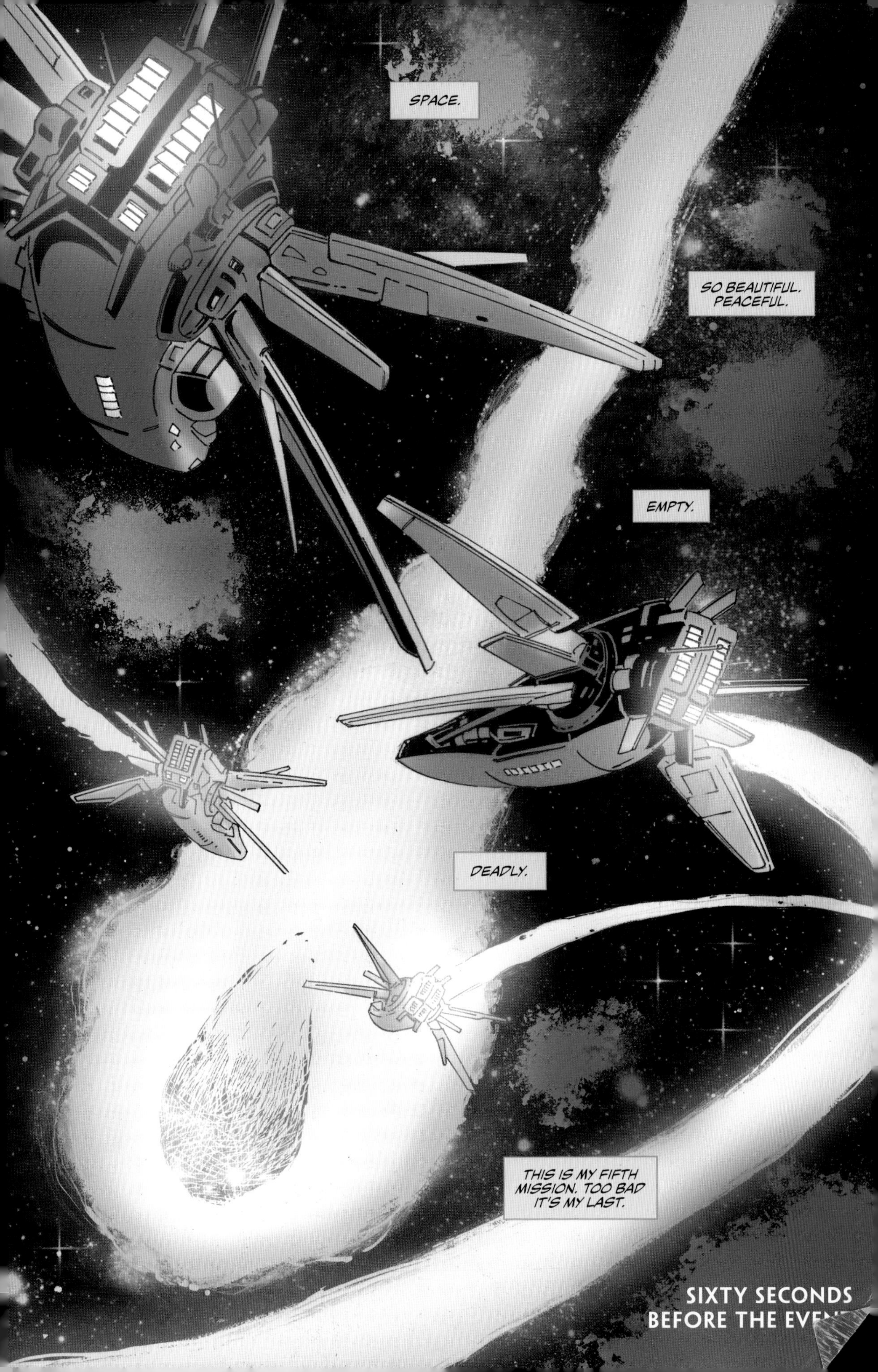
SPACE.
SO BEAUTIFUL. PEACEFUL.
EMPTY.
DEADLY.
THIS IS MY FIFTH MISSION. TOO BAD IT'S MY LAST.
SIXTY SECONDS BEFORE THE EVE

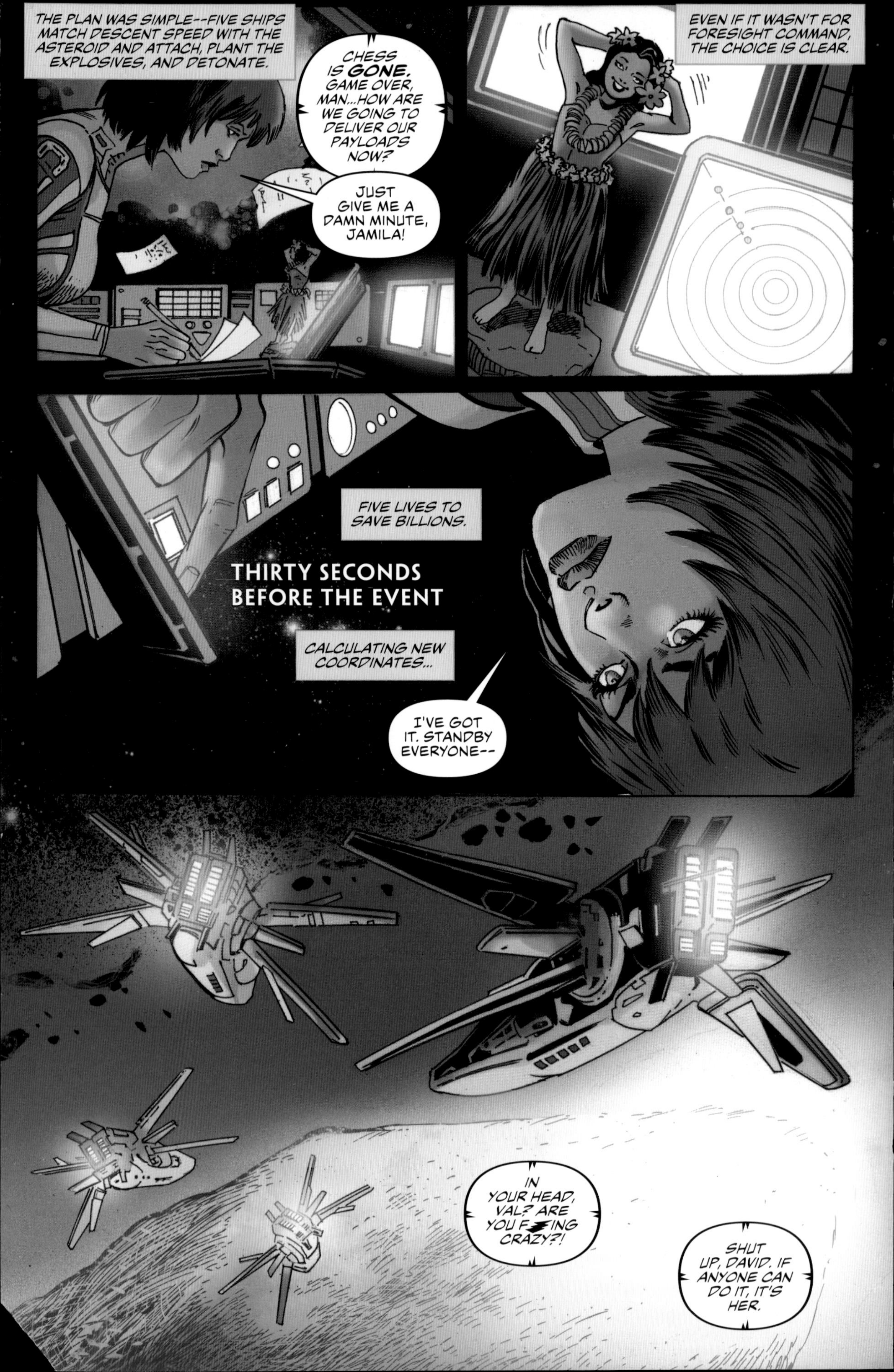
THE PLAN WAS SIMPLE--FIVE SHIPS MATCH DESCENT SPEED WITH THE ASTEROID AND ATTACH, PLANT THE EXPLOSIVES, AND DETONATE.
CHESS IS GONE. GAME OVER, MAN...HOW ARE WE GOING TO DELIVER OUR PAYLOADS NOW?
JUST GIVE ME A DAMN MINUTE, JAMILA!
EVEN IF IT WASN'T FOR FORESIGHT COMMAND, THE CHOICE IS CLEAR.
FIVE LIVES TO SAVE BILLIONS.
THIRTY SECONDS BEFORE THE EVENT
CALCULATING NEW COORDINATES...
I'VE GOT IT. STANDBY EVERYONE--
IN YOUR HEAD, VAL? ARE YOU F⚡ING CRAZY?!
SHUT UP, DAVID. IF ANYONE CAN DO IT, IT'S HER.

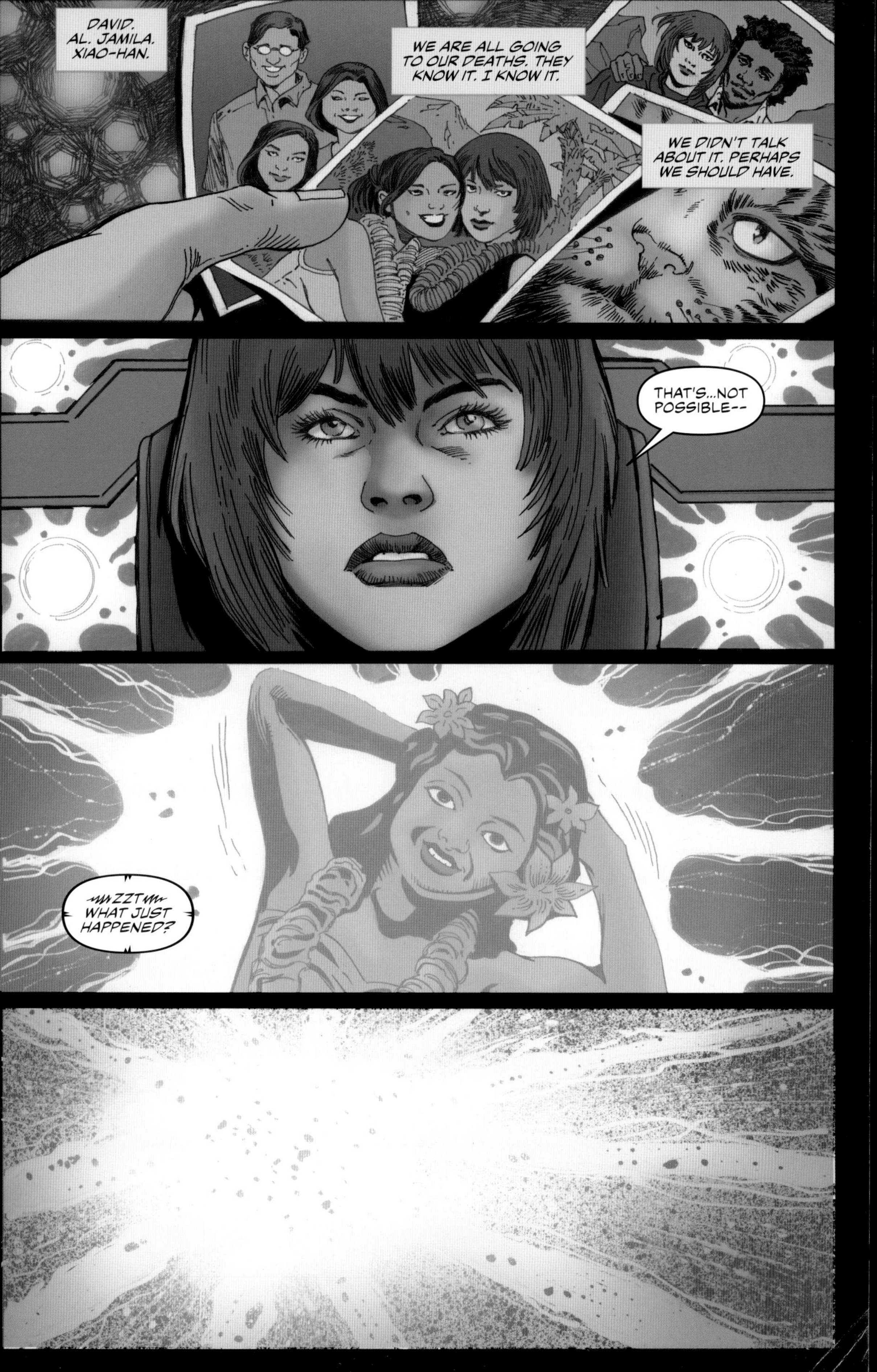
DAVID. AL. JAMILA. XIAO-HAN.
WE ARE ALL GOING TO OUR DEATHS. THEY KNOW IT. I KNOW IT.
WE DIDN'T TALK ABOUT IT. PERHAPS WE SHOULD HAVE.
THAT'S...NOT POSSIBLE--
ZZT WHAT JUST HAPPENED?

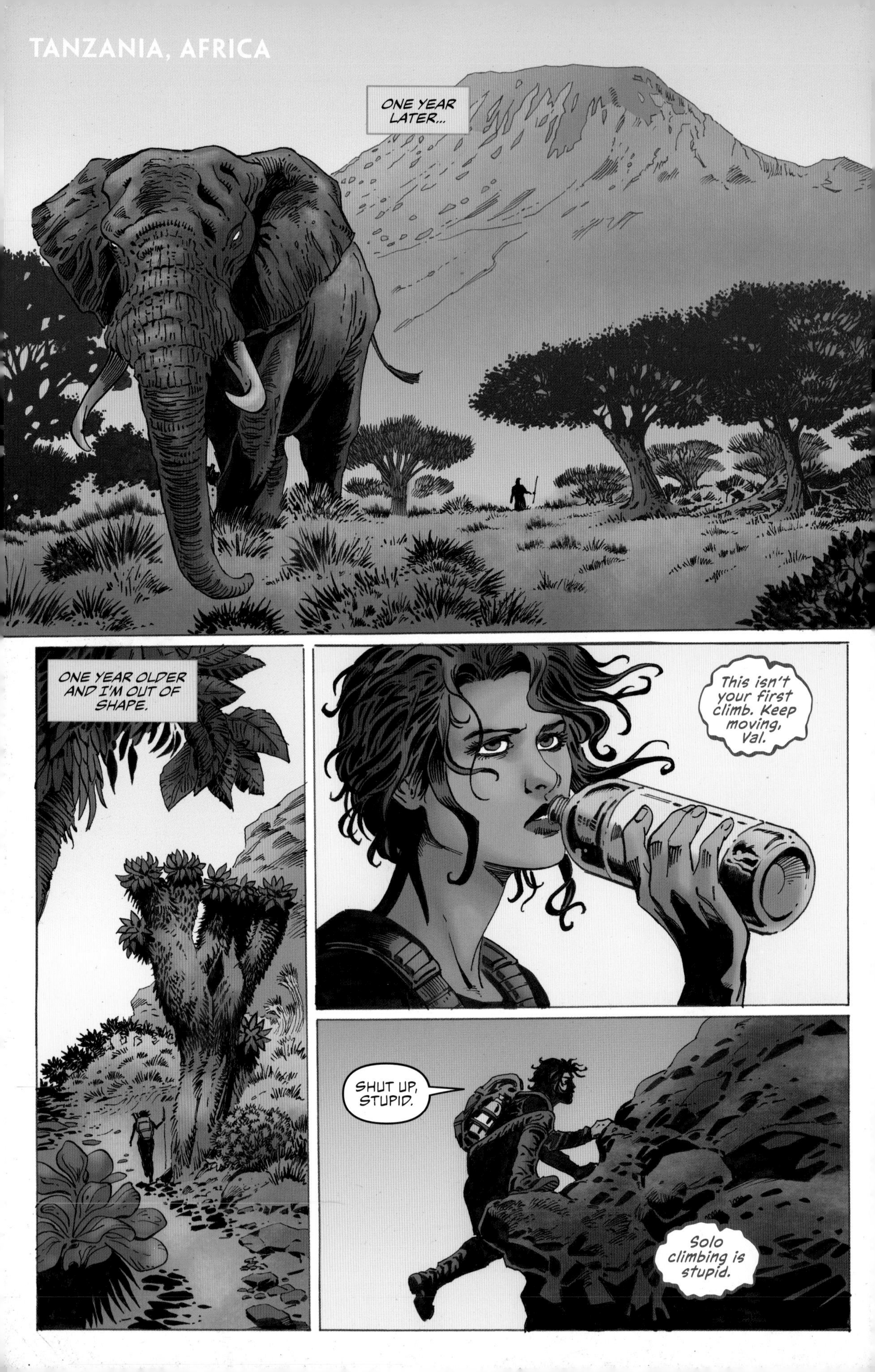
TANZANIA, AFRICA
ONE YEAR LATER...
ONE YEAR OLDER AND I'M OUT OF SHAPE.
This isn't your first climb. Keep moving, Val.
SHUT UP, STUPID.
Solo climbing is stupid.

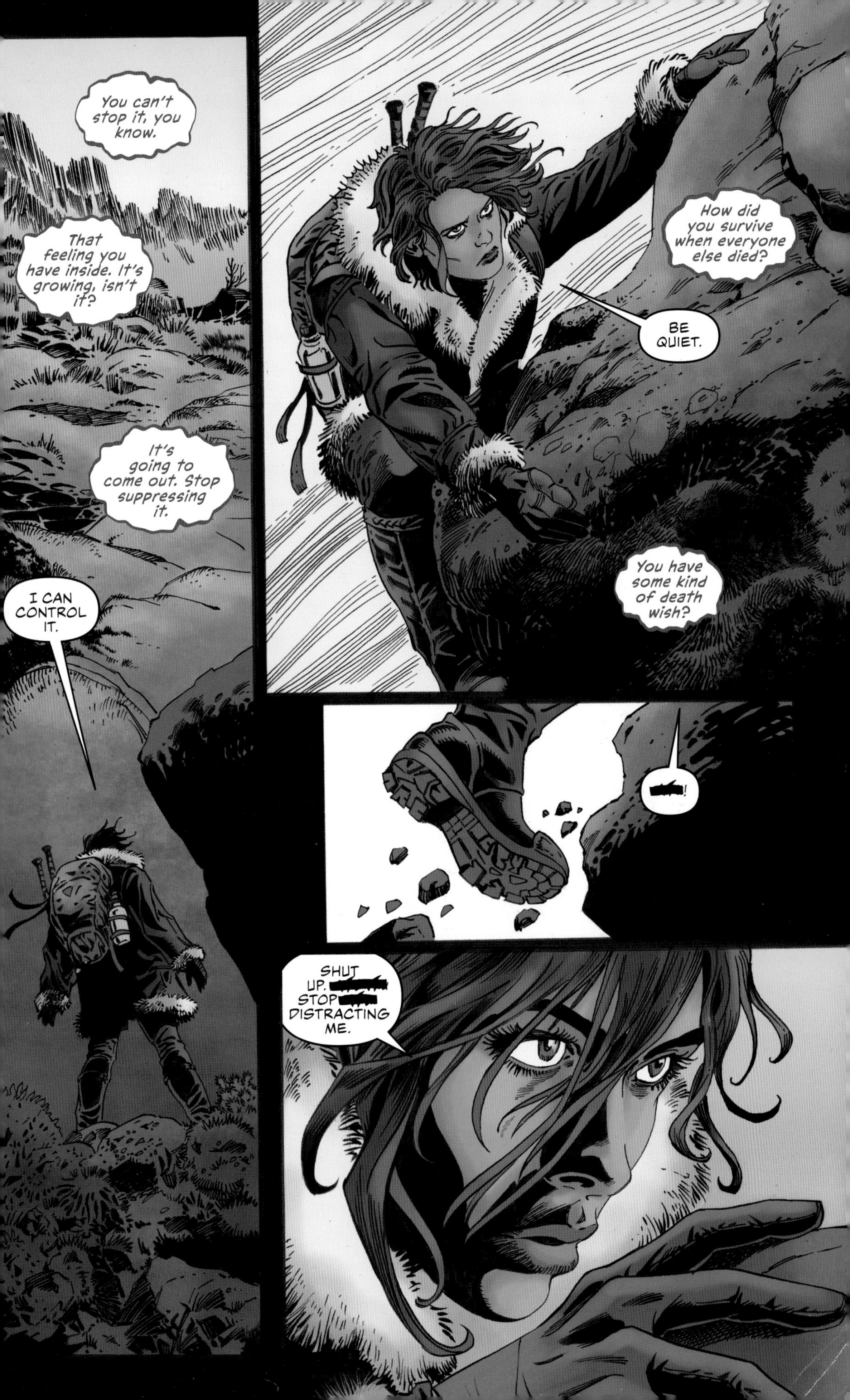
You can't stop it, you know.
That feeling you have inside. It's growing, isn't it?
It's going to come out. Stop suppressing it.
I CAN CONTROL IT.
How did you survive when everyone else died?
BE QUIET.
You have some kind of death wish?
[redacted]!
SHUT UP. [redacted] STOP [redacted] DISTRACTING ME.

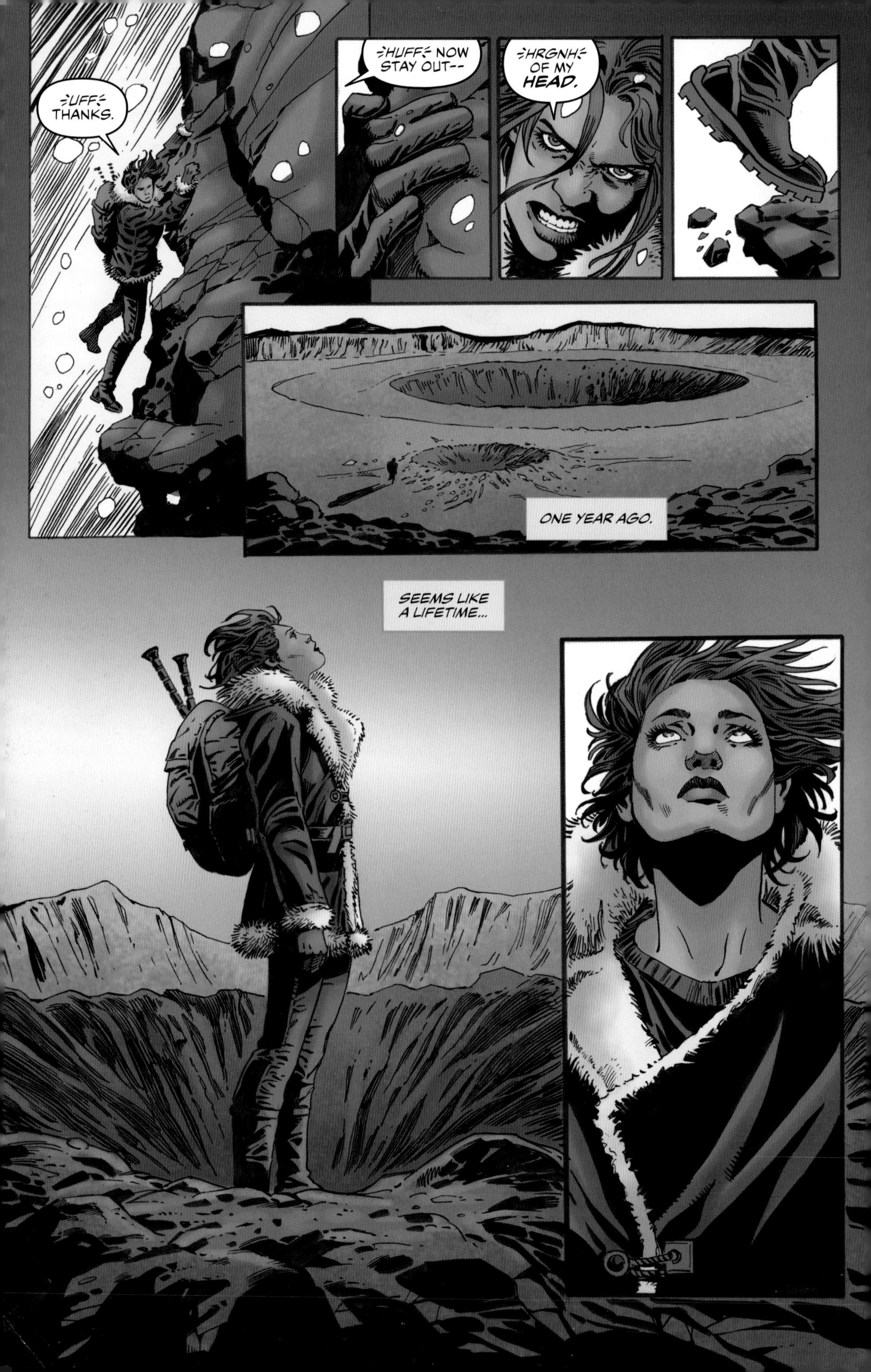

-UFF- THANKS.
-HUFF- NOW STAY OUT--
-HRGNH- OF MY **HEAD.**
ONE YEAR AGO.
SEEMS LIKE A LIFETIME...

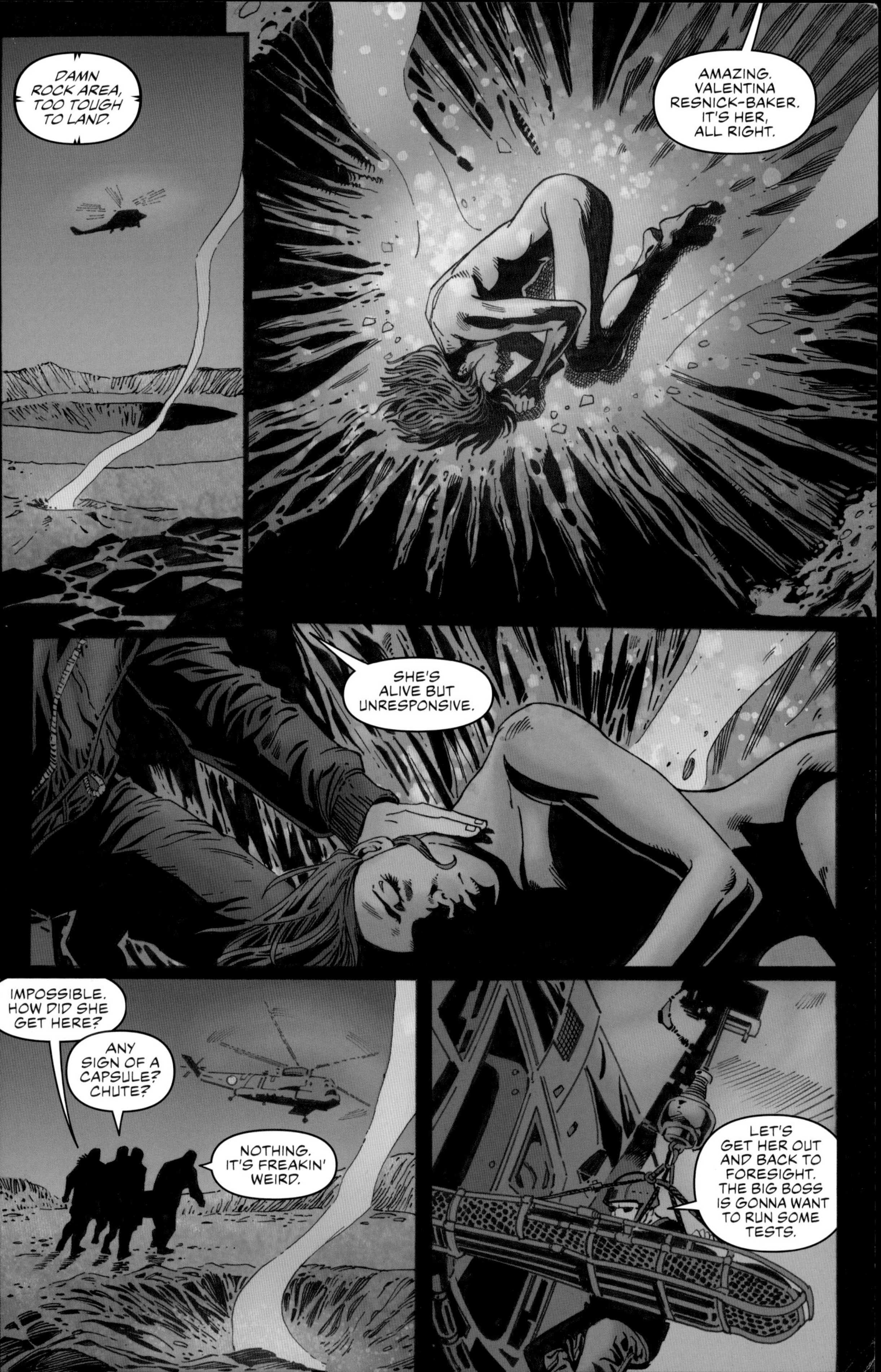
DAMN ROCK AREA, TOO TOUGH TO LAND.
AMAZING. VALENTINA RESNICK-BAKER. IT'S HER, ALL RIGHT.
SHE'S ALIVE BUT UNRESPONSIVE.
IMPOSSIBLE. HOW DID SHE GET HERE?
ANY SIGN OF A CAPSULE? CHUTE?
NOTHING. IT'S FREAKIN' WEIRD.
LET'S GET HER OUT AND BACK TO FORESIGHT. THE BIG BOSS IS GONNA WANT TO RUN SOME TESTS.

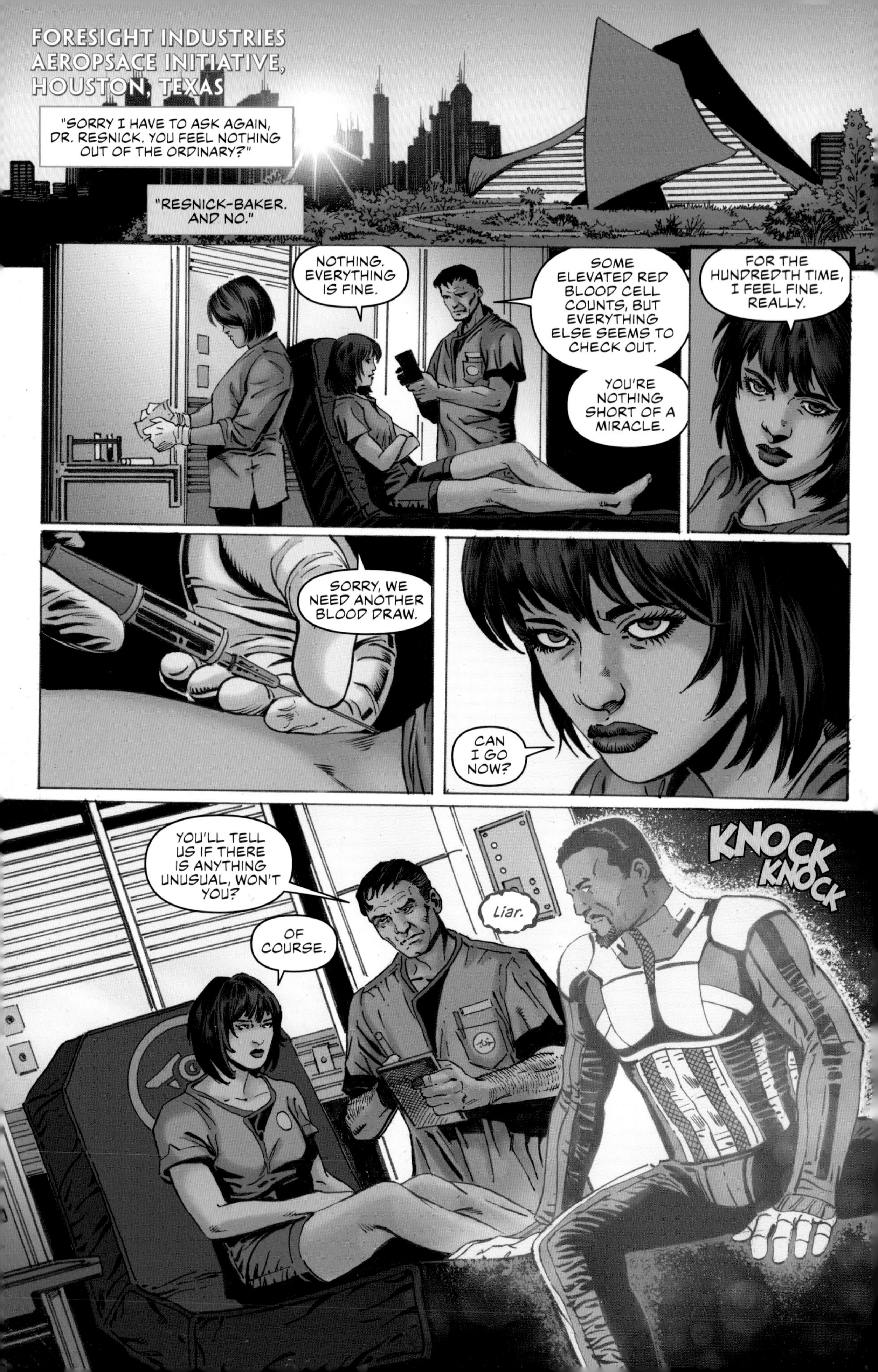
FORESIGHT INDUSTRIES AEROPSACE INITIATIVE, HOUSTON, TEXAS
"SORRY I HAVE TO ASK AGAIN, DR. RESNICK. YOU FEEL NOTHING OUT OF THE ORDINARY?"
"RESNICK-BAKER. AND NO."
NOTHING. EVERYTHING IS FINE.
SOME ELEVATED RED BLOOD CELL COUNTS, BUT EVERYTHING ELSE SEEMS TO CHECK OUT.
YOU'RE NOTHING SHORT OF A MIRACLE.
FOR THE HUNDREDTH TIME, I FEEL FINE. REALLY.
SORRY, WE NEED ANOTHER BLOOD DRAW.
CAN I GO NOW?
YOU'LL TELL US IF THERE IS ANYTHING UNUSUAL, WON'T YOU?
OF COURSE.
Liar.
KNOCK KNOCK

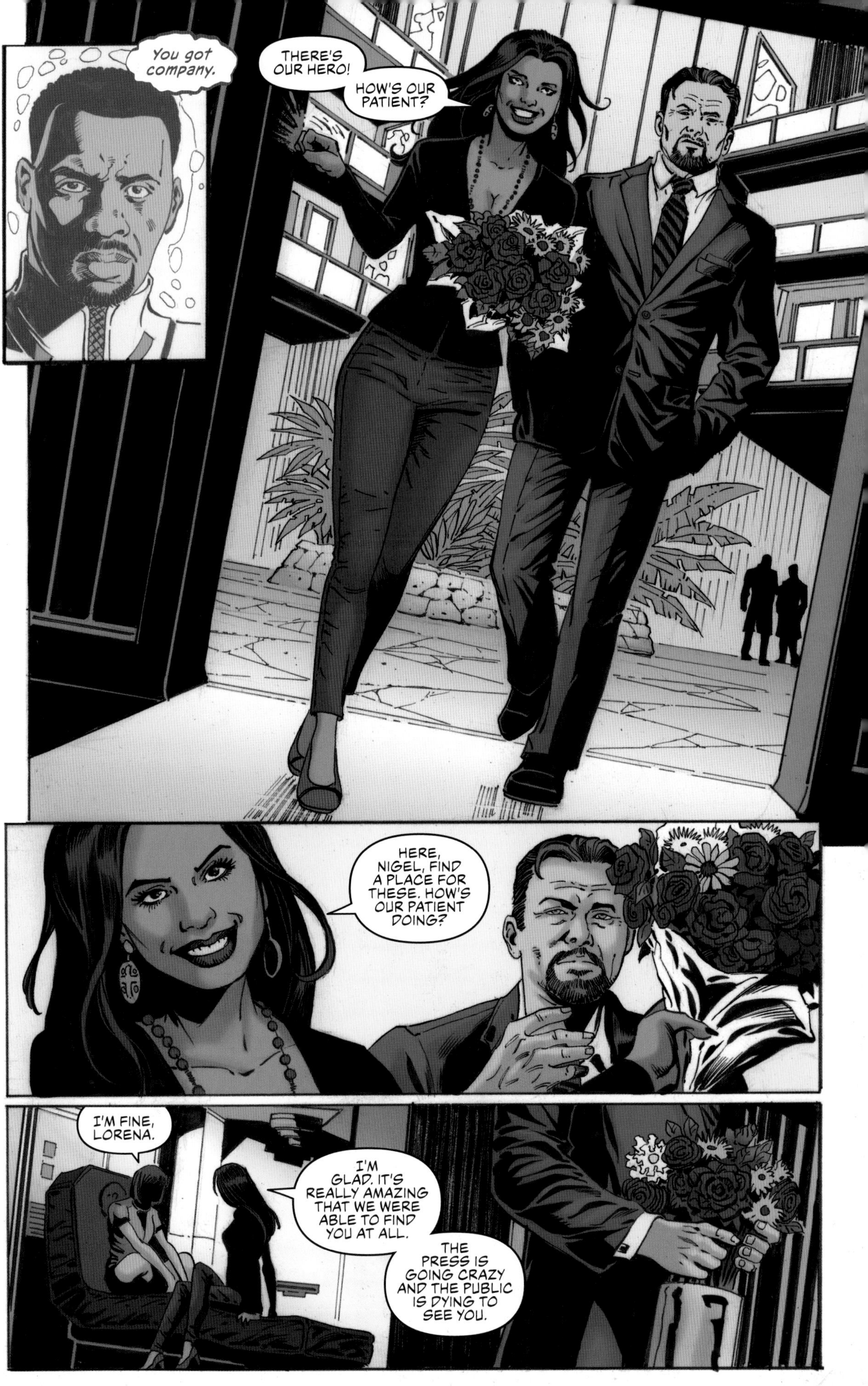
You got company.
THERE'S OUR HERO!
HOW'S OUR PATIENT?
HERE, NIGEL, FIND A PLACE FOR THESE. HOW'S OUR PATIENT DOING?
I'M FINE, LORENA.
I'M GLAD. IT'S REALLY AMAZING THAT WE WERE ABLE TO FIND YOU AT ALL.
THE PRESS IS GOING CRAZY AND THE PUBLIC IS DYING TO SEE YOU.

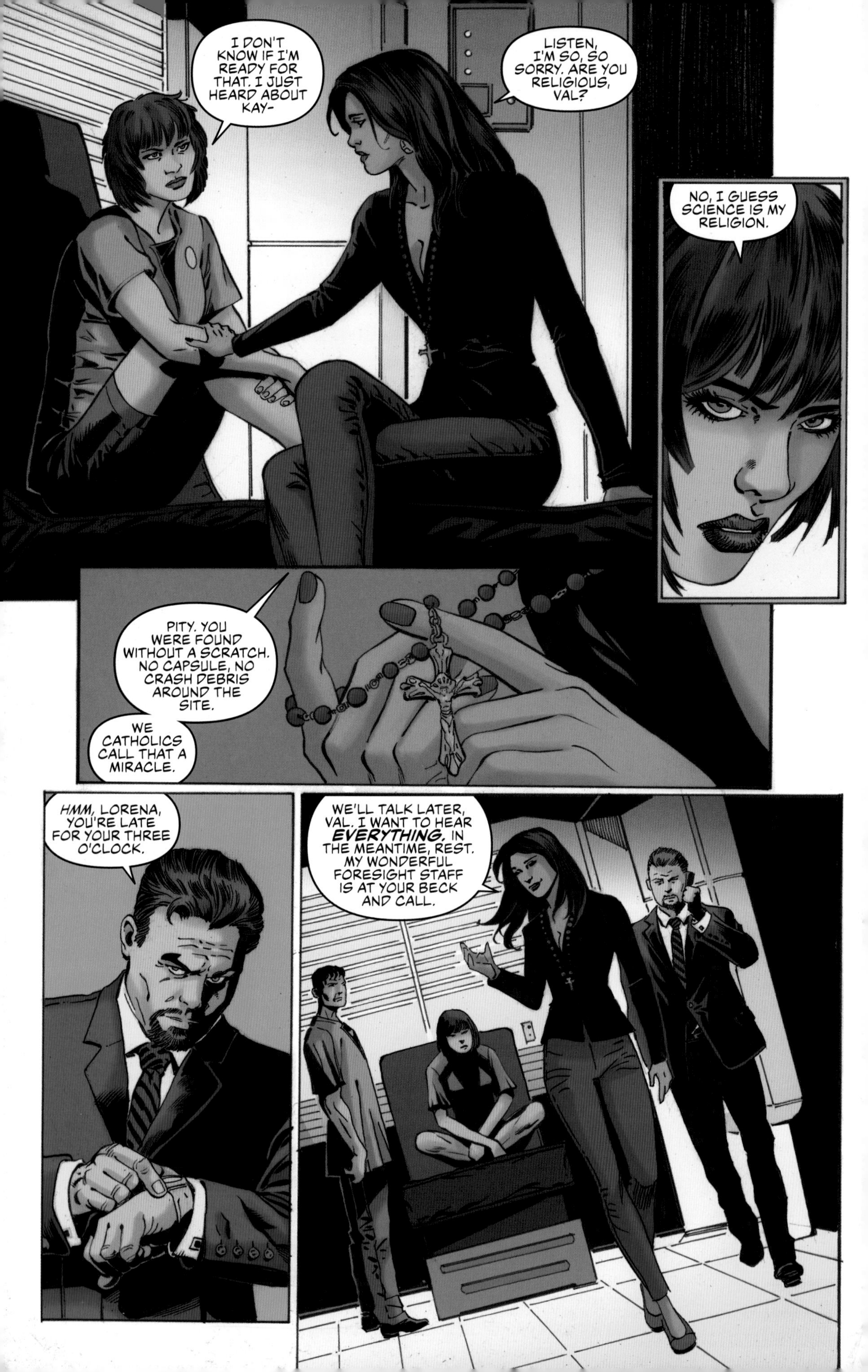
I DON'T KNOW IF I'M READY FOR THAT. I JUST HEARD ABOUT KAY-
LISTEN, I'M SO, SO SORRY. ARE YOU RELIGIOUS, VAL?
NO, I GUESS SCIENCE IS MY RELIGION.
PITY. YOU WERE FOUND WITHOUT A SCRATCH. NO CAPSULE, NO CRASH DEBRIS AROUND THE SITE.
WE CATHOLICS CALL THAT A MIRACLE.
HMM, LORENA, YOU'RE LATE FOR YOUR THREE O'CLOCK.
WE'LL TALK LATER, VAL. I WANT TO HEAR ***EVERYTHING.*** IN THE MEANTIME, REST. MY WONDERFUL FORESIGHT STAFF IS AT YOUR BECK AND CALL.

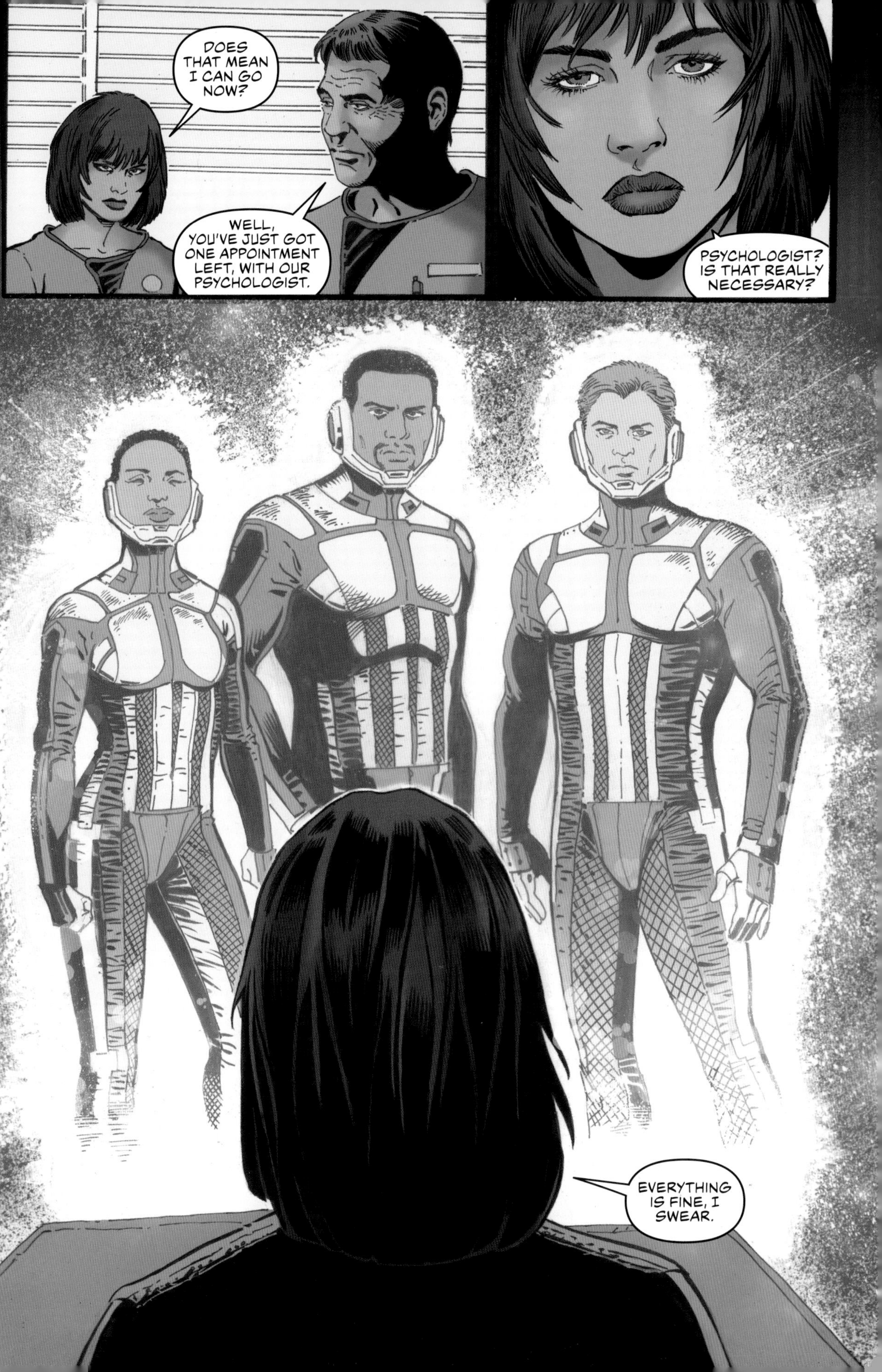
DOES THAT MEAN I CAN GO NOW?
WELL, YOU'VE JUST GOT ONE APPOINTMENT LEFT, WITH OUR PSYCHOLOGIST.
PSYCHOLOGIST? IS THAT REALLY NECESSARY?
EVERYTHING IS FINE, I SWEAR.

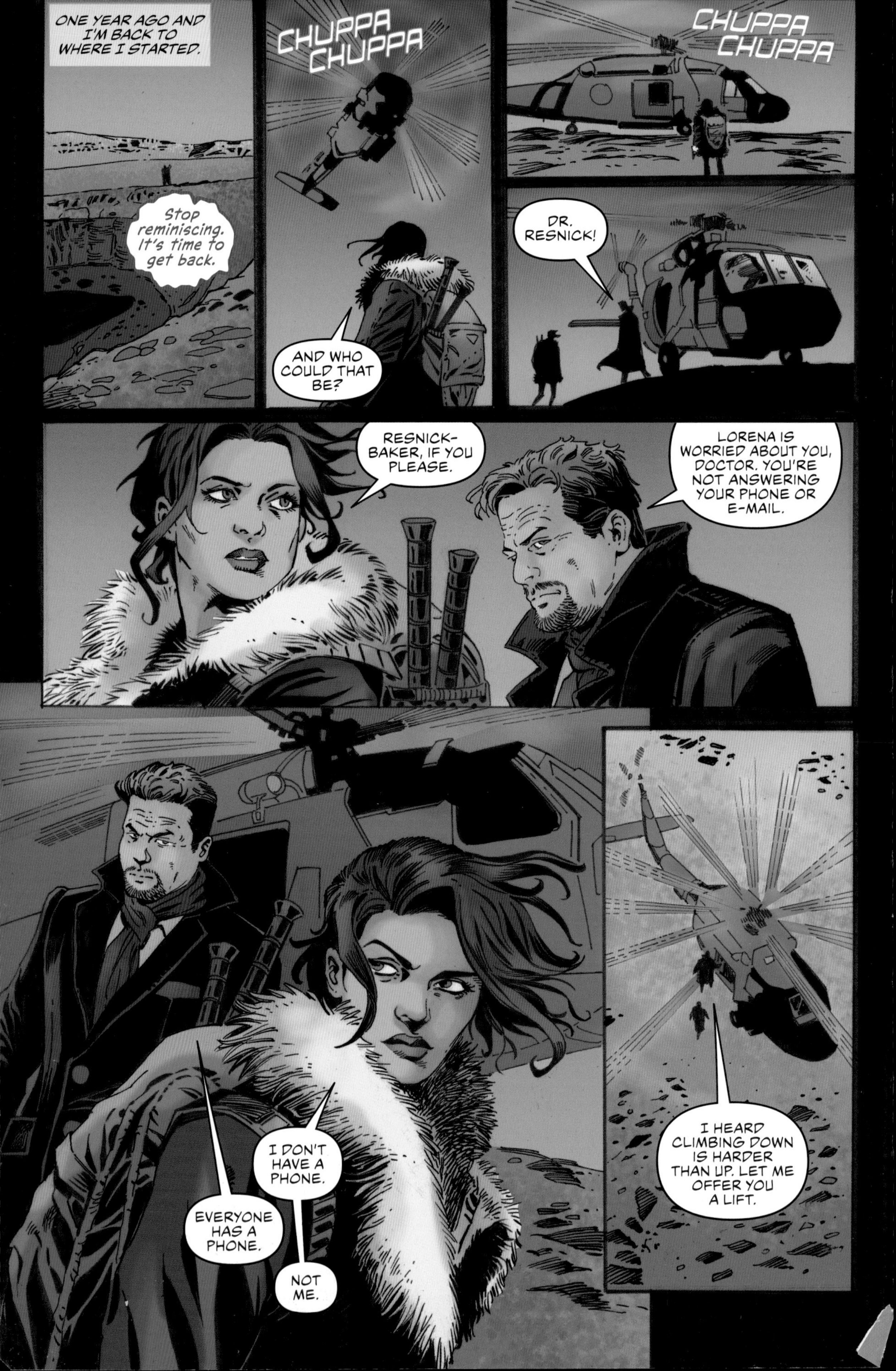
ONE YEAR AGO AND I'M BACK TO WHERE I STARTED.
Stop reminiscing. It's time to get back.
CHUPPA CHUPPA
AND WHO COULD THAT BE?
CHUPPA CHUPPA
DR. RESNICK!
RESNICK-BAKER, IF YOU PLEASE.
LORENA IS WORRIED ABOUT YOU, DOCTOR. YOU'RE NOT ANSWERING YOUR PHONE OR E-MAIL.
I DON'T HAVE A PHONE.
EVERYONE HAS A PHONE.
NOT ME.
I HEARD CLIMBING DOWN IS HARDER THAN UP. LET ME OFFER YOU A LIFT.

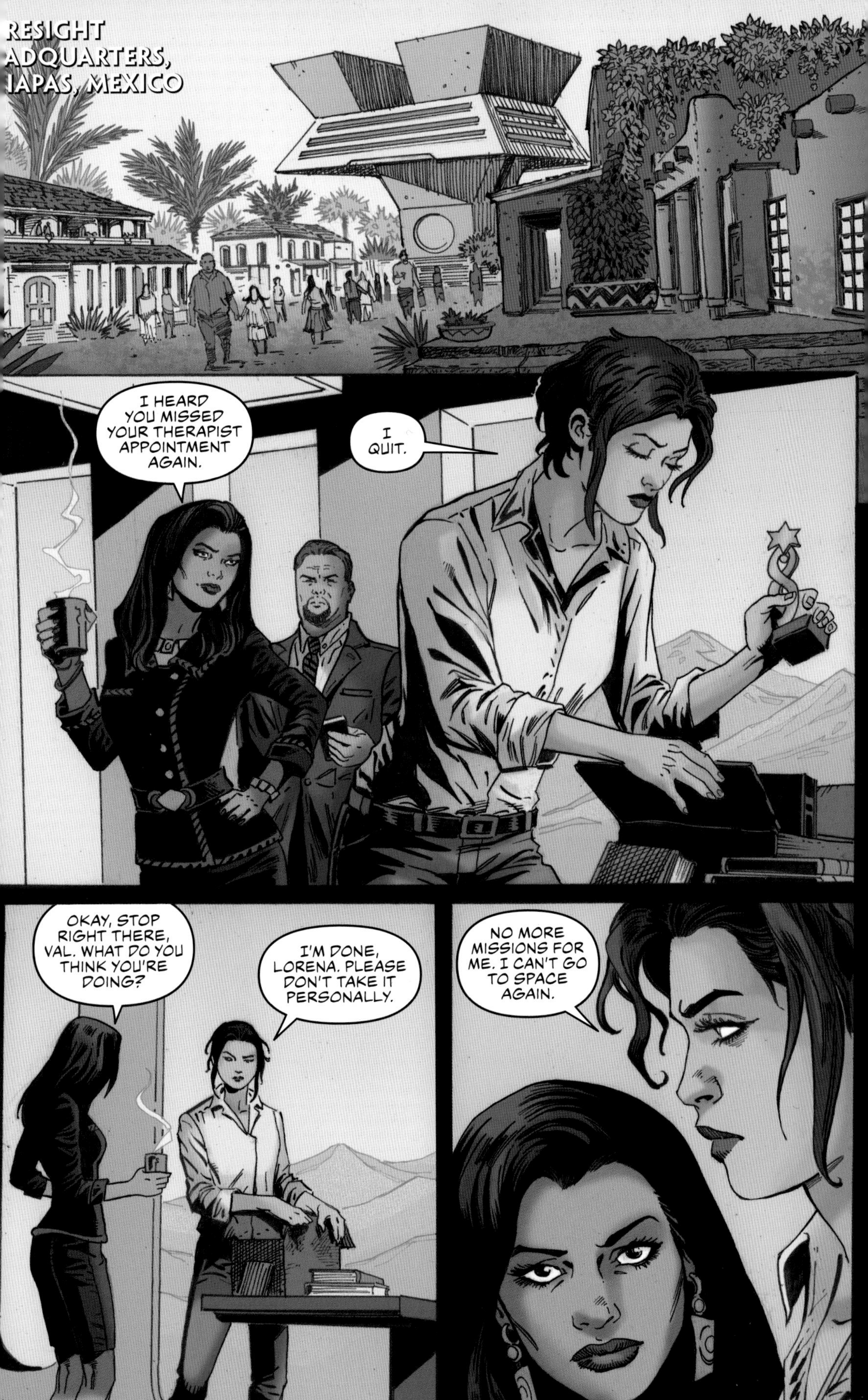
RESIGHT
ADQUARTERS,
IAPAS, MEXICO
I HEARD YOU MISSED YOUR THERAPIST APPOINTMENT AGAIN.
I QUIT.
OKAY, STOP RIGHT THERE, VAL. WHAT DO YOU THINK YOU'RE DOING?
I'M DONE, LORENA. PLEASE DON'T TAKE IT PERSONALLY.
NO MORE MISSIONS FOR ME. I CAN'T GO TO SPACE AGAIN.

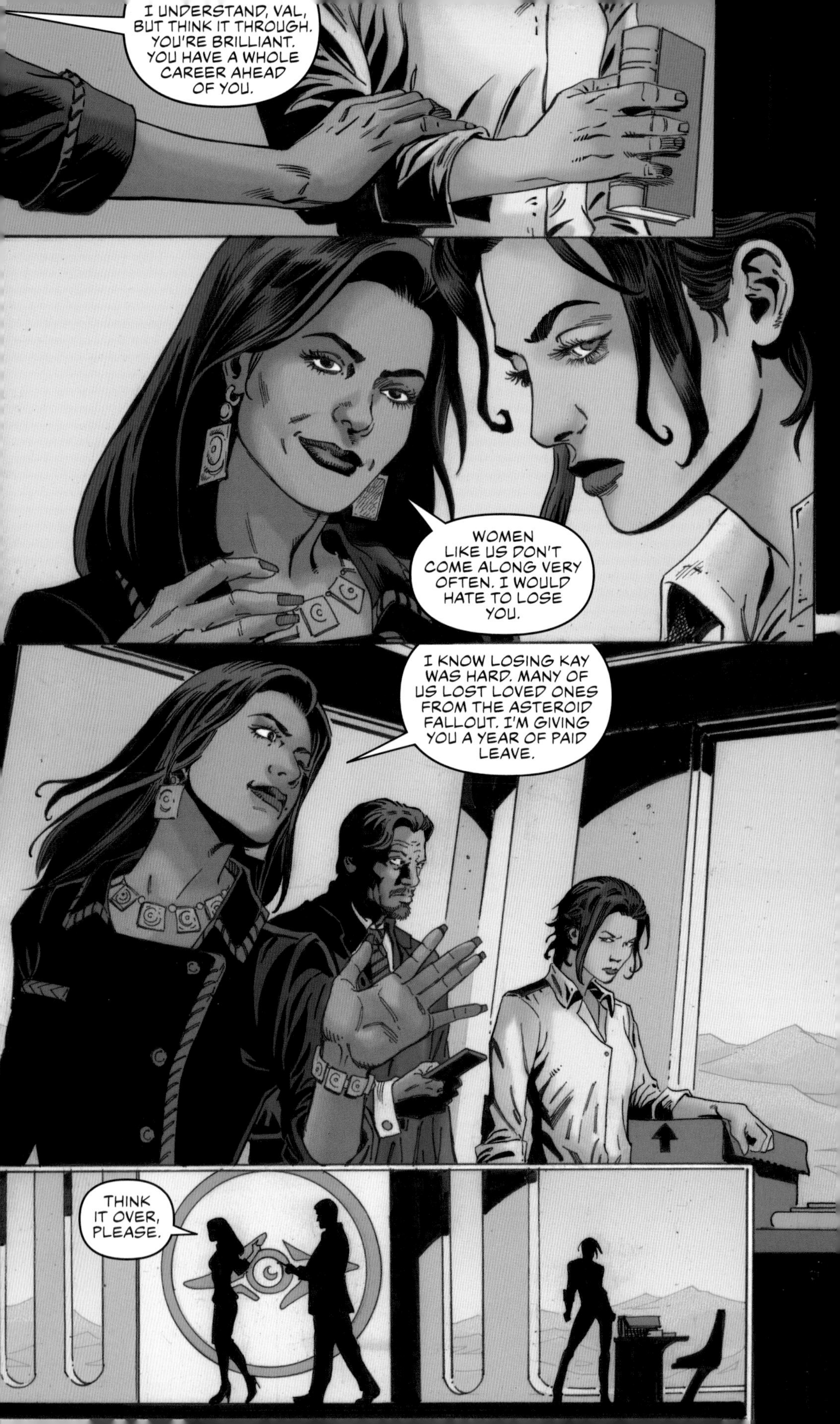
I UNDERSTAND, VAL, BUT THINK IT THROUGH. YOU'RE BRILLIANT. YOU HAVE A WHOLE CAREER AHEAD OF YOU.
WOMEN LIKE US DON'T COME ALONG VERY OFTEN. I WOULD HATE TO LOSE YOU.
I KNOW LOSING KAY WAS HARD. MANY OF US LOST LOVED ONES FROM THE ASTEROID FALLOUT. I'M GIVING YOU A YEAR OF PAID LEAVE.
THINK IT OVER, PLEASE.

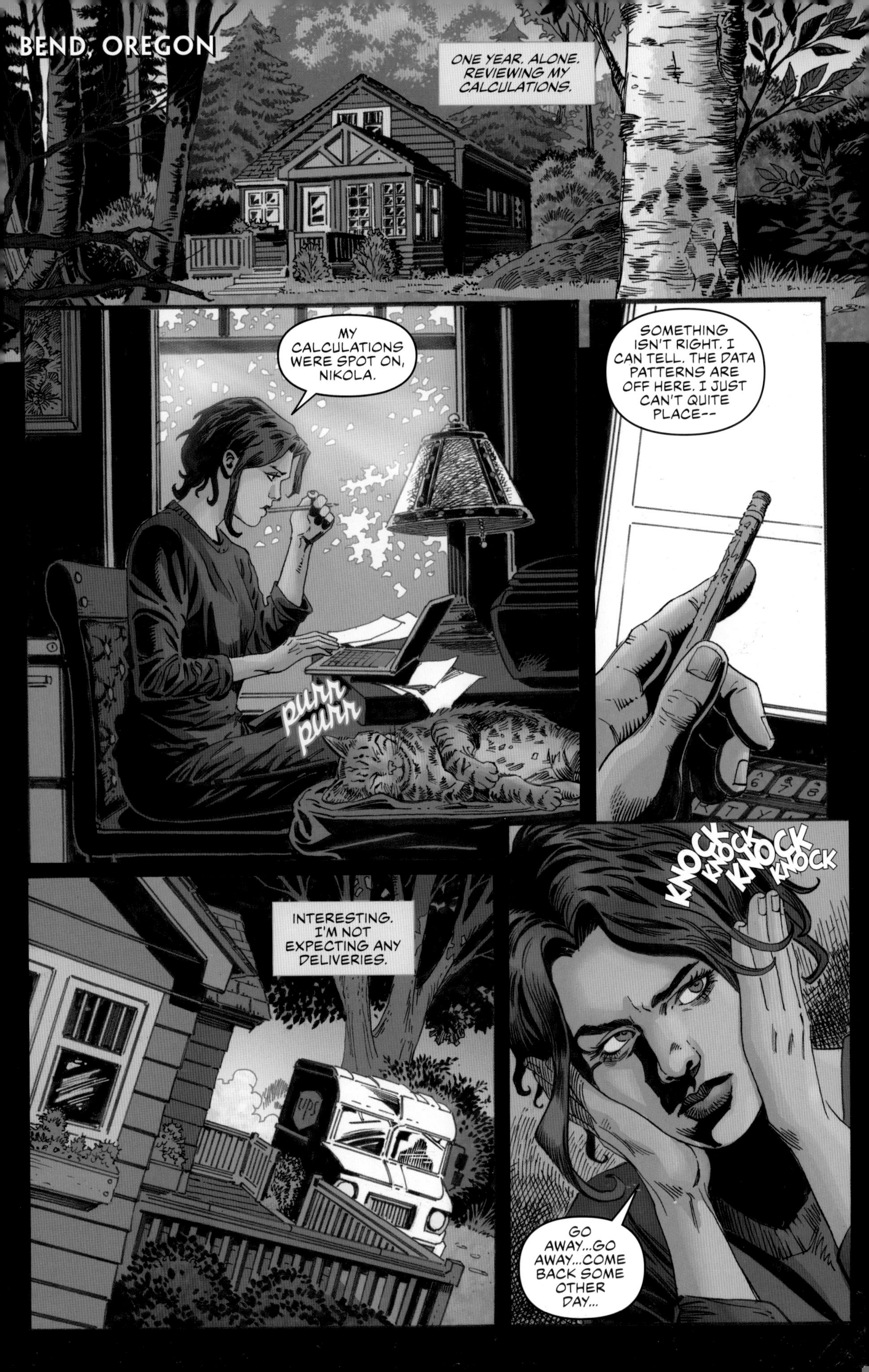
BEND, OREGON
ONE YEAR. ALONE. REVIEWING MY CALCULATIONS.
MY CALCULATIONS WERE SPOT ON, NIKOLA.
purr purr
SOMETHING ISN'T RIGHT. I CAN TELL. THE DATA PATTERNS ARE OFF HERE. I JUST CAN'T QUITE PLACE--
KNOCK KNOCK KNOCK KNOCK
INTERESTING. I'M NOT EXPECTING ANY DELIVERIES.
GO AWAY...GO AWAY...COME BACK SOME OTHER DAY...

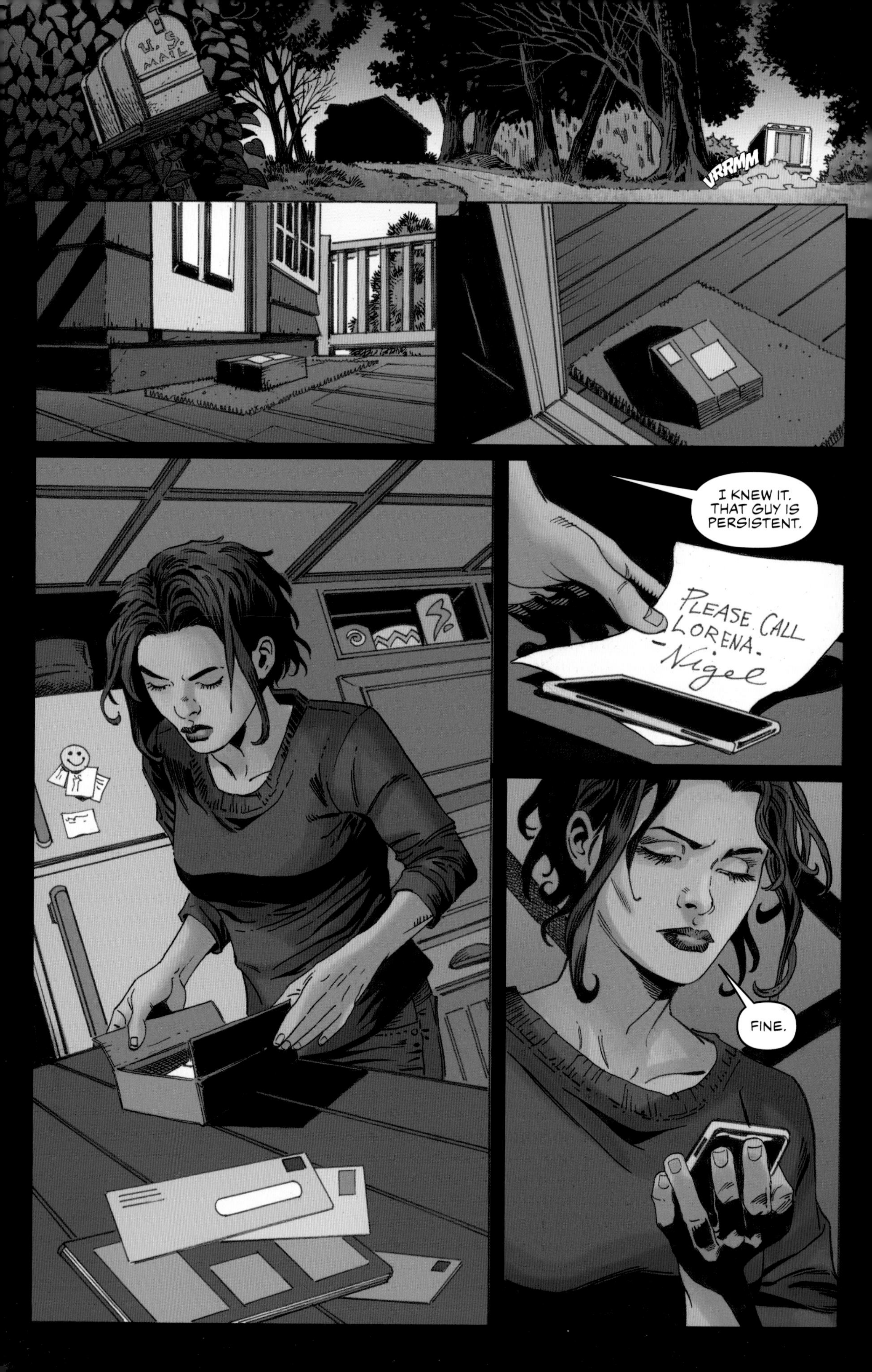
U.S. MAIL
VRRMM
I KNEW IT. THAT GUY IS PERSISTENT.
PLEASE CALL LORENA. -Nigel
FINE.

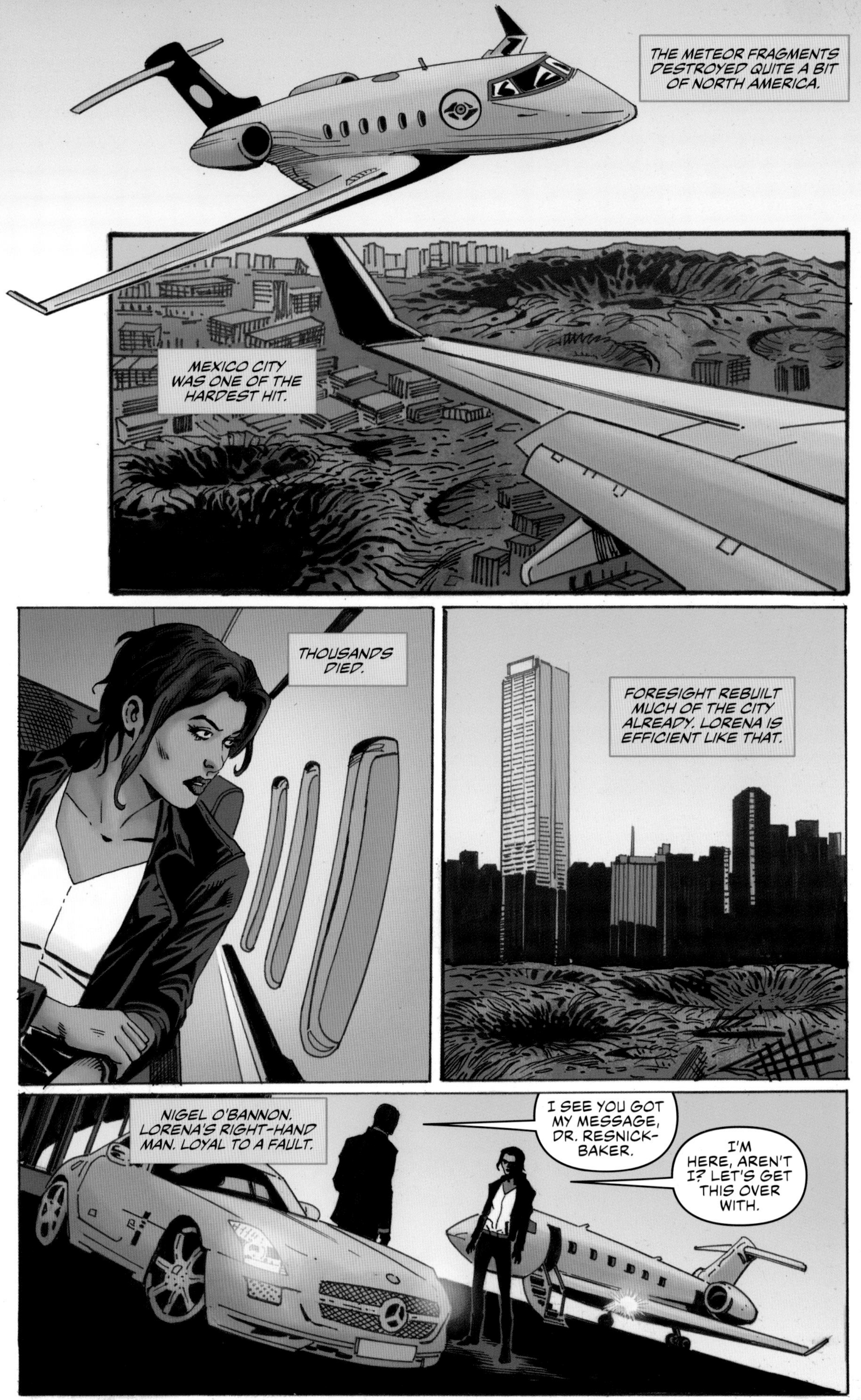
THE METEOR FRAGMENTS DESTROYED QUITE A BIT OF NORTH AMERICA.
MEXICO CITY WAS ONE OF THE HARDEST HIT.
THOUSANDS DIED.
FORESIGHT REBUILT MUCH OF THE CITY ALREADY. LORENA IS EFFICIENT LIKE THAT.
NIGEL O'BANNON. LORENA'S RIGHT-HAND MAN. LOYAL TO A FAULT.
I SEE YOU GOT MY MESSAGE, DR. RESNICK-BAKER.
I'M HERE, AREN'T I? LET'S GET THIS OVER WITH.

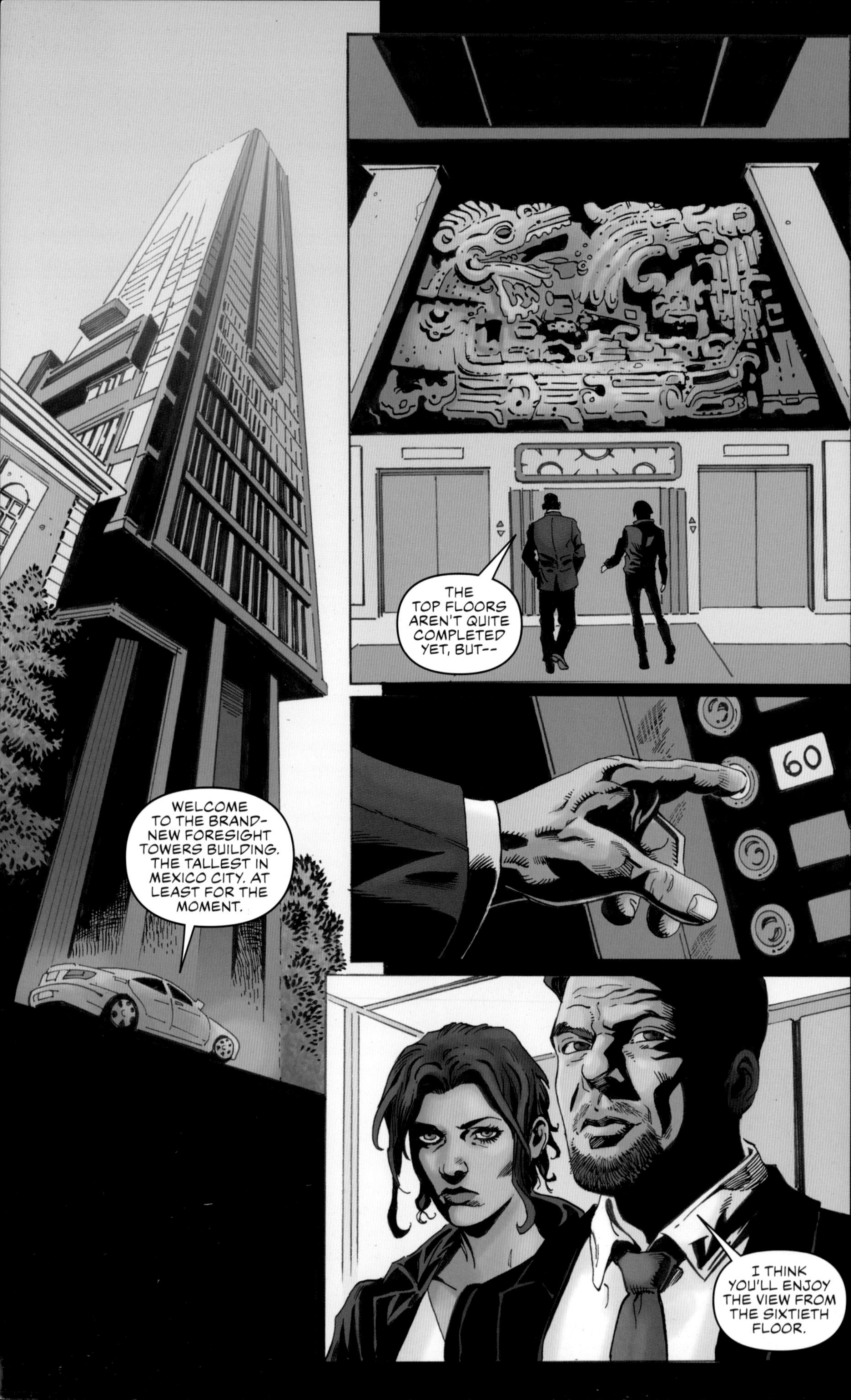
WELCOME TO THE BRAND-NEW FORESIGHT TOWERS BUILDING. THE TALLEST IN MEXICO CITY. AT LEAST FOR THE MOMENT.
THE TOP FLOORS AREN'T QUITE COMPLETED YET, BUT--
60
I THINK YOU'LL ENJOY THE VIEW FROM THE SIXTIETH FLOOR.

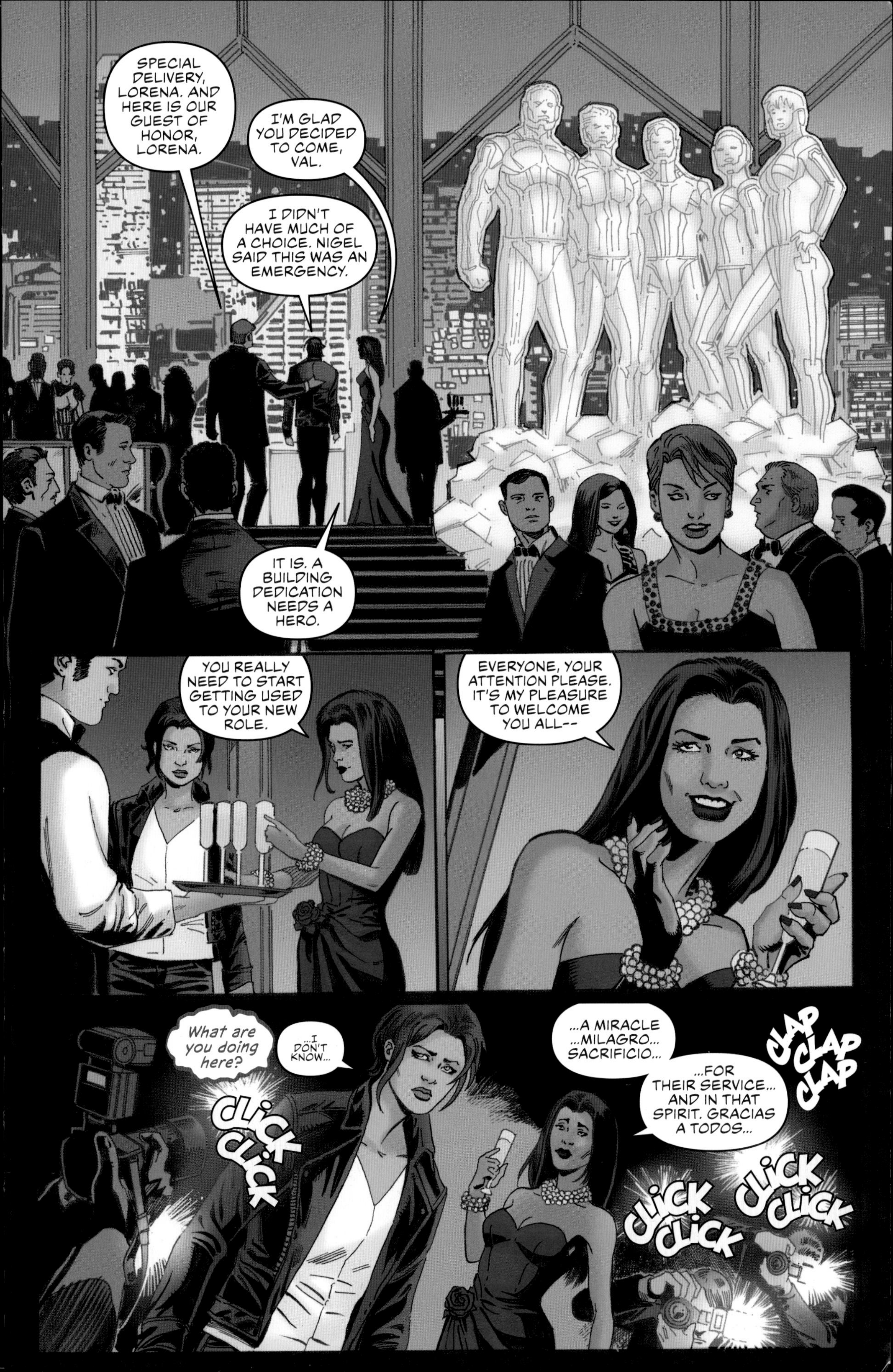
SPECIAL DELIVERY, LORENA. AND HERE IS OUR GUEST OF HONOR, LORENA.
I'M GLAD YOU DECIDED TO COME, VAL.
I DIDN'T HAVE MUCH OF A CHOICE. NIGEL SAID THIS WAS AN EMERGENCY.
IT IS. A BUILDING DEDICATION NEEDS A HERO.
YOU REALLY NEED TO START GETTING USED TO YOUR NEW ROLE.
EVERYONE, YOUR ATTENTION PLEASE. IT'S MY PLEASURE TO WELCOME YOU ALL--
What are you doing here?
...I DON'T KNOW...
CLICK CLICK
...A MIRACLE ...MILAGRO... SACRIFICIO...
...FOR THEIR SERVICE... AND IN THAT SPIRIT. GRACIAS A TODOS...
CLAP CLAP CLAP
CLICK CLICK
CLICK CLICK

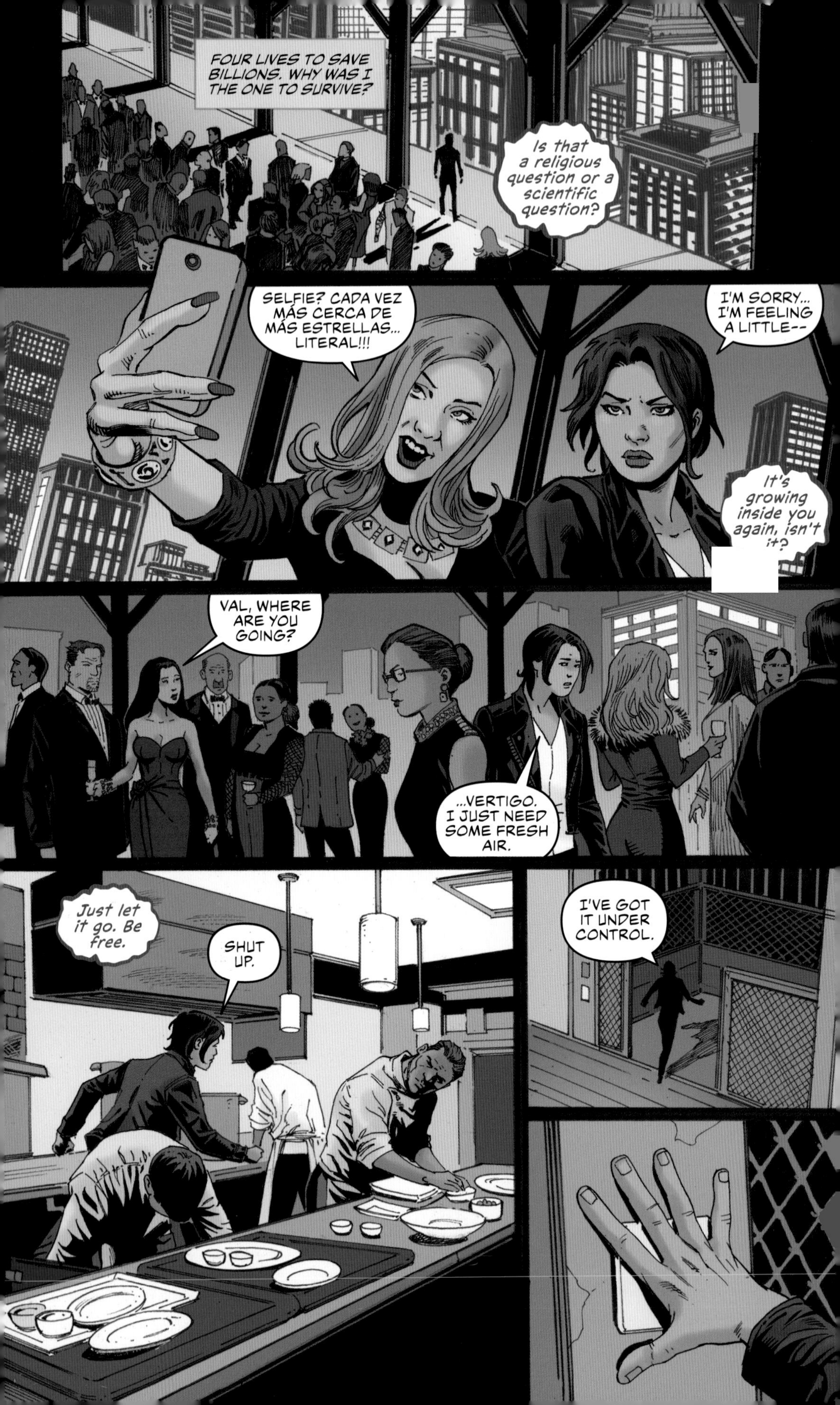
FOUR LIVES TO SAVE BILLIONS. WHY WAS I THE ONE TO SURVIVE?
Is that a religious question or a scientific question?
SELFIE? CADA VEZ MÁS CERCA DE MÁS ESTRELLAS... LITERAL!!!
I'M SORRY... I'M FEELING A LITTLE--
It's growing inside you again, isn't it?
VAL, WHERE ARE YOU GOING?
...VERTIGO. I JUST NEED SOME FRESH AIR.
Just let it go. Be free.
SHUT UP.
I'VE GOT IT UNDER CONTROL.

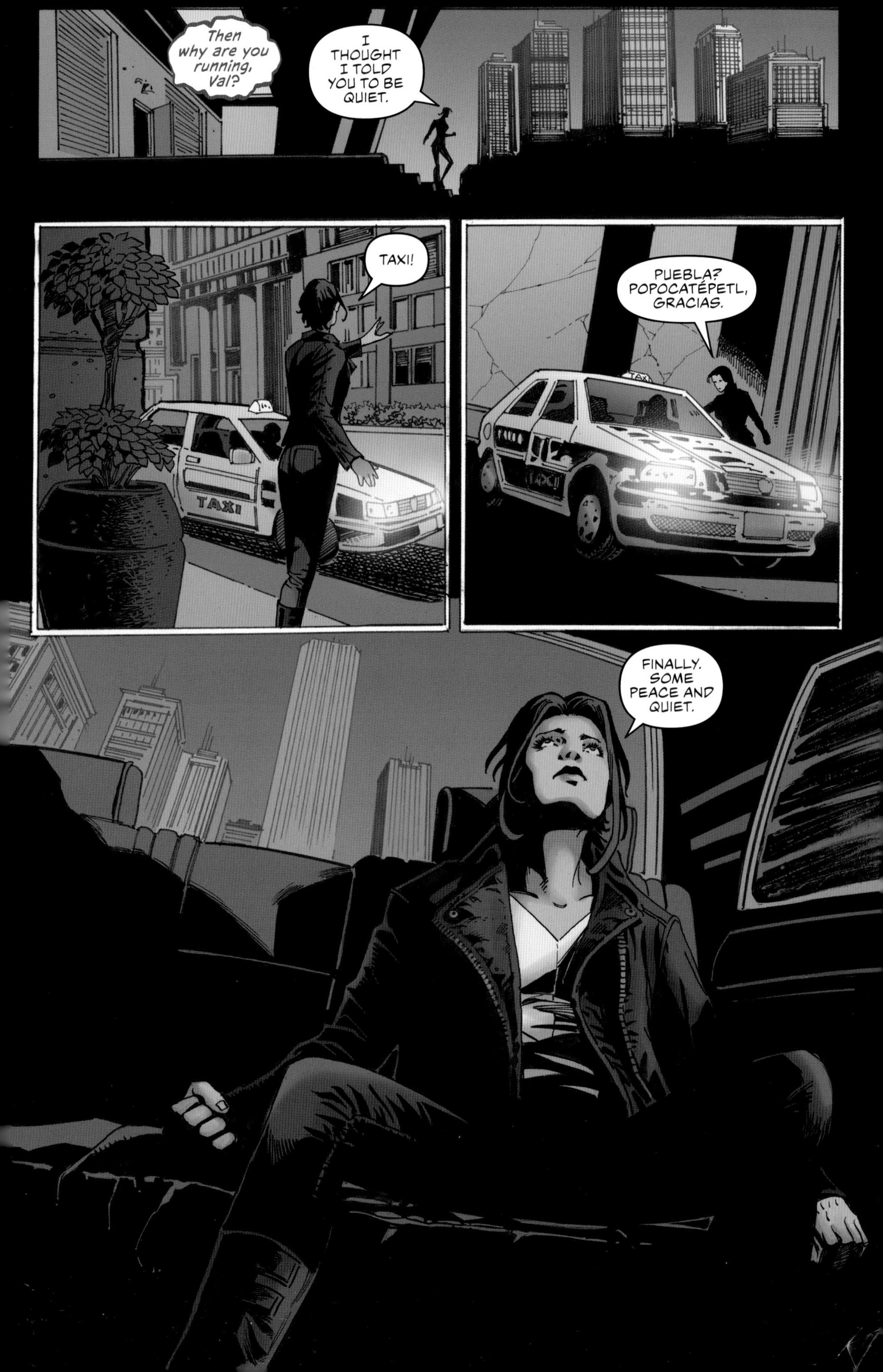
Then why are you running, Val?
I THOUGHT I TOLD YOU TO BE QUIET.
TAXI!
PUEBLA? POPOCATÉPETL, GRACIAS.
FINALLY. SOME PEACE AND QUIET.

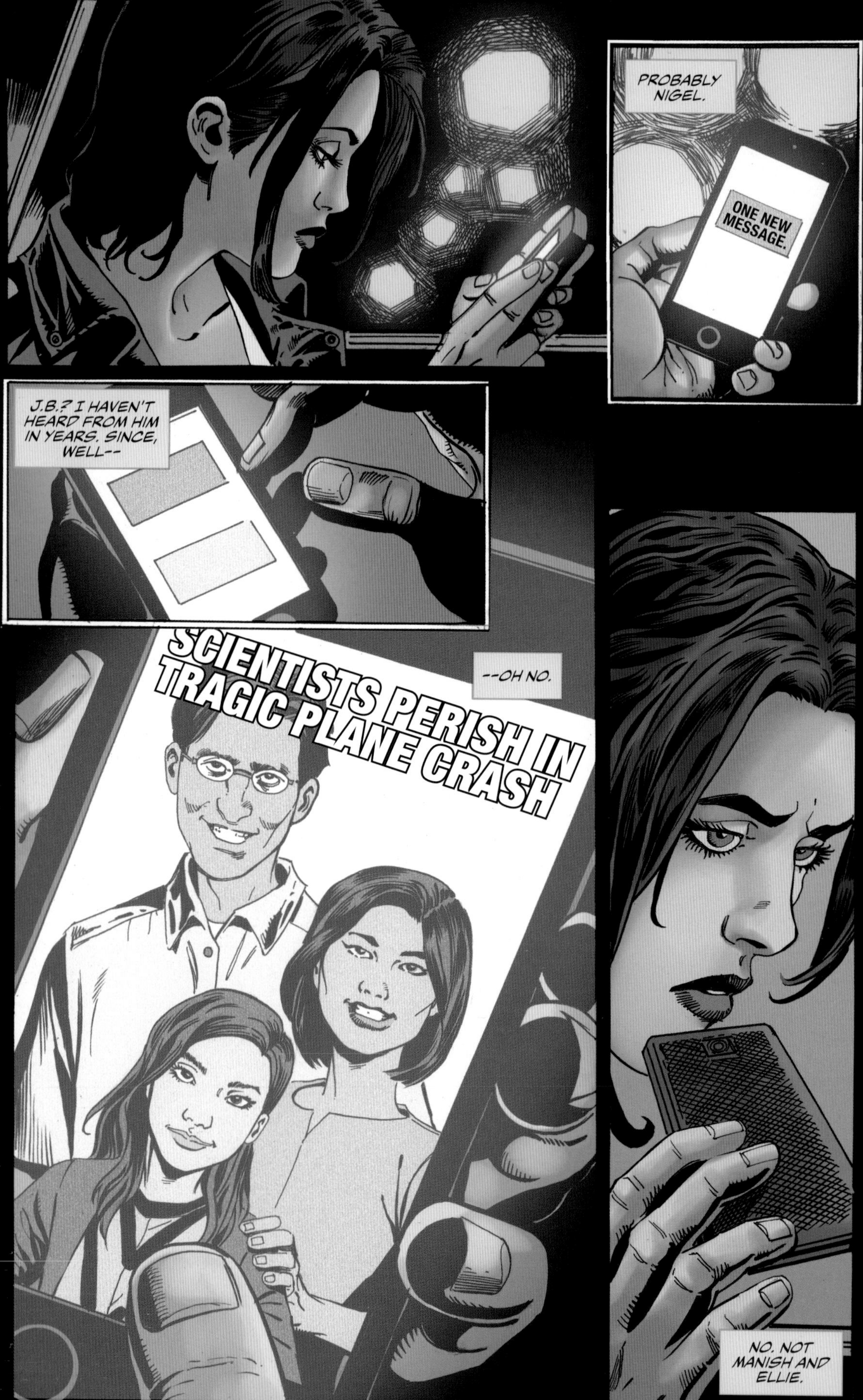
PROBABLY NIGEL.
ONE NEW MESSAGE.
J.B.? I HAVEN'T HEARD FROM HIM IN YEARS. SINCE, WELL--
SCIENTISTS PERISH IN TRAGIC PLANE CRASH
--OH NO.
NO. NOT MANISH AND ELLIE.

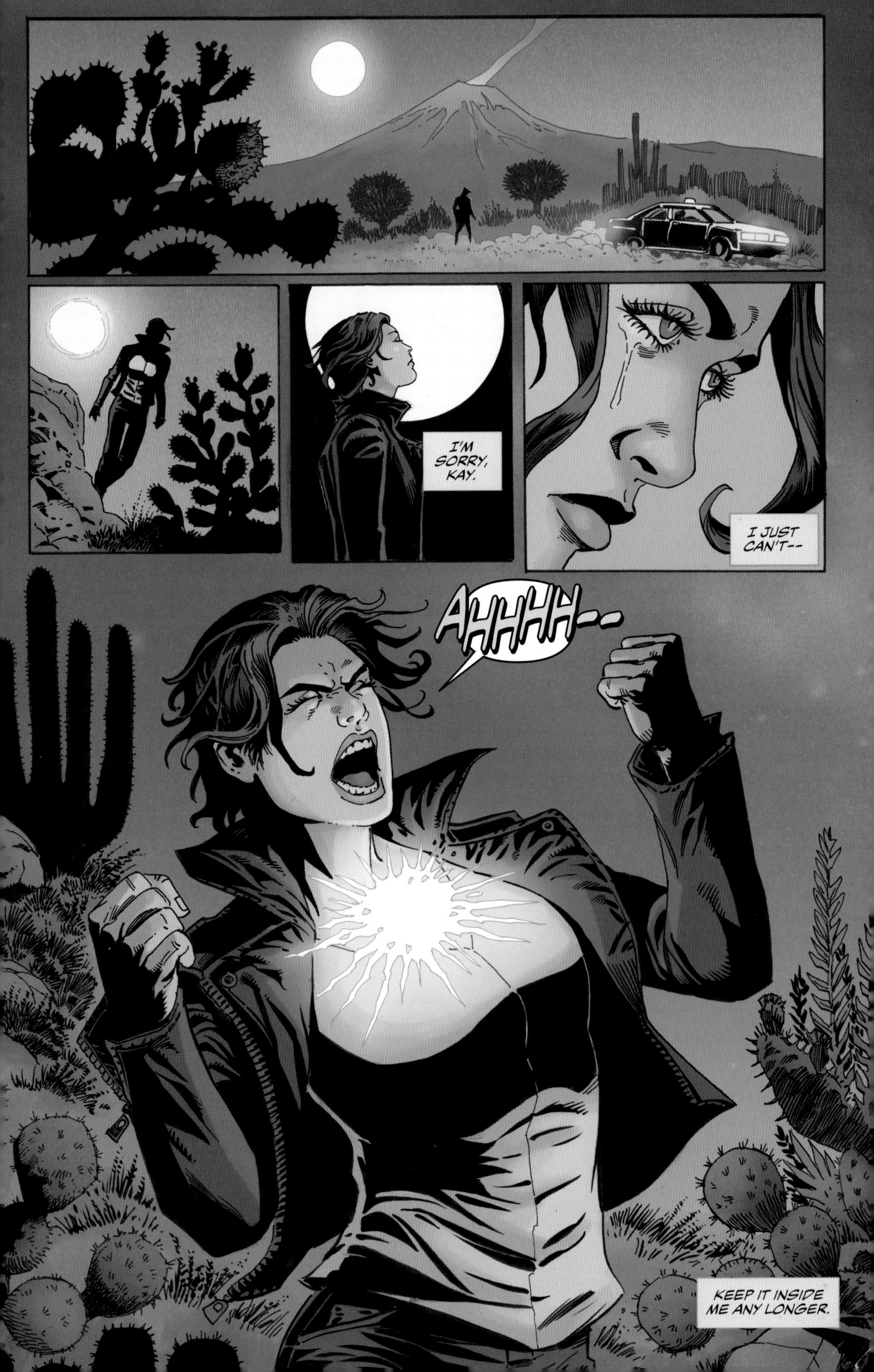
I'M SORRY, KAY.
I JUST CAN'T--
AHHHH--
KEEP IT INSIDE ME ANY LONGER.

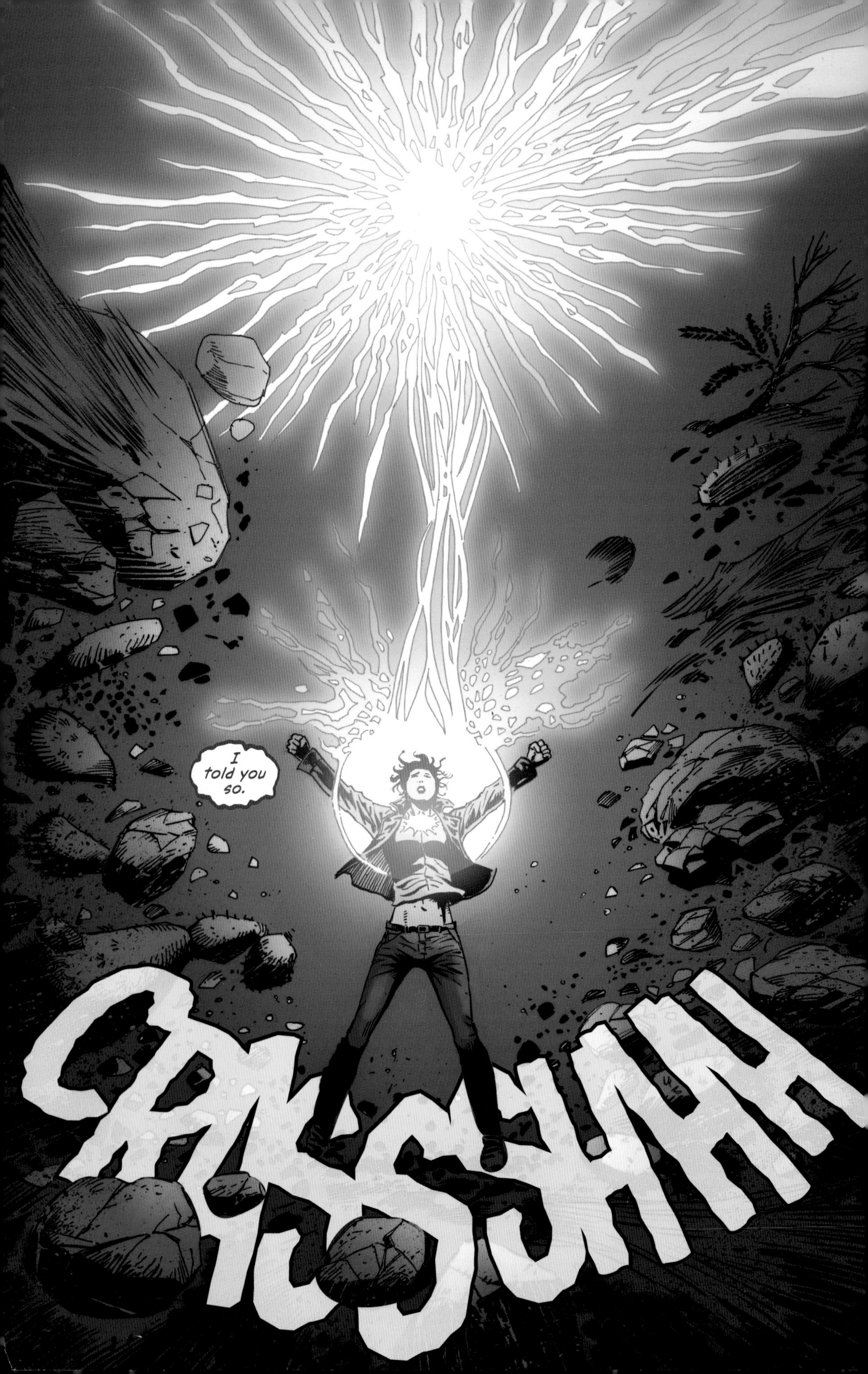
I told you so.
CRASSHH

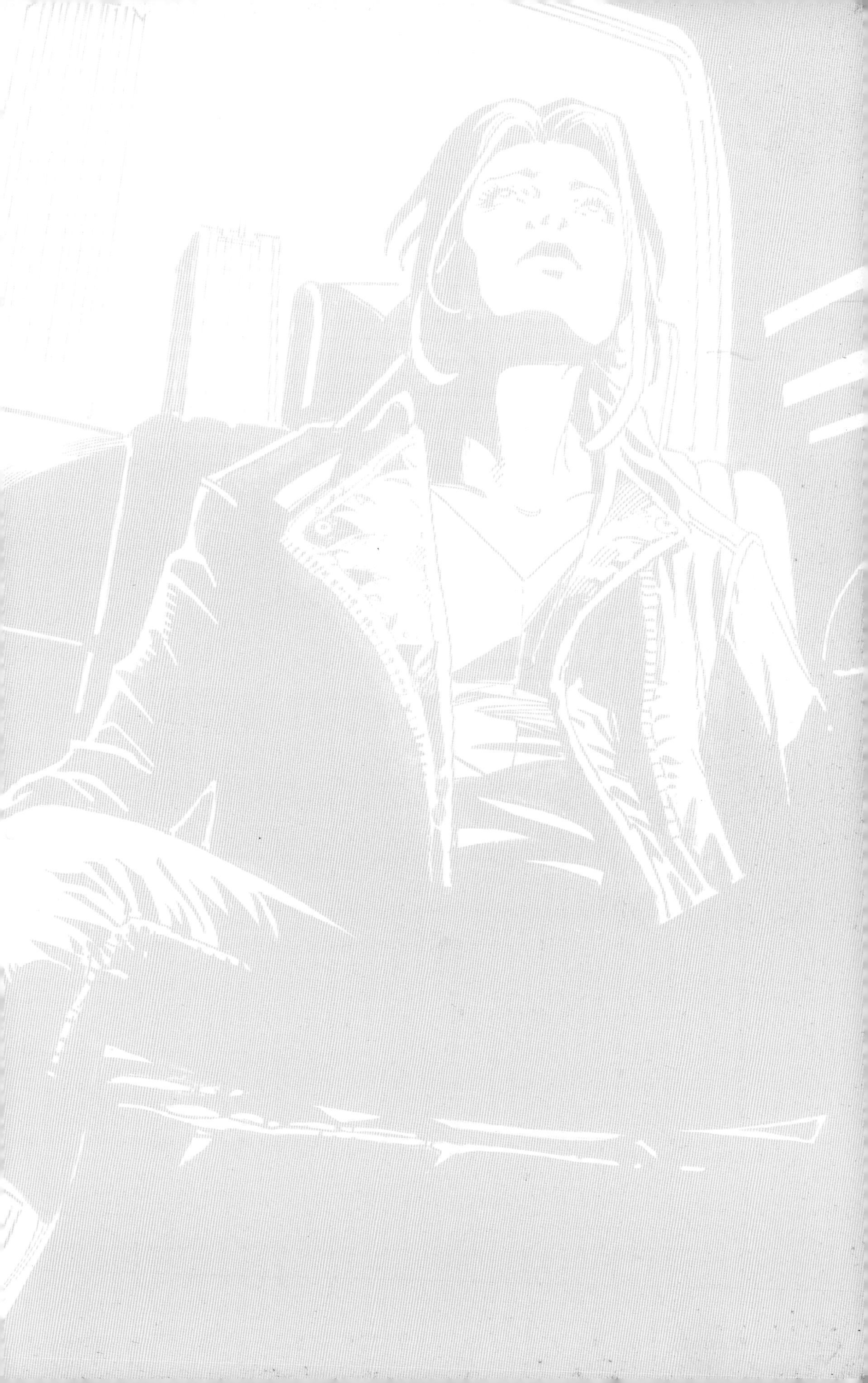

CHAPTER TWO

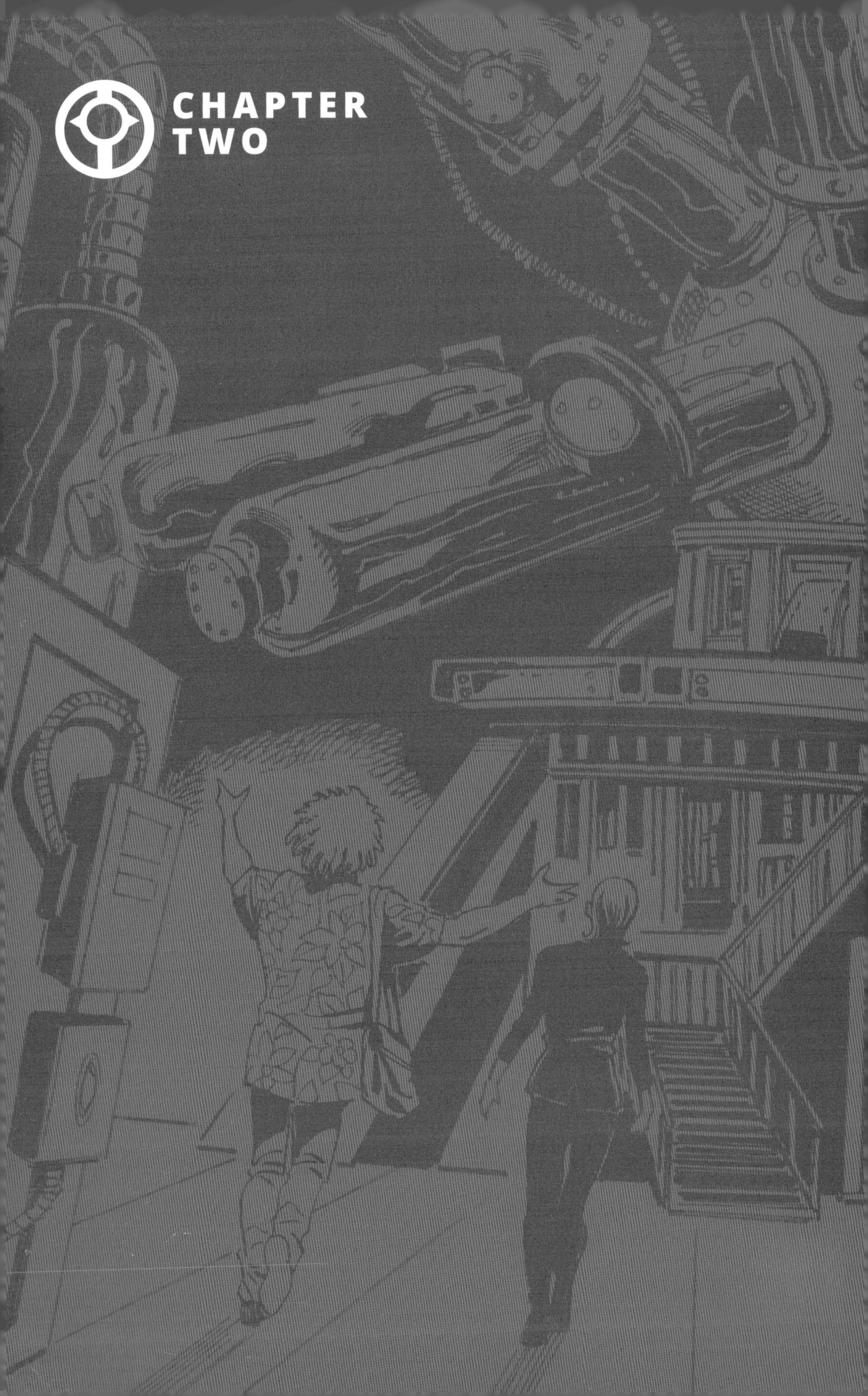

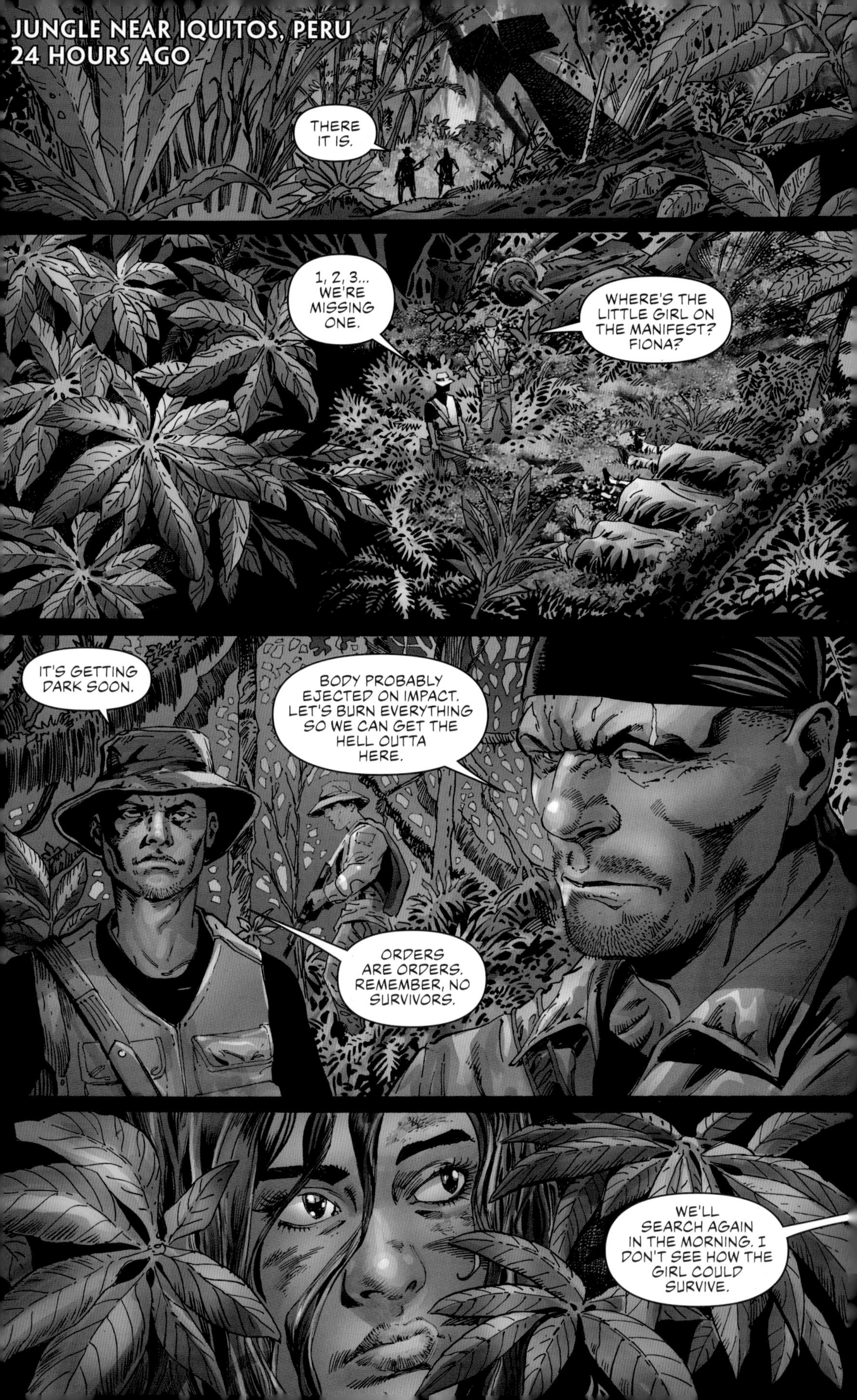
JUNGLE NEAR IQUITOS, PERU
24 HOURS AGO
THERE IT IS.
1, 2, 3... WE'RE MISSING ONE.
WHERE'S THE LITTLE GIRL ON THE MANIFEST? FIONA?
IT'S GETTING DARK SOON.
BODY PROBABLY EJECTED ON IMPACT. LET'S BURN EVERYTHING SO WE CAN GET THE HELL OUTTA HERE.
ORDERS ARE ORDERS. REMEMBER, NO SURVIVORS.
WE'LL SEARCH AGAIN IN THE MORNING. I DON'T SEE HOW THE GIRL COULD SURVIVE.

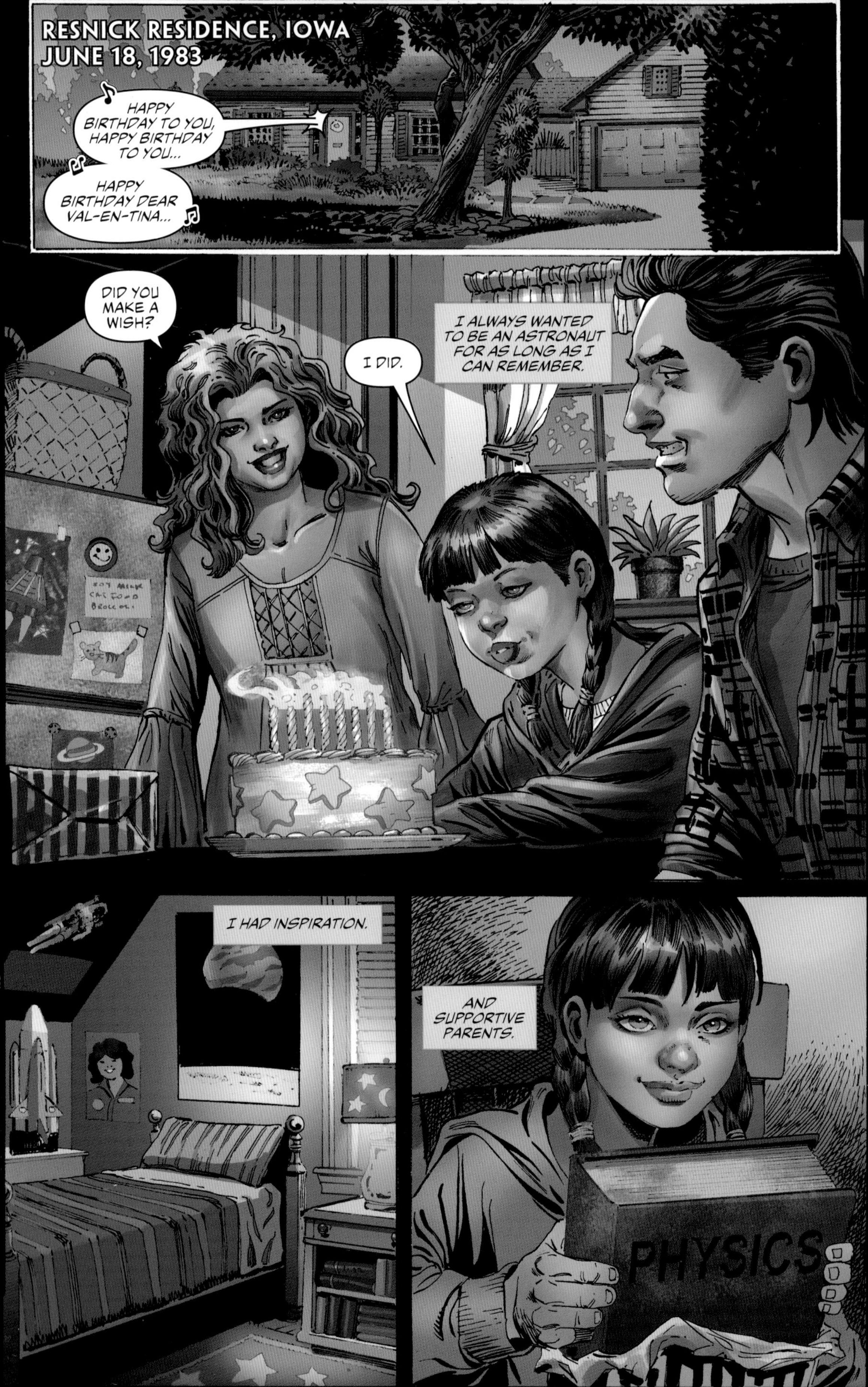
RESNICK RESIDENCE, IOWA
JUNE 18, 1983
HAPPY BIRTHDAY TO YOU, HAPPY BIRTHDAY TO YOU...
HAPPY BIRTHDAY DEAR VAL-EN-TINA...
DID YOU MAKE A WISH?
I DID.
I ALWAYS WANTED TO BE AN ASTRONAUT FOR AS LONG AS I CAN REMEMBER.
I HAD INSPIRATION.
AND SUPPORTIVE PARENTS.
PHYSICS

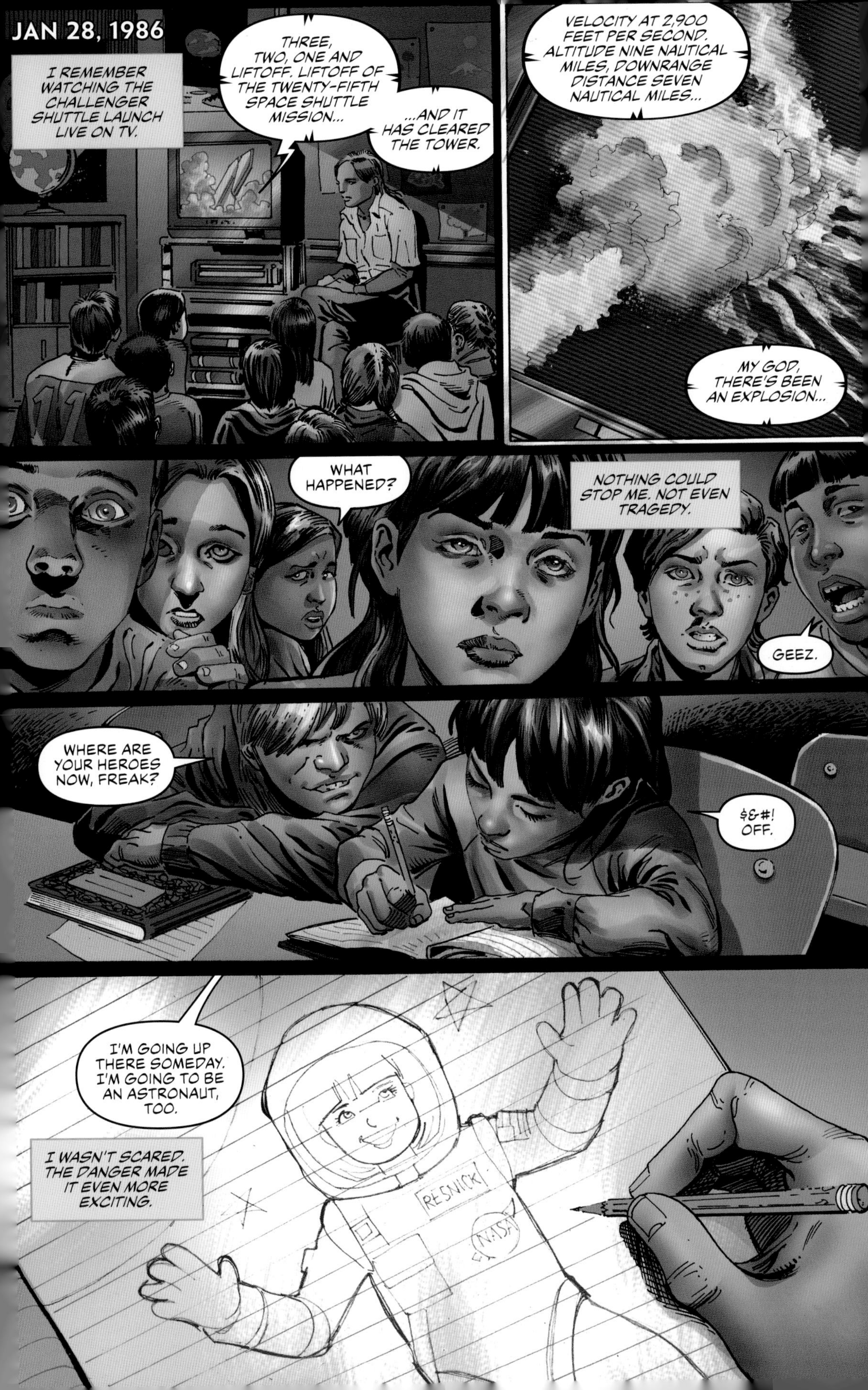
JAN 28, 1986
I REMEMBER WATCHING THE CHALLENGER SHUTTLE LAUNCH LIVE ON TV.
THREE, TWO, ONE AND LIFTOFF. LIFTOFF OF THE TWENTY-FIFTH SPACE SHUTTLE MISSION...
...AND IT HAS CLEARED THE TOWER.
VELOCITY AT 2,900 FEET PER SECOND. ALTITUDE NINE NAUTICAL MILES, DOWNRANGE DISTANCE SEVEN NAUTICAL MILES...
MY GOD, THERE'S BEEN AN EXPLOSION...
WHAT HAPPENED?
NOTHING COULD STOP ME. NOT EVEN TRAGEDY.
GEEZ.
WHERE ARE YOUR HEROES NOW, FREAK?
$&#! OFF.
I'M GOING UP THERE SOMEDAY. I'M GOING TO BE AN ASTRONAUT, TOO.
I WASN'T SCARED. THE DANGER MADE IT EVEN MORE EXCITING.
RESNICK
NASA

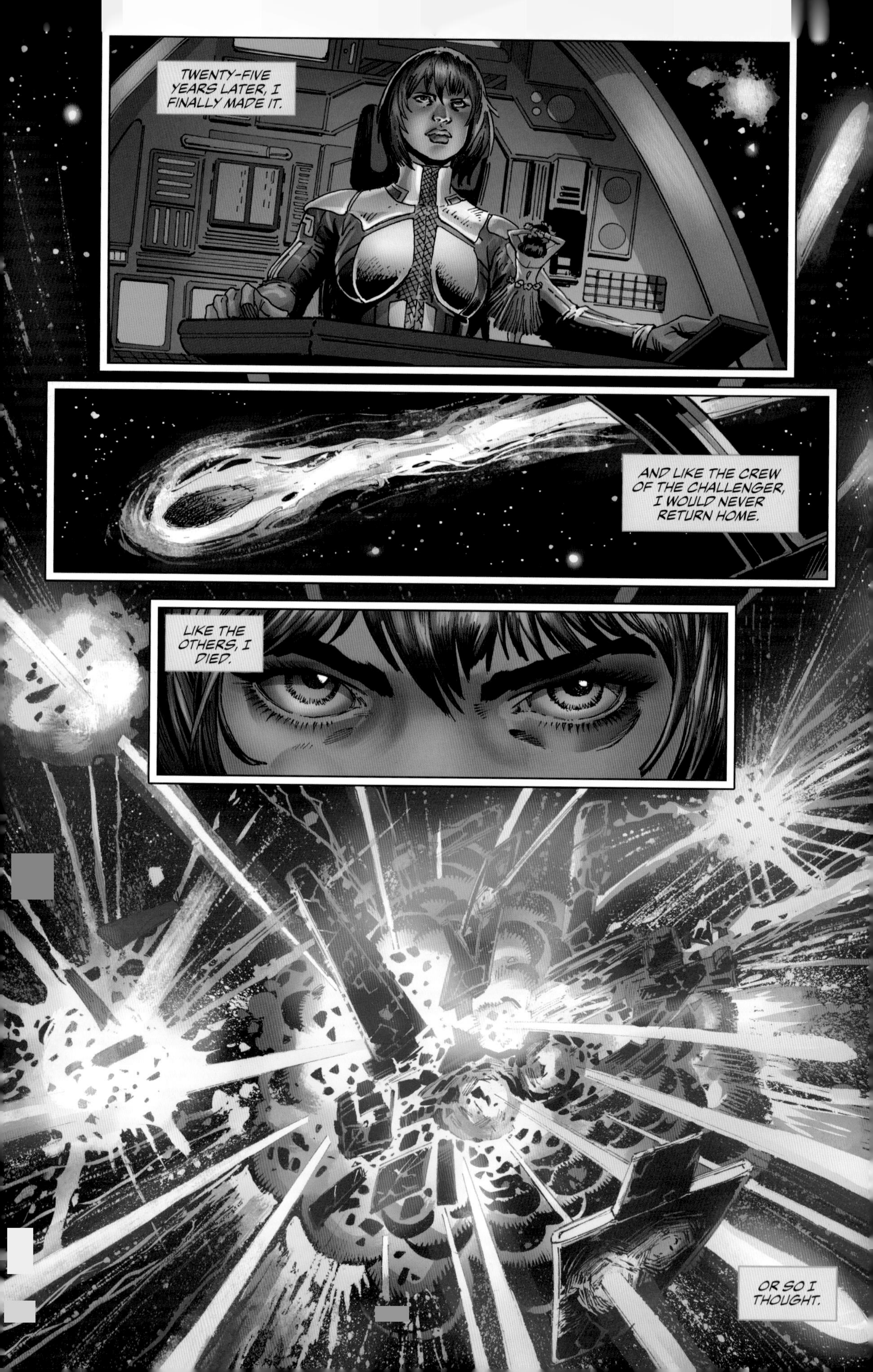
TWENTY-FIVE YEARS LATER, I FINALLY MADE IT.
AND LIKE THE CREW OF THE CHALLENGER, I WOULD NEVER RETURN HOME.
LIKE THE OTHERS, I DIED.
OR SO I THOUGHT.

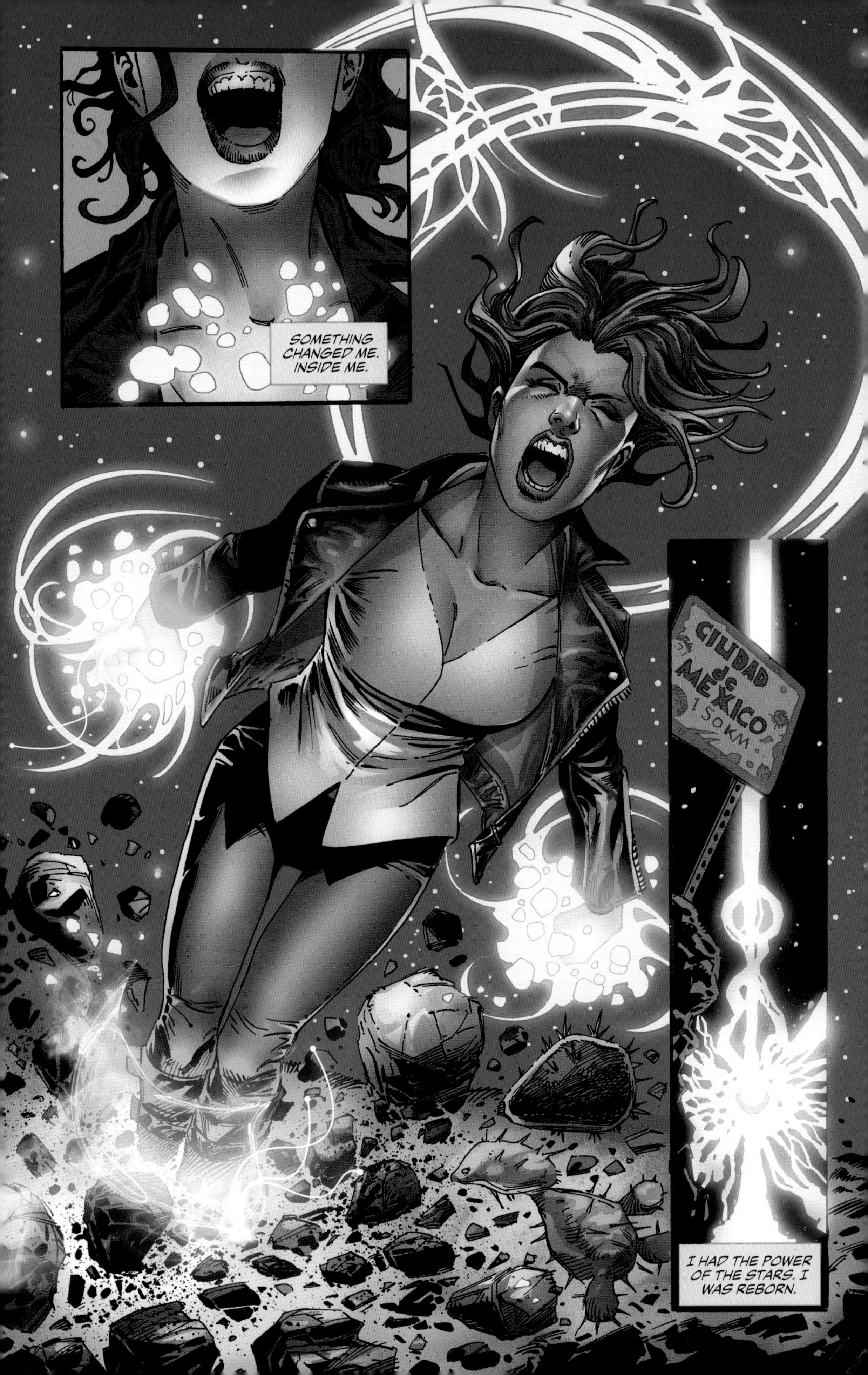
SOMETHING CHANGED ME. INSIDE ME.
CIUDAD de MEXICO 150KM
I HAD THE POWER OF THE STARS. I WAS REBORN.

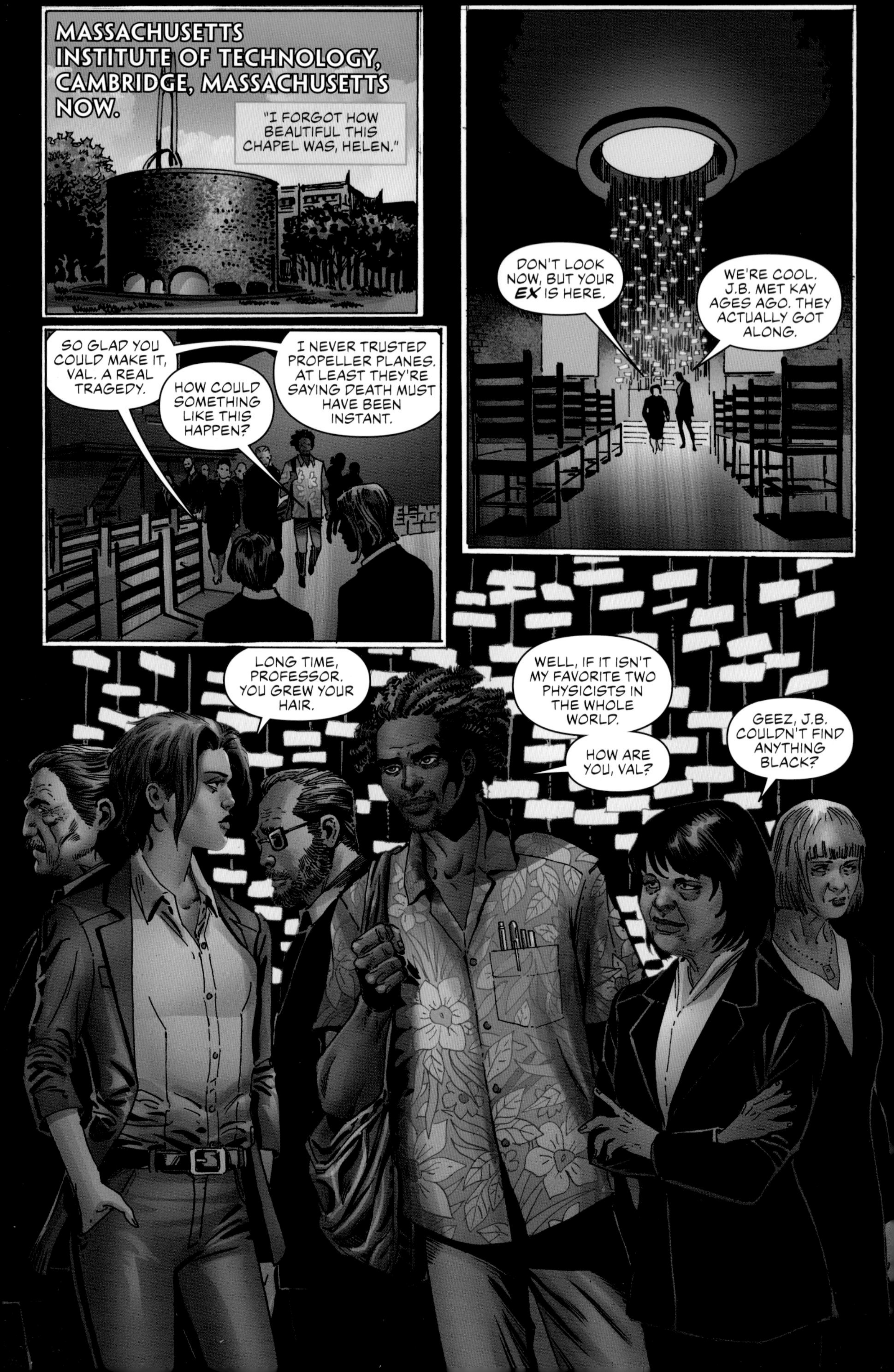
MASSACHUSETTS INSTITUTE OF TECHNOLOGY, CAMBRIDGE, MASSACHUSETTS NOW.
"I FORGOT HOW BEAUTIFUL THIS CHAPEL WAS, HELEN."
DON'T LOOK NOW, BUT YOUR EX IS HERE.
WE'RE COOL. J.B. MET KAY AGES AGO. THEY ACTUALLY GOT ALONG.
SO GLAD YOU COULD MAKE IT, VAL. A REAL TRAGEDY.
HOW COULD SOMETHING LIKE THIS HAPPEN?
I NEVER TRUSTED PROPELLER PLANES. AT LEAST THEY'RE SAYING DEATH MUST HAVE BEEN INSTANT.
LONG TIME, PROFESSOR. YOU GREW YOUR HAIR.
WELL, IF IT ISN'T MY FAVORITE TWO PHYSICISTS IN THE WHOLE WORLD.
HOW ARE YOU, VAL?
GEEZ, J.B. COULDN'T FIND ANYTHING BLACK?

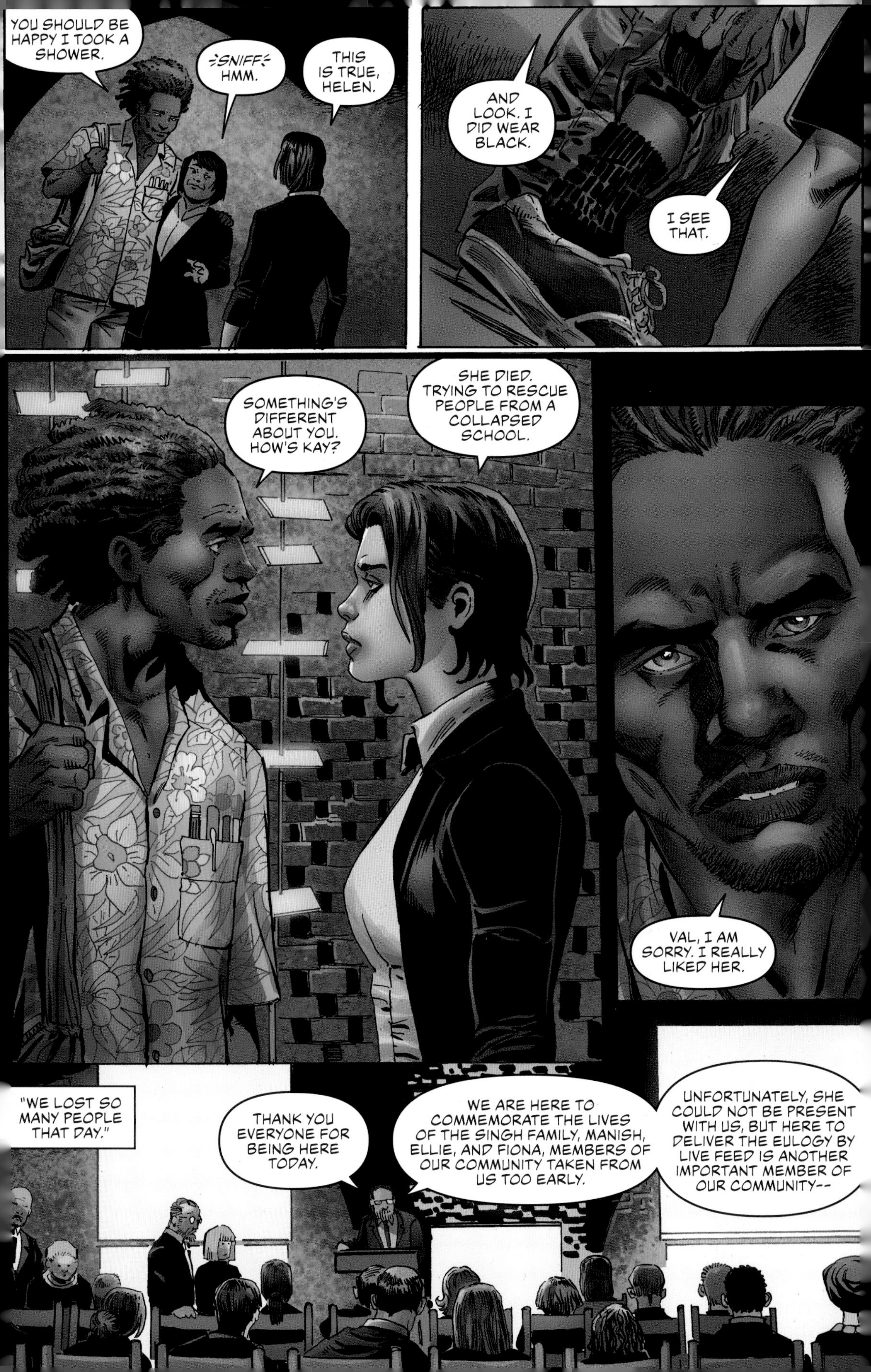
YOU SHOULD BE HAPPY I TOOK A SHOWER.
SNIFF HMM.
THIS IS TRUE, HELEN.
AND LOOK. I DID WEAR BLACK.
I SEE THAT.
SOMETHING'S DIFFERENT ABOUT YOU. HOW'S KAY?
SHE DIED. TRYING TO RESCUE PEOPLE FROM A COLLAPSED SCHOOL.
VAL, I AM SORRY. I REALLY LIKED HER.
"WE LOST SO MANY PEOPLE THAT DAY."
THANK YOU EVERYONE FOR BEING HERE TODAY.
WE ARE HERE TO COMMEMORATE THE LIVES OF THE SINGH FAMILY, MANISH, ELLIE, AND FIONA, MEMBERS OF OUR COMMUNITY TAKEN FROM US TOO EARLY.
UNFORTUNATELY, SHE COULD NOT BE PRESENT WITH US, BUT HERE TO DELIVER THE EULOGY BY LIVE FEED IS ANOTHER IMPORTANT MEMBER OF OUR COMMUNITY--

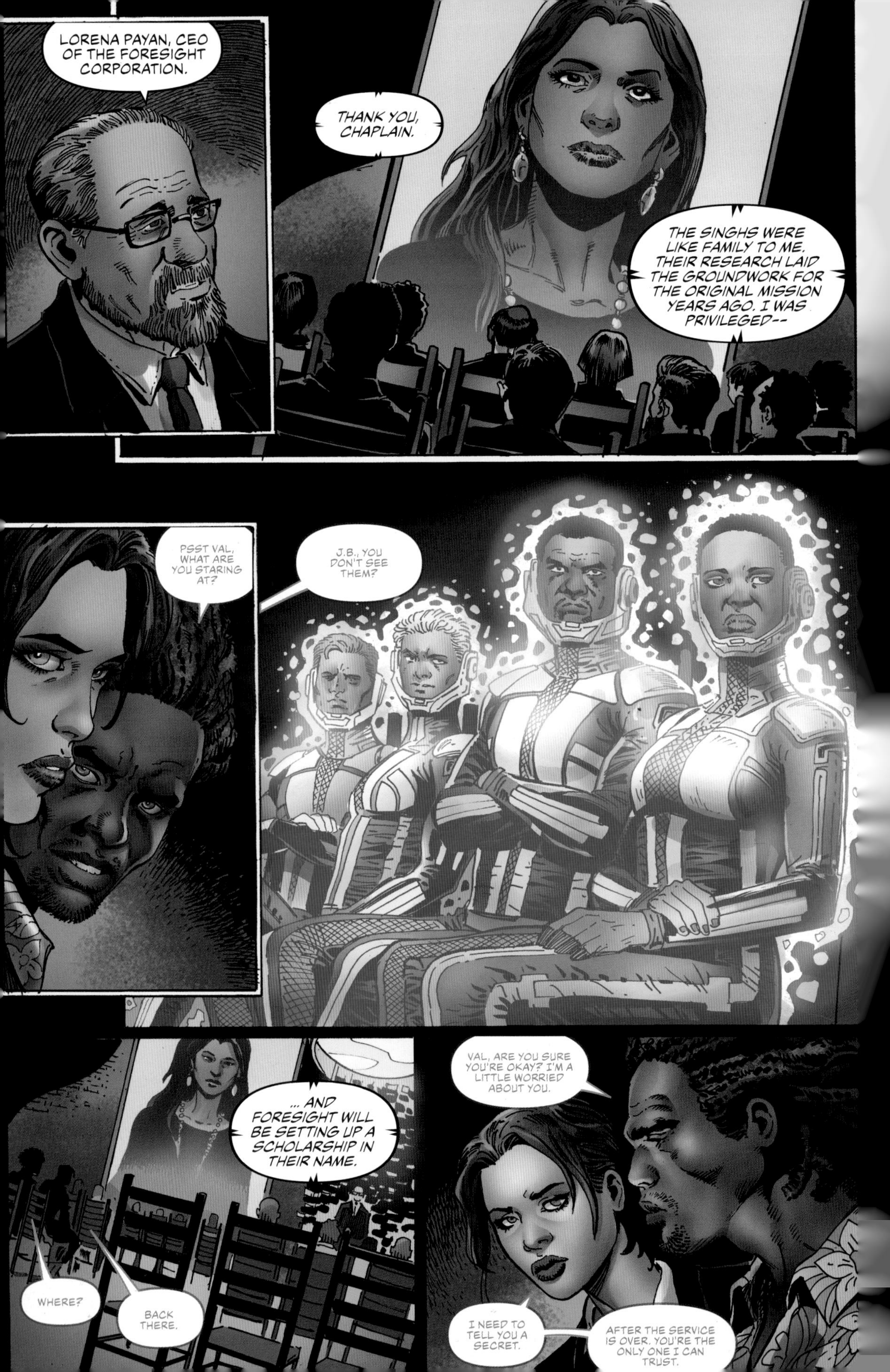
LORENA PAYAN, CEO OF THE FORESIGHT CORPORATION.
THANK YOU, CHAPLAIN.
THE SINGHS WERE LIKE FAMILY TO ME. THEIR RESEARCH LAID THE GROUNDWORK FOR THE ORIGINAL MISSION YEARS AGO. I WAS PRIVILEGED--
PSST VAL, WHAT ARE YOU STARING AT?
J.B., YOU DON'T SEE THEM?
... AND FORESIGHT WILL BE SETTING UP A SCHOLARSHIP IN THEIR NAME.
WHERE?
BACK THERE.
VAL, ARE YOU SURE YOU'RE OKAY? I'M A LITTLE WORRIED ABOUT YOU.
I NEED TO TELL YOU A SECRET.
AFTER THE SERVICE IS OVER. YOU'RE THE ONLY ONE I CAN TRUST.

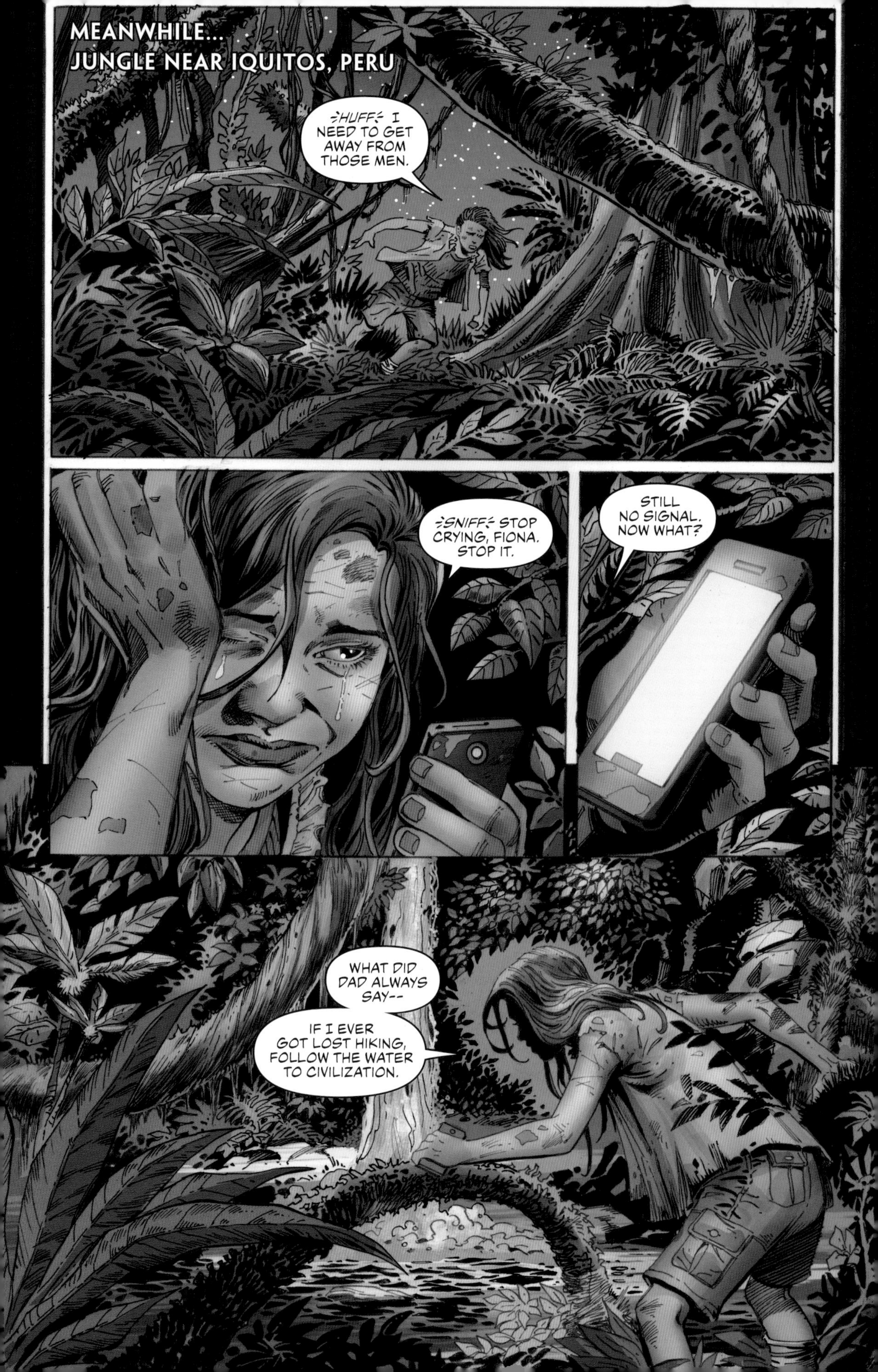
MEANWHILE...
JUNGLE NEAR IQUITOS, PERU
HUFF I NEED TO GET AWAY FROM THOSE MEN.
SNIFF STOP CRYING, FIONA. STOP IT.
STILL NO SIGNAL. NOW WHAT?
WHAT DID DAD ALWAYS SAY--
IF I EVER GOT LOST HIKING, FOLLOW THE WATER TO CIVILIZATION.

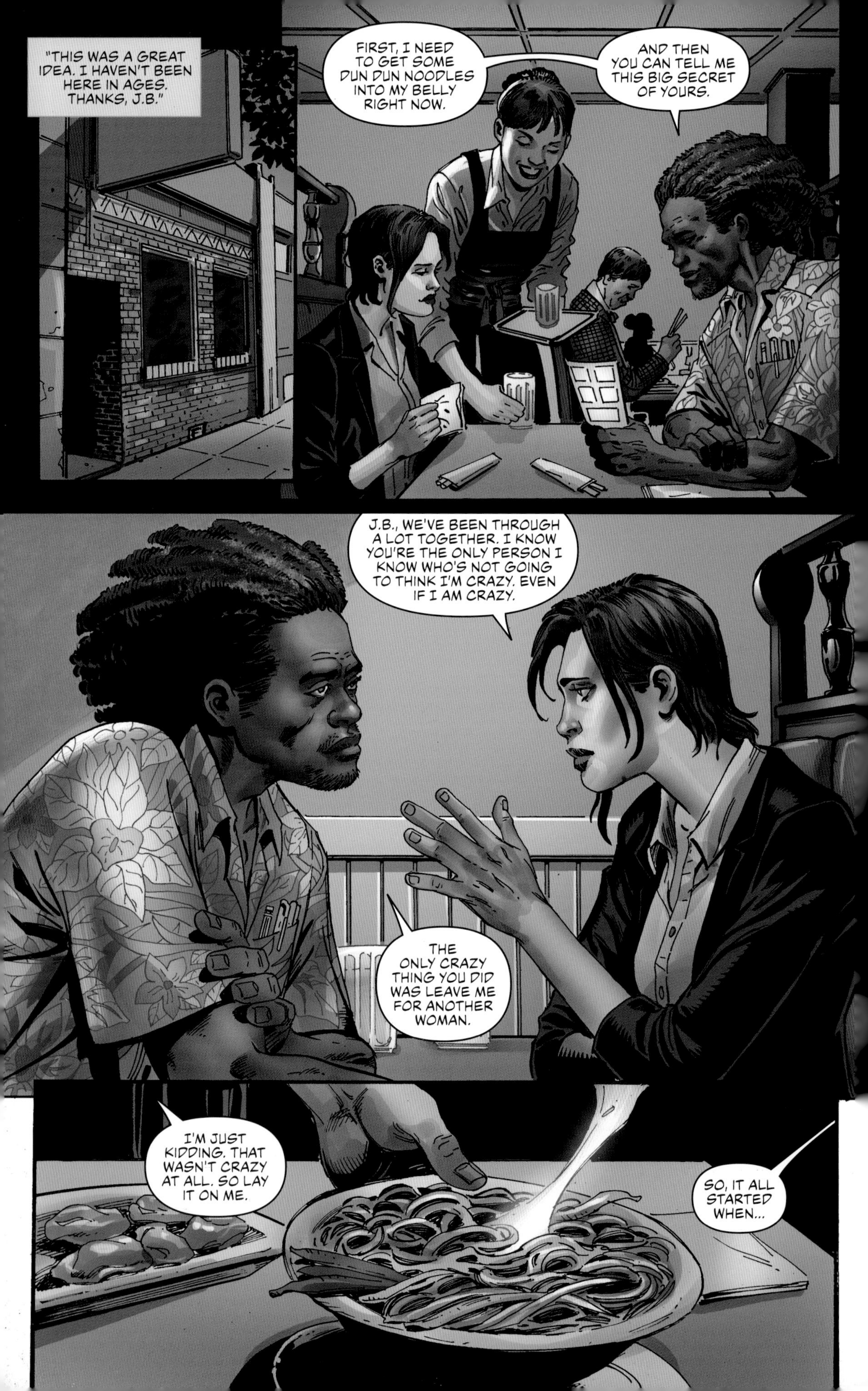
"THIS WAS A GREAT IDEA. I HAVEN'T BEEN HERE IN AGES. THANKS, J.B."
FIRST, I NEED TO GET SOME DUN DUN NOODLES INTO MY BELLY RIGHT NOW.
AND THEN YOU CAN TELL ME THIS BIG SECRET OF YOURS.
J.B., WE'VE BEEN THROUGH A LOT TOGETHER. I KNOW YOU'RE THE ONLY PERSON I KNOW WHO'S NOT GOING TO THINK I'M CRAZY. EVEN IF I AM CRAZY.
THE ONLY CRAZY THING YOU DID WAS LEAVE ME FOR ANOTHER WOMAN.
I'M JUST KIDDING. THAT WASN'T CRAZY AT ALL. SO LAY IT ON ME.
SO, IT ALL STARTED WHEN...

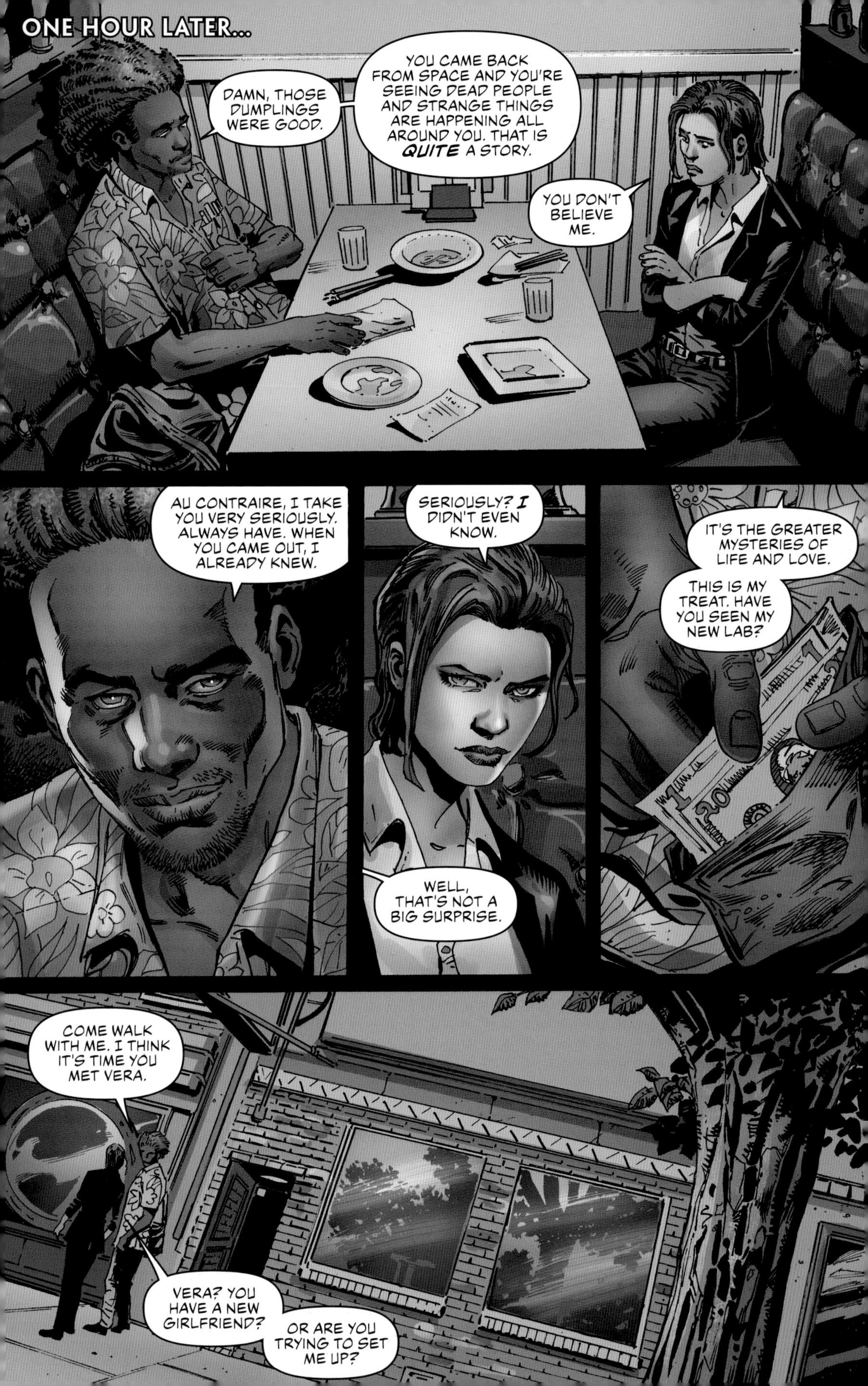
ONE HOUR LATER...
DAMN, THOSE DUMPLINGS WERE GOOD.
YOU CAME BACK FROM SPACE AND YOU'RE SEEING DEAD PEOPLE AND STRANGE THINGS ARE HAPPENING ALL AROUND YOU. THAT IS *QUITE* A STORY.
YOU DON'T BELIEVE ME.
AU CONTRAIRE, I TAKE YOU VERY SERIOUSLY. ALWAYS HAVE. WHEN YOU CAME OUT, I ALREADY KNEW.
SERIOUSLY? *I* DIDN'T EVEN KNOW.
WELL, THAT'S NOT A BIG SURPRISE.
IT'S THE GREATER MYSTERIES OF LIFE AND LOVE.
THIS IS MY TREAT. HAVE YOU SEEN MY NEW LAB?
COME WALK WITH ME. I THINK IT'S TIME YOU MET VERA.
VERA? YOU HAVE A NEW GIRLFRIEND?
OR ARE YOU TRYING TO SET ME UP?

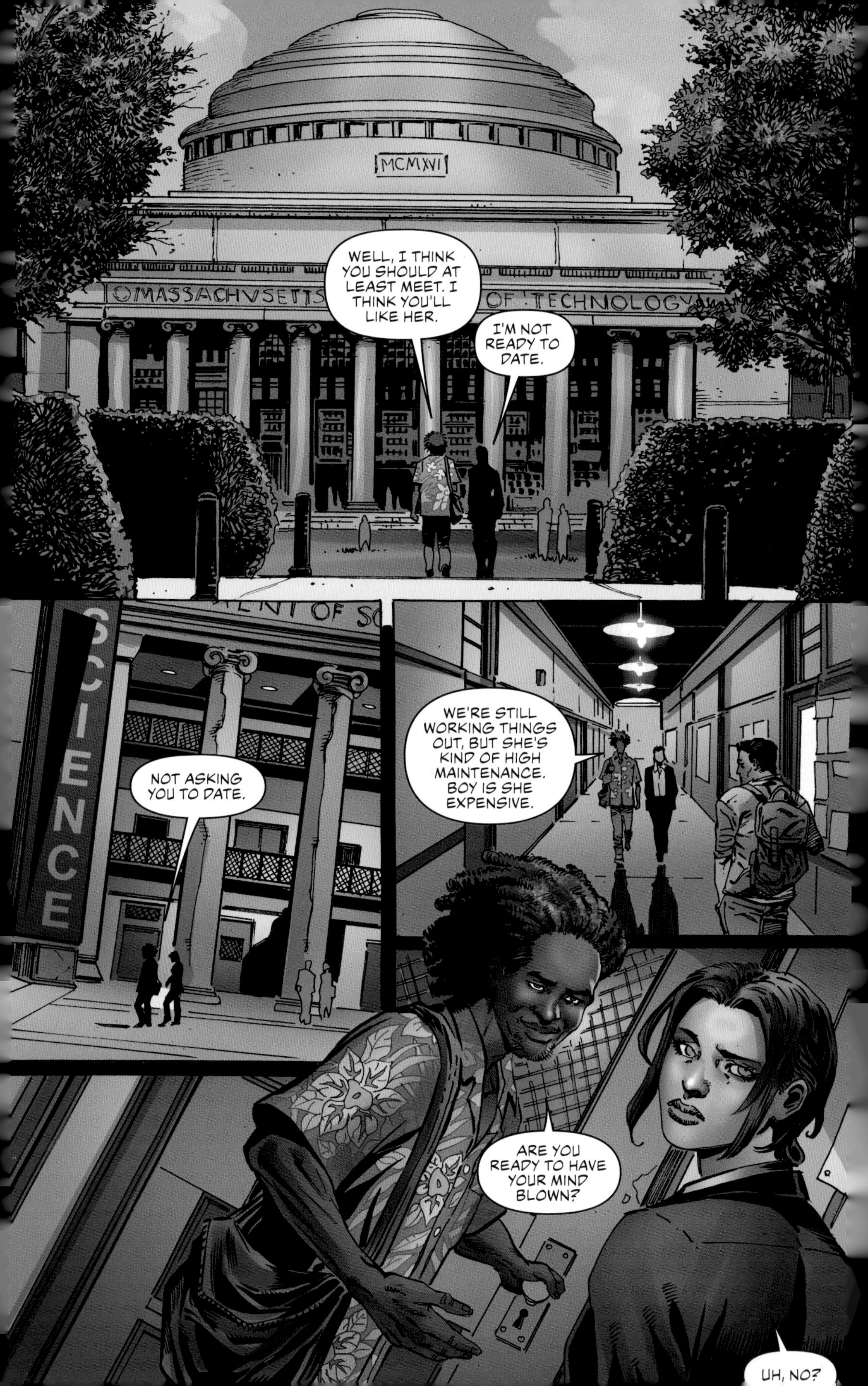
MCMXVI
MASSACHVSETTS OF TECHNOLOGY
WELL, I THINK YOU SHOULD AT LEAST MEET. I THINK YOU'LL LIKE HER.
I'M NOT READY TO DATE.
SCIENCE
NOT ASKING YOU TO DATE.
WE'RE STILL WORKING THINGS OUT, BUT SHE'S KIND OF HIGH MAINTENANCE. BOY IS SHE EXPENSIVE.
ARE YOU READY TO HAVE YOUR MIND BLOWN?
UH, NO?

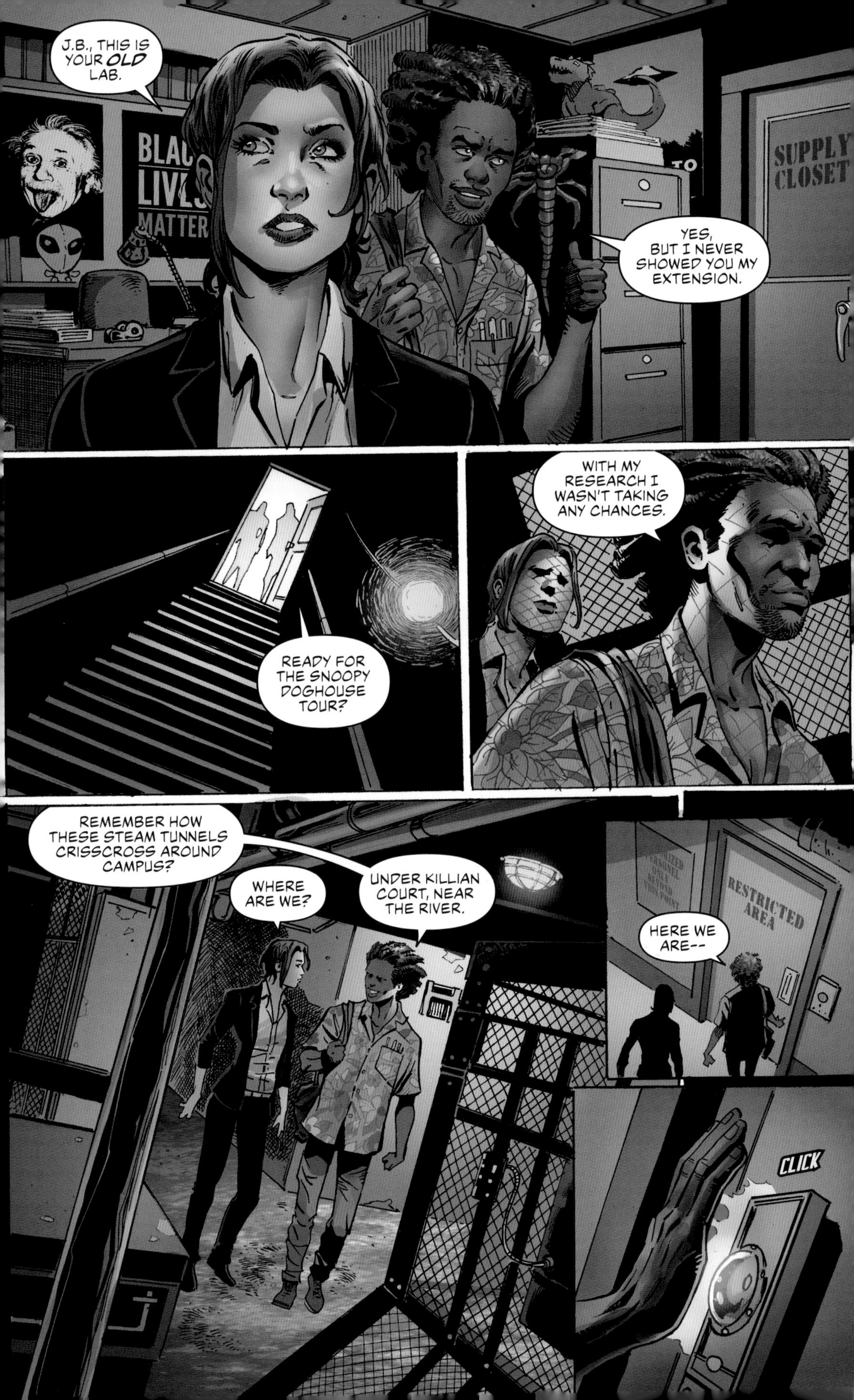
J.B., THIS IS YOUR OLD LAB.
SUPPLY CLOSET
YES, BUT I NEVER SHOWED YOU MY EXTENSION.
READY FOR THE SNOOPY DOGHOUSE TOUR?
WITH MY RESEARCH I WASN'T TAKING ANY CHANCES.
REMEMBER HOW THESE STEAM TUNNELS CRISSCROSS AROUND CAMPUS?
WHERE ARE WE?
UNDER KILLIAN COURT, NEAR THE RIVER.
RESTRICTED AREA
HERE WE ARE--
CLICK

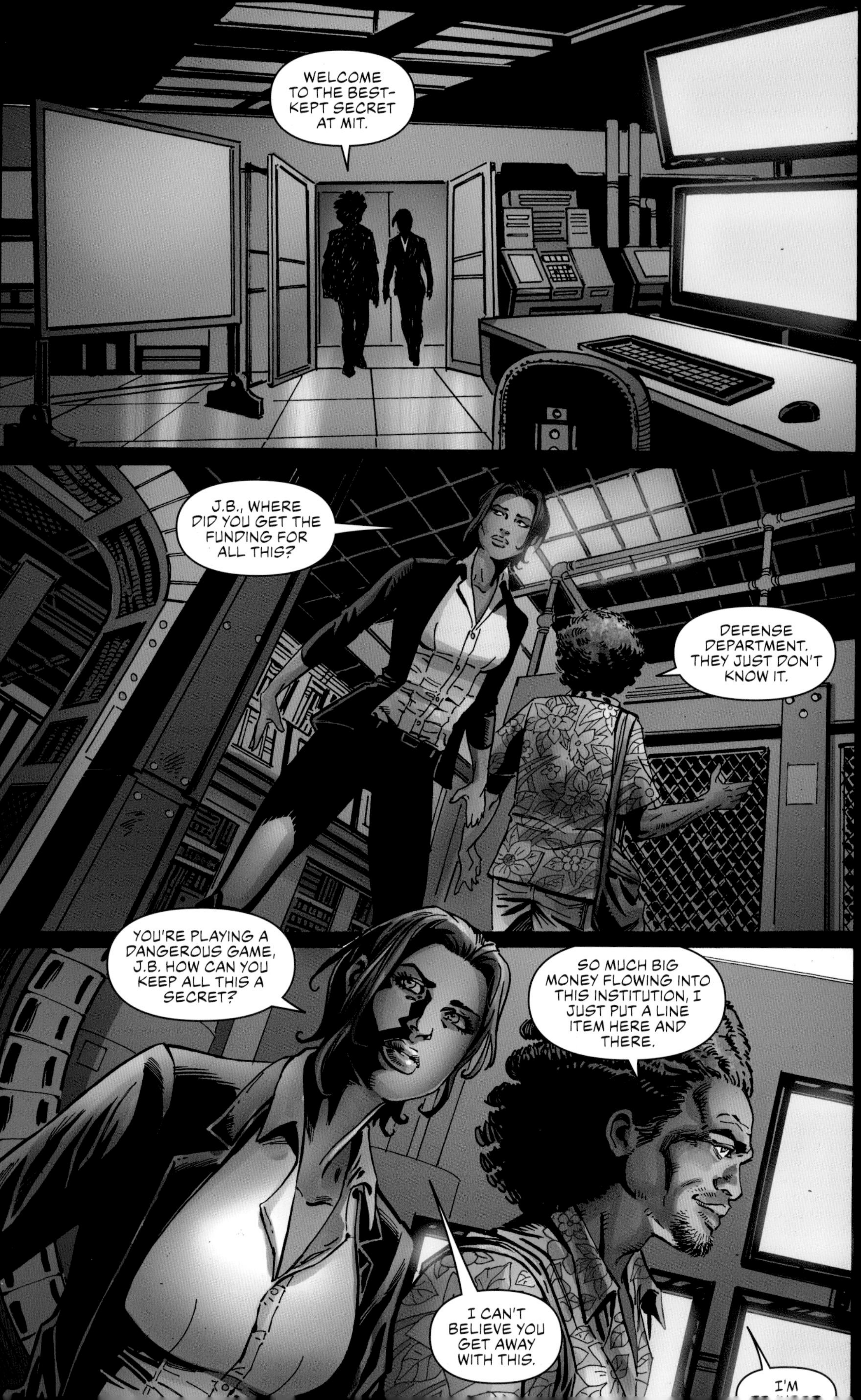
WELCOME TO THE BEST-KEPT SECRET AT MIT.
J.B., WHERE DID YOU GET THE FUNDING FOR ALL THIS?
DEFENSE DEPARTMENT. THEY JUST DON'T KNOW IT.
YOU'RE PLAYING A DANGEROUS GAME, J.B. HOW CAN YOU KEEP ALL THIS A SECRET?
SO MUCH BIG MONEY FLOWING INTO THIS INSTITUTION, I JUST PUT A LINE ITEM HERE AND THERE.
I CAN'T BELIEVE YOU GET AWAY WITH THIS.
I'M

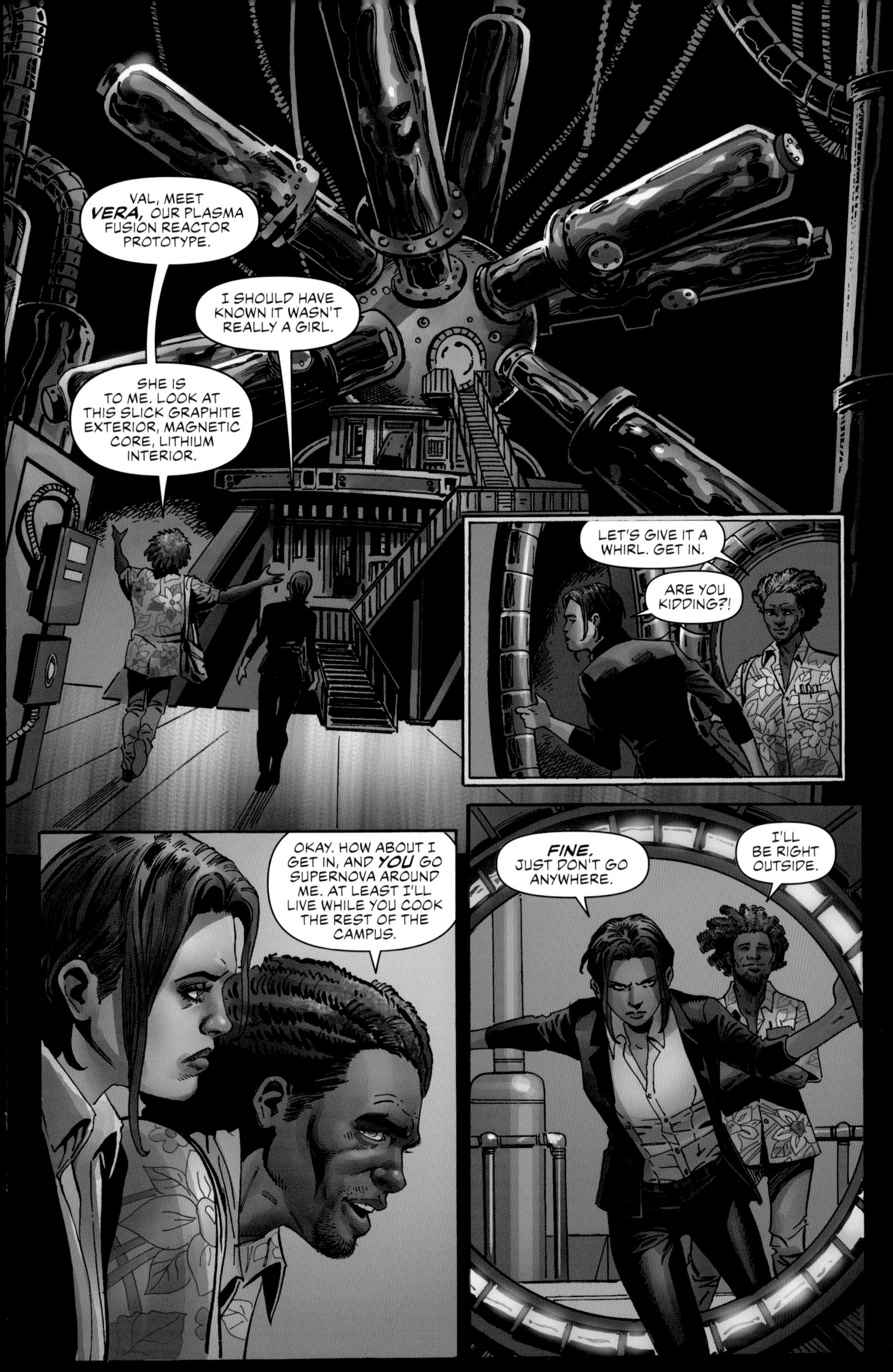
VAL, MEET VERA, OUR PLASMA FUSION REACTOR PROTOTYPE.
I SHOULD HAVE KNOWN IT WASN'T REALLY A GIRL.
SHE IS TO ME. LOOK AT THIS SLICK GRAPHITE EXTERIOR, MAGNETIC CORE, LITHIUM INTERIOR.
LET'S GIVE IT A WHIRL. GET IN.
ARE YOU KIDDING?!
OKAY. HOW ABOUT I GET IN, AND YOU GO SUPERNOVA AROUND ME. AT LEAST I'LL LIVE WHILE YOU COOK THE REST OF THE CAMPUS.
FINE. JUST DON'T GO ANYWHERE.
I'LL BE RIGHT OUTSIDE.

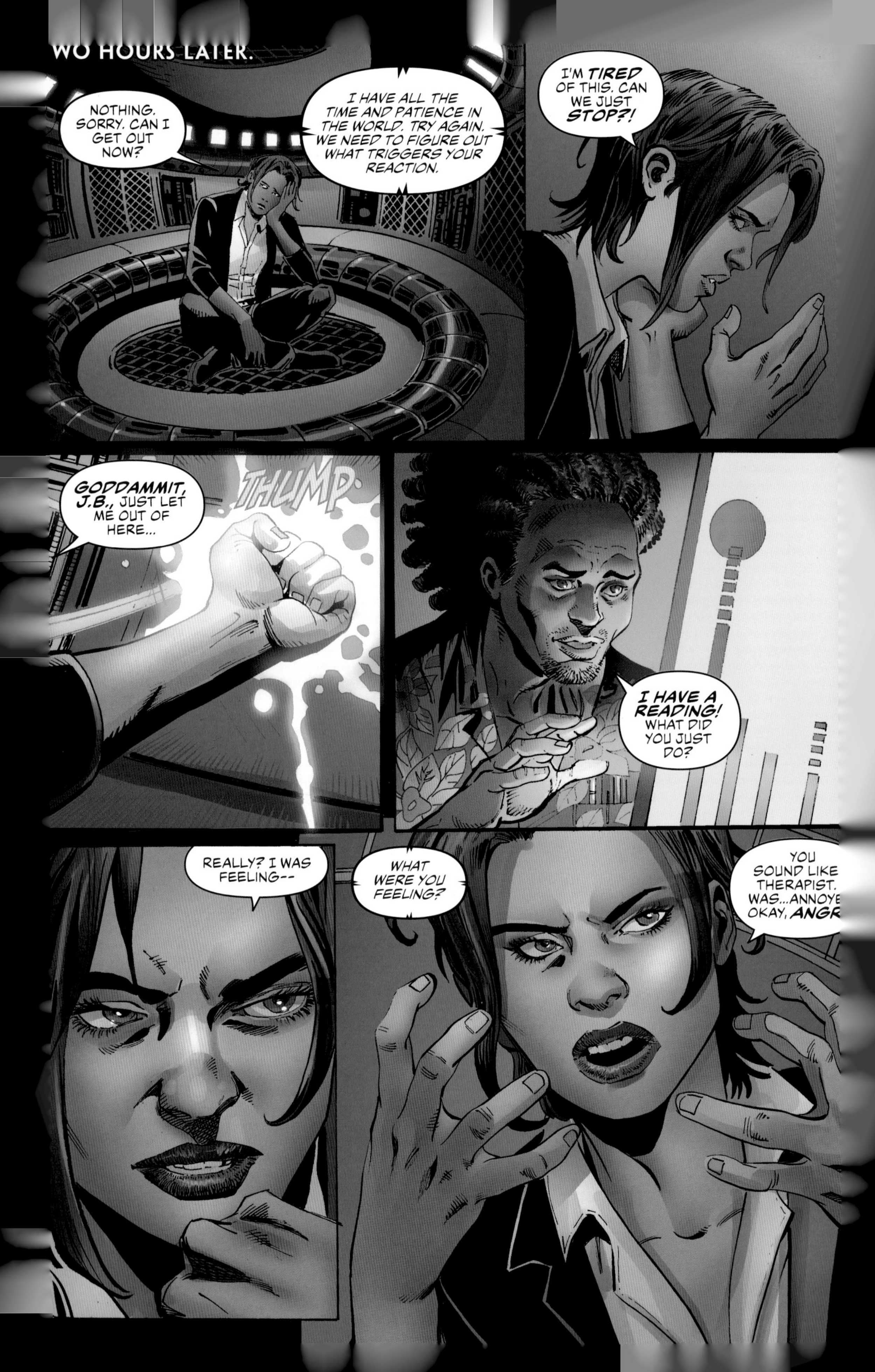
WO HOURS LATER.
NOTHING. SORRY. CAN I GET OUT NOW?
I HAVE ALL THE TIME AND PATIENCE IN THE WORLD. TRY AGAIN. WE NEED TO FIGURE OUT WHAT TRIGGERS YOUR REACTION.
I'M TIRED OF THIS. CAN WE JUST STOP?!
GODDAMMIT, J.B., JUST LET ME OUT OF HERE...
THUMP
I HAVE A READING! WHAT DID YOU JUST DO?
REALLY? I WAS FEELING--
WHAT WERE YOU FEELING?
YOU SOUND LIKE THERAPIST. WAS...ANNOYE OKAY, ANGR

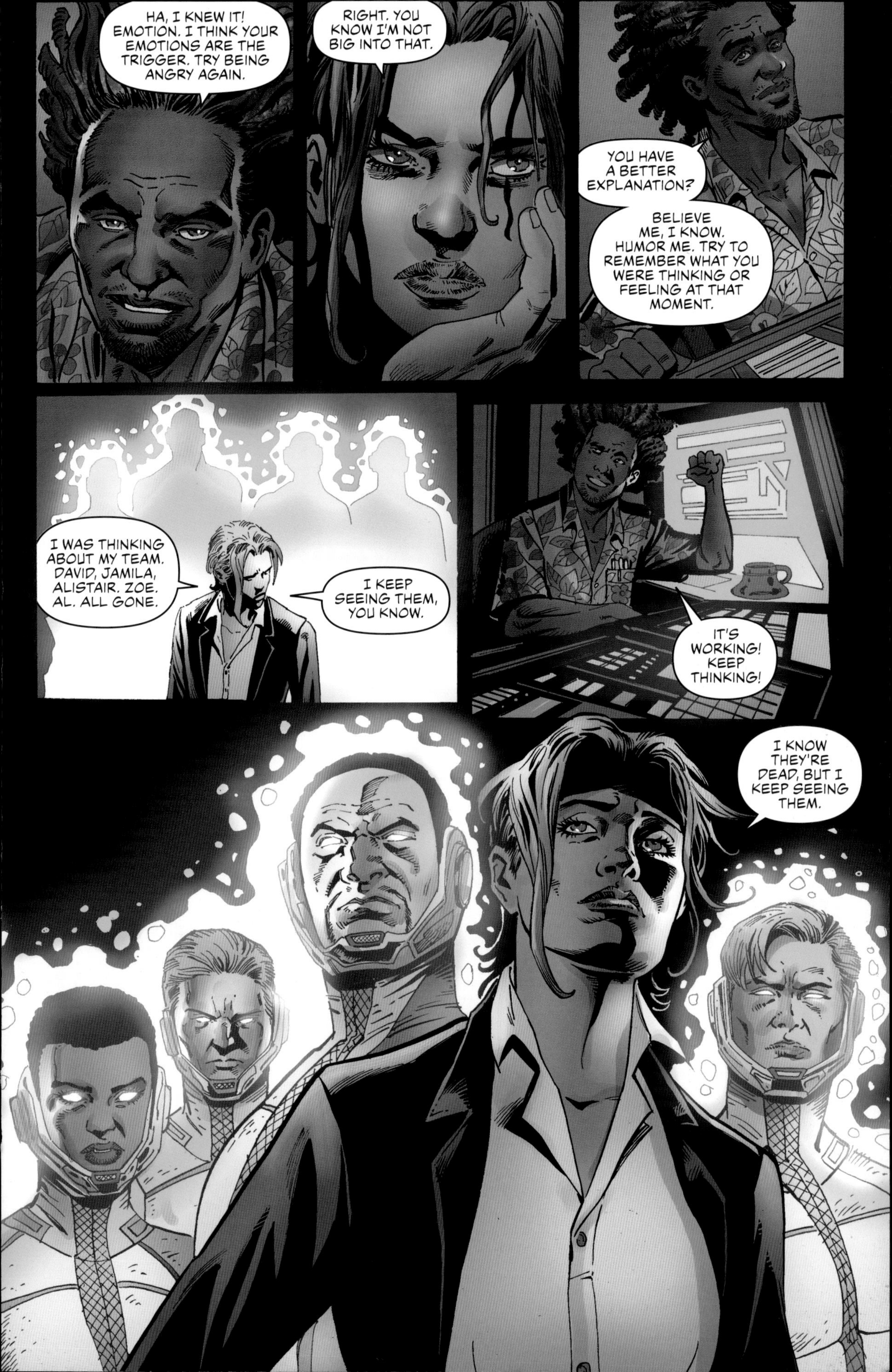
HA, I KNEW IT! EMOTION. I THINK YOUR EMOTIONS ARE THE TRIGGER. TRY BEING ANGRY AGAIN.
RIGHT. YOU KNOW I'M NOT BIG INTO THAT.
YOU HAVE A BETTER EXPLANATION?
BELIEVE ME, I KNOW. HUMOR ME. TRY TO REMEMBER WHAT YOU WERE THINKING OR FEELING AT THAT MOMENT.
I WAS THINKING ABOUT MY TEAM. DAVID, JAMILA, ALISTAIR. ZOE. AL. ALL GONE.
I KEEP SEEING THEM, YOU KNOW.
IT'S WORKING! KEEP THINKING!
I KNOW THEY'RE DEAD, BUT I KEEP SEEING THEM.

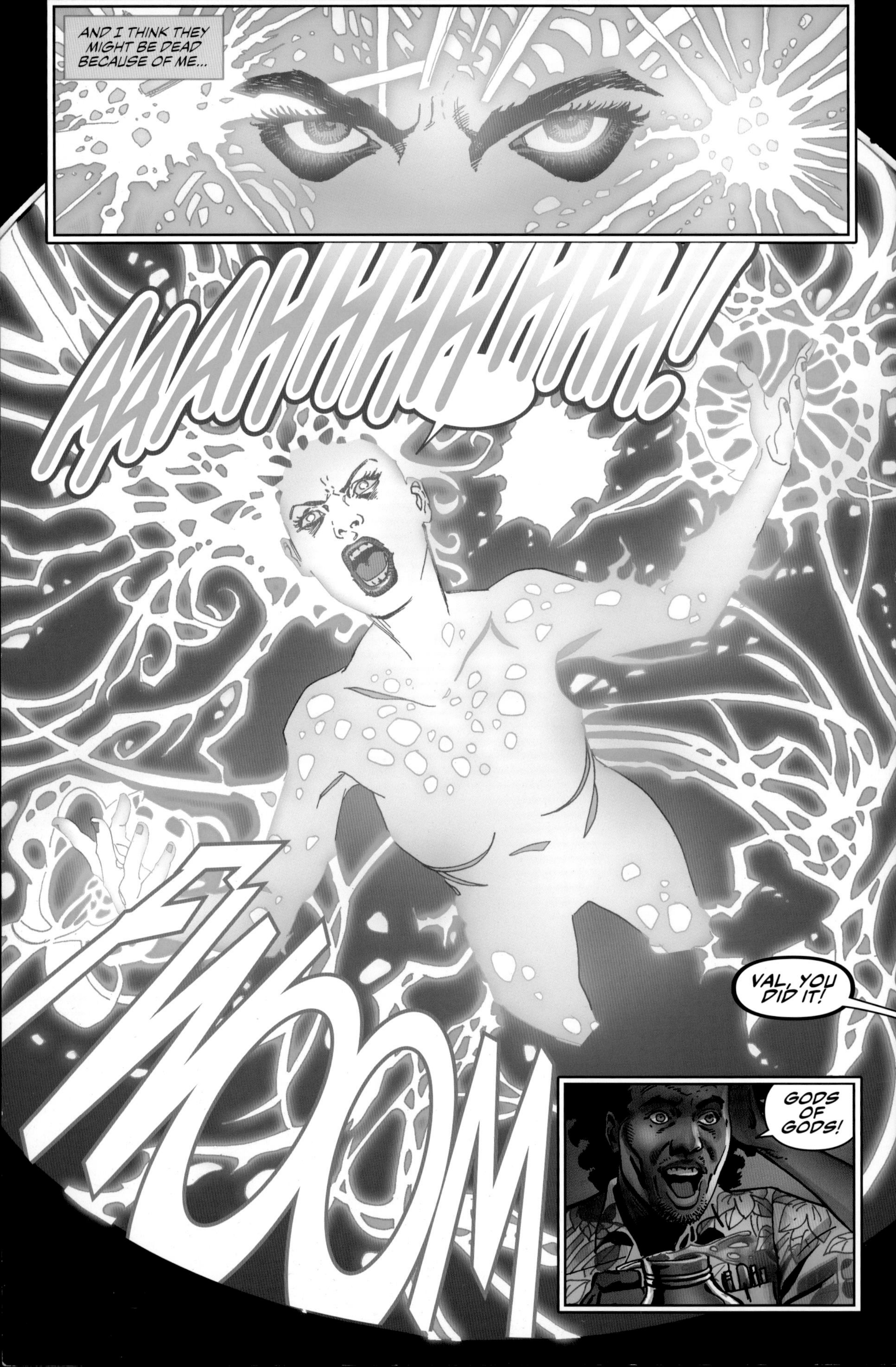
AND I THINK THEY MIGHT BE DEAD BECAUSE OF ME...
AAAAHHHHHHHHH!
VAL, YOU DID IT!
GODS OF GODS!

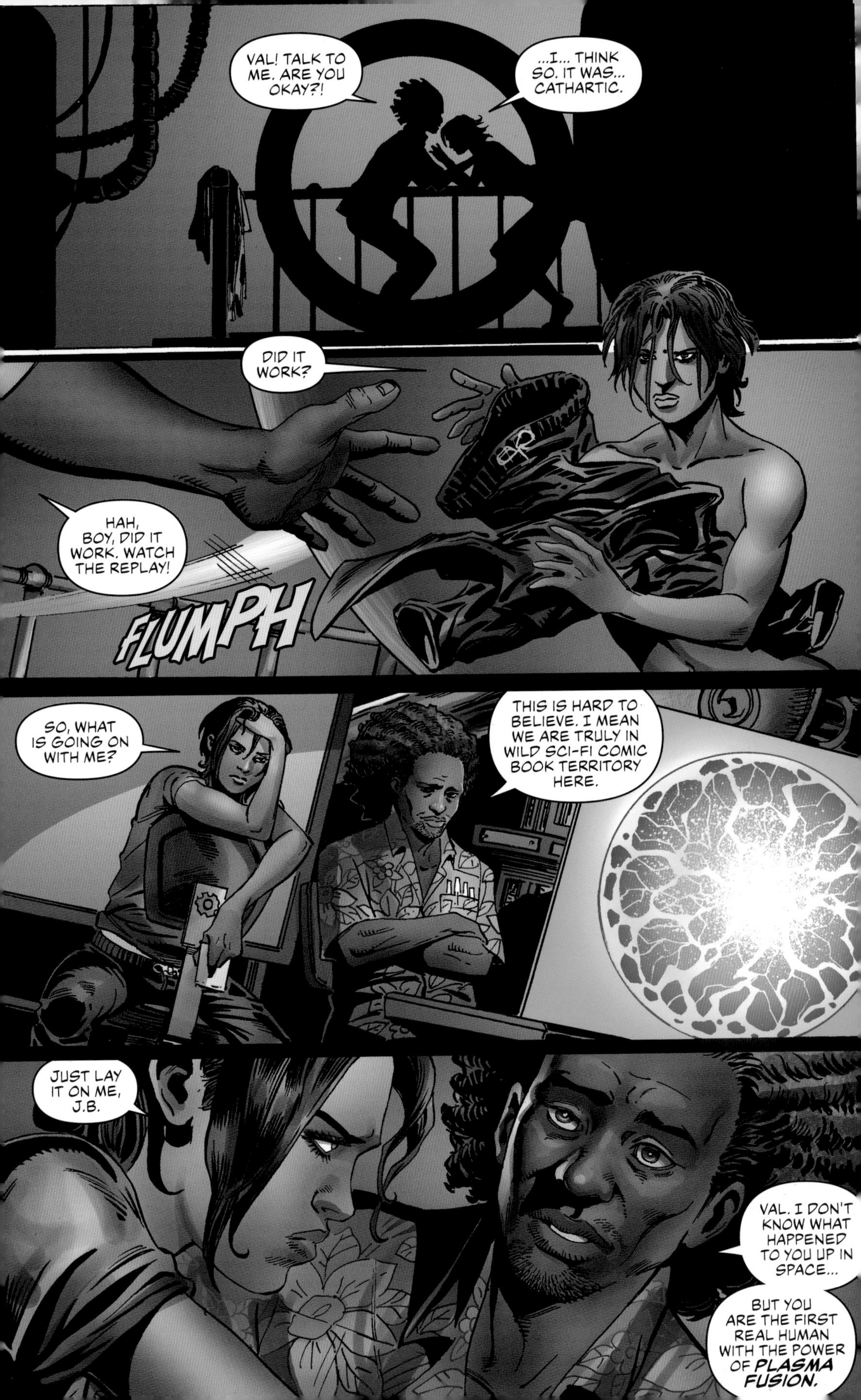

VAL! TALK TO ME. ARE YOU OKAY?!
...I... THINK SO. IT WAS... CATHARTIC.
DID IT WORK?
HAH, BOY, DID IT WORK. WATCH THE REPLAY!
FLUMPH
SO, WHAT IS GOING ON WITH ME?
THIS IS HARD TO BELIEVE. I MEAN WE ARE TRULY IN WILD SCI-FI COMIC BOOK TERRITORY HERE.
JUST LAY IT ON ME, J.B.
VAL. I DON'T KNOW WHAT HAPPENED TO YOU UP IN SPACE...
BUT YOU ARE THE FIRST REAL HUMAN WITH THE POWER OF PLASMA FUSION.

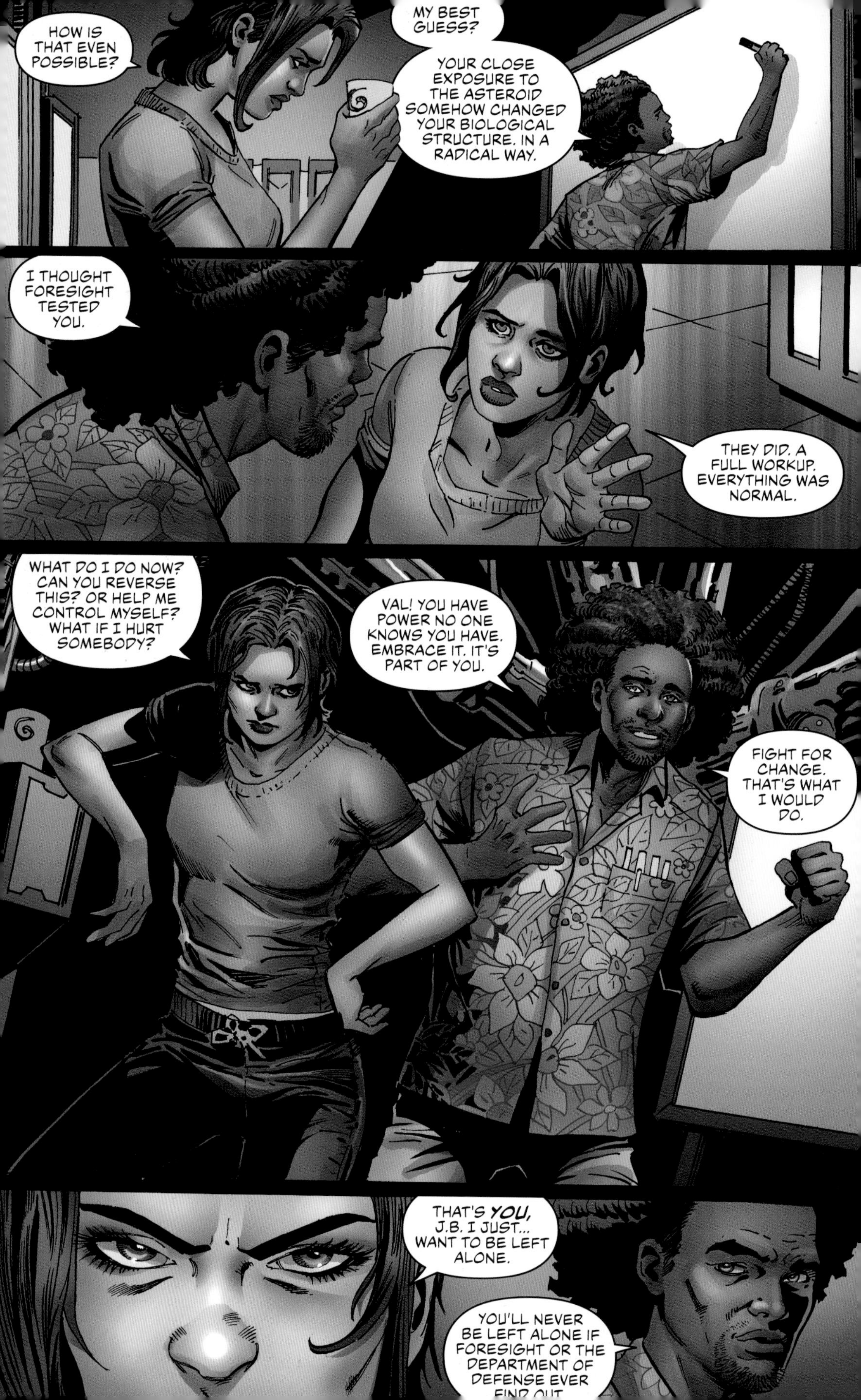
HOW IS THAT EVEN POSSIBLE?
MY BEST GUESS?
YOUR CLOSE EXPOSURE TO THE ASTEROID SOMEHOW CHANGED YOUR BIOLOGICAL STRUCTURE. IN A RADICAL WAY.
I THOUGHT FORESIGHT TESTED YOU.
THEY DID. A FULL WORKUP. EVERYTHING WAS NORMAL.
WHAT DO I DO NOW? CAN YOU REVERSE THIS? OR HELP ME CONTROL MYSELF? WHAT IF I HURT SOMEBODY?
VAL! YOU HAVE POWER NO ONE KNOWS YOU HAVE. EMBRACE IT. IT'S PART OF YOU.
FIGHT FOR CHANGE. THAT'S WHAT I WOULD DO.
THAT'S *YOU,* J.B. I JUST... WANT TO BE LEFT ALONE.
YOU'LL NEVER BE LEFT ALONE IF FORESIGHT OR THE DEPARTMENT OF DEFENSE EVER

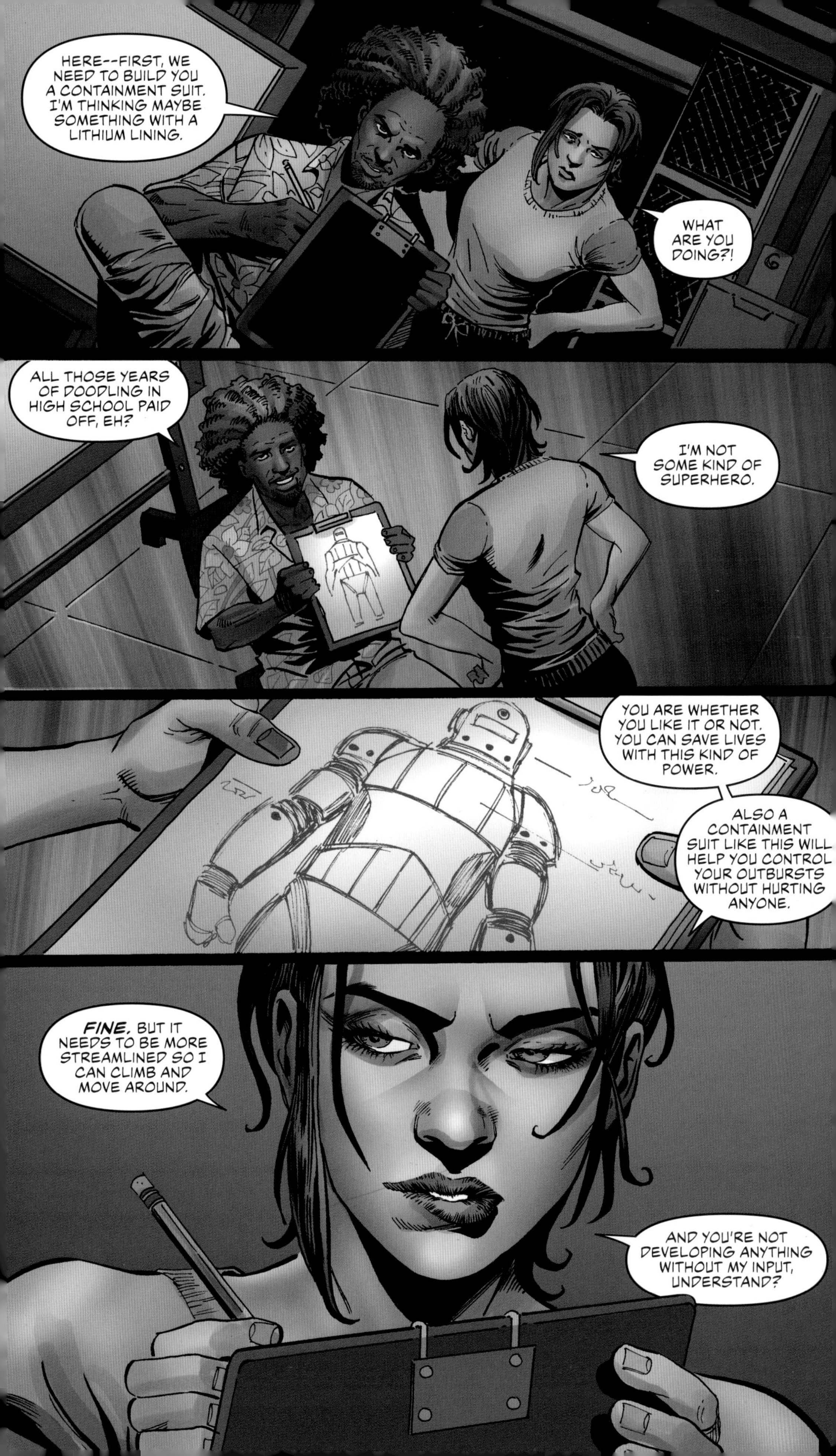
HERE--FIRST, WE NEED TO BUILD YOU A CONTAINMENT SUIT. I'M THINKING MAYBE SOMETHING WITH A LITHIUM LINING.
WHAT ARE YOU DOING?!
ALL THOSE YEARS OF DOODLING IN HIGH SCHOOL PAID OFF, EH?
I'M NOT SOME KIND OF SUPERHERO.
YOU ARE WHETHER YOU LIKE IT OR NOT. YOU CAN SAVE LIVES WITH THIS KIND OF POWER.
ALSO A CONTAINMENT SUIT LIKE THIS WILL HELP YOU CONTROL YOUR OUTBURSTS WITHOUT HURTING ANYONE.
FINE. BUT IT NEEDS TO BE MORE STREAMLINED SO I CAN CLIMB AND MOVE AROUND.
AND YOU'RE NOT DEVELOPING ANYTHING WITHOUT MY INPUT, UNDERSTAND?

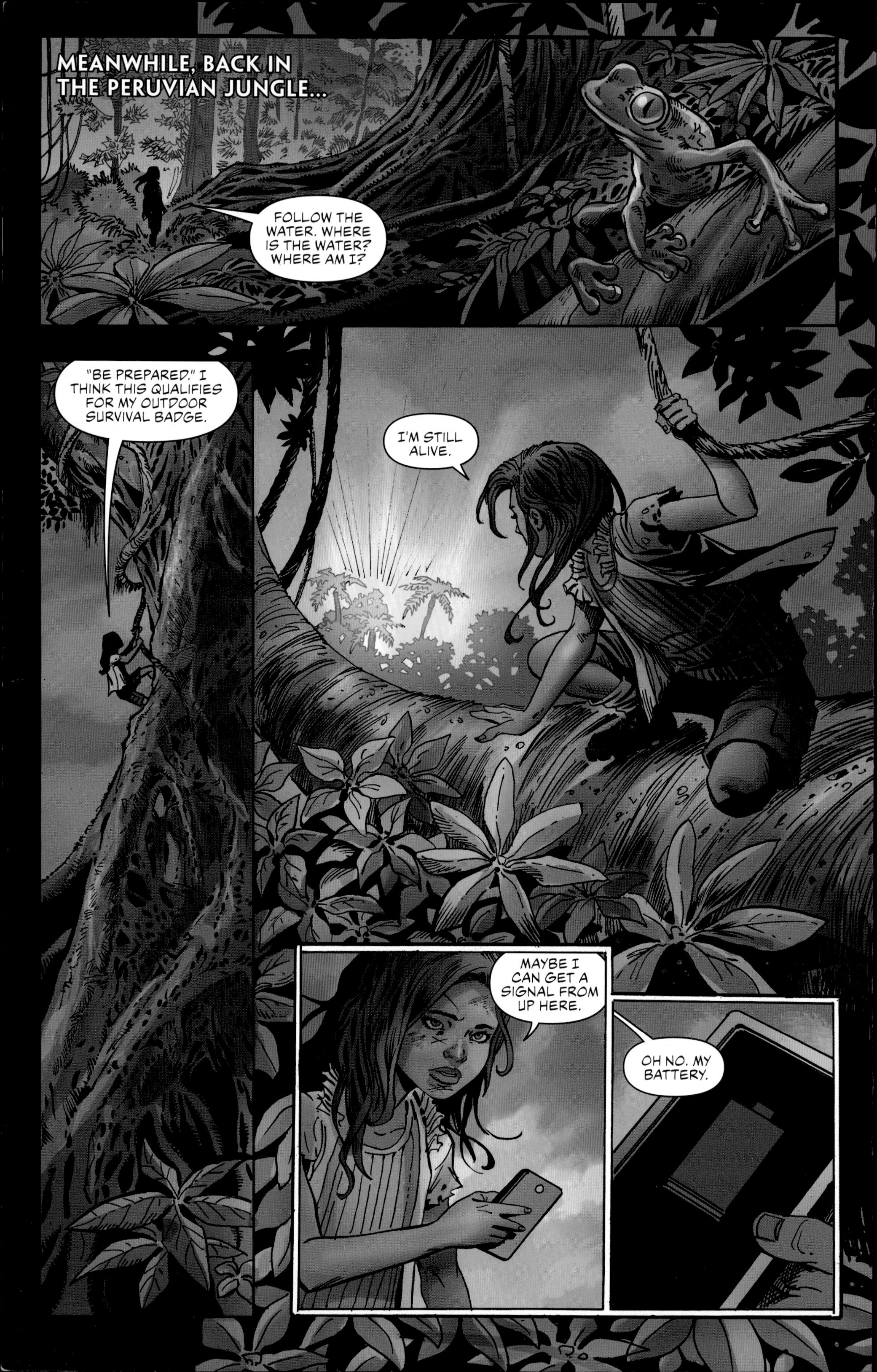
MEANWHILE, BACK IN THE PERUVIAN JUNGLE...
FOLLOW THE WATER. WHERE IS THE WATER? WHERE AM I?
"BE PREPARED." I THINK THIS QUALIFIES FOR MY OUTDOOR SURVIVAL BADGE.
I'M STILL ALIVE.
MAYBE I CAN GET A SIGNAL FROM UP HERE.
OH NO. MY BATTERY.

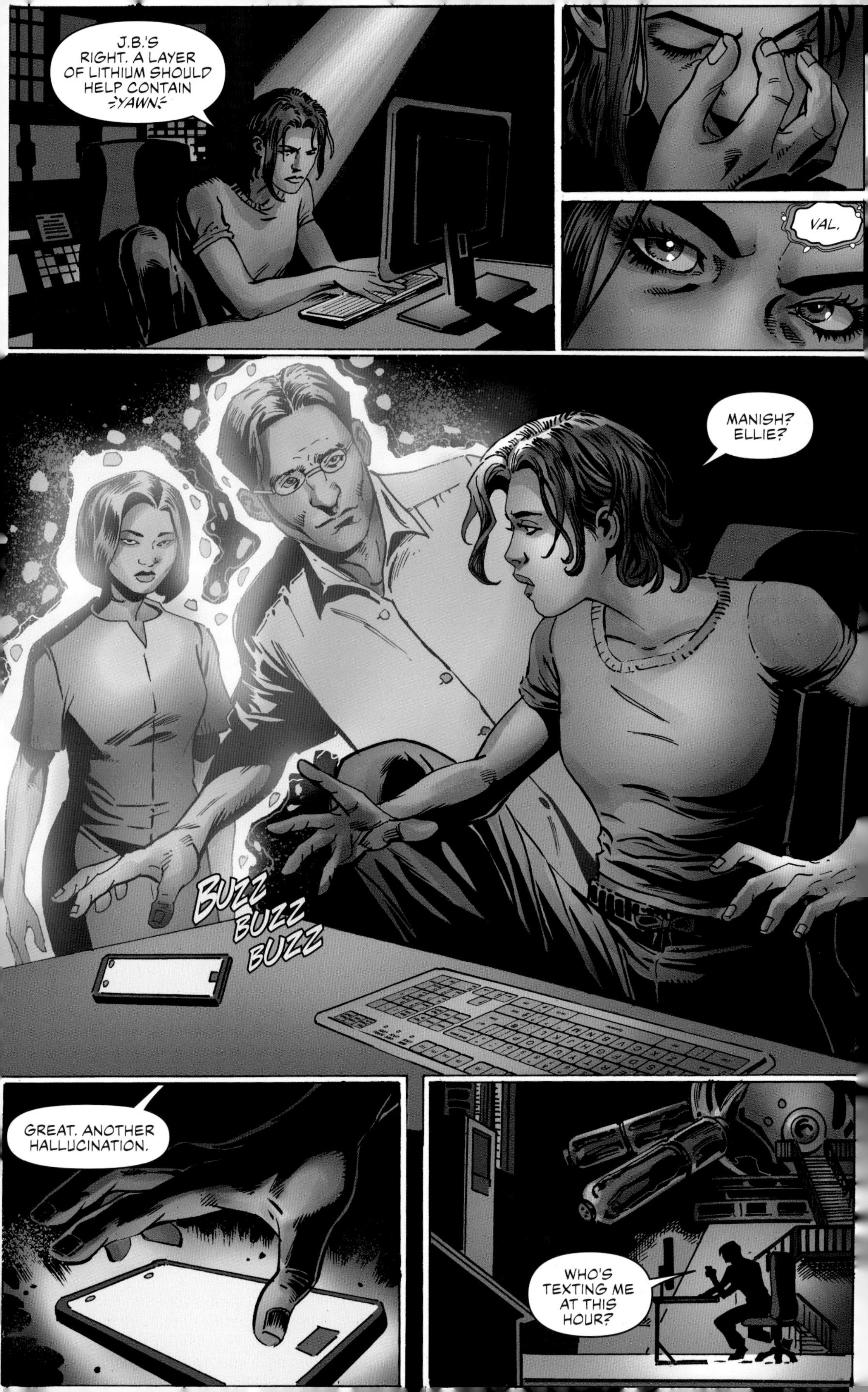
J.B.'S RIGHT. A LAYER OF LITHIUM SHOULD HELP CONTAIN =YAWN=
VAL.
MANISH? ELLIE?
BUZZ
BUZZ
BUZZ
GREAT. ANOTHER HALLUCINATION.
WHO'S TEXTING ME AT THIS HOUR?

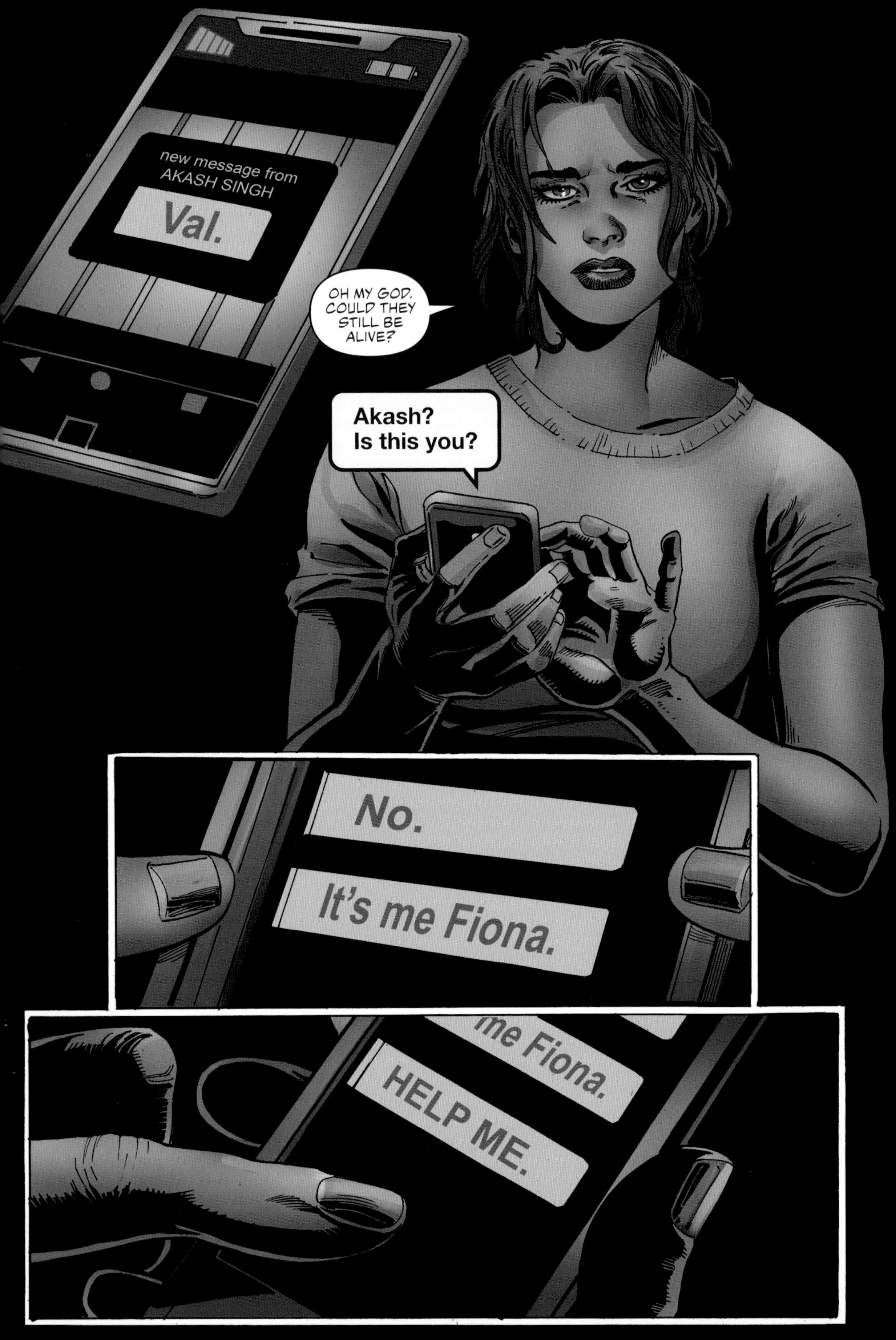
new message from
AKASH SINGH
Val.
OH MY GOD. COULD THEY STILL BE ALIVE?
Akash? Is this you?
No.
It's me Fiona.
me Fiona.
HELP ME.

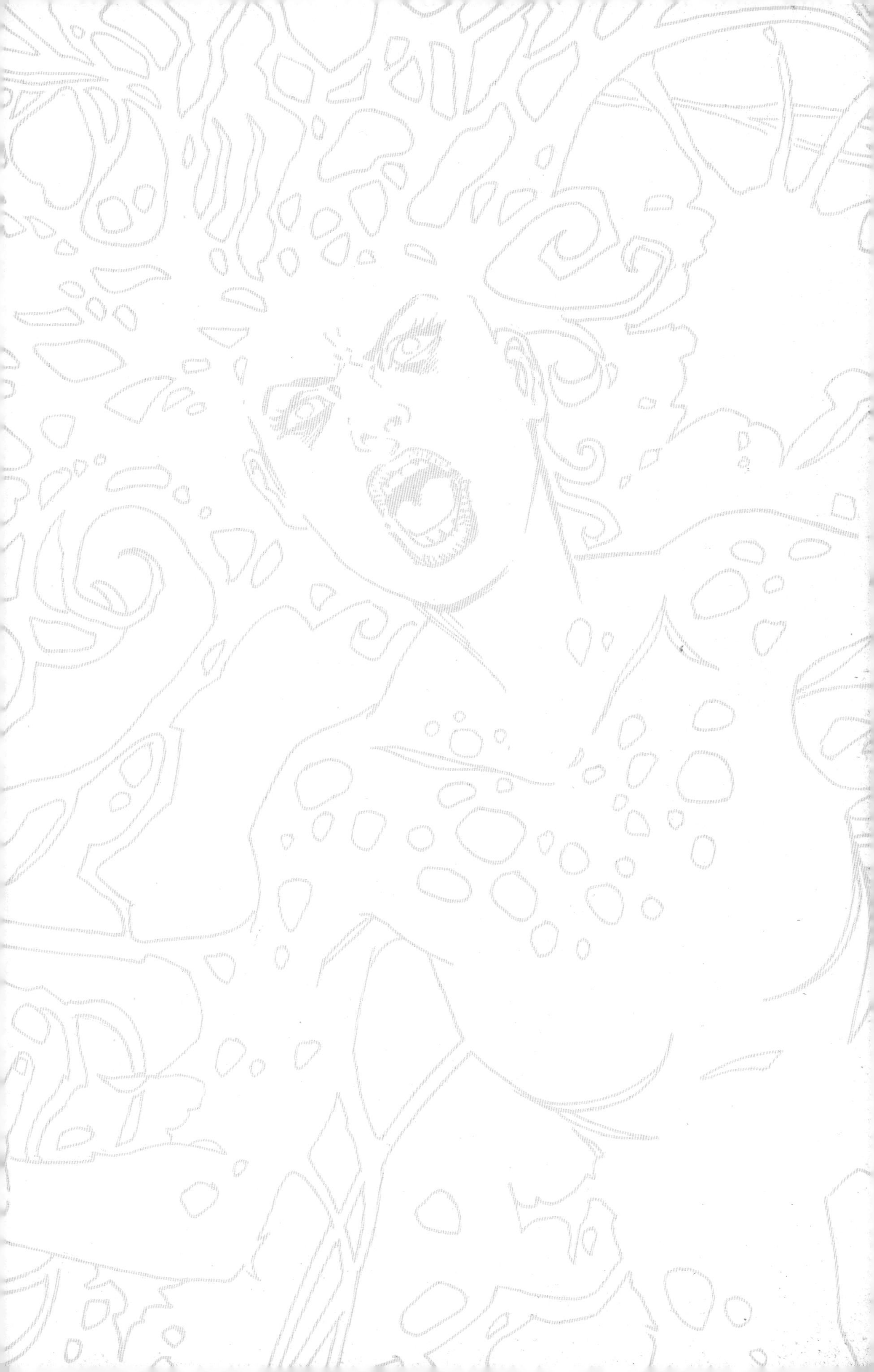

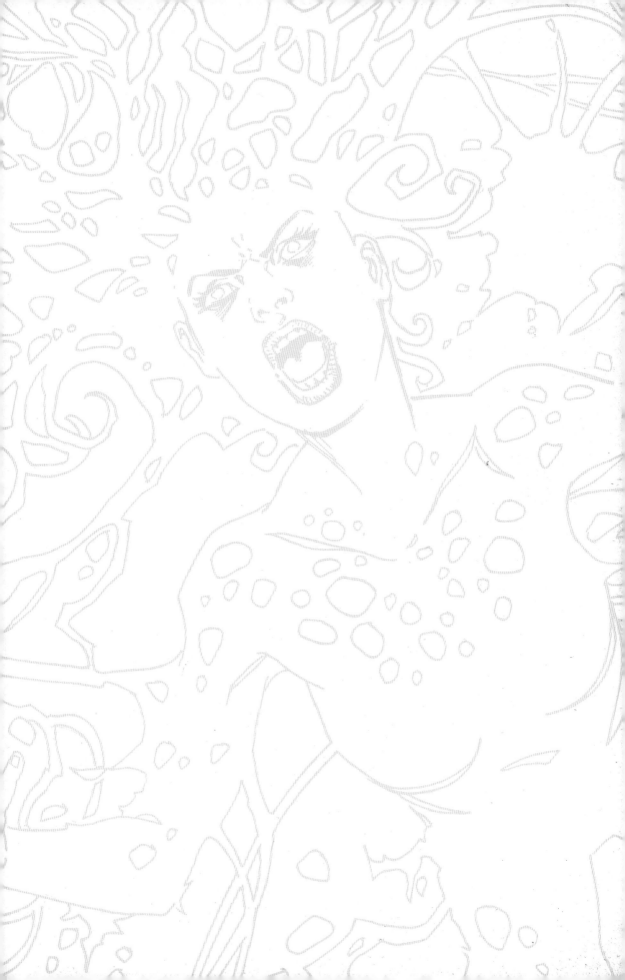

CHAPTER THREE

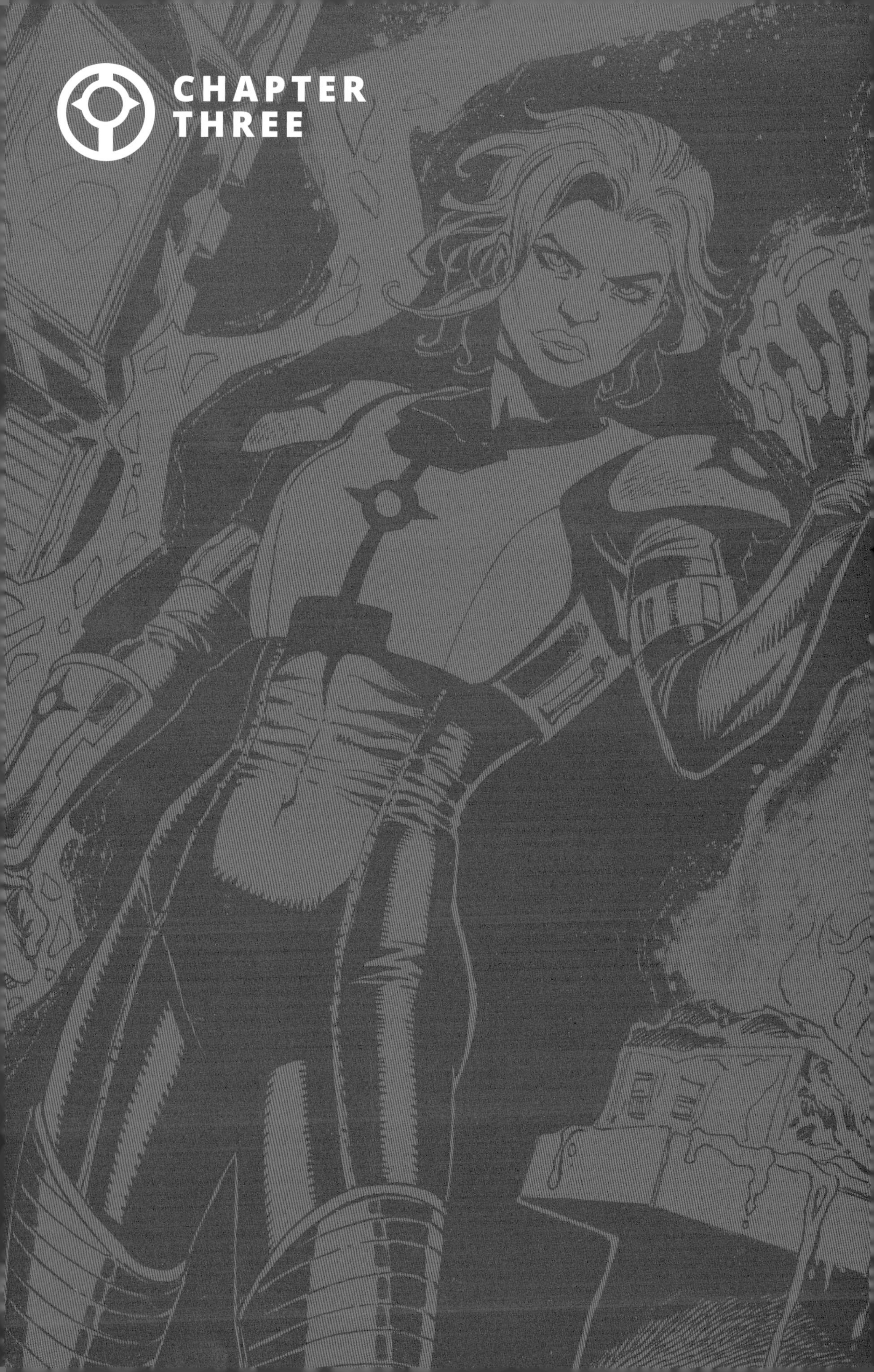

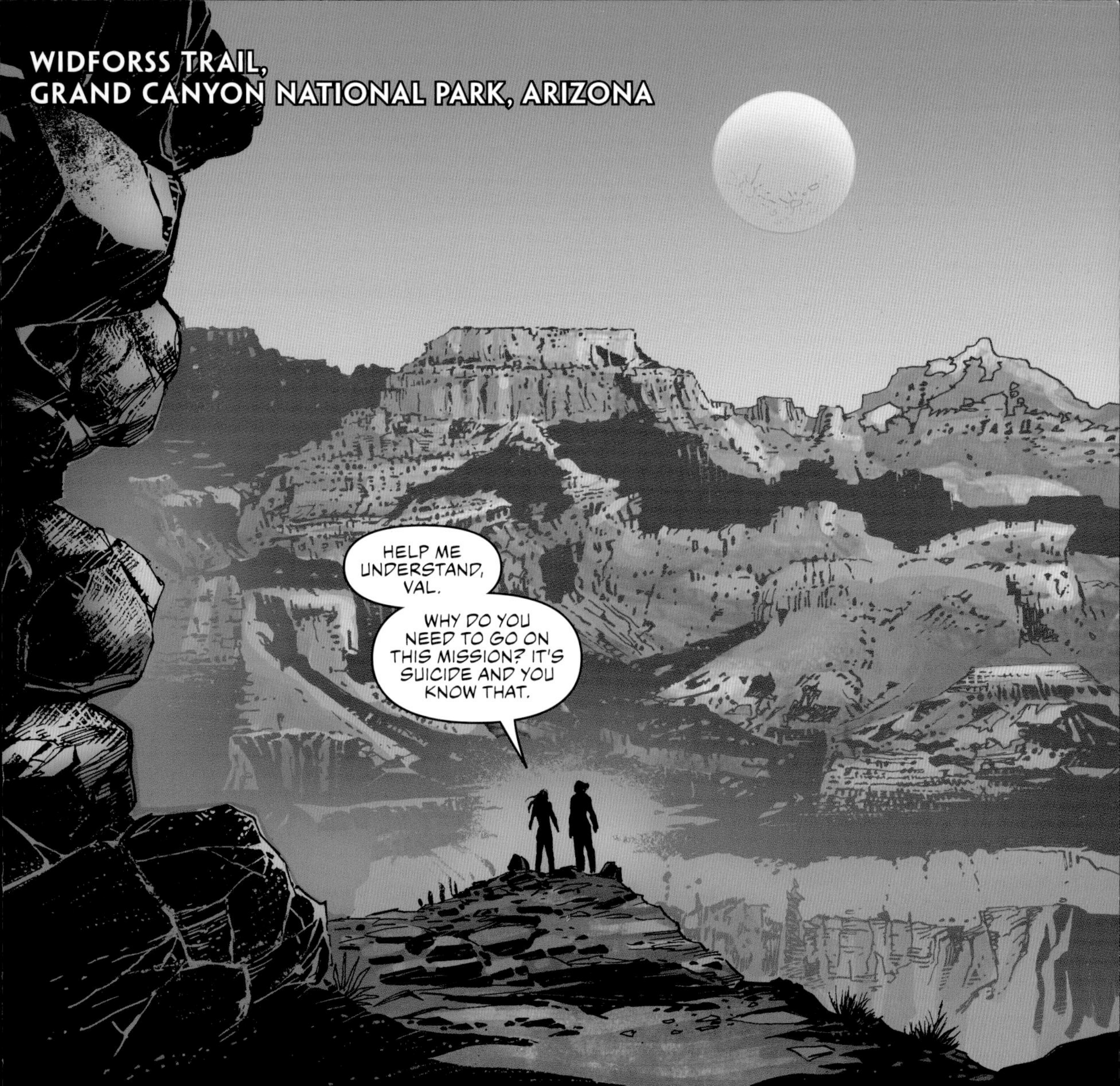
WIDFORSS TRAIL,
GRAND CANYON NATIONAL PARK, ARIZONA
HELP ME UNDERSTAND, VAL.
WHY DO YOU NEED TO GO ON THIS MISSION? IT'S SUICIDE AND YOU KNOW THAT.

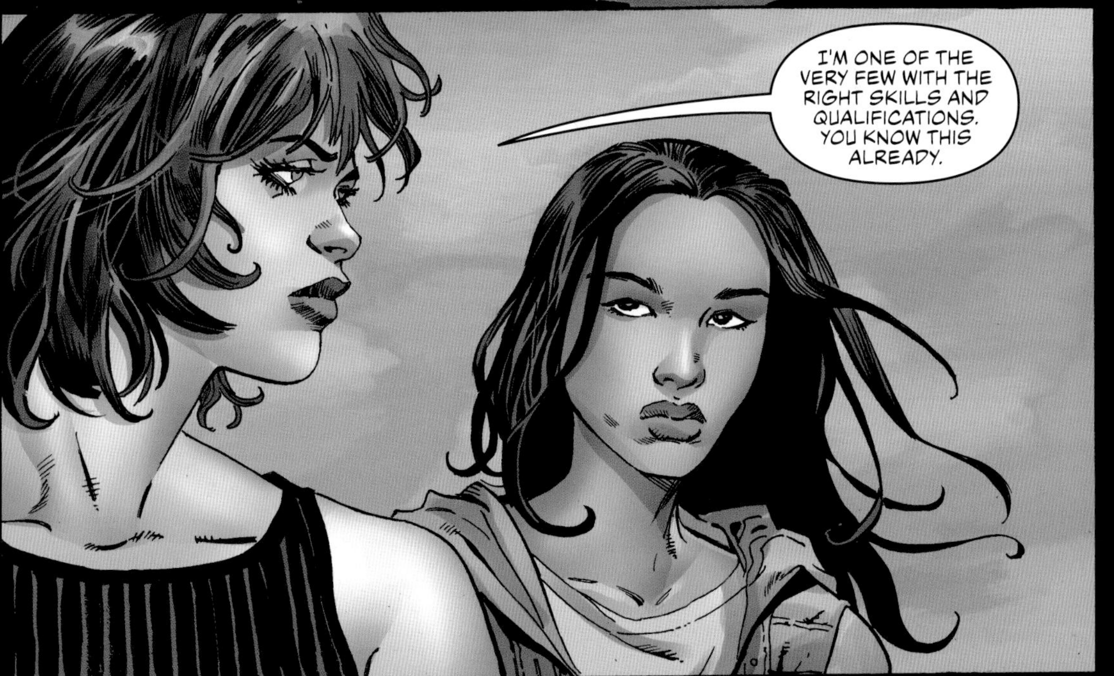
I'M ONE OF THE VERY FEW WITH THE RIGHT SKILLS AND QUALIFICATIONS. YOU KNOW THIS ALREADY.

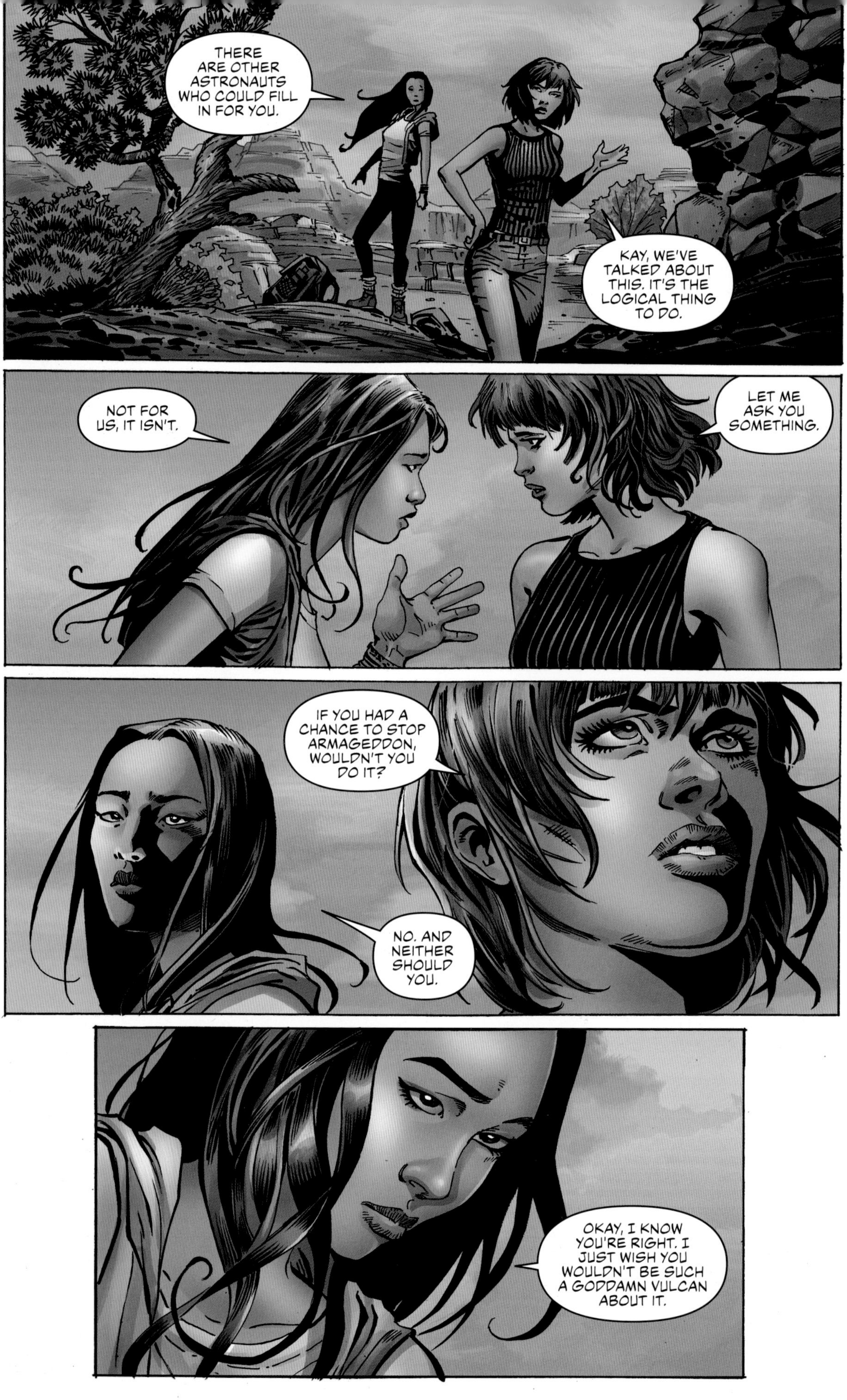
THERE ARE OTHER ASTRONAUTS WHO COULD FILL IN FOR YOU.
KAY, WE'VE TALKED ABOUT THIS. IT'S THE LOGICAL THING TO DO.
NOT FOR US, IT ISN'T.
LET ME ASK YOU SOMETHING.
IF YOU HAD A CHANCE TO STOP ARMAGEDDON, WOULDN'T YOU DO IT?
NO. AND NEITHER SHOULD YOU.
OKAY, I KNOW YOU'RE RIGHT. I JUST WISH YOU WOULDN'T BE SUCH A GODDAMN VULCAN ABOUT IT.

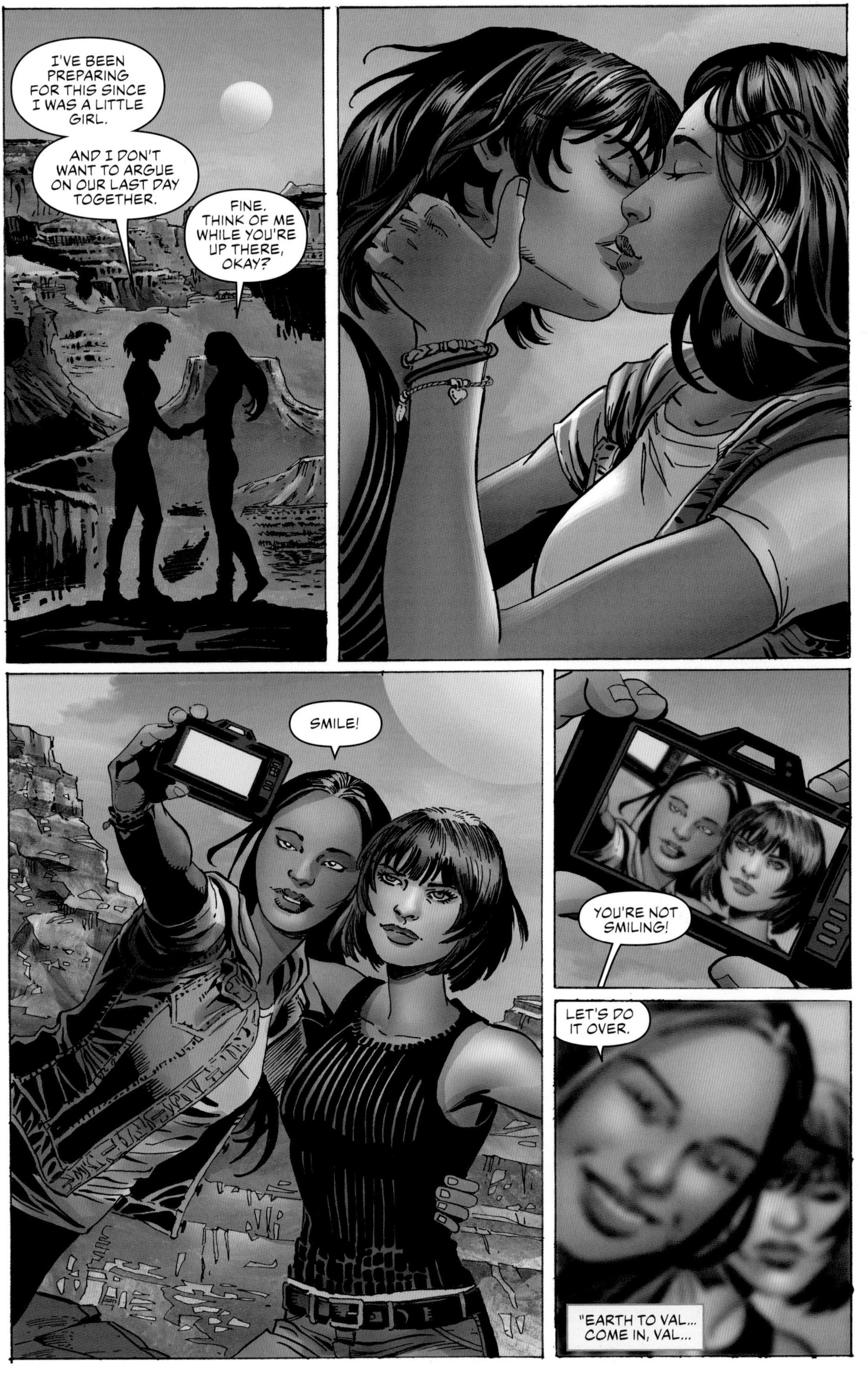
I'VE BEEN PREPARING FOR THIS SINCE I WAS A LITTLE GIRL.
AND I DON'T WANT TO ARGUE ON OUR LAST DAY TOGETHER.
FINE. THINK OF ME WHILE YOU'RE UP THERE, OKAY?
SMILE!
YOU'RE NOT SMILING!
LET'S DO IT OVER.
"EARTH TO VAL... COME IN, VAL...

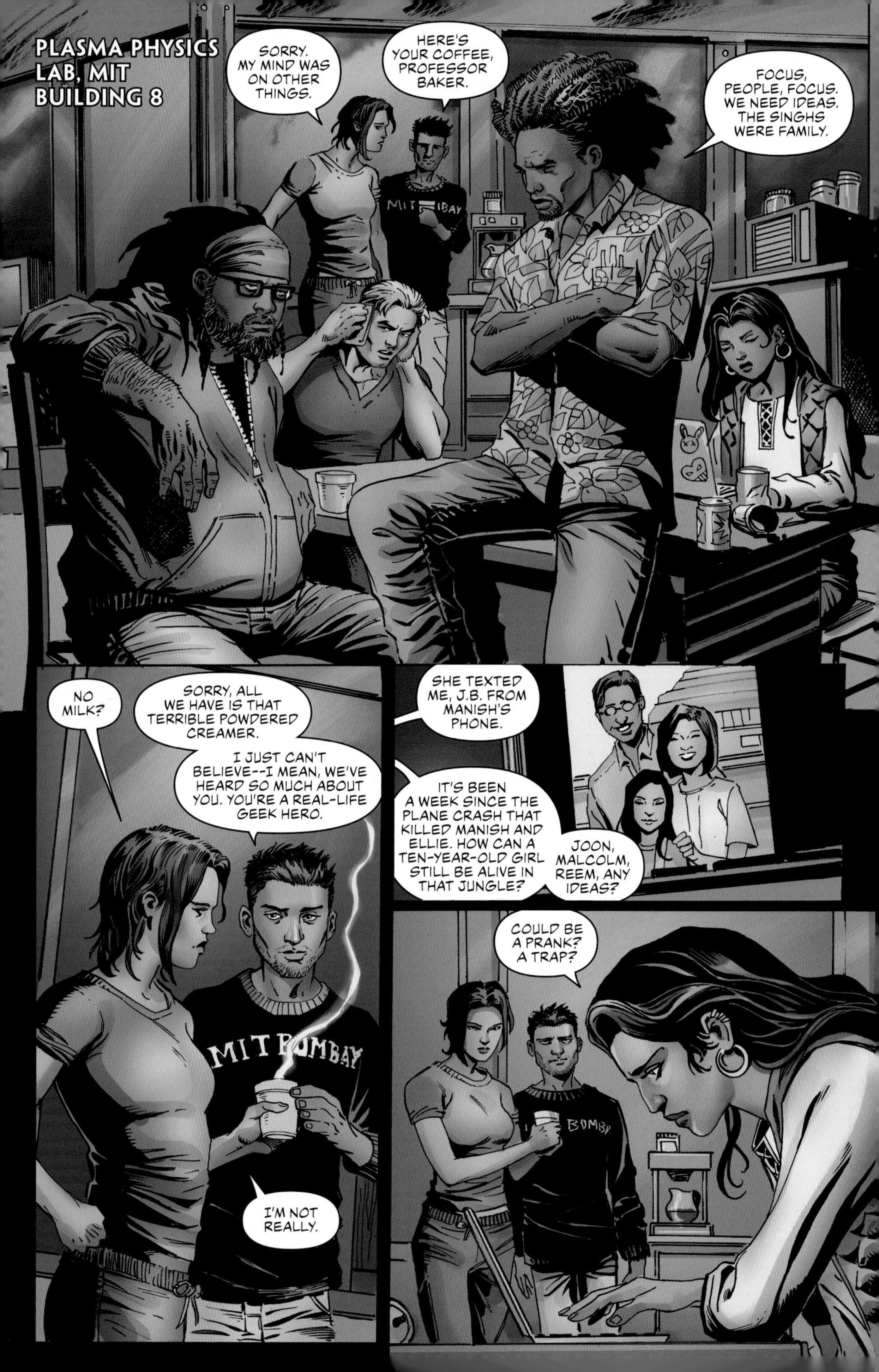
PLASMA PHYSICS LAB, MIT BUILDING 8
SORRY. MY MIND WAS ON OTHER THINGS.
HERE'S YOUR COFFEE, PROFESSOR BAKER.
FOCUS, PEOPLE, FOCUS. WE NEED IDEAS. THE SINGHS WERE FAMILY.
MIT BAY
NO MILK?
SORRY, ALL WE HAVE IS THAT TERRIBLE POWDERED CREAMER.
I JUST CAN'T BELIEVE--I MEAN, WE'VE HEARD SO MUCH ABOUT YOU. YOU'RE A REAL-LIFE GEEK HERO.
MIT BOMBAY
I'M NOT REALLY.
SHE TEXTED ME, J.B. FROM MANISH'S PHONE.
IT'S BEEN A WEEK SINCE THE PLANE CRASH THAT KILLED MANISH AND ELLIE. HOW CAN A TEN-YEAR-OLD GIRL STILL BE ALIVE IN THAT JUNGLE?
JOON, MALCOLM, REEM, ANY IDEAS?
COULD BE A PRANK? A TRAP?
BOMBY

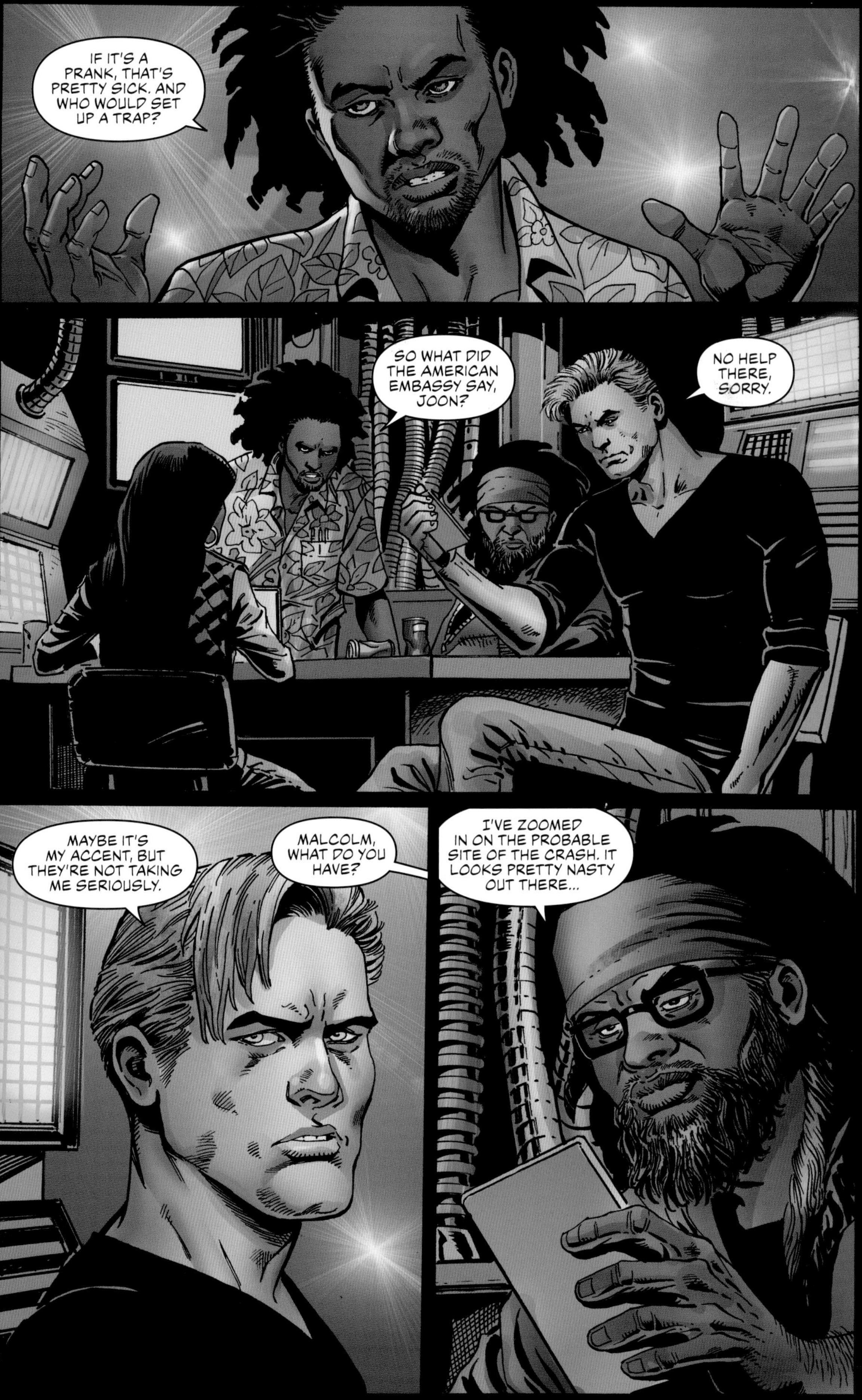
IF IT'S A PRANK, THAT'S PRETTY SICK. AND WHO WOULD SET UP A TRAP?
SO WHAT DID THE AMERICAN EMBASSY SAY, JOON?
NO HELP THERE, SORRY.
MAYBE IT'S MY ACCENT, BUT THEY'RE NOT TAKING ME SERIOUSLY.
MALCOLM, WHAT DO YOU HAVE?
I'VE ZOOMED IN ON THE PROBABLE SITE OF THE CRASH. IT LOOKS PRETTY NASTY OUT THERE...

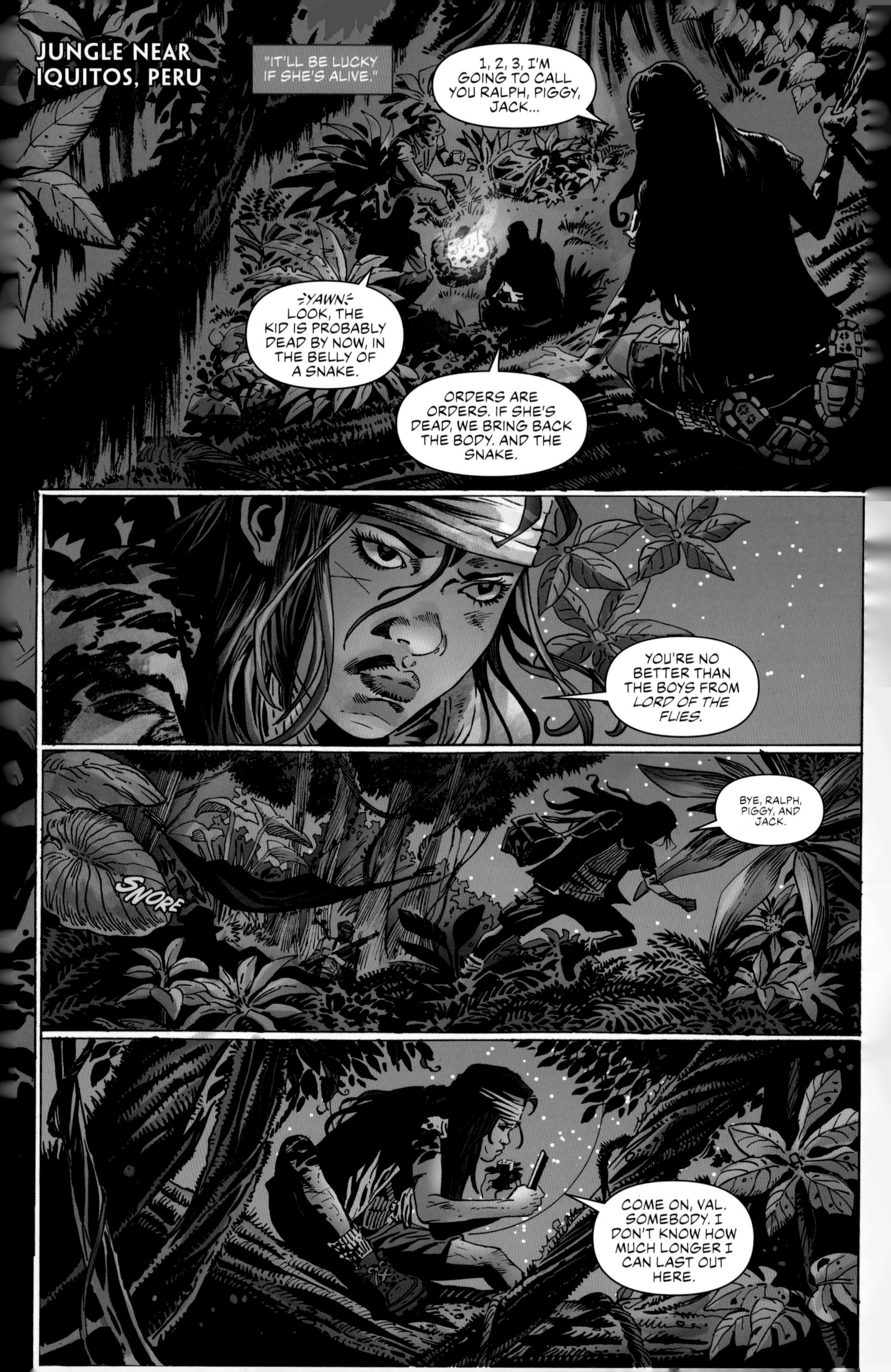
JUNGLE NEAR IQUITOS, PERU
"IT'LL BE LUCKY IF SHE'S ALIVE."
1, 2, 3, I'M GOING TO CALL YOU RALPH, PIGGY, JACK...
YAWN
LOOK, THE KID IS PROBABLY DEAD BY NOW, IN THE BELLY OF A SNAKE.
ORDERS ARE ORDERS. IF SHE'S DEAD, WE BRING BACK THE BODY. AND THE SNAKE.
YOU'RE NO BETTER THAN THE BOYS FROM LORD OF THE FLIES.
SNORE
BYE, RALPH, PIGGY, AND JACK.
COME ON, VAL. SOMEBODY. I DON'T KNOW HOW MUCH LONGER I CAN LAST OUT HERE.

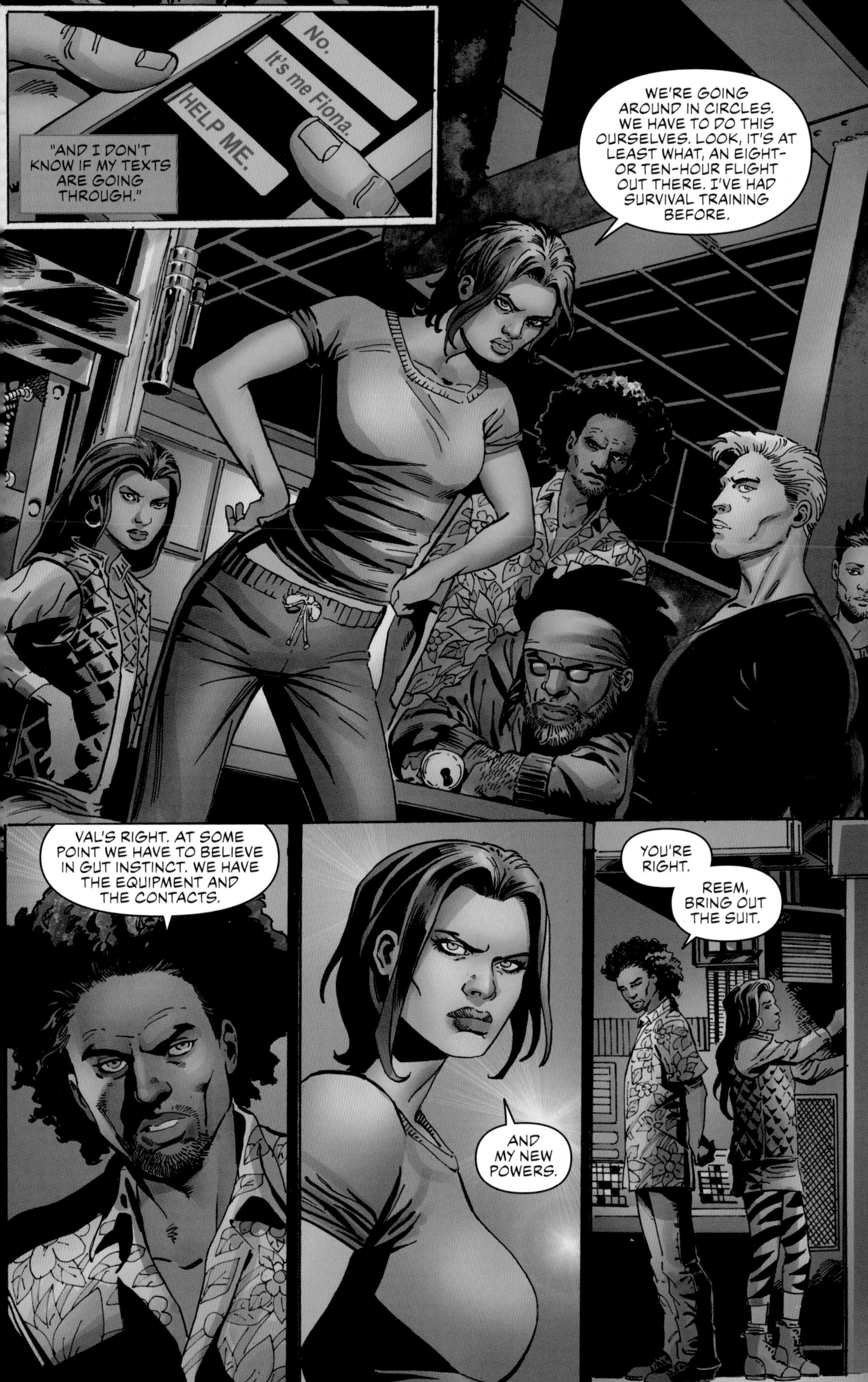
No.
It's me Fiona.
HELP ME.
"AND I DON'T KNOW IF MY TEXTS ARE GOING THROUGH."
WE'RE GOING AROUND IN CIRCLES. WE HAVE TO DO THIS OURSELVES. LOOK, IT'S AT LEAST WHAT, AN EIGHT- OR TEN-HOUR FLIGHT OUT THERE. I'VE HAD SURVIVAL TRAINING BEFORE.
VAL'S RIGHT. AT SOME POINT WE HAVE TO BELIEVE IN GUT INSTINCT. WE HAVE THE EQUIPMENT AND THE CONTACTS.
AND MY NEW POWERS.
YOU'RE RIGHT.
REEM, BRING OUT THE SUIT.

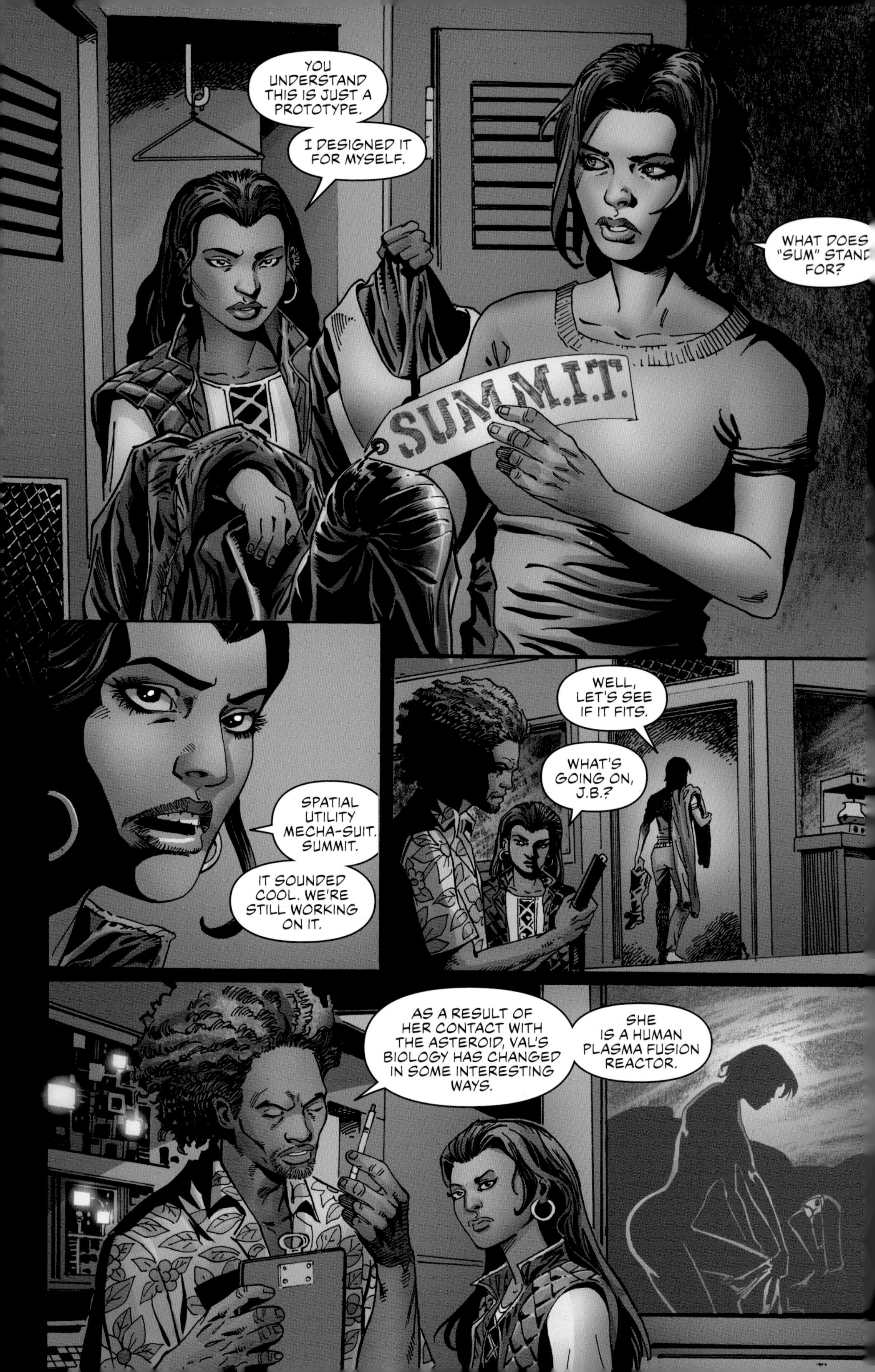
YOU UNDERSTAND THIS IS JUST A PROTOTYPE.
I DESIGNED IT FOR MYSELF.
WHAT DOES "SUM" STAND FOR?
SUMM.I.T.
SPATIAL UTILITY MECHA-SUIT. SUMMIT.
IT SOUNDED COOL. WE'RE STILL WORKING ON IT.
WELL, LET'S SEE IF IT FITS.
WHAT'S GOING ON, J.B.?
AS A RESULT OF HER CONTACT WITH THE ASTEROID, VAL'S BIOLOGY HAS CHANGED IN SOME INTERESTING WAYS.
SHE IS A HUMAN PLASMA FUSION REACTOR.

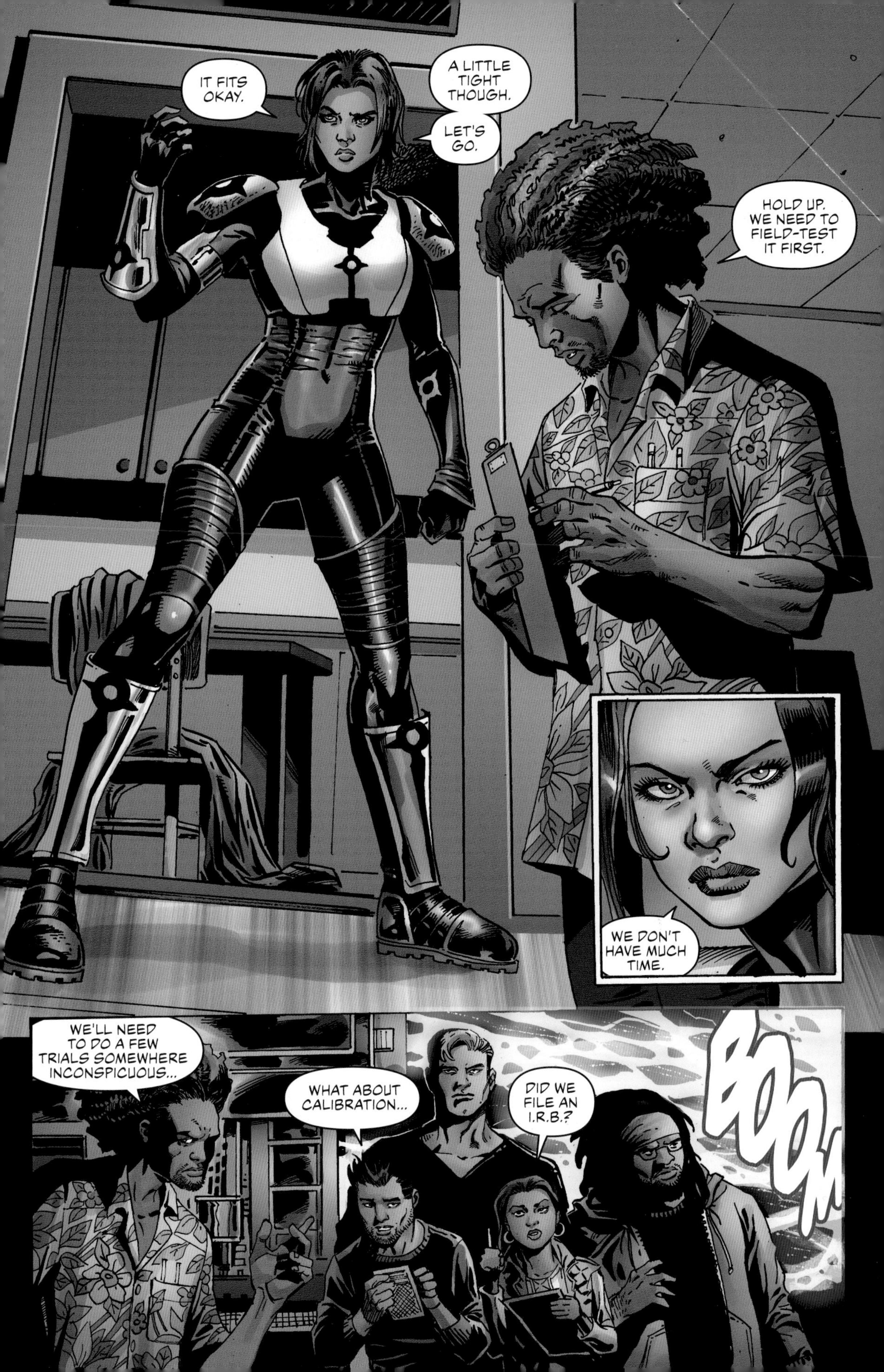
IT FITS OKAY.
A LITTLE TIGHT THOUGH.
LET'S GO.
HOLD UP. WE NEED TO FIELD-TEST IT FIRST.
WE DON'T HAVE MUCH TIME.
WE'LL NEED TO DO A FEW TRIALS SOMEWHERE INCONSPICUOUS...
WHAT ABOUT CALIBRATION...
DID WE FILE AN I.R.B.?
BOOM

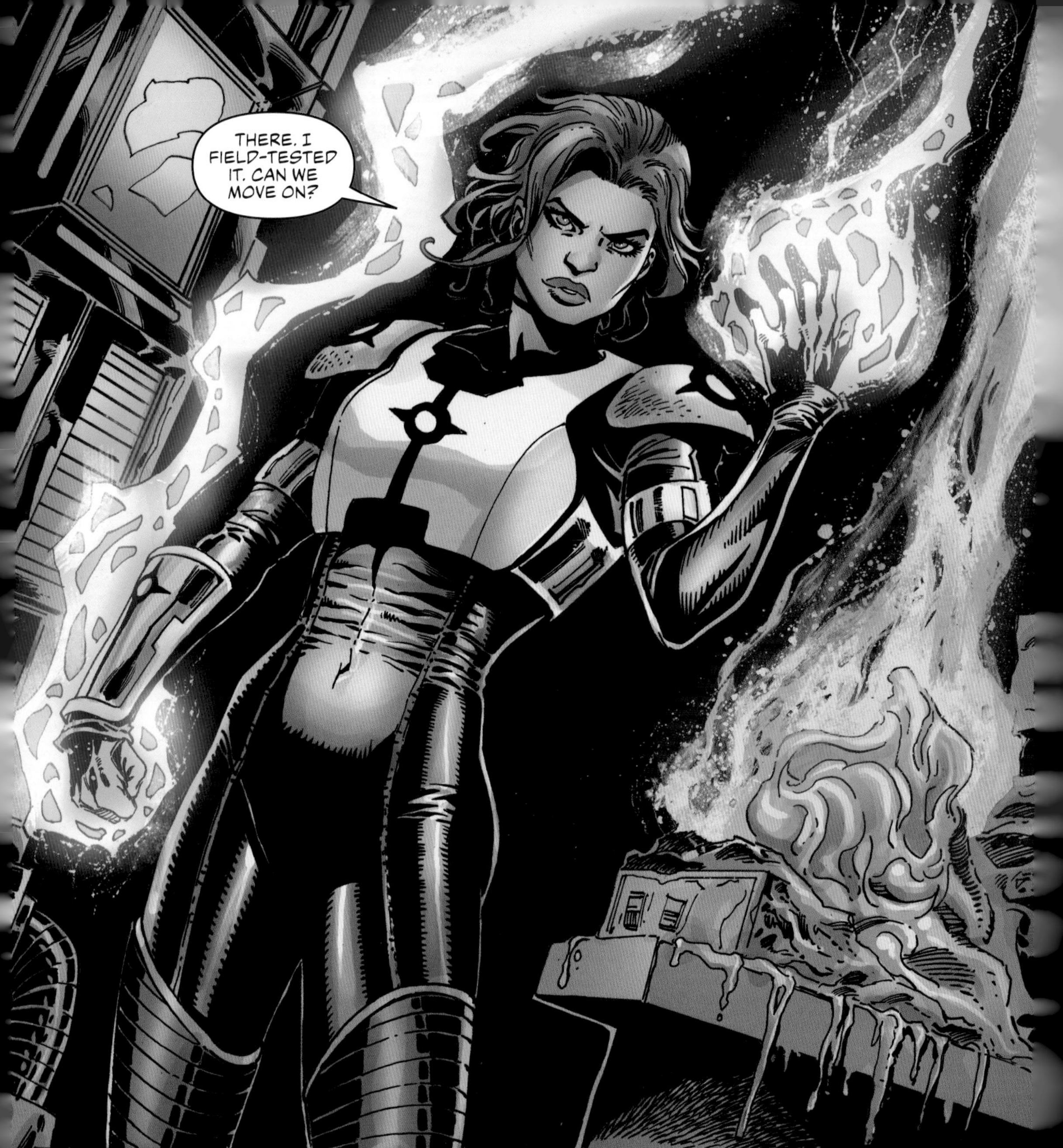
THERE. I FIELD-TESTED IT. CAN WE MOVE ON?

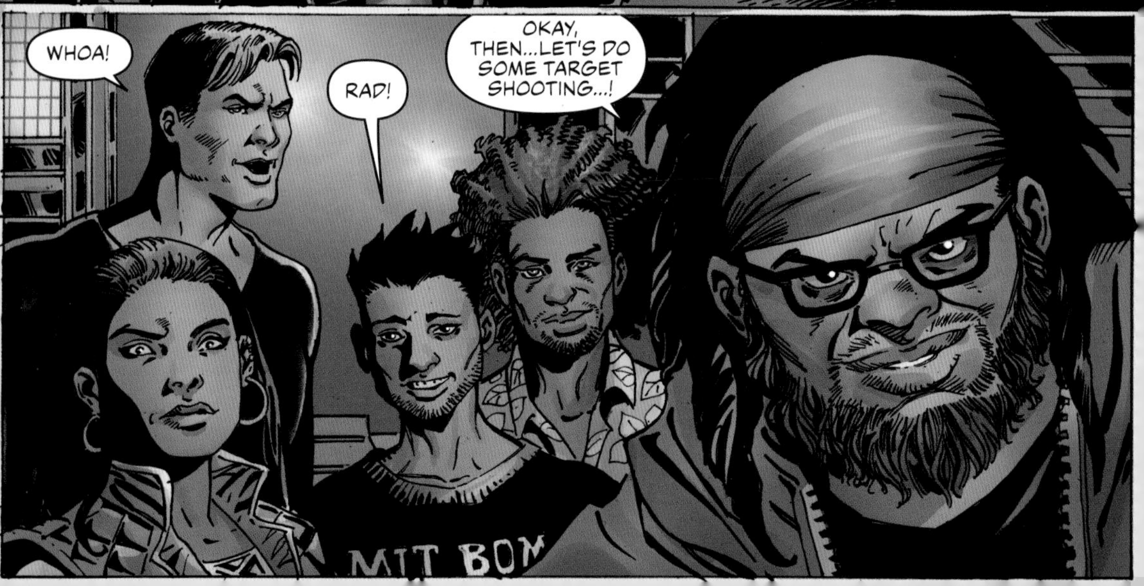
WHOA!
RAD!
OKAY, THEN...LET'S DO SOME TARGET SHOOTING...!
MIT BOM

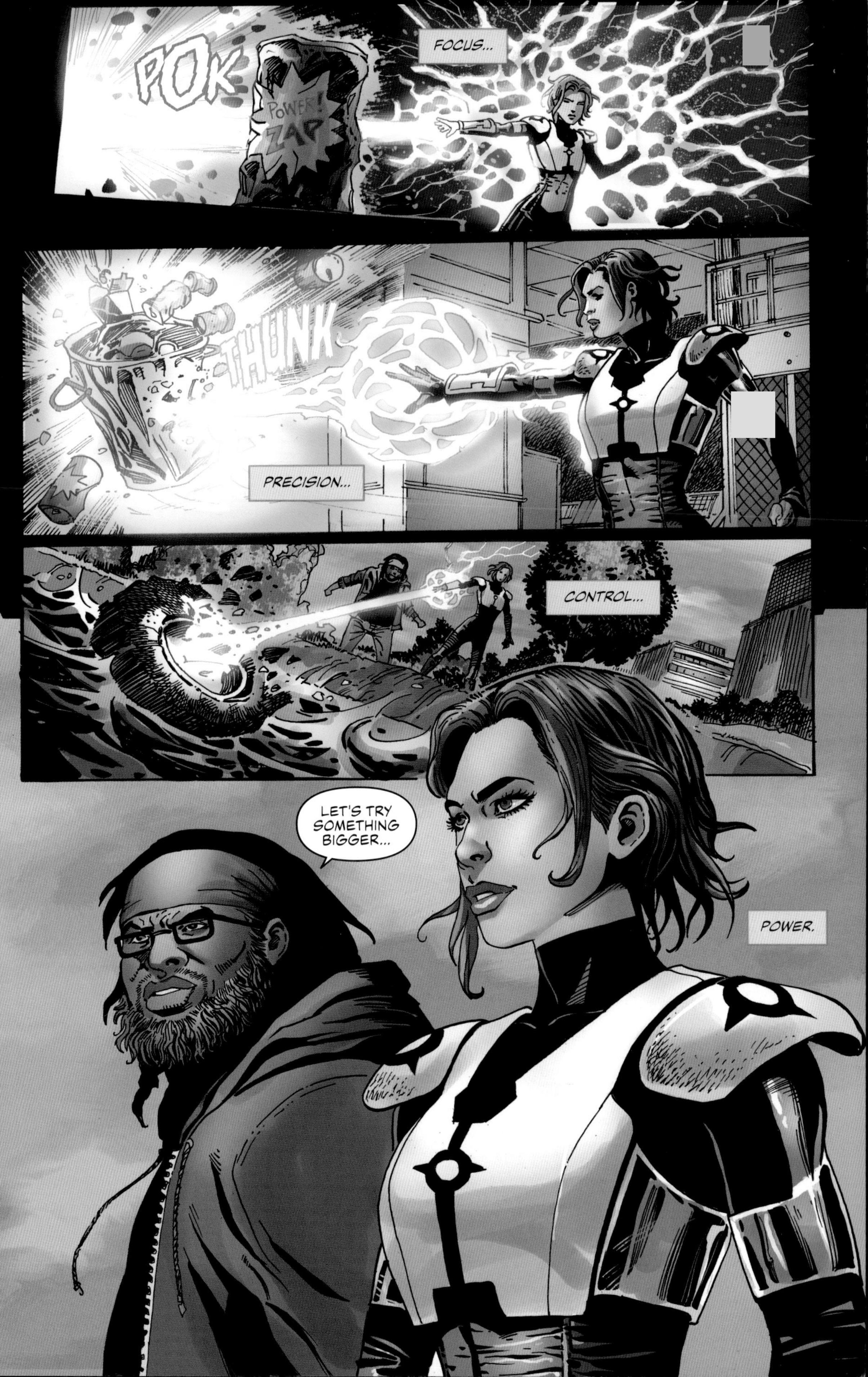
POK
POWER!
ZAP
FOCUS...
THUNK
PRECISION...
CONTROL...
LET'S TRY SOMETHING BIGGER...
POWER.

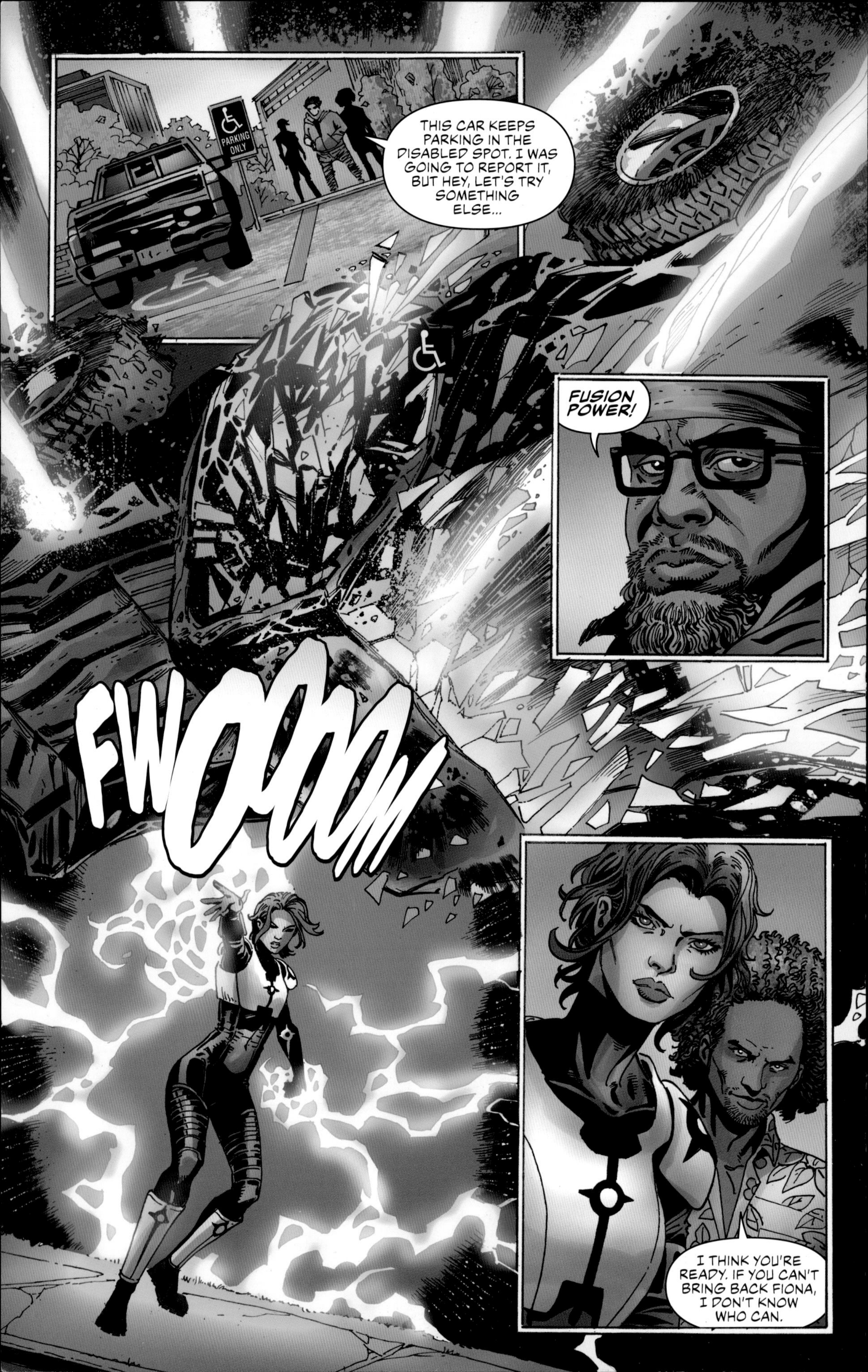
PARKING ONLY
THIS CAR KEEPS PARKING IN THE DISABLED SPOT. I WAS GOING TO REPORT IT, BUT HEY, LET'S TRY SOMETHING ELSE...
FUSION POWER!
FWOOOM
I THINK YOU'RE READY. IF YOU CAN'T BRING BACK FIONA, I DON'T KNOW WHO CAN.

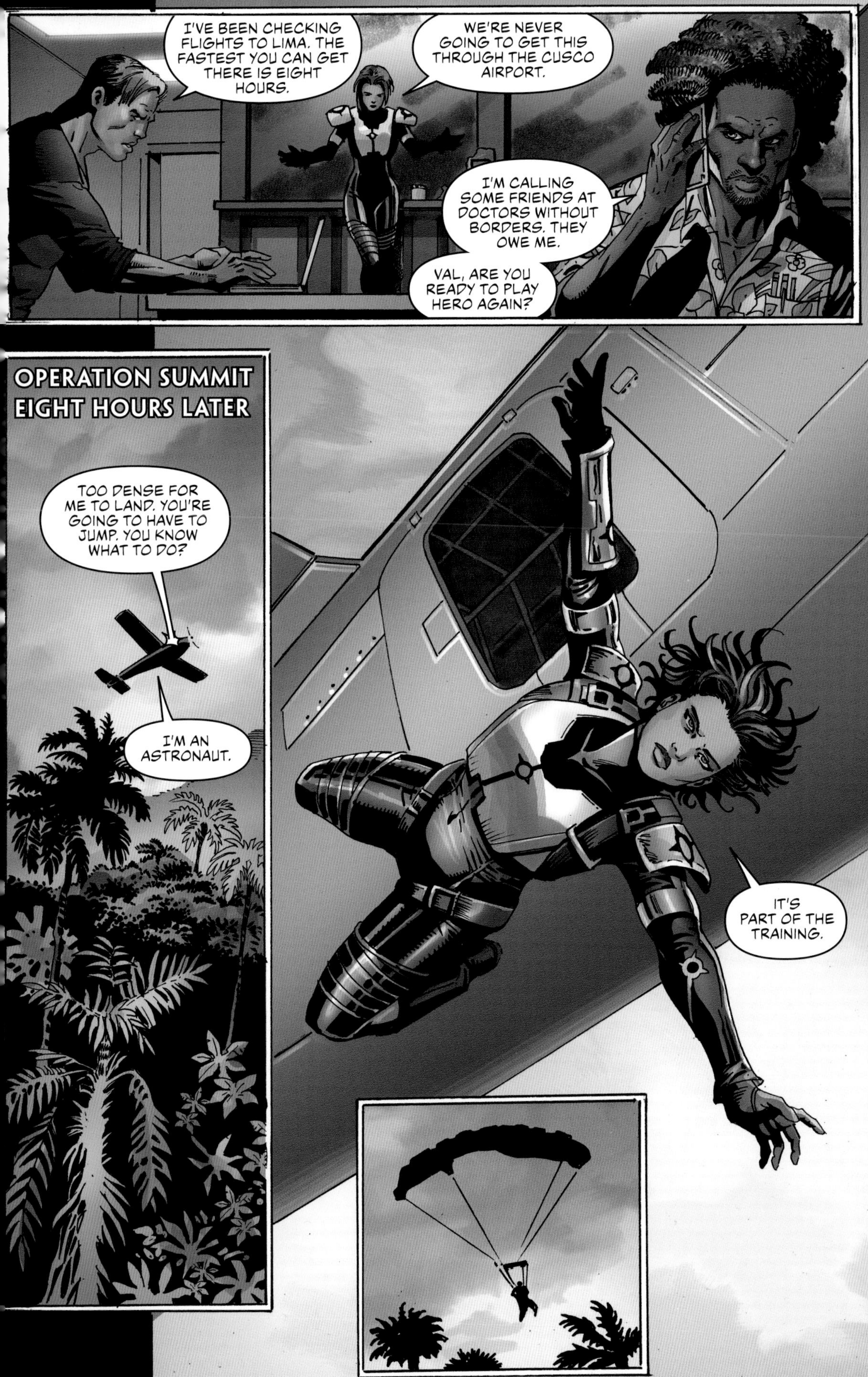
I'VE BEEN CHECKING FLIGHTS TO LIMA. THE FASTEST YOU CAN GET THERE IS EIGHT HOURS.
WE'RE NEVER GOING TO GET THIS THROUGH THE CUSCO AIRPORT.
I'M CALLING SOME FRIENDS AT DOCTORS WITHOUT BORDERS. THEY OWE ME.
VAL, ARE YOU READY TO PLAY HERO AGAIN?
OPERATION SUMMIT
EIGHT HOURS LATER
TOO DENSE FOR ME TO LAND. YOU'RE GOING TO HAVE TO JUMP. YOU KNOW WHAT TO DO?
I'M AN ASTRONAUT.
IT'S PART OF THE TRAINING.

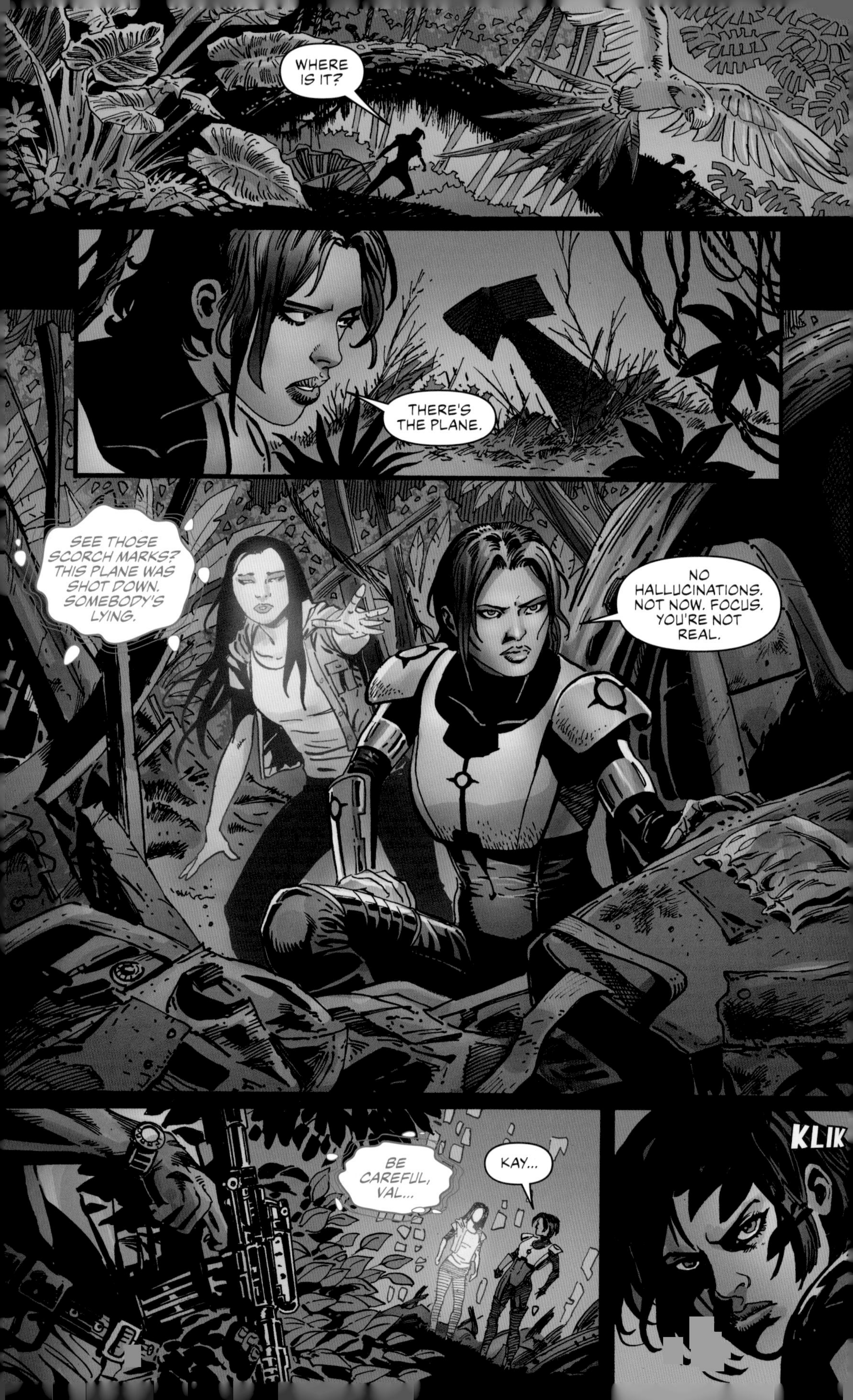
WHERE IS IT?
THERE'S THE PLANE.
SEE THOSE SCORCH MARKS? THIS PLANE WAS SHOT DOWN. SOMEBODY'S LYING.
NO HALLUCINATIONS. NOT NOW. FOCUS. YOU'RE NOT REAL.
BE CAREFUL, VAL...
KAY...
KLIK

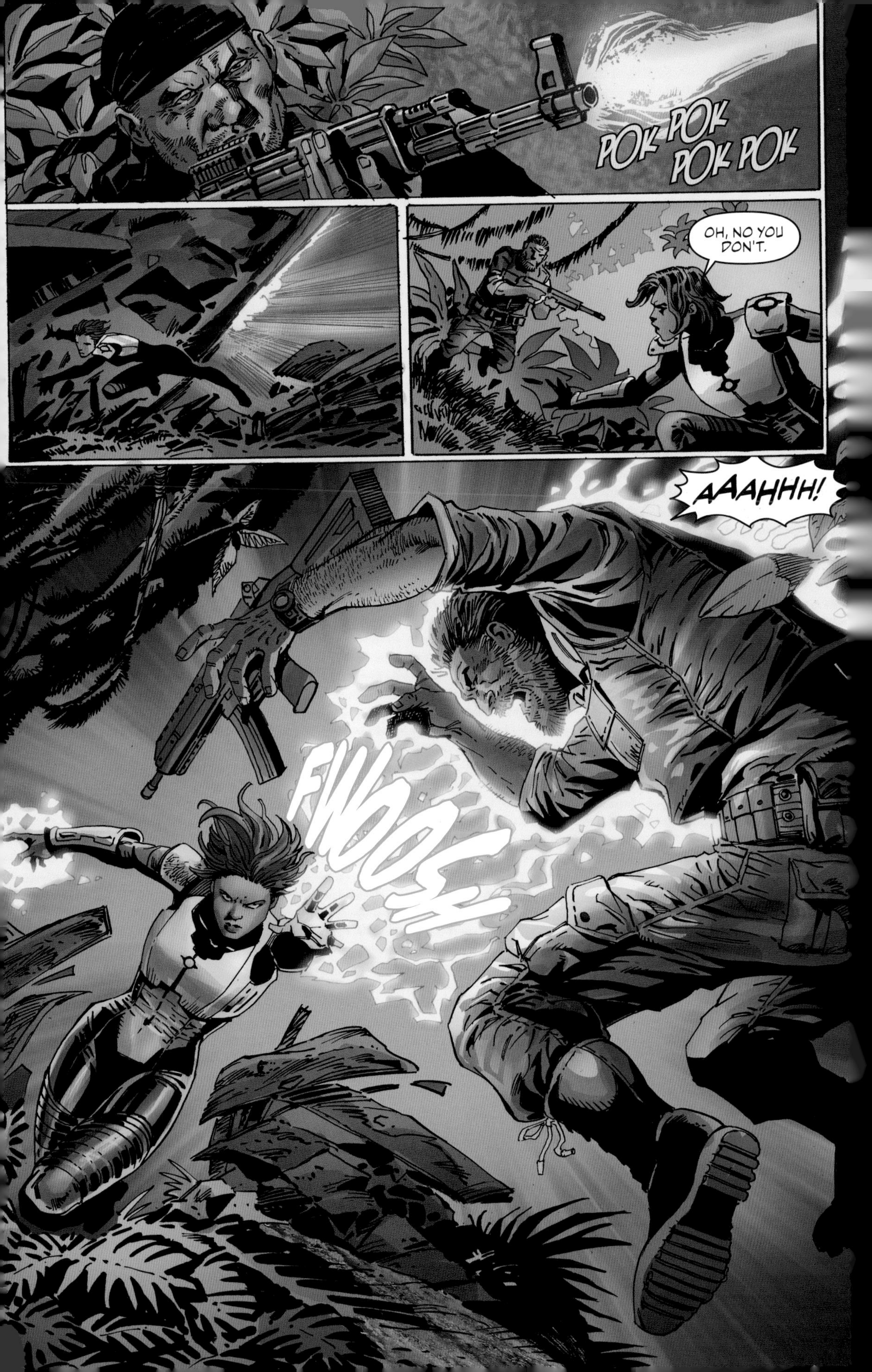
POK POK
POK POK
OH, NO YOU DON'T.
AAAHHH!
FWOOSH!

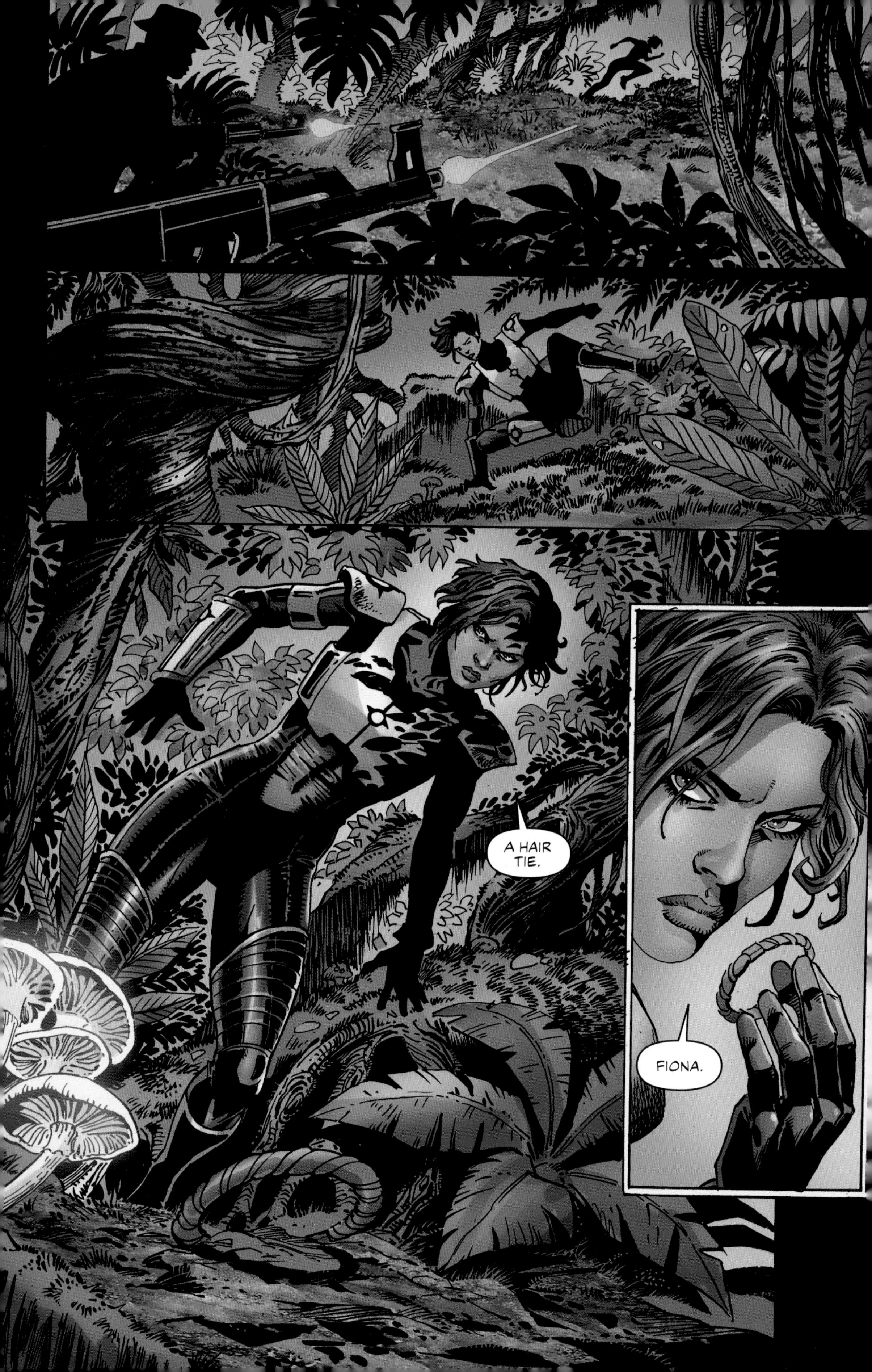
A HAIR TIE.
FIONA.

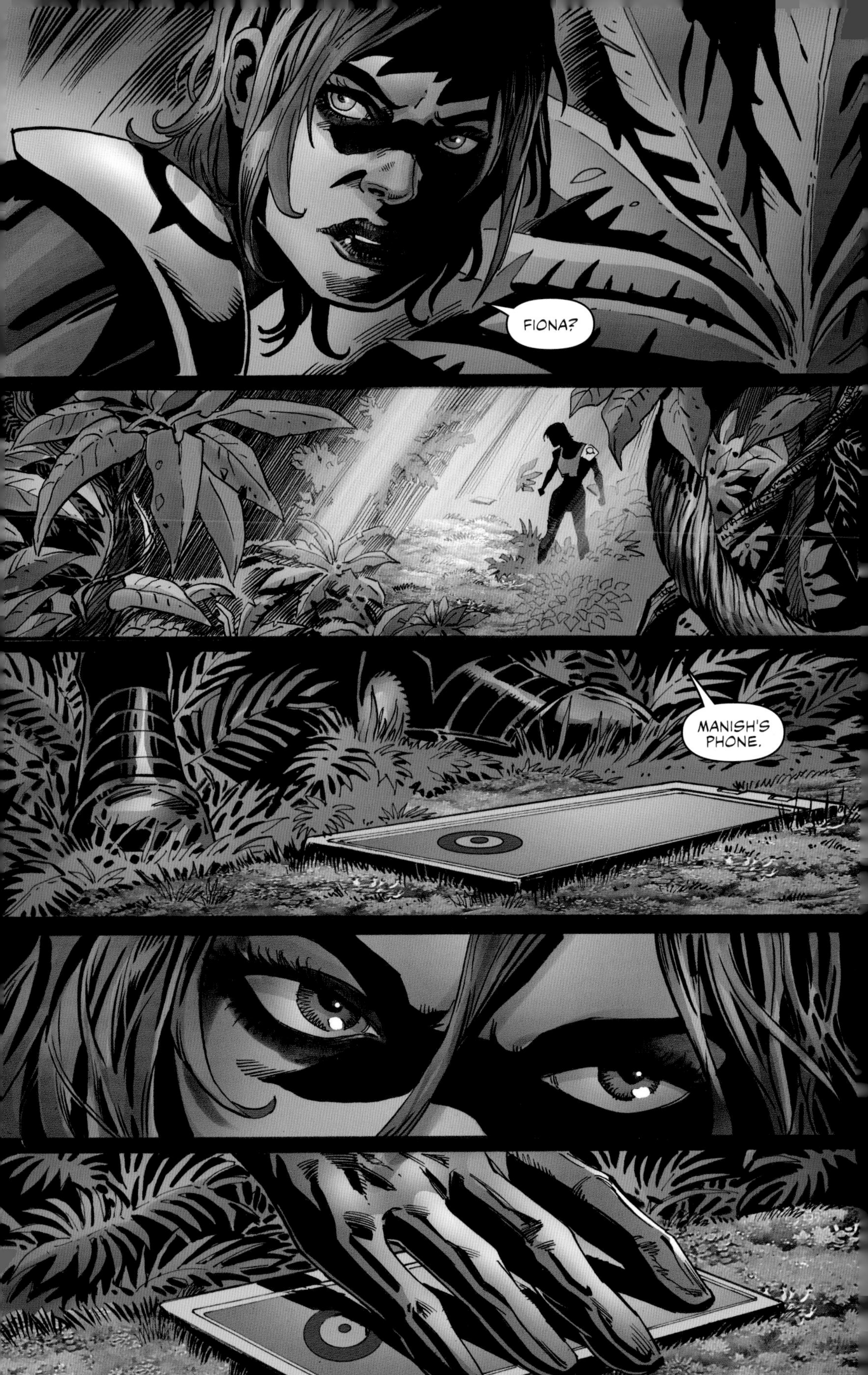
FIONA?
MANISH'S PHONE.

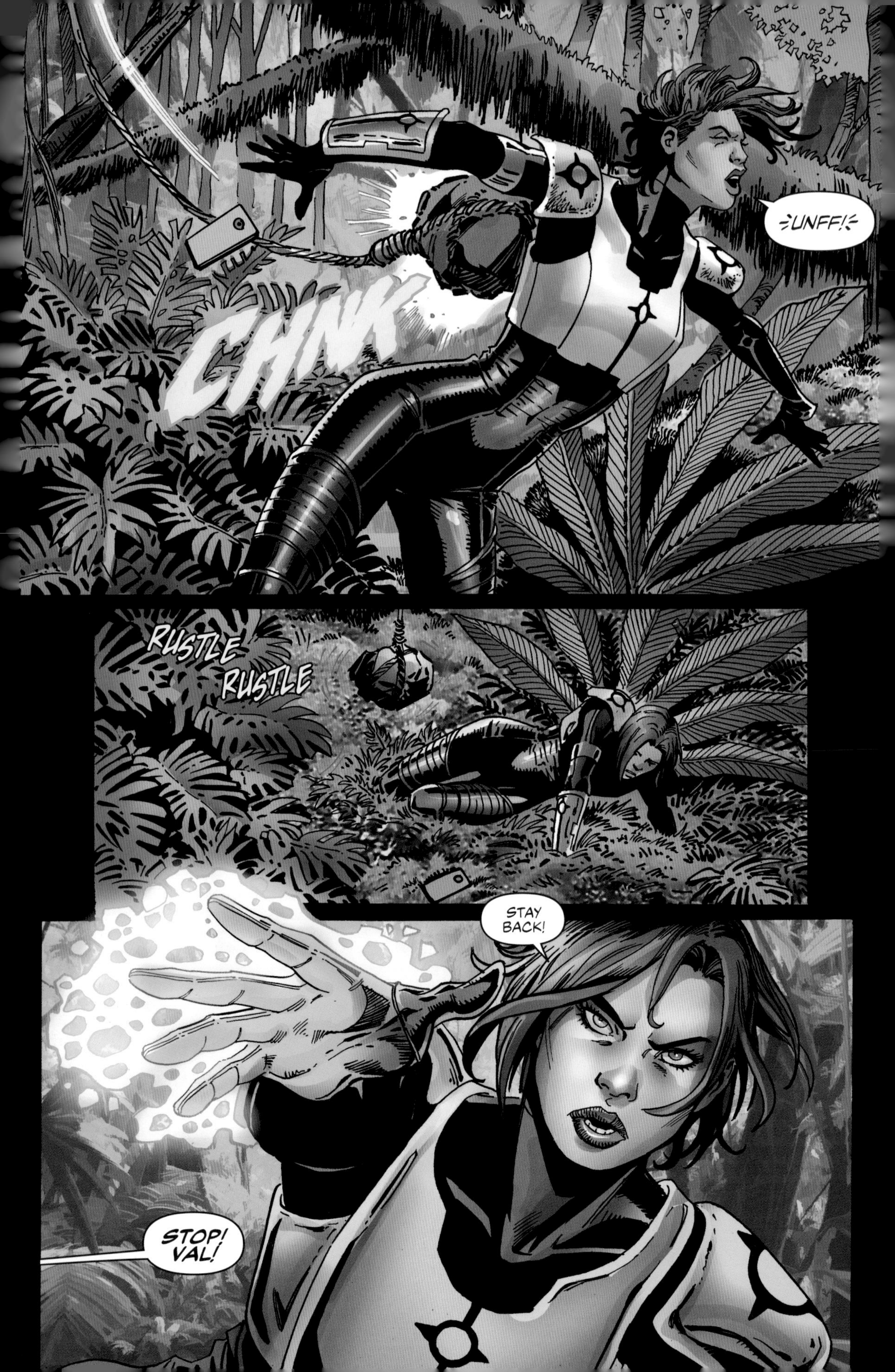
UNFF!
CHNK
RUSTLE
RUSTLE
STAY BACK!
STOP! VAL!

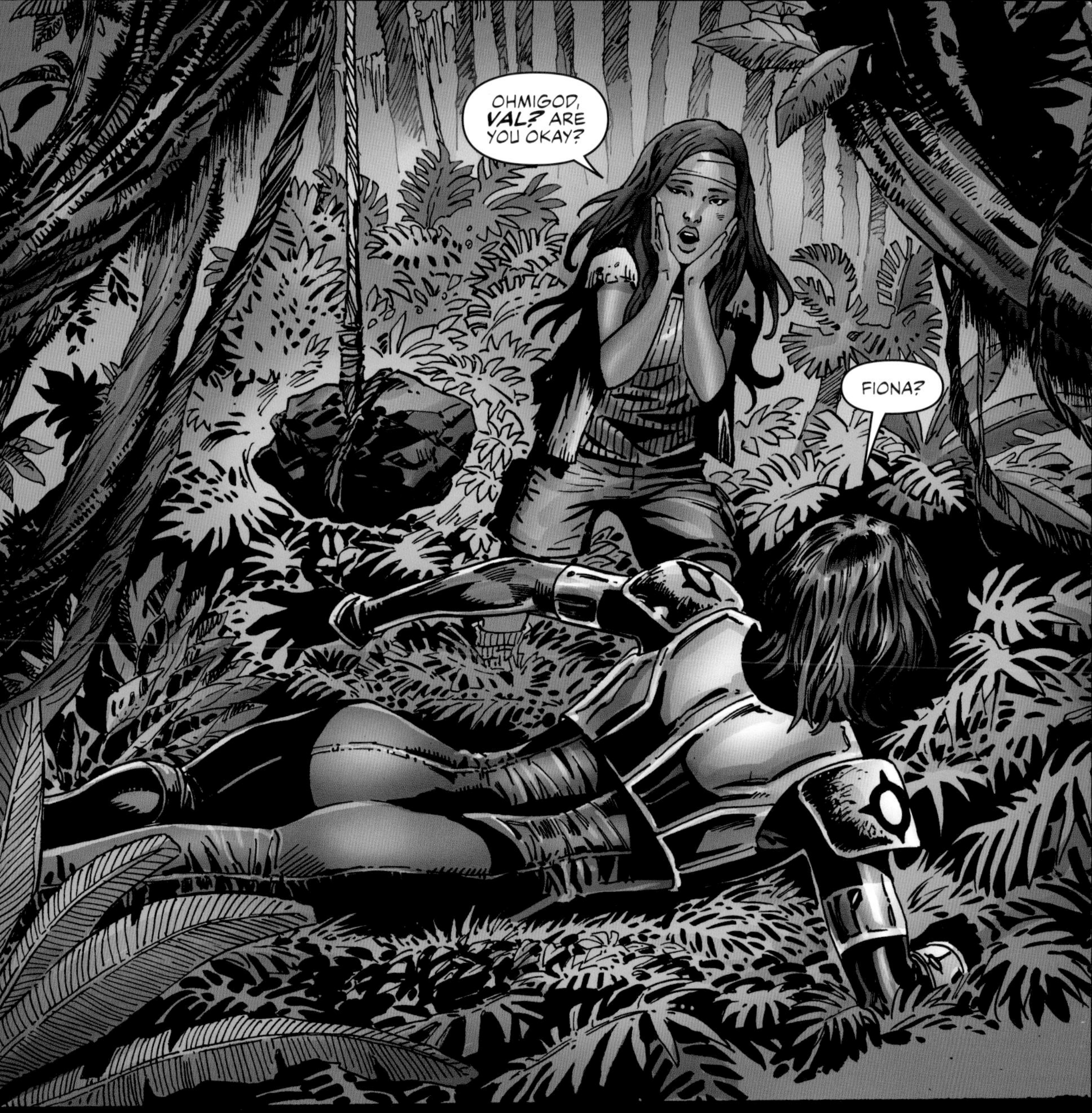
OHMIGOD, VAL? ARE YOU OKAY?
FIONA?

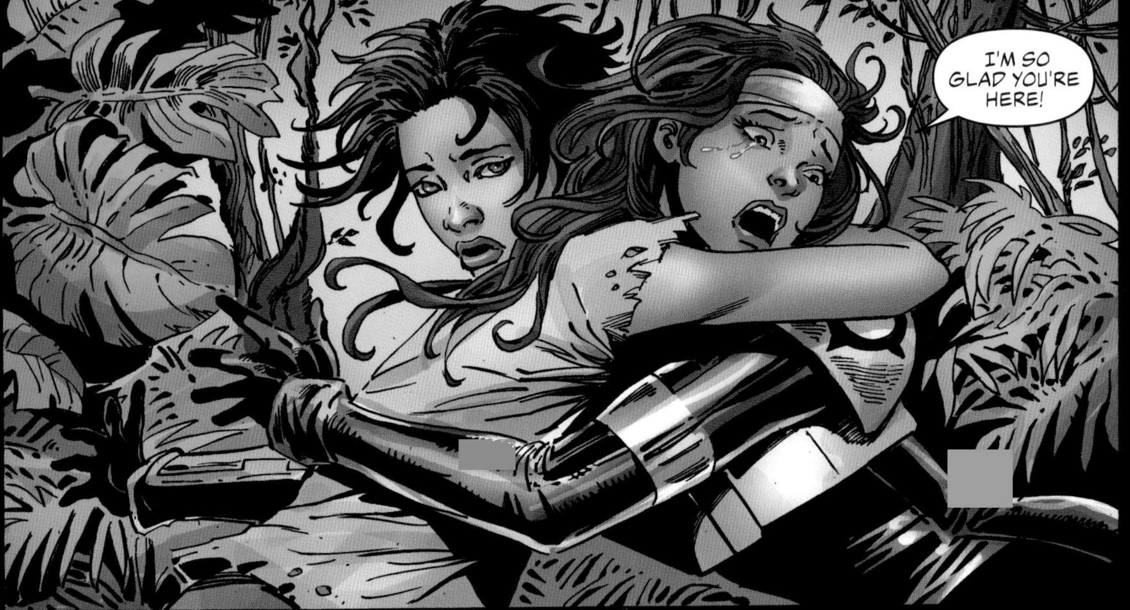
I'M SO GLAD YOU'RE HERE!

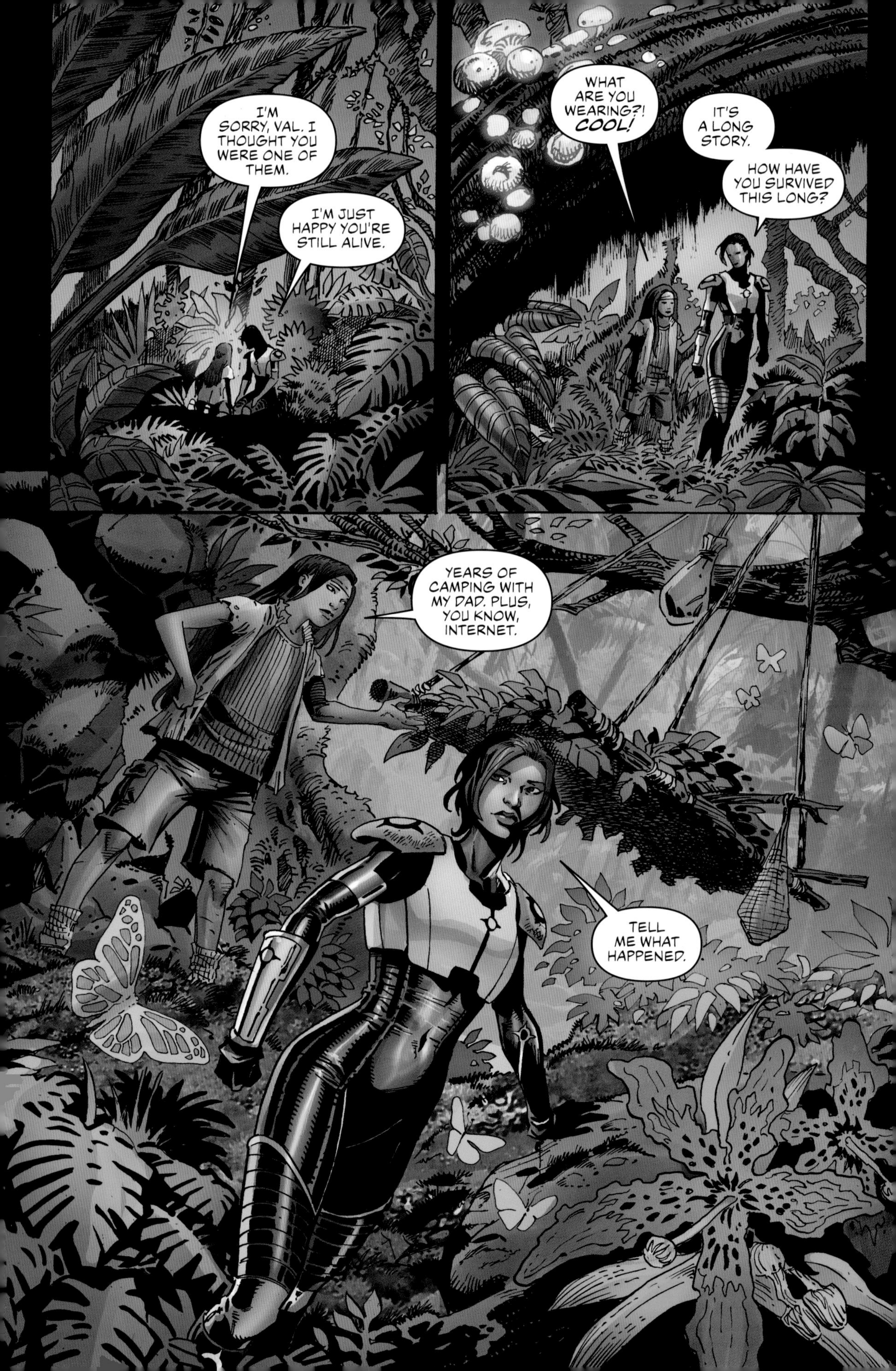
I'M SORRY, VAL. I THOUGHT YOU WERE ONE OF THEM.
I'M JUST HAPPY YOU'RE STILL ALIVE.
WHAT ARE YOU WEARING?! COOL!
IT'S A LONG STORY.
HOW HAVE YOU SURVIVED THIS LONG?
YEARS OF CAMPING WITH MY DAD. PLUS, YOU KNOW, INTERNET.
TELL ME WHAT HAPPENED.

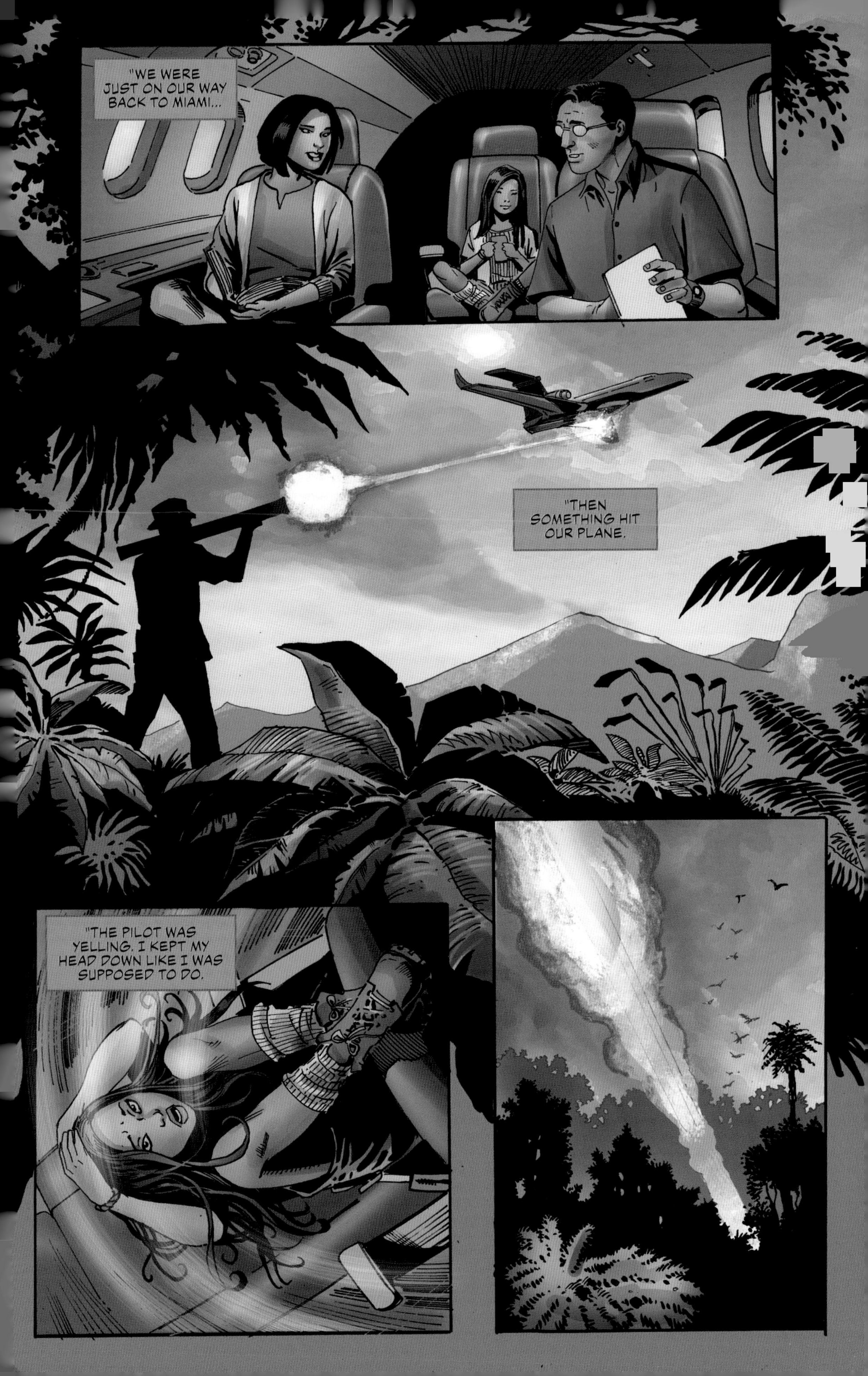
"WE WERE JUST ON OUR WAY BACK TO MIAMI...
"THEN SOMETHING HIT OUR PLANE.
"THE PILOT WAS YELLING. I KEPT MY HEAD DOWN LIKE I WAS SUPPOSED TO DO.

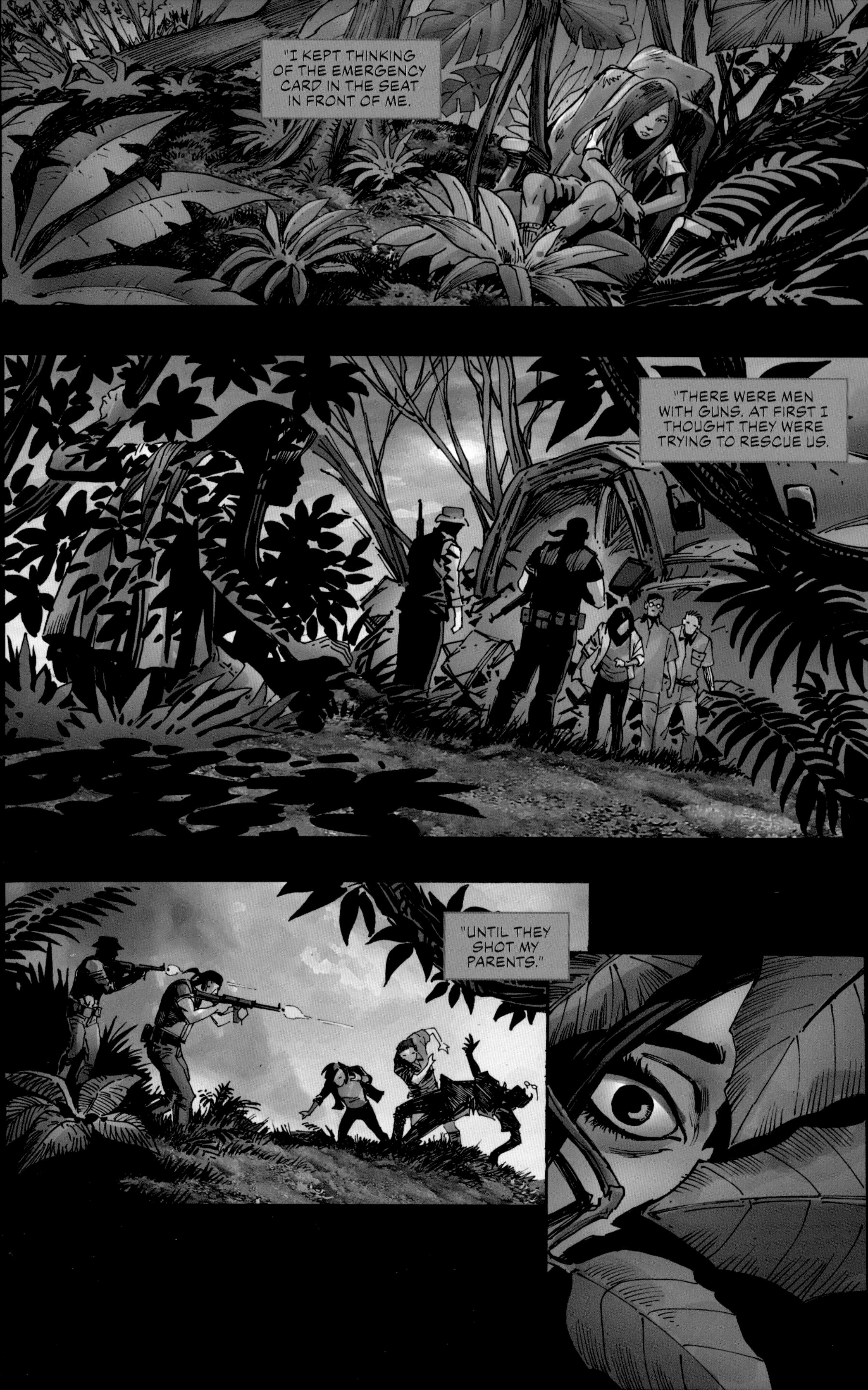
"I KEPT THINKING OF THE EMERGENCY CARD IN THE SEAT IN FRONT OF ME.
"THERE WERE MEN WITH GUNS. AT FIRST I THOUGHT THEY WERE TRYING TO RESCUE US.
"UNTIL THEY SHOT MY PARENTS."

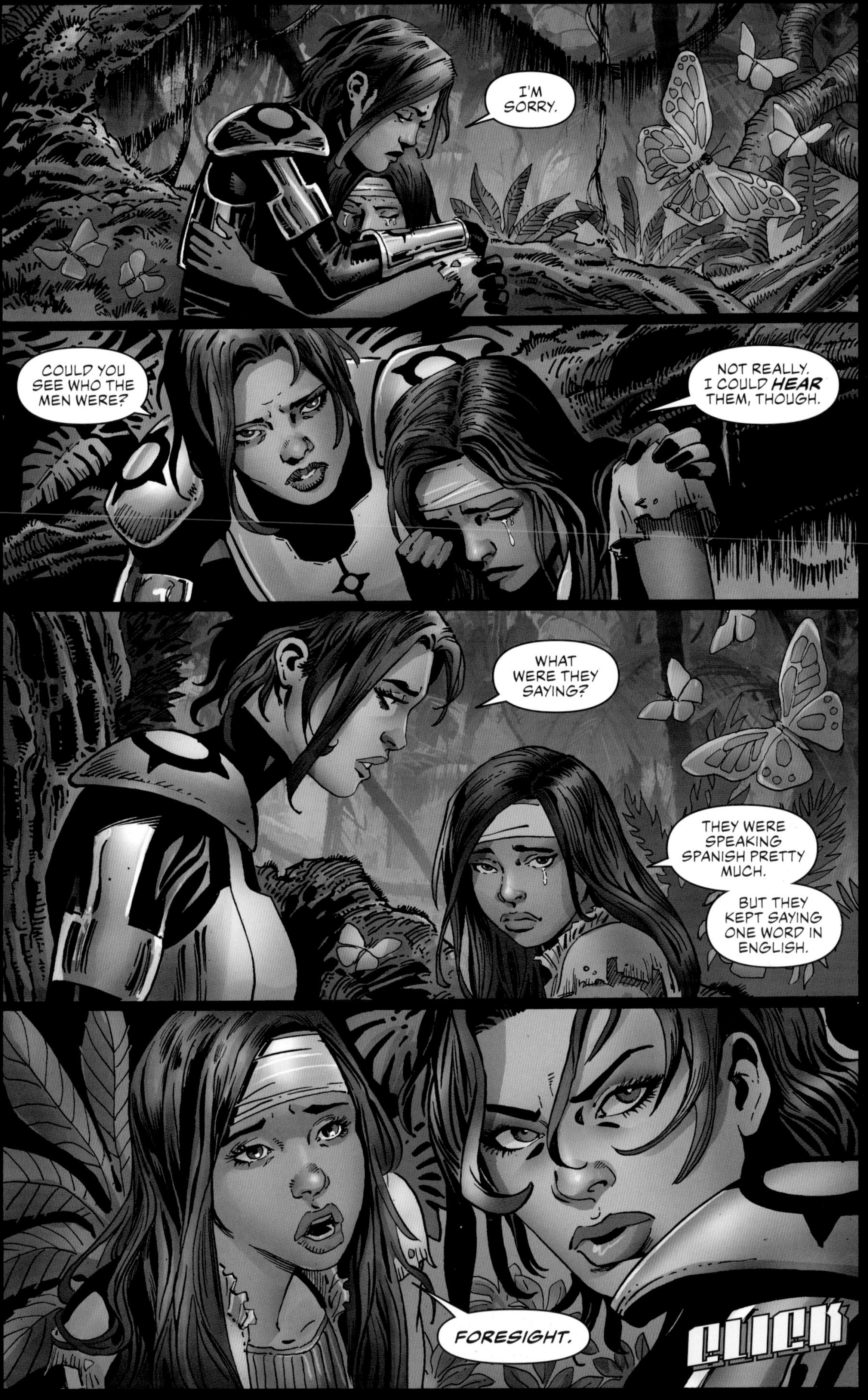
I'M SORRY.
COULD YOU SEE WHO THE MEN WERE?
NOT REALLY. I COULD HEAR THEM, THOUGH.
WHAT WERE THEY SAYING?
THEY WERE SPEAKING SPANISH PRETTY MUCH.
BUT THEY KEPT SAYING ONE WORD IN ENGLISH.
FORESIGHT.
CLICK

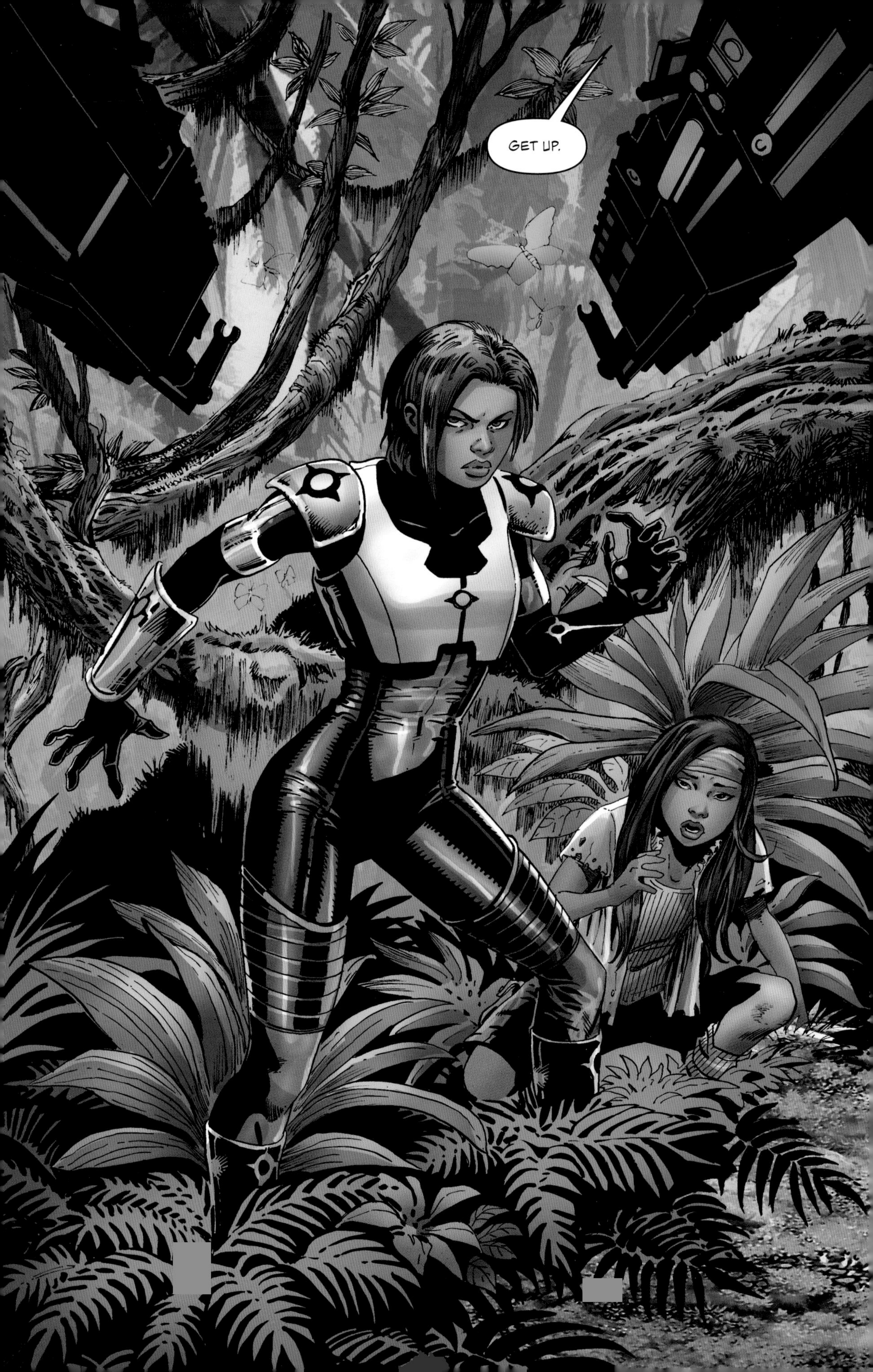
GET UP.

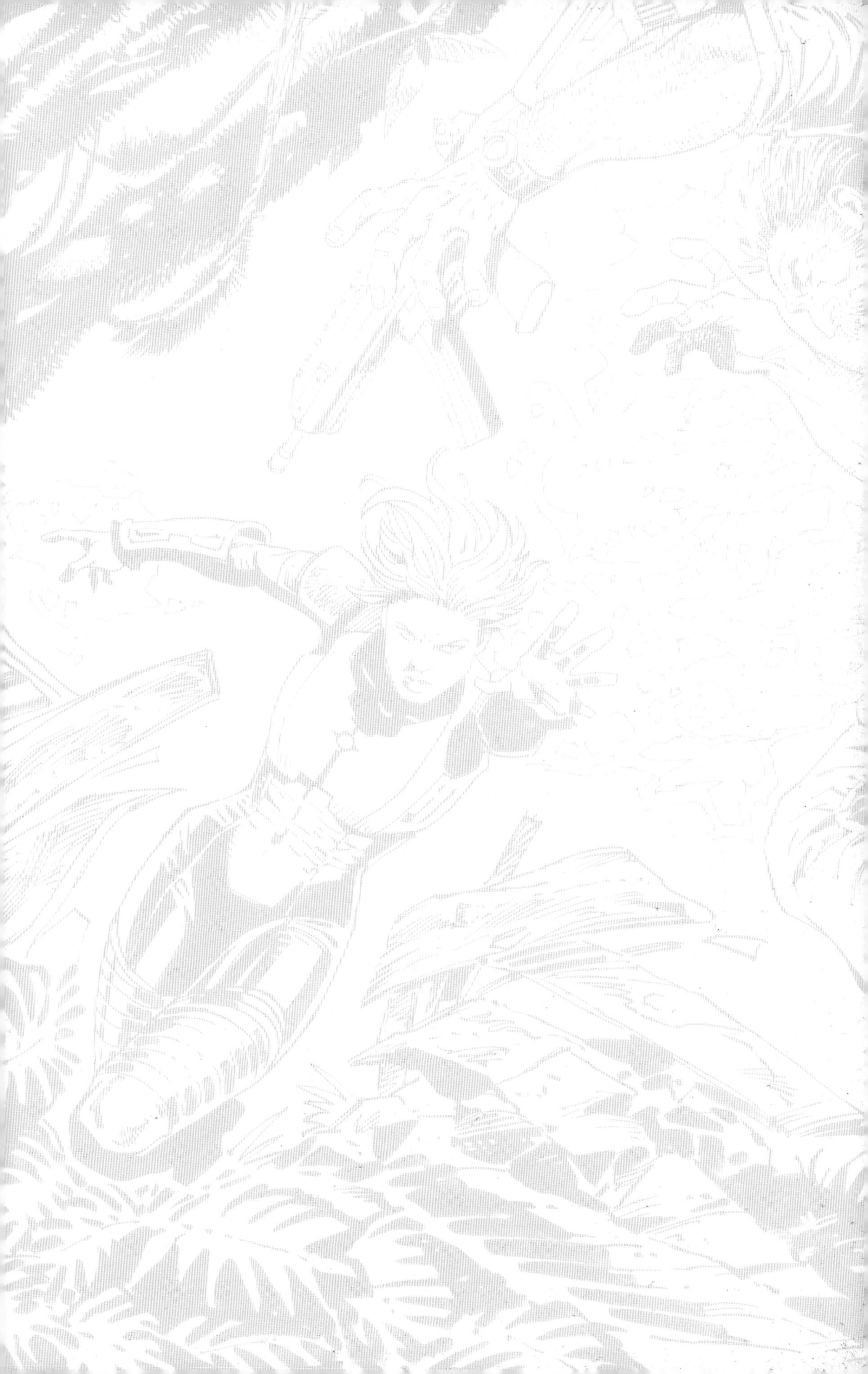

CHAPTER FOUR

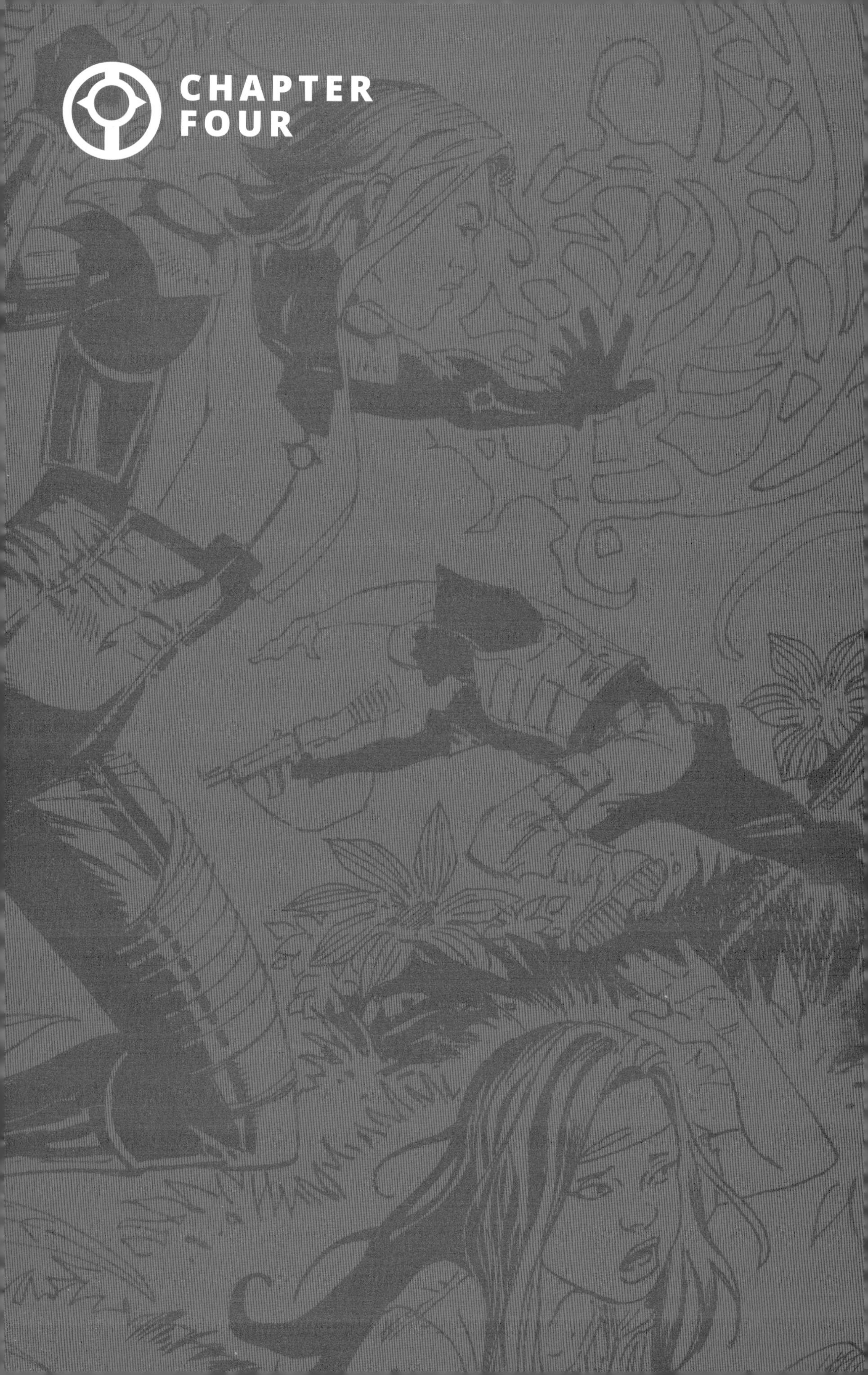

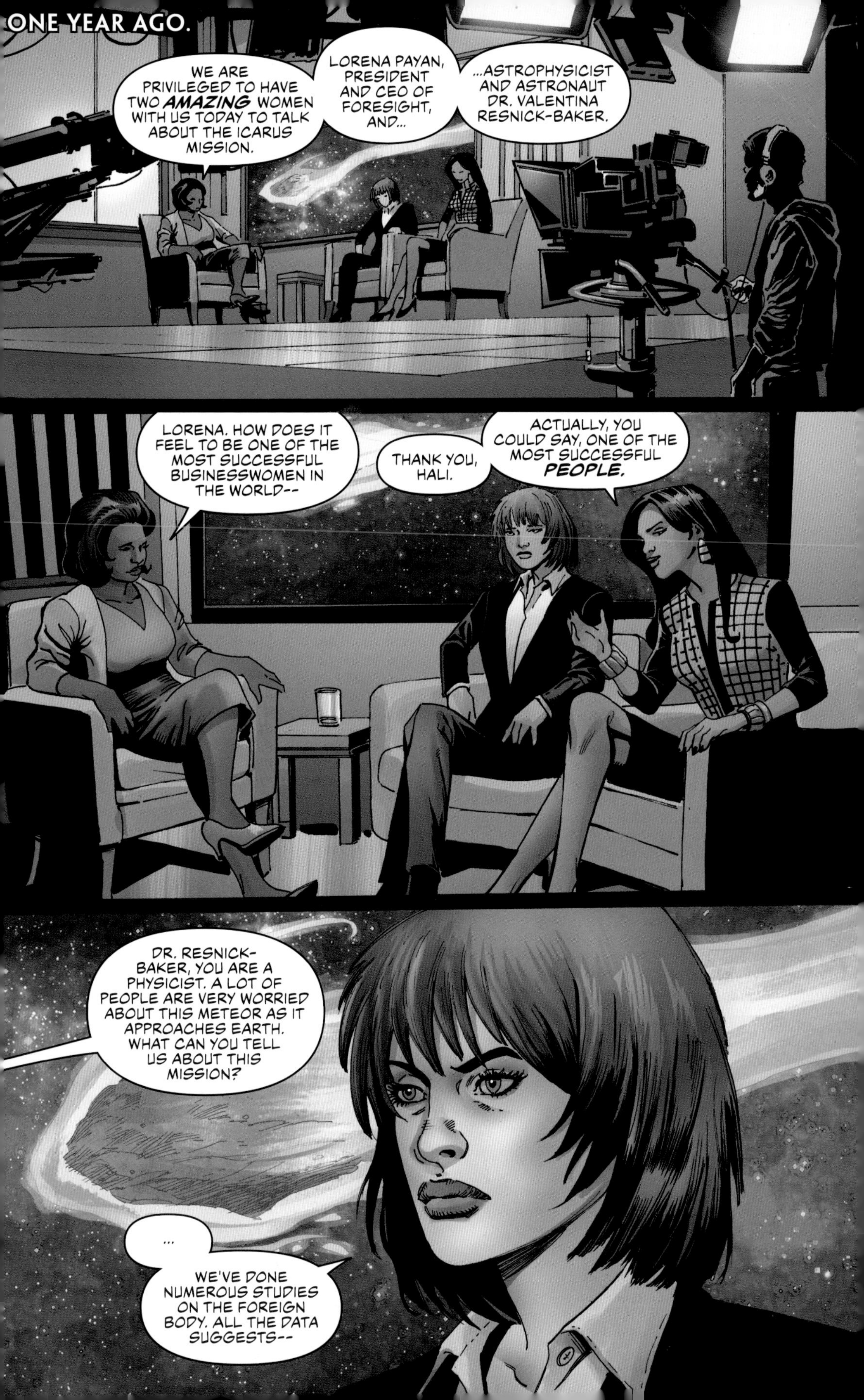
ONE YEAR AGO.
WE ARE PRIVILEGED TO HAVE TWO AMAZING WOMEN WITH US TODAY TO TALK ABOUT THE ICARUS MISSION.
LORENA PAYAN, PRESIDENT AND CEO OF FORESIGHT, AND...
...ASTROPHYSICIST AND ASTRONAUT DR. VALENTINA RESNICK-BAKER.
LORENA. HOW DOES IT FEEL TO BE ONE OF THE MOST SUCCESSFUL BUSINESSWOMEN IN THE WORLD--
THANK YOU, HALI.
ACTUALLY, YOU COULD SAY, ONE OF THE MOST SUCCESSFUL PEOPLE.
DR. RESNICK-BAKER, YOU ARE A PHYSICIST. A LOT OF PEOPLE ARE VERY WORRIED ABOUT THIS METEOR AS IT APPROACHES EARTH. WHAT CAN YOU TELL US ABOUT THIS MISSION?
...
WE'VE DONE NUMEROUS STUDIES ON THE FOREIGN BODY. ALL THE DATA SUGGESTS--

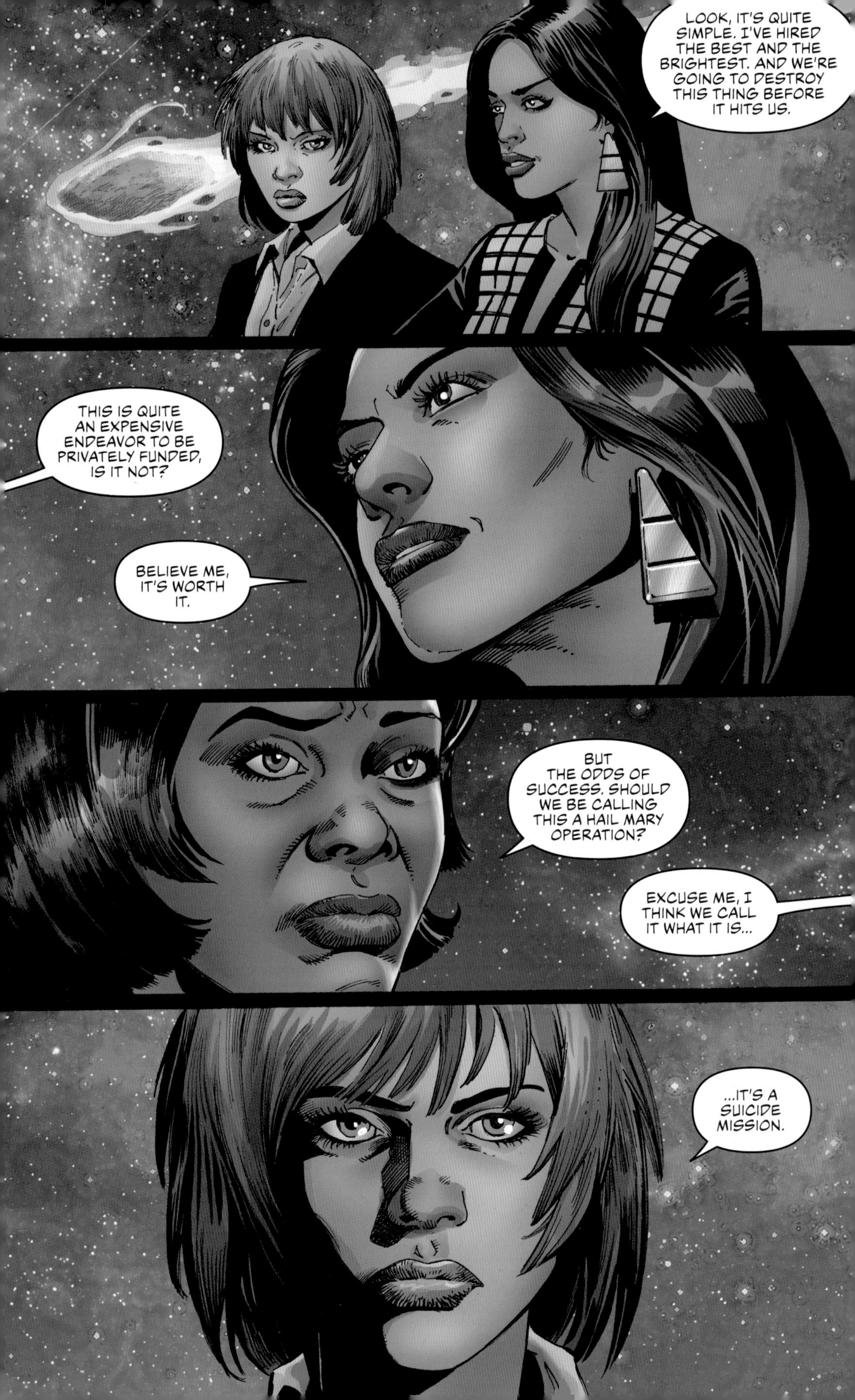
LOOK, IT'S QUITE SIMPLE. I'VE HIRED THE BEST AND THE BRIGHTEST. AND WE'RE GOING TO DESTROY THIS THING BEFORE IT HITS US.
THIS IS QUITE AN EXPENSIVE ENDEAVOR TO BE PRIVATELY FUNDED, IS IT NOT?
BELIEVE ME, IT'S WORTH IT.
BUT THE ODDS OF SUCCESS. SHOULD WE BE CALLING THIS A HAIL MARY OPERATION?
EXCUSE ME, I THINK WE CALL IT WHAT IT IS...
...IT'S A SUICIDE MISSION.

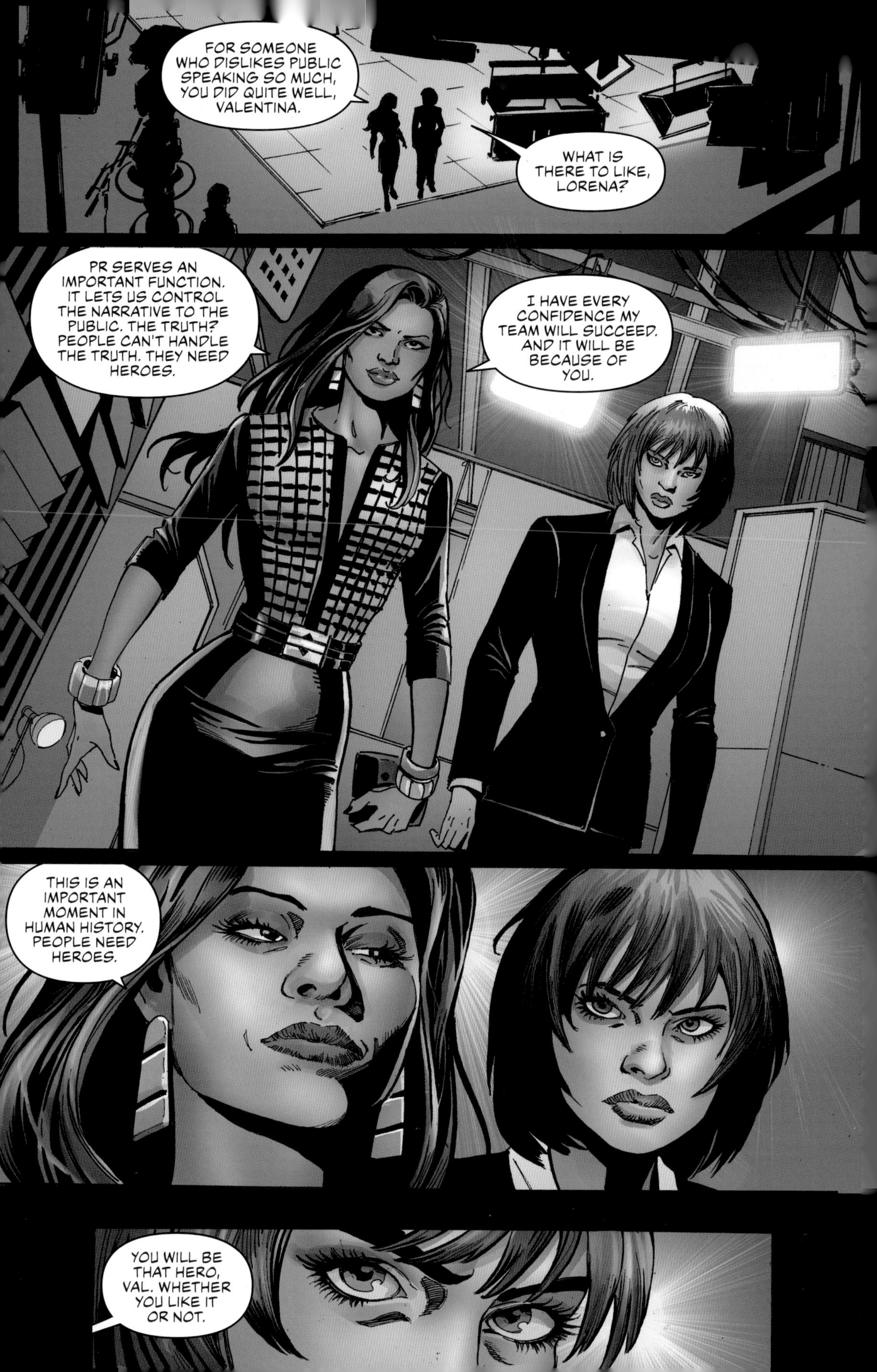
FOR SOMEONE WHO DISLIKES PUBLIC SPEAKING SO MUCH, YOU DID QUITE WELL, VALENTINA.
WHAT IS THERE TO LIKE, LORENA?
PR SERVES AN IMPORTANT FUNCTION. IT LETS US CONTROL THE NARRATIVE TO THE PUBLIC. THE TRUTH? PEOPLE CAN'T HANDLE THE TRUTH. THEY NEED HEROES.
I HAVE EVERY CONFIDENCE MY TEAM WILL SUCCEED. AND IT WILL BE BECAUSE OF YOU.
THIS IS AN IMPORTANT MOMENT IN HUMAN HISTORY. PEOPLE NEED HEROES.
YOU WILL BE THAT HERO, VAL. WHETHER YOU LIKE IT OR NOT.

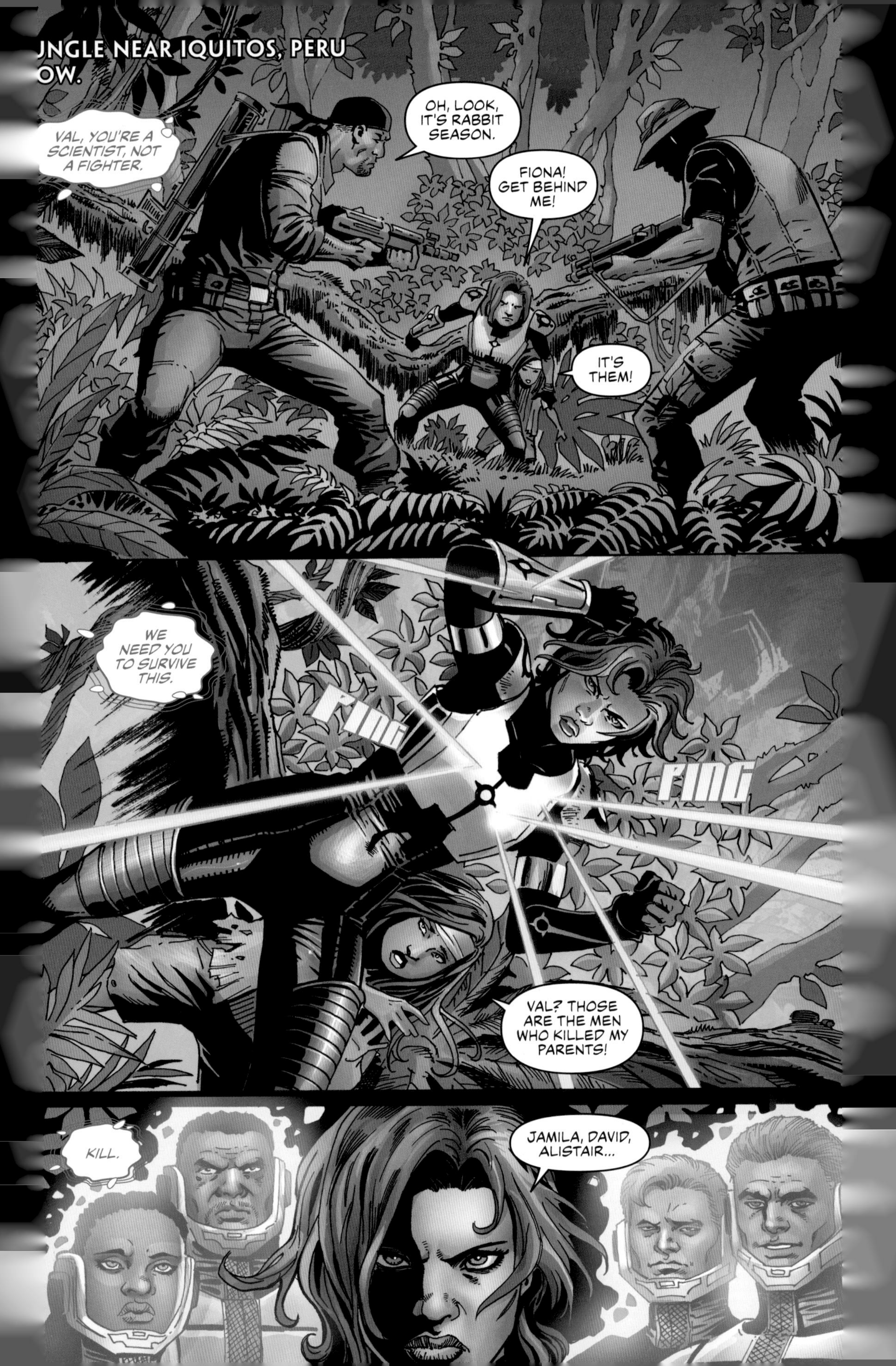
JNGLE NEAR IQUITOS, PERU
OW.
VAL, YOU'RE A SCIENTIST, NOT A FIGHTER.
OH, LOOK, IT'S RABBIT SEASON.
FIONA! GET BEHIND ME!
IT'S THEM!
WE NEED YOU TO SURVIVE THIS.
PING
PING
VAL? THOSE ARE THE MEN WHO KILLED MY PARENTS!
KILL.
JAMILA, DAVID, ALISTAIR...

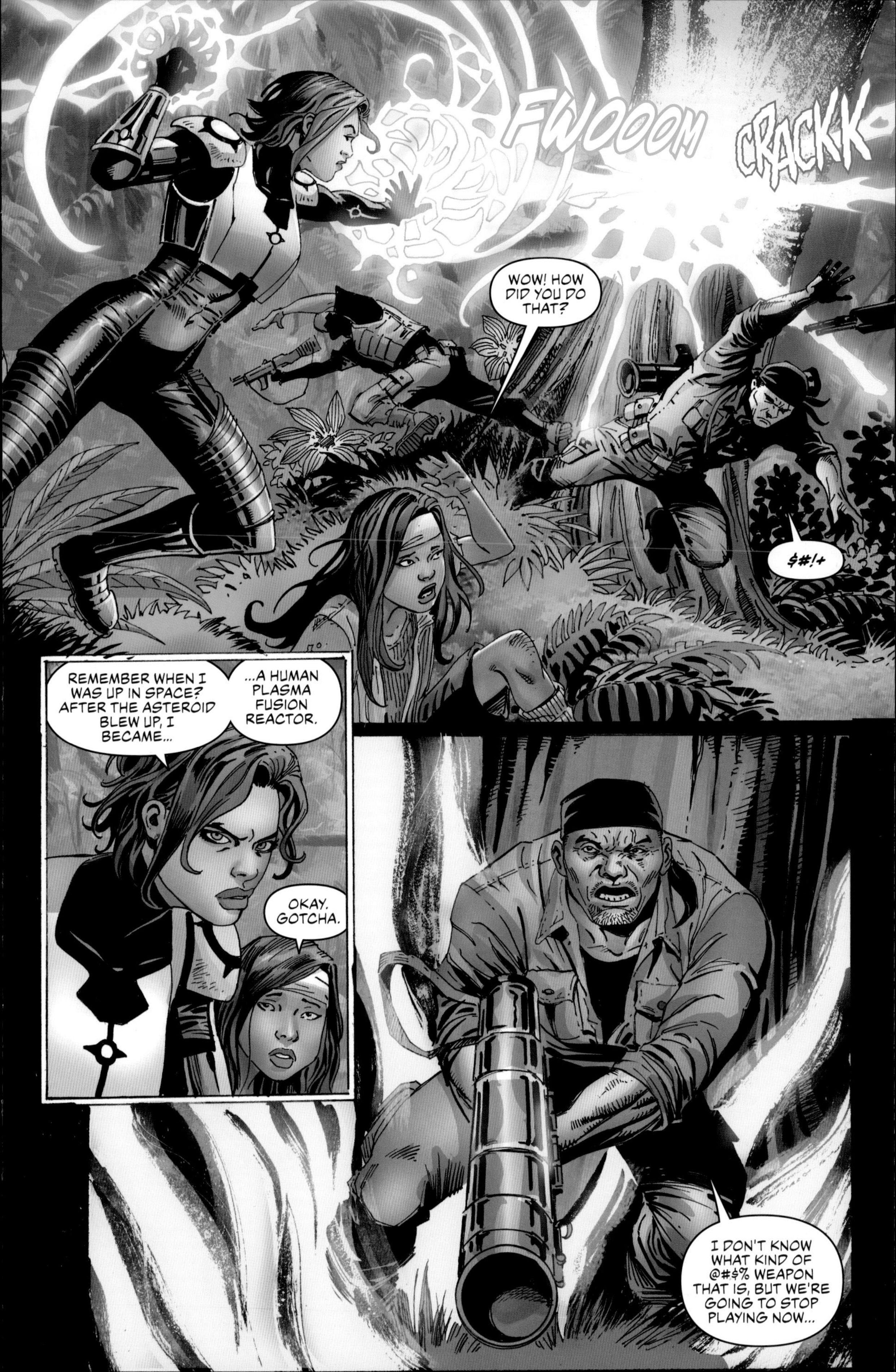
FWOOOM
CRACKK
WOW! HOW DID YOU DO THAT?
$#!+
REMEMBER WHEN I WAS UP IN SPACE? AFTER THE ASTEROID BLEW UP, I BECAME...
...A HUMAN PLASMA FUSION REACTOR.
OKAY. GOTCHA.
I DON'T KNOW WHAT KIND OF @#$% WEAPON THAT IS, BUT WE'RE GOING TO STOP PLAYING NOW...

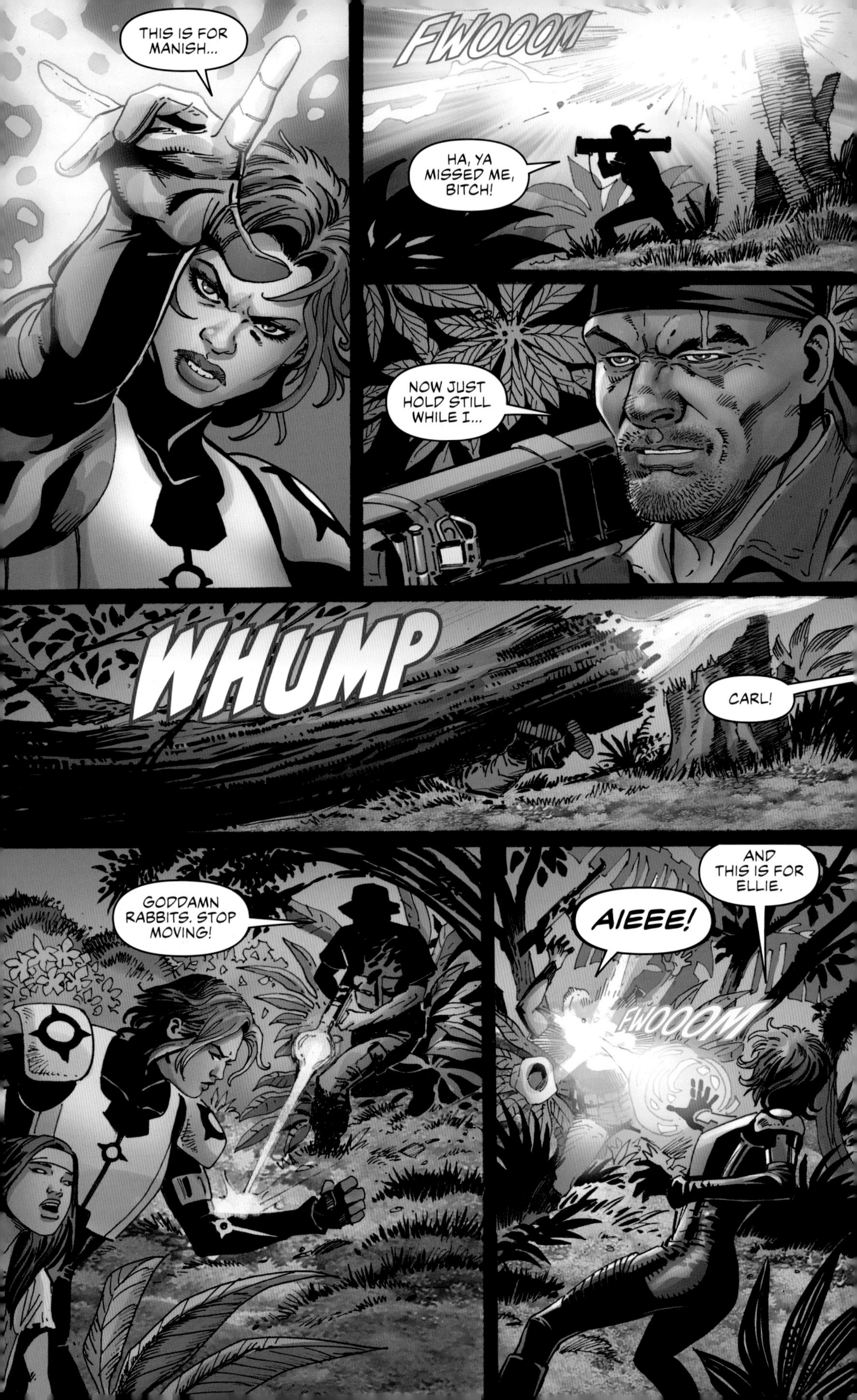
THIS IS FOR MANISH...
FWOOOM
HA, YA MISSED ME, BITCH!
NOW JUST HOLD STILL WHILE I...
WHUMP
CARL!
GODDAMN RABBITS. STOP MOVING!
AND THIS IS FOR ELLIE.
AIEEE!
FWOOOM

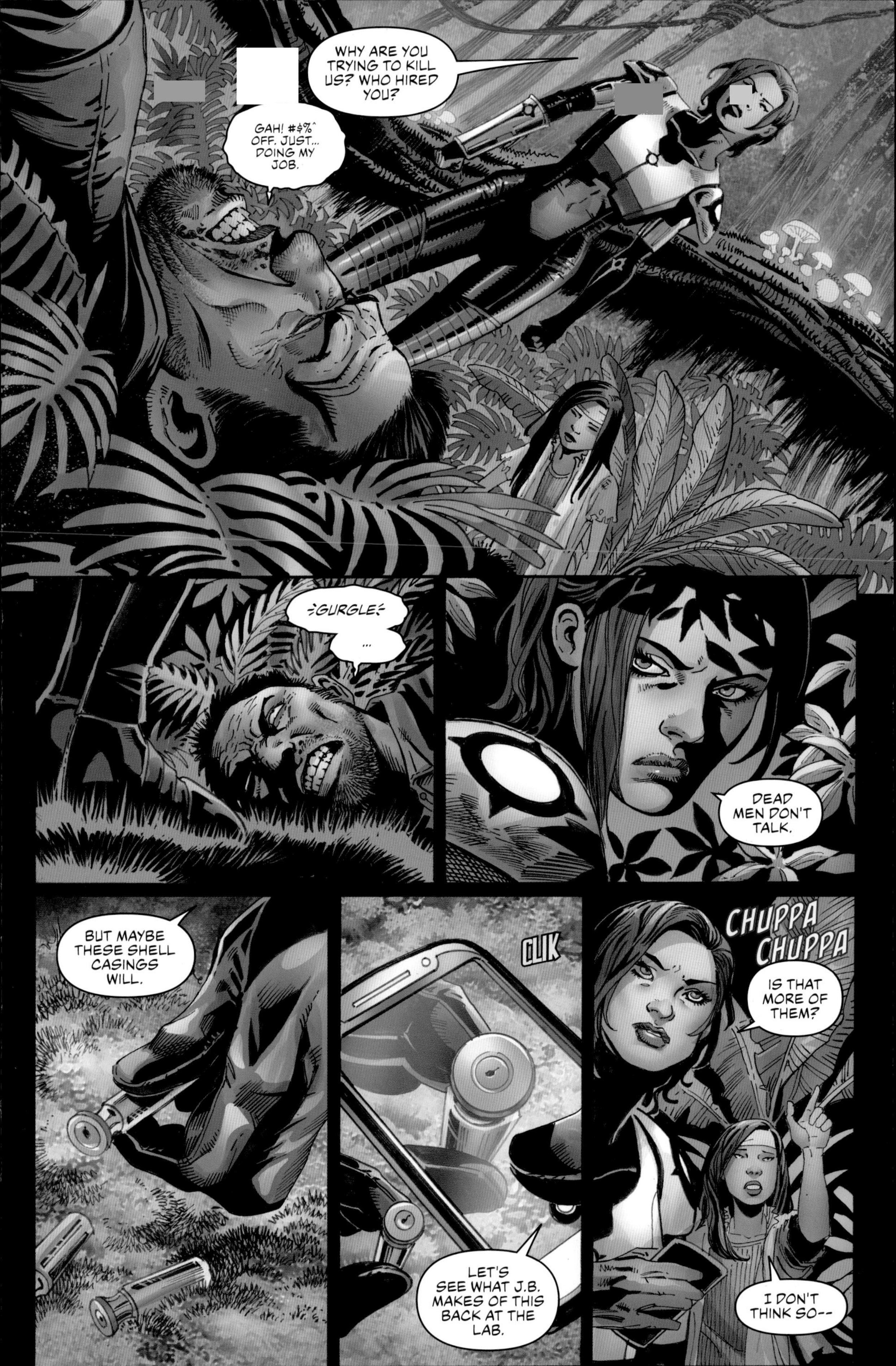
WHY ARE YOU TRYING TO KILL US? WHO HIRED YOU?
GAH! #$%^ OFF. JUST... DOING MY JOB.
GURGLE
...
DEAD MEN DON'T TALK.
BUT MAYBE THESE SHELL CASINGS WILL.
CLIK
LET'S SEE WHAT J.B. MAKES OF THIS BACK AT THE LAB.
CHUPPA CHUPPA
IS THAT MORE OF THEM?
I DON'T THINK SO--

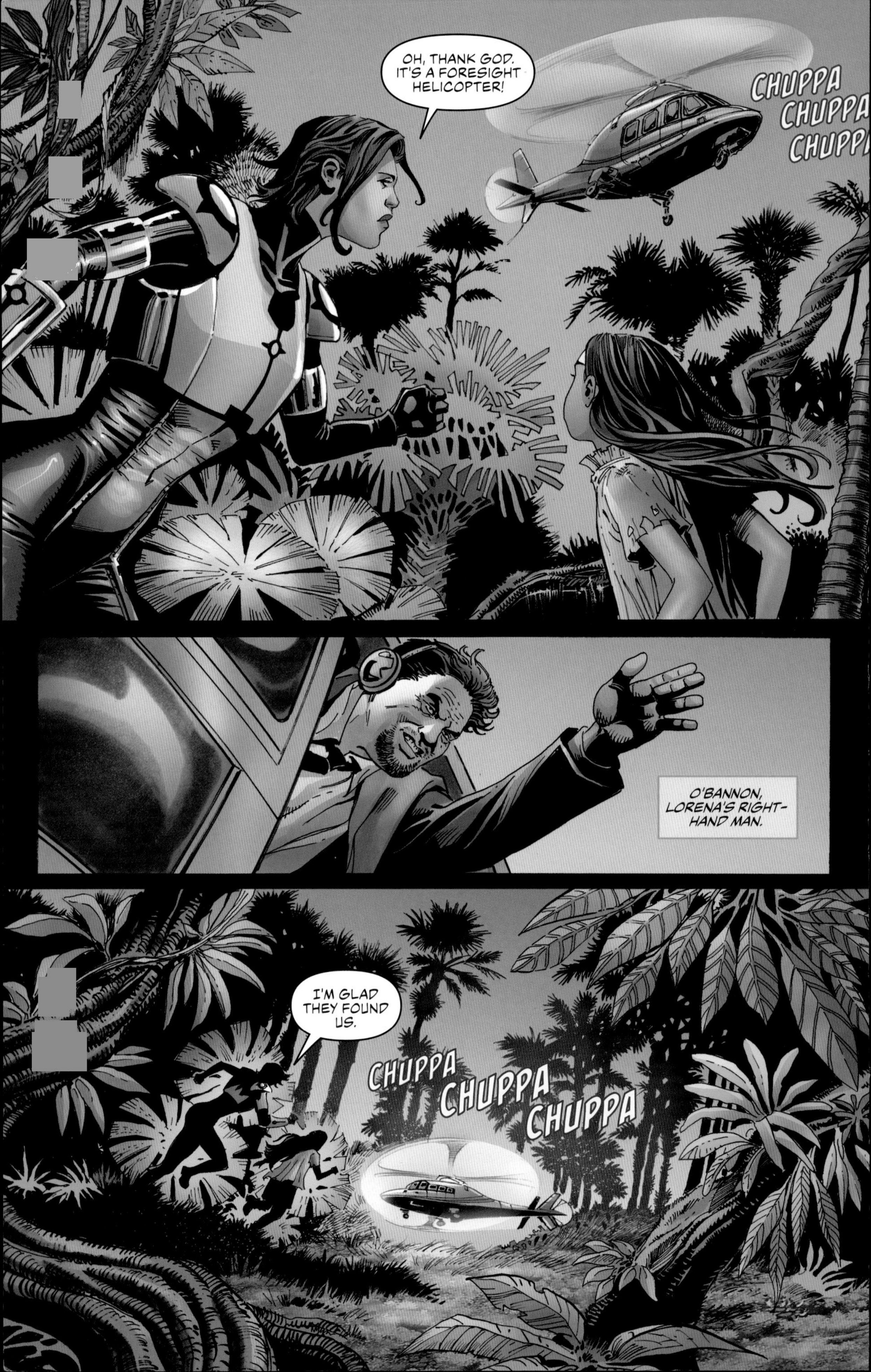
OH, THANK GOD. IT'S A FORESIGHT HELICOPTER!
CHUPPA CHUPPA CHUPP
O'BANNON, LORENA'S RIGHT-HAND MAN.
I'M GLAD THEY FOUND US.
CHUPPA CHUPPA CHUPPA

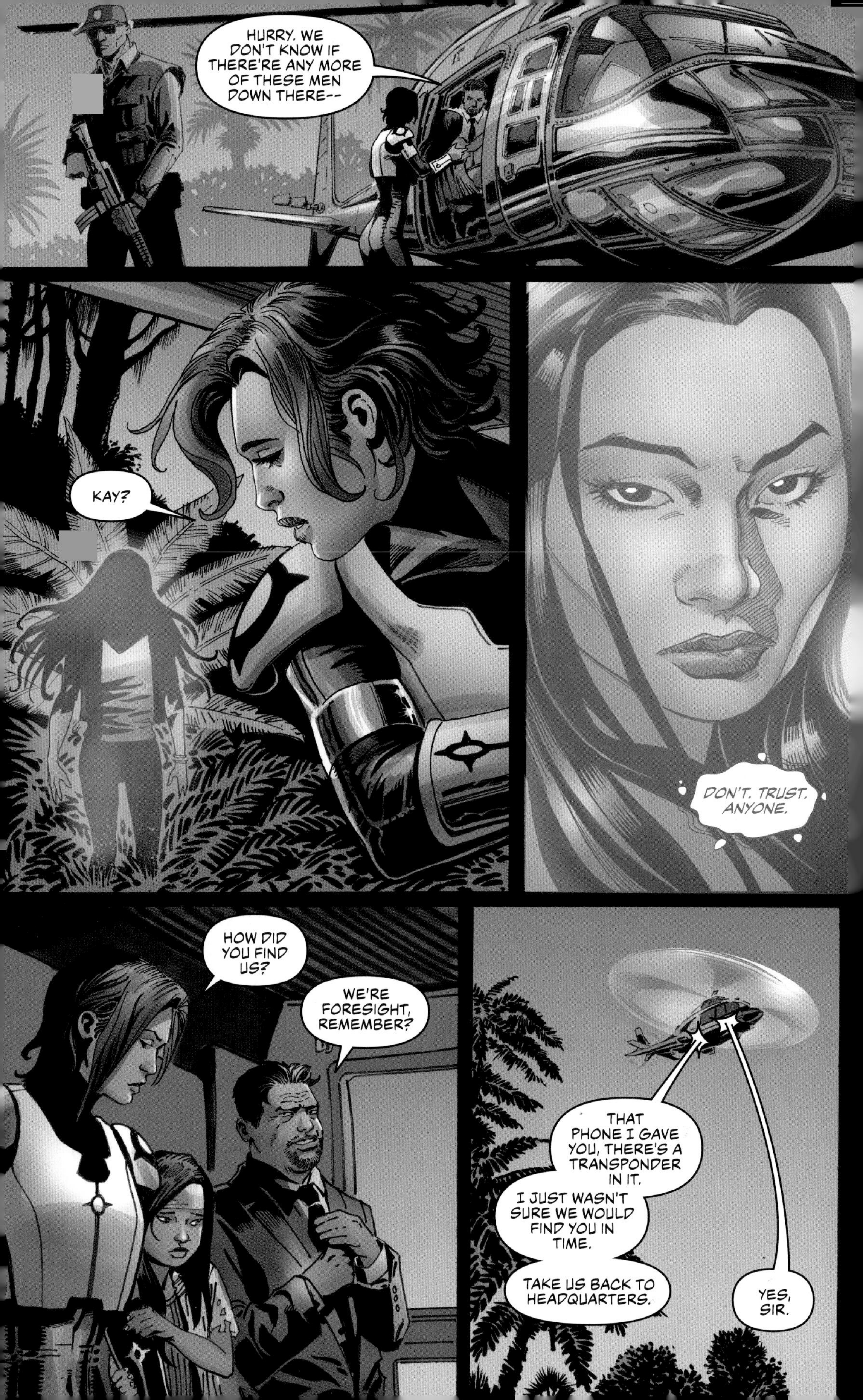
HURRY. WE DON'T KNOW IF THERE'RE ANY MORE OF THESE MEN DOWN THERE--
KAY?
DON'T. TRUST. ANYONE.
HOW DID YOU FIND US?
WE'RE FORESIGHT, REMEMBER?
THAT PHONE I GAVE YOU, THERE'S A TRANSPONDER IN IT.
I JUST WASN'T SURE WE WOULD FIND YOU IN TIME.
TAKE US BACK TO HEADQUARTERS.
YES, SIR.

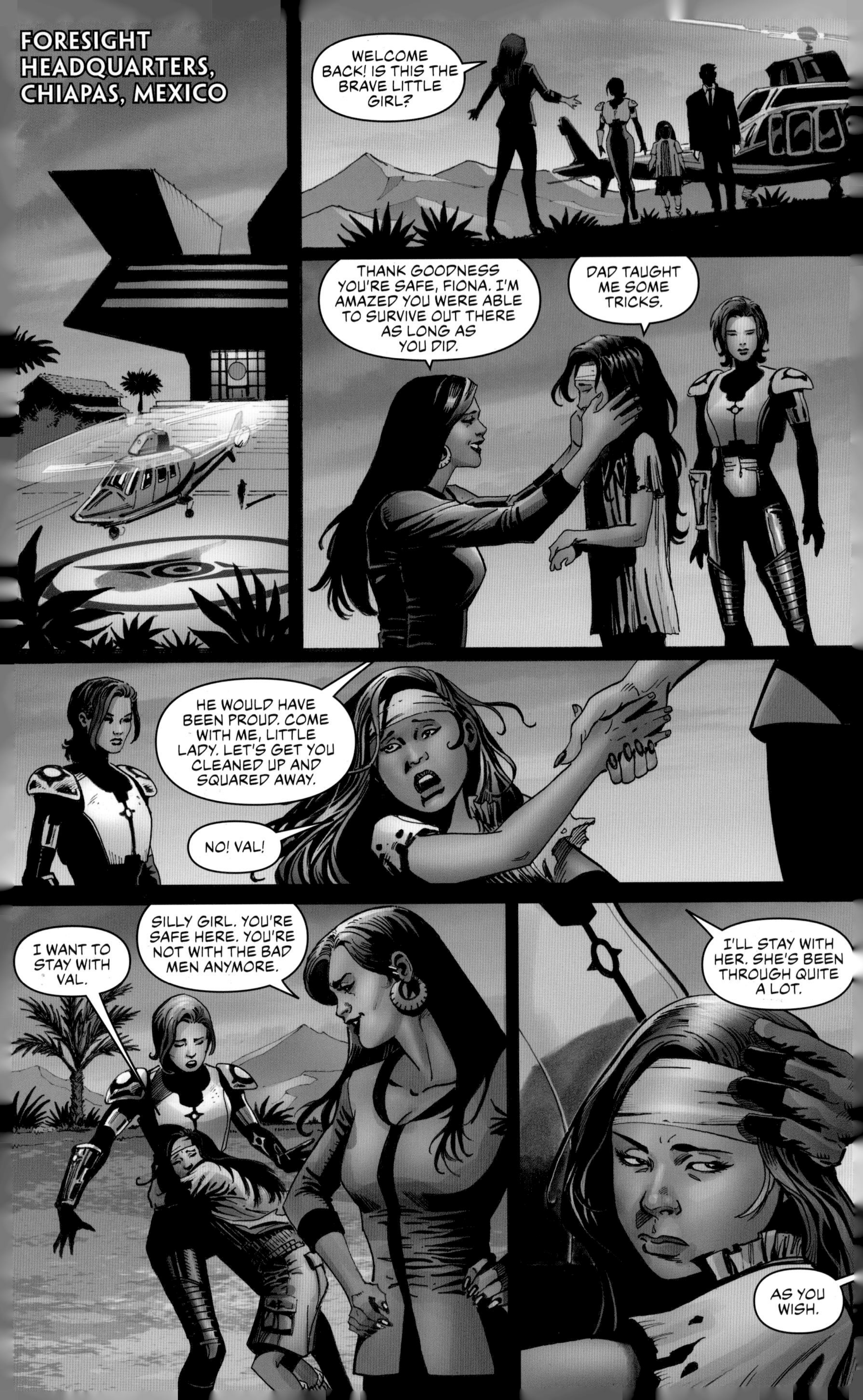
FORESIGHT HEADQUARTERS, CHIAPAS, MEXICO
WELCOME BACK! IS THIS THE BRAVE LITTLE GIRL?
THANK GOODNESS YOU'RE SAFE, FIONA. I'M AMAZED YOU WERE ABLE TO SURVIVE OUT THERE AS LONG AS YOU DID.
DAD TAUGHT ME SOME TRICKS.
HE WOULD HAVE BEEN PROUD. COME WITH ME, LITTLE LADY. LET'S GET YOU CLEANED UP AND SQUARED AWAY.
NO! VAL!
I WANT TO STAY WITH VAL.
SILLY GIRL. YOU'RE SAFE HERE. YOU'RE NOT WITH THE BAD MEN ANYMORE.
I'LL STAY WITH HER. SHE'S BEEN THROUGH QUITE A LOT.
AS YOU WISH.

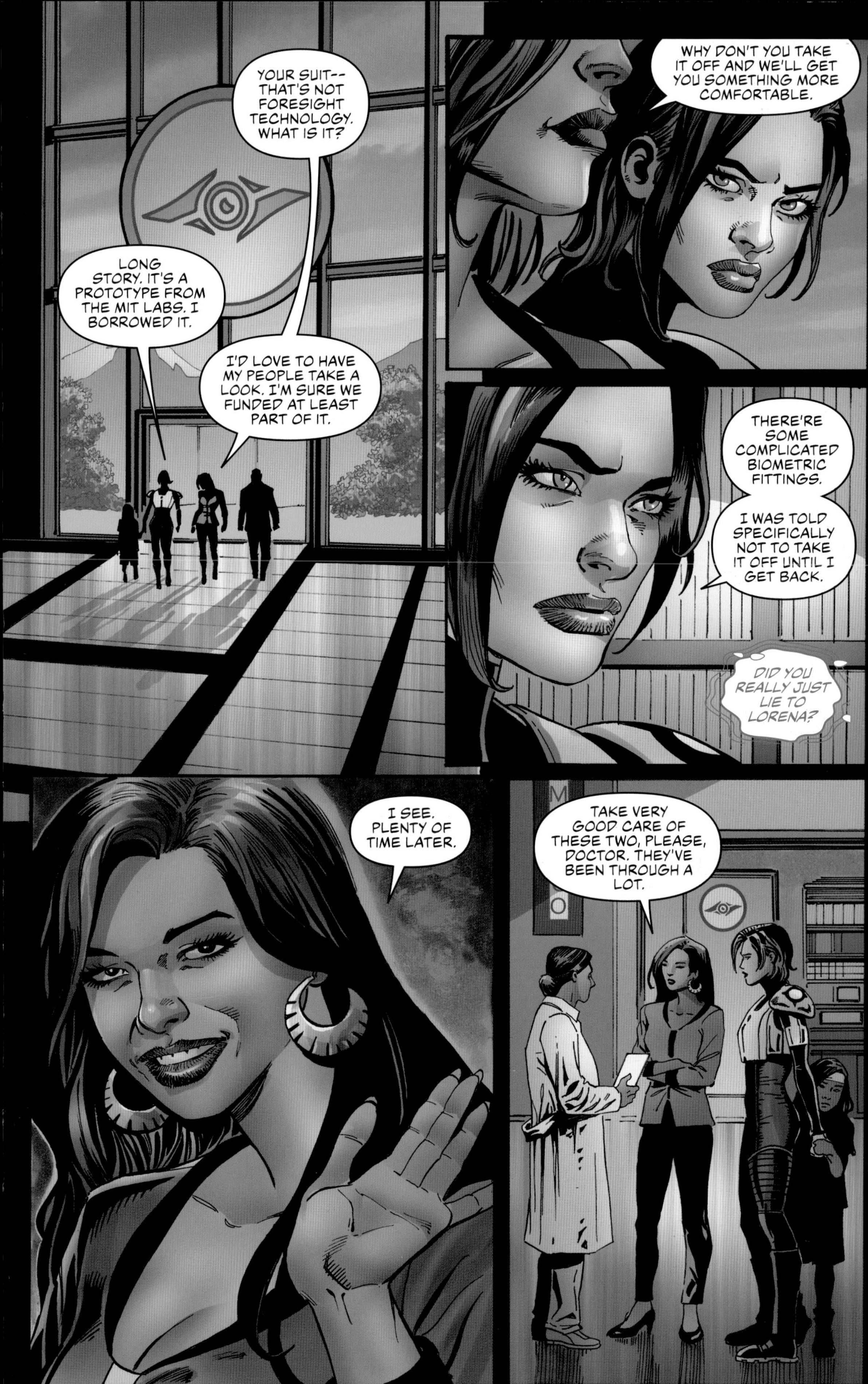
YOUR SUIT--THAT'S NOT FORESIGHT TECHNOLOGY. WHAT IS IT?
LONG STORY. IT'S A PROTOTYPE FROM THE MIT LABS. I BORROWED IT.
I'D LOVE TO HAVE MY PEOPLE TAKE A LOOK. I'M SURE WE FUNDED AT LEAST PART OF IT.
WHY DON'T YOU TAKE IT OFF AND WE'LL GET YOU SOMETHING MORE COMFORTABLE.
THERE'RE SOME COMPLICATED BIOMETRIC FITTINGS.
I WAS TOLD SPECIFICALLY NOT TO TAKE IT OFF UNTIL I GET BACK.
DID YOU REALLY JUST LIE TO LORENA?
I SEE. PLENTY OF TIME LATER.
TAKE VERY GOOD CARE OF THESE TWO, PLEASE, DOCTOR. THEY'VE BEEN THROUGH A LOT.

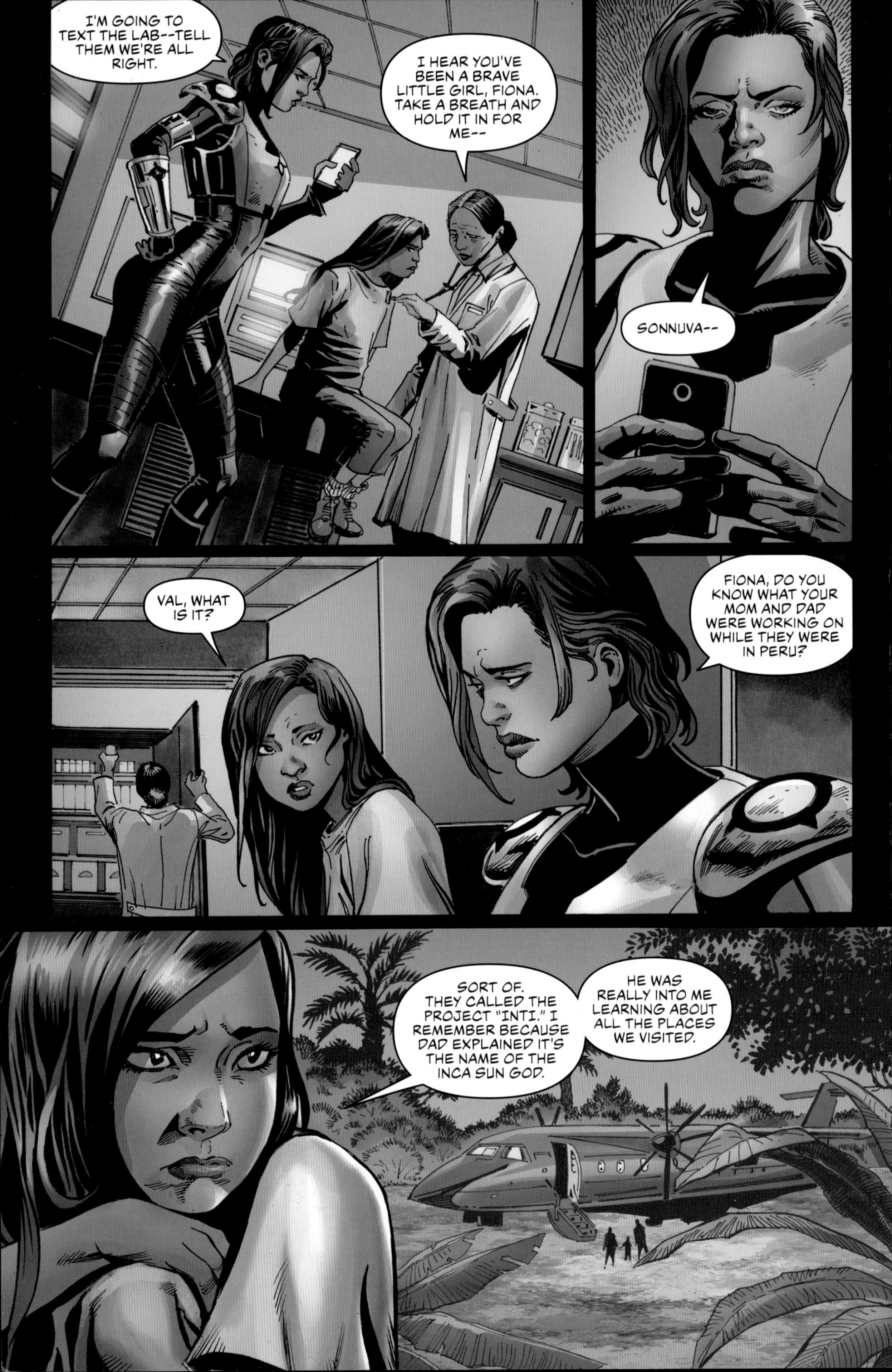
I'M GOING TO TEXT THE LAB--TELL THEM WE'RE ALL RIGHT.
I HEAR YOU'VE BEEN A BRAVE LITTLE GIRL, FIONA. TAKE A BREATH AND HOLD IT IN FOR ME--
SONNUVA--
VAL, WHAT IS IT?
FIONA, DO YOU KNOW WHAT YOUR MOM AND DAD WERE WORKING ON WHILE THEY WERE IN PERU?
SORT OF. THEY CALLED THE PROJECT "INTI." I REMEMBER BECAUSE DAD EXPLAINED IT'S THE NAME OF THE INCA SUN GOD.
HE WAS REALLY INTO ME LEARNING ABOUT ALL THE PLACES WE VISITED.

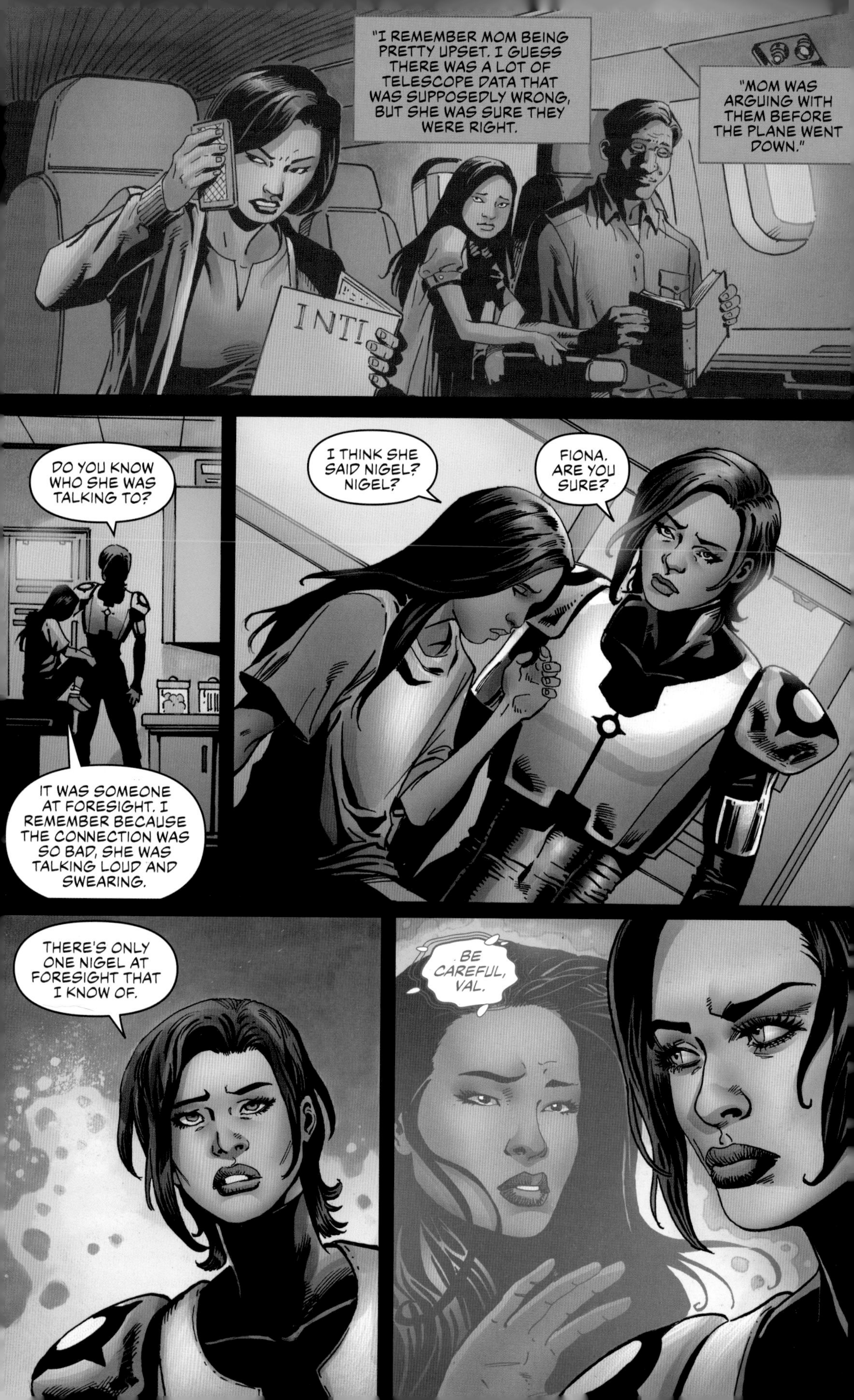
"I REMEMBER MOM BEING PRETTY UPSET. I GUESS THERE WAS A LOT OF TELESCOPE DATA THAT WAS SUPPOSEDLY WRONG, BUT SHE WAS SURE THEY WERE RIGHT.
"MOM WAS ARGUING WITH THEM BEFORE THE PLANE WENT DOWN."
INTI
DO YOU KNOW WHO SHE WAS TALKING TO?
IT WAS SOMEONE AT FORESIGHT. I REMEMBER BECAUSE THE CONNECTION WAS SO BAD, SHE WAS TALKING LOUD AND SWEARING.
I THINK SHE SAID NIGEL? NIGEL?
FIONA. ARE YOU SURE?
THERE'S ONLY ONE NIGEL AT FORESIGHT THAT I KNOW OF.
BE CAREFUL, VAL.

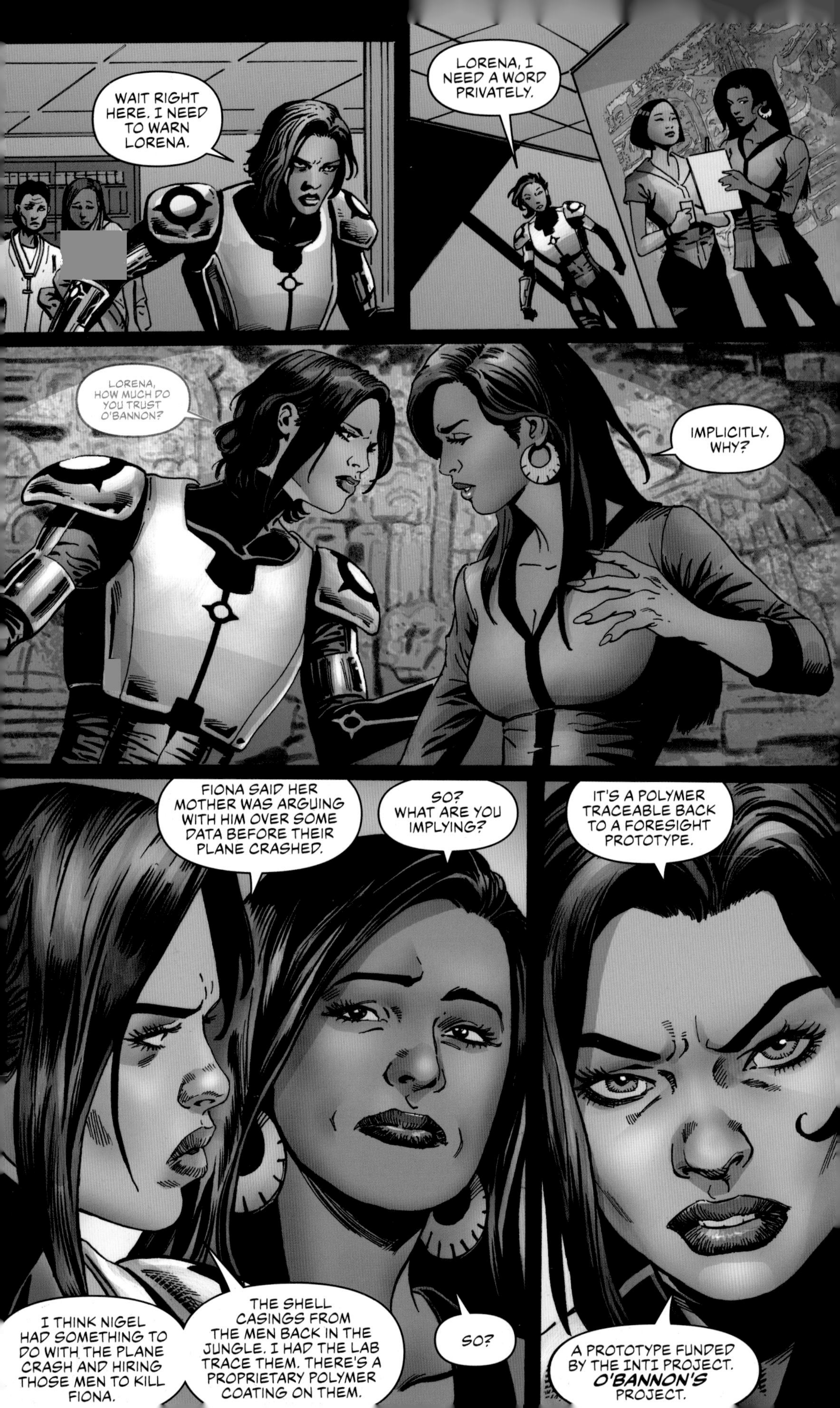
WAIT RIGHT HERE. I NEED TO WARN LORENA.
LORENA, I NEED A WORD PRIVATELY.
LORENA, HOW MUCH DO YOU TRUST O'BANNON?
IMPLICITLY. WHY?
FIONA SAID HER MOTHER WAS ARGUING WITH HIM OVER SOME DATA BEFORE THEIR PLANE CRASHED.
SO? WHAT ARE YOU IMPLYING?
I THINK NIGEL HAD SOMETHING TO DO WITH THE PLANE CRASH AND HIRING THOSE MEN TO KILL FIONA.
THE SHELL CASINGS FROM THE MEN BACK IN THE JUNGLE. I HAD THE LAB TRACE THEM. THERE'S A PROPRIETARY POLYMER COATING ON THEM.
SO?
IT'S A POLYMER TRACEABLE BACK TO A FORESIGHT PROTOTYPE.
A PROTOTYPE FUNDED BY THE INTI PROJECT. O'BANNON'S PROJECT.

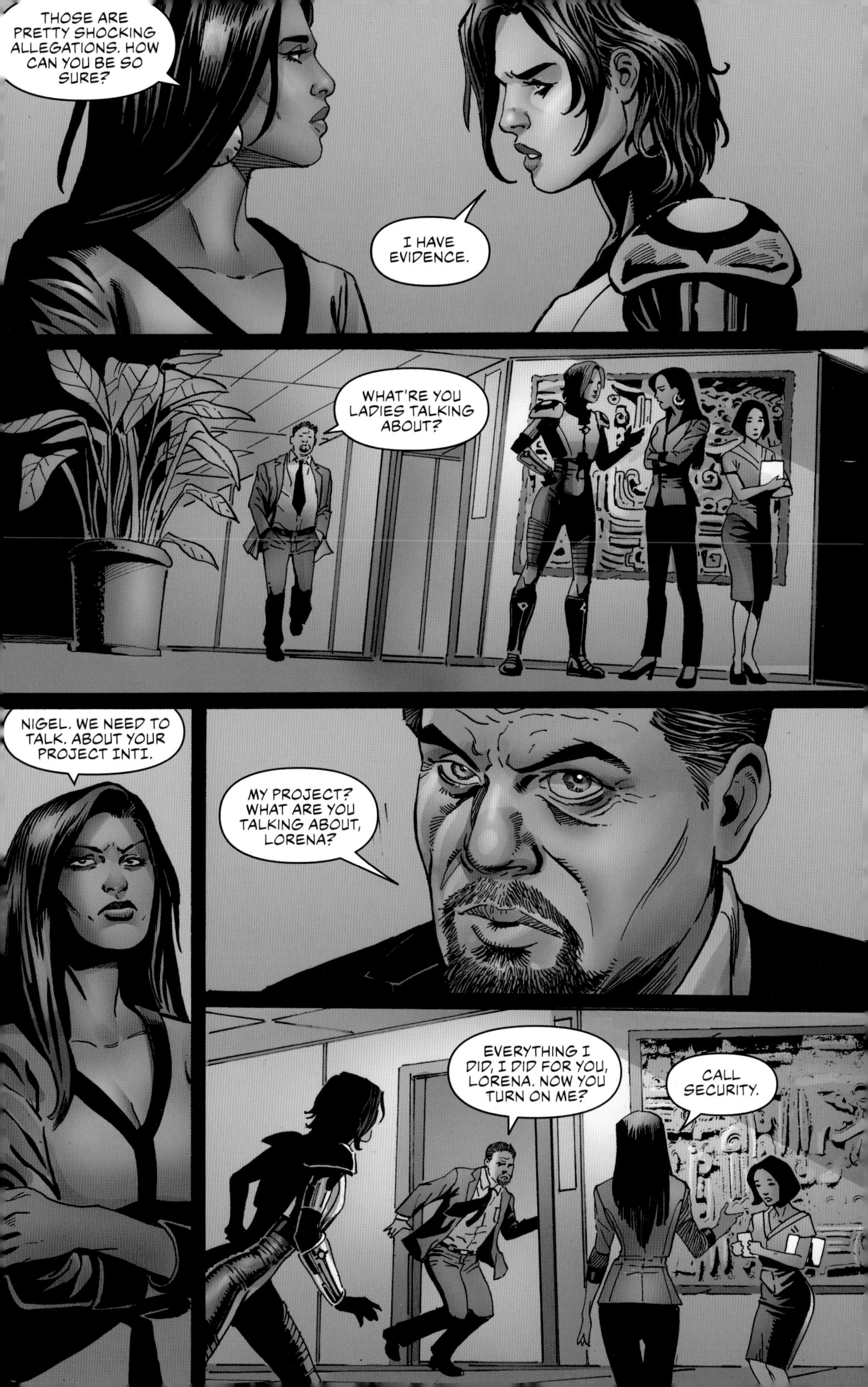
THOSE ARE PRETTY SHOCKING ALLEGATIONS. HOW CAN YOU BE SO SURE?
I HAVE EVIDENCE.
WHAT'RE YOU LADIES TALKING ABOUT?
NIGEL. WE NEED TO TALK. ABOUT YOUR PROJECT INTI.
MY PROJECT? WHAT ARE YOU TALKING ABOUT, LORENA?
EVERYTHING I DID, I DID FOR YOU, LORENA. NOW YOU TURN ON ME?
CALL SECURITY.

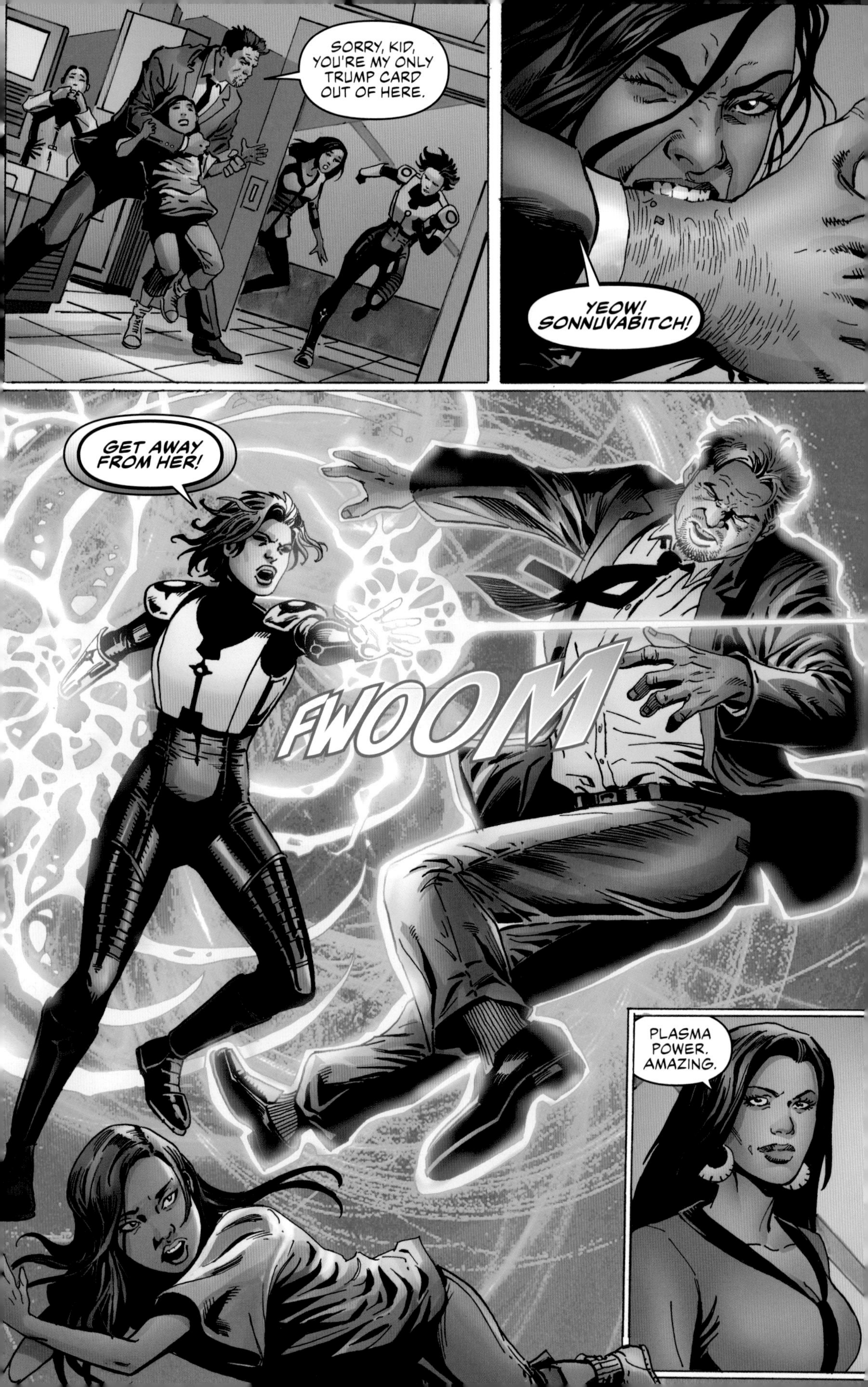
SORRY, KID, YOU'RE MY ONLY TRUMP CARD OUT OF HERE.
YEOW! SONNUVABITCH!
GET AWAY FROM HER!
FWOOM
PLASMA POWER. AMAZING.

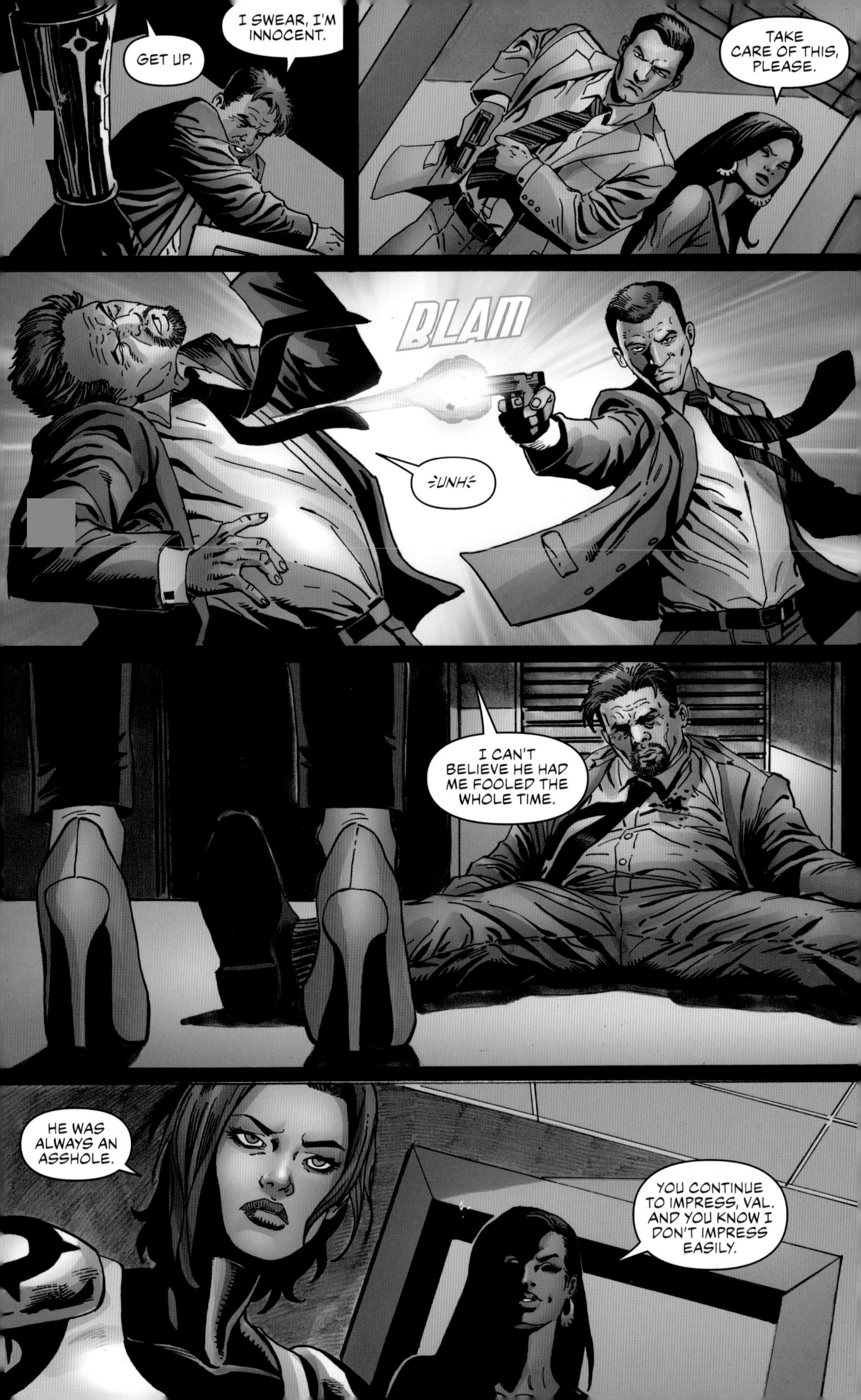
GET UP.
I SWEAR, I'M INNOCENT.
TAKE CARE OF THIS, PLEASE.
BLAM
UNH
I CAN'T BELIEVE HE HAD ME FOOLED THE WHOLE TIME.
HE WAS ALWAYS AN ASSHOLE.
YOU CONTINUE TO IMPRESS, VAL. AND YOU KNOW I DON'T IMPRESS EASILY.

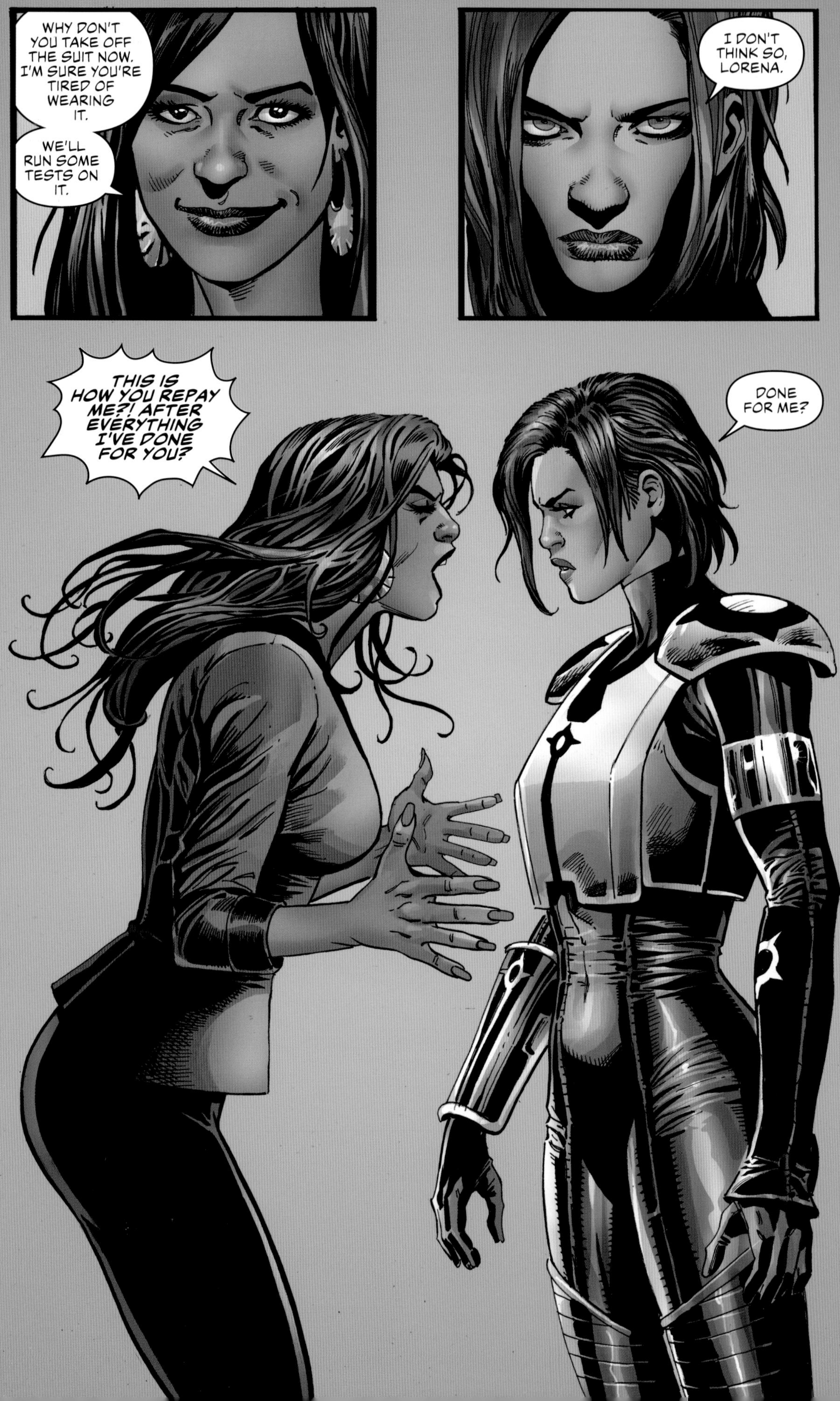
WHY DON'T YOU TAKE OFF THE SUIT NOW. I'M SURE YOU'RE TIRED OF WEARING IT.
WE'LL RUN SOME TESTS ON IT.
I DON'T THINK SO, LORENA.
THIS IS HOW YOU REPAY ME?! AFTER EVERYTHING I'VE DONE FOR YOU?
DONE FOR ME?

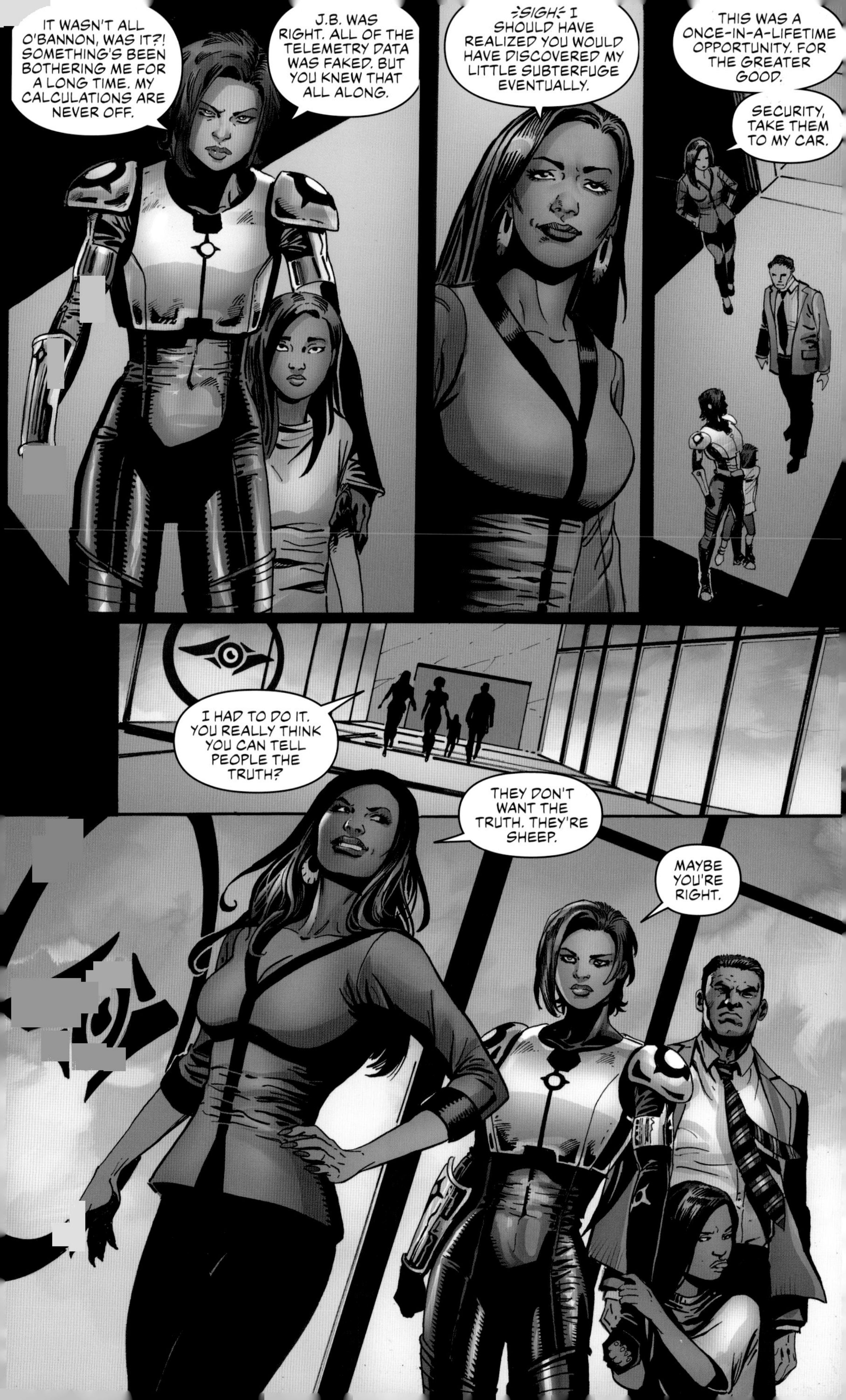
IT WASN'T ALL O'BANNON, WAS IT?! SOMETHING'S BEEN BOTHERING ME FOR A LONG TIME. MY CALCULATIONS ARE NEVER OFF.
J.B. WAS RIGHT. ALL OF THE TELEMETRY DATA WAS FAKED. BUT YOU KNEW THAT ALL ALONG.
SIGH I SHOULD HAVE REALIZED YOU WOULD HAVE DISCOVERED MY LITTLE SUBTERFUGE EVENTUALLY.
THIS WAS A ONCE-IN-A-LIFETIME OPPORTUNITY. FOR THE GREATER GOOD.
SECURITY, TAKE THEM TO MY CAR.
I HAD TO DO IT. YOU REALLY THINK YOU CAN TELL PEOPLE THE TRUTH?
THEY DON'T WANT THE TRUTH. THEY'RE SHEEP.
MAYBE YOU'RE RIGHT.

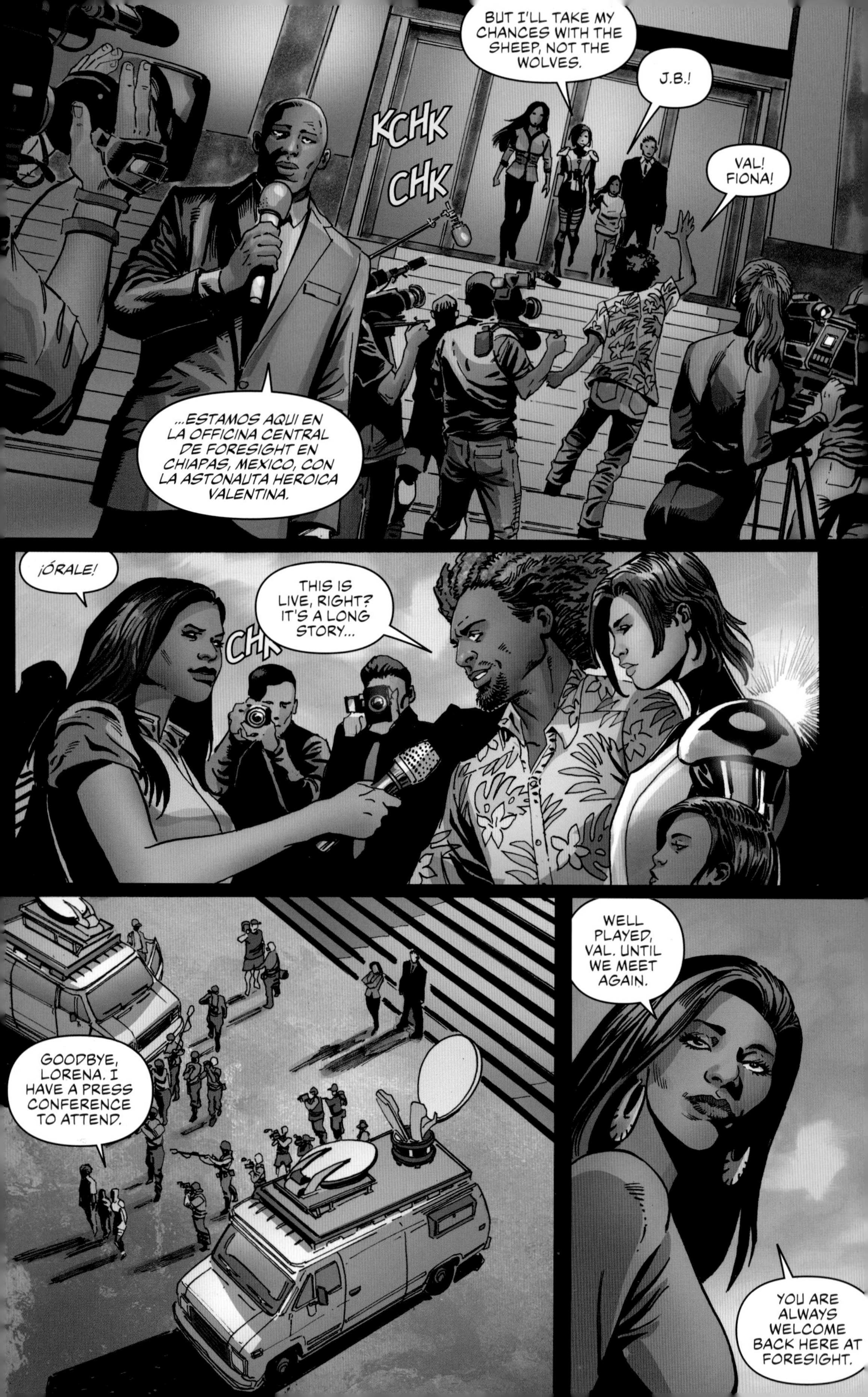
BUT I'LL TAKE MY CHANCES WITH THE SHEEP, NOT THE WOLVES.
J.B.!
VAL! FIONA!
KCHK
CHK
...ESTAMOS AQUI EN LA OFFICINA CENTRAL DE FORESIGHT EN CHIAPAS, MEXICO, CON LA ASTONAUTA HEROICA VALENTINA.
¡ÓRALE!
THIS IS LIVE, RIGHT? IT'S A LONG STORY...
GOODBYE, LORENA. I HAVE A PRESS CONFERENCE TO ATTEND.
WELL PLAYED, VAL. UNTIL WE MEET AGAIN.
YOU ARE ALWAYS WELCOME BACK HERE AT FORESIGHT.

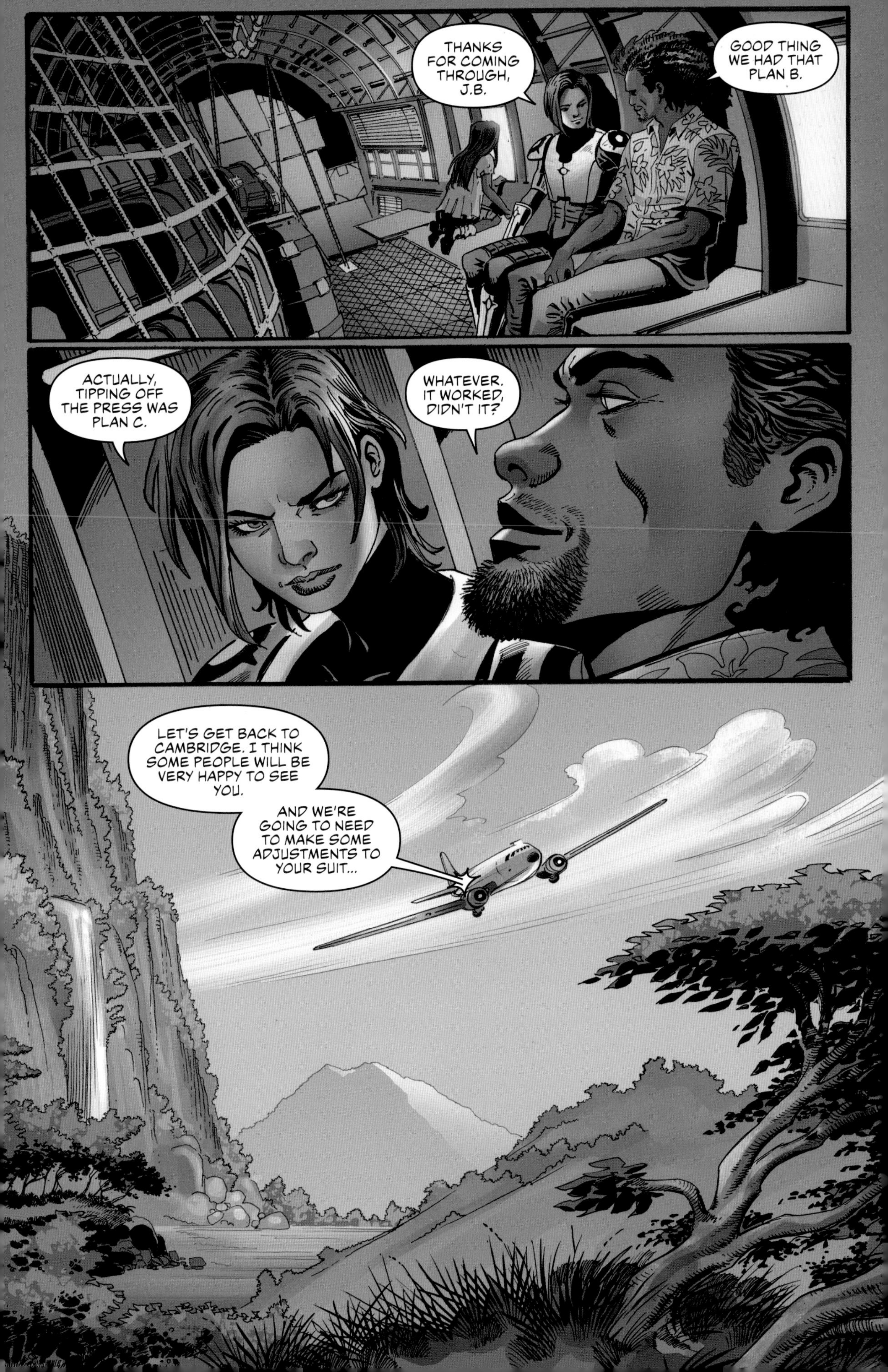
THANKS FOR COMING THROUGH, J.B.
GOOD THING WE HAD THAT PLAN B.
ACTUALLY, TIPPING OFF THE PRESS WAS PLAN C.
WHATEVER. IT WORKED, DIDN'T IT?
LET'S GET BACK TO CAMBRIDGE. I THINK SOME PEOPLE WILL BE VERY HAPPY TO SEE YOU.
AND WE'RE GOING TO NEED TO MAKE SOME ADJUSTMENTS TO YOUR SUIT...

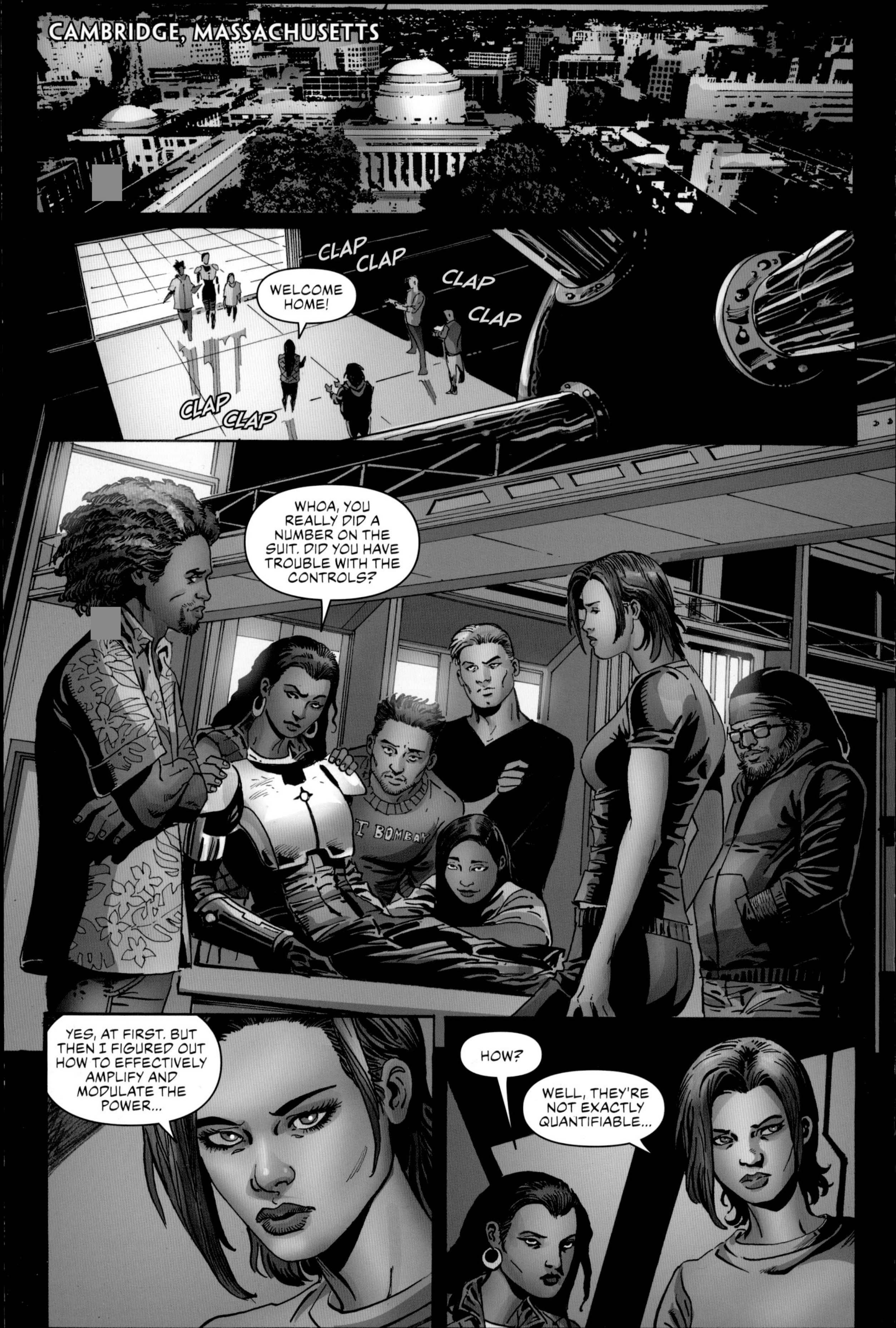
CAMBRIDGE, MASSACHUSETTS
CLAP CLAP
WELCOME HOME!
CLAP
CLAP
CLAP CLAP
WHOA, YOU REALLY DID A NUMBER ON THE SUIT. DID YOU HAVE TROUBLE WITH THE CONTROLS?
I BOMBAY
YES, AT FIRST. BUT THEN I FIGURED OUT HOW TO EFFECTIVELY AMPLIFY AND MODULATE THE POWER...
HOW?
WELL, THEY'RE NOT EXACTLY QUANTIFIABLE...

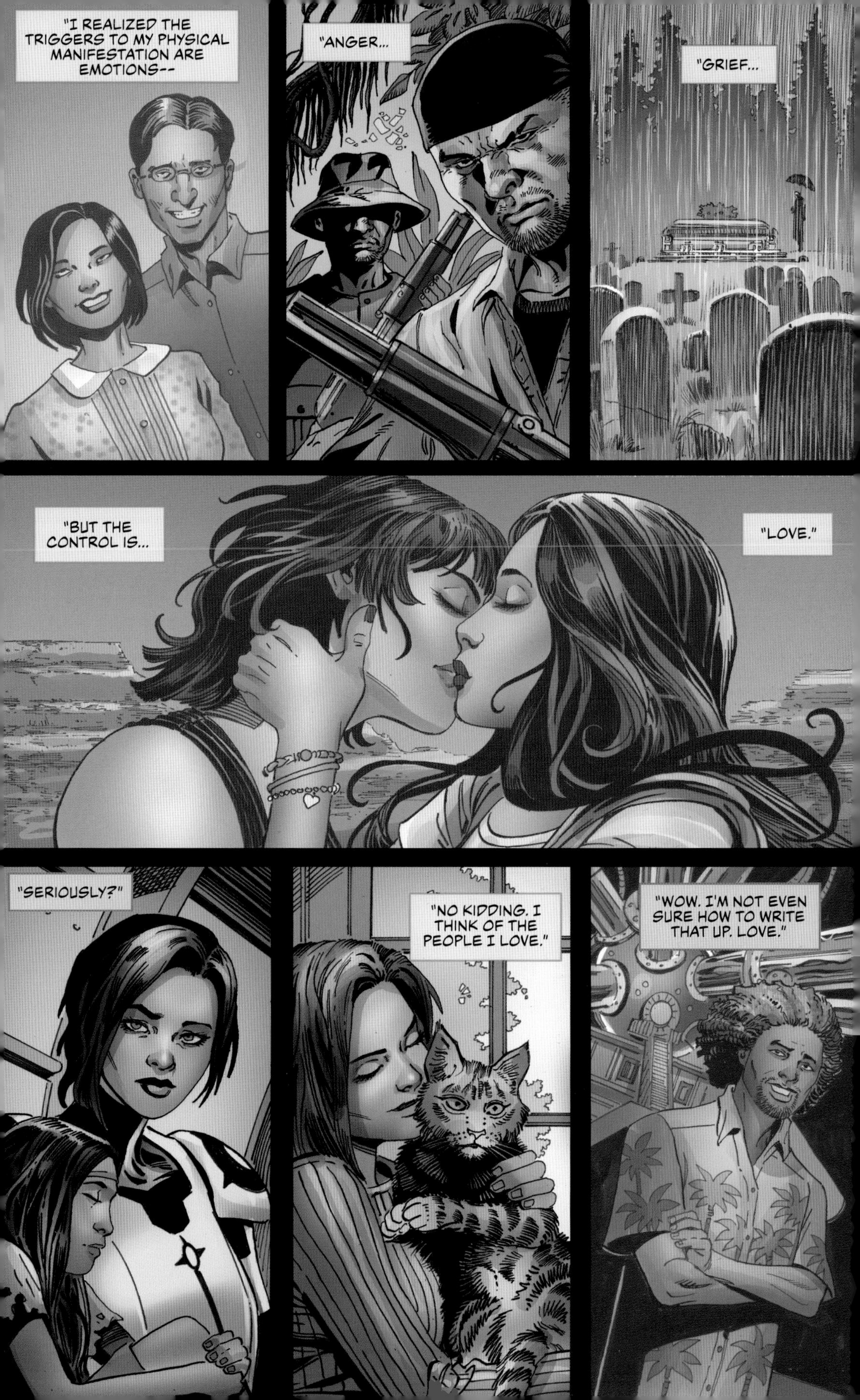
"I REALIZED THE TRIGGERS TO MY PHYSICAL MANIFESTATION ARE EMOTIONS--
"ANGER...
"GRIEF...
"BUT THE CONTROL IS...
"LOVE."
"SERIOUSLY?"
"NO KIDDING. I THINK OF THE PEOPLE I LOVE."
"WOW. I'M NOT EVEN SURE HOW TO WRITE THAT UP. LOVE."

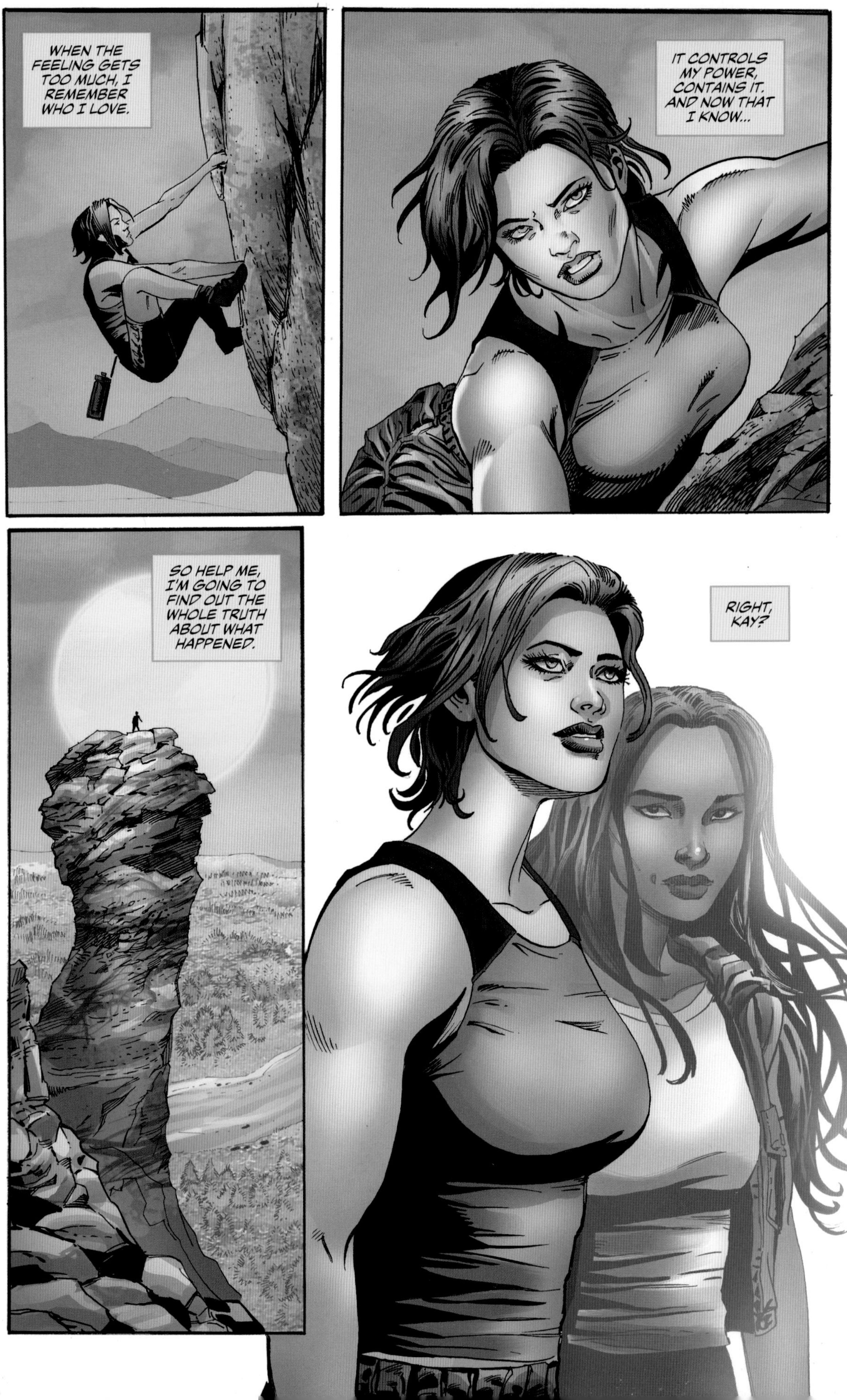
WHEN THE FEELING GETS TOO MUCH, I REMEMBER WHO I LOVE.
IT CONTROLS MY POWER, CONTAINS IT. AND NOW THAT I KNOW...
SO HELP ME, I'M GOING TO FIND OUT THE WHOLE TRUTH ABOUT WHAT HAPPENED.
RIGHT, KAY?

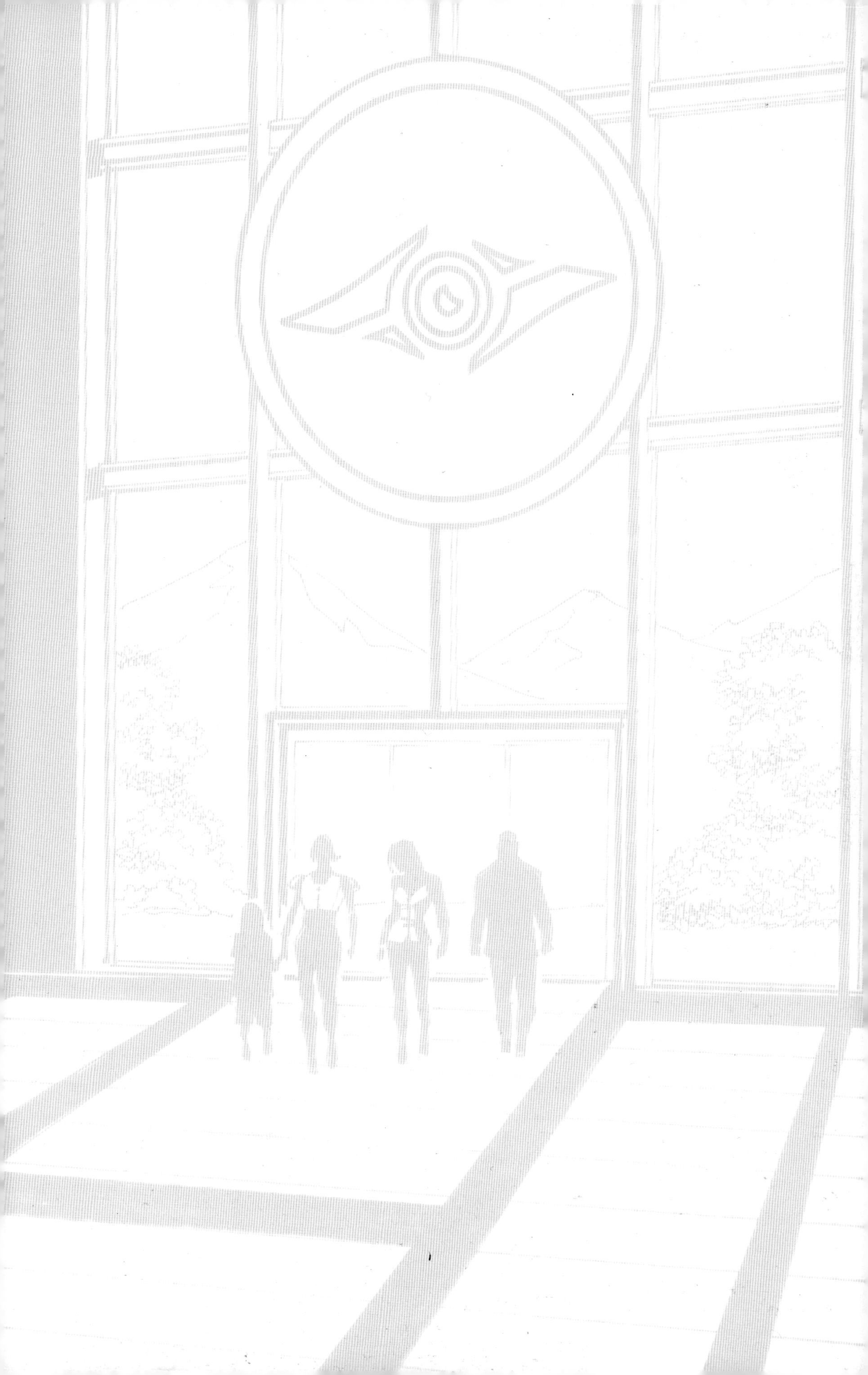

"THE EVENT"

One year before the story of SUMMIT, humanity was on the verge of extinction. An asteroid detected in space was on a collision course with Earth.

Foresight Corporation, the world's most advanced high-tech humanitarian company led by CEO Lorena Payan, developed the science and ships needed to destroy the asteroid.

A team of astronauts flew into space on a suicide mission to save the world.

This is the story of that heroic mission, and "The Event" from which a new generation of heroes emerged in the world.

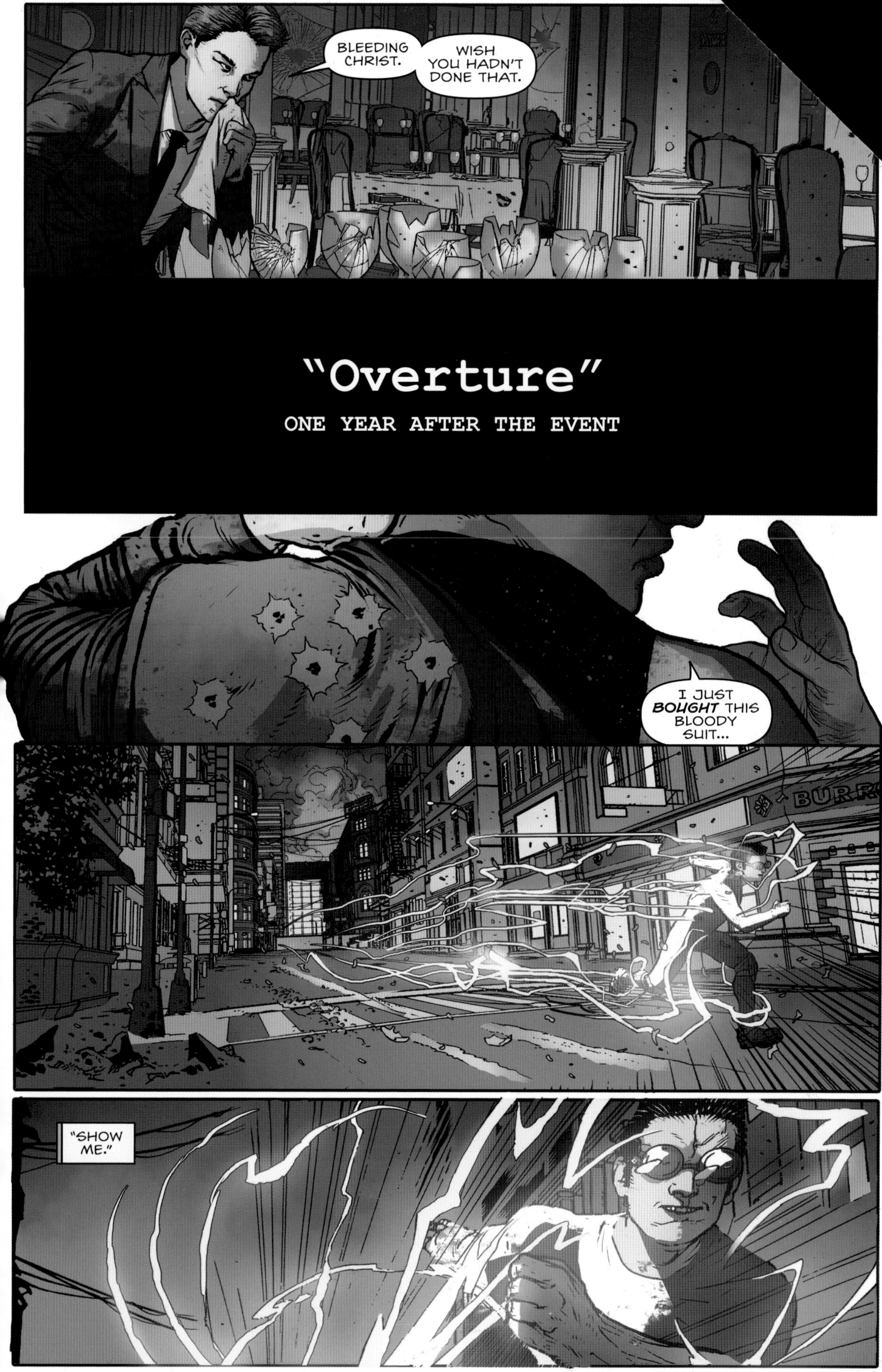
BLEEDING CHRIST.
WISH YOU HADN'T DONE THAT.
"Overture"
ONE YEAR AFTER THE EVENT
I JUST BOUGHT THIS BLOODY SUIT...
"SHOW ME."

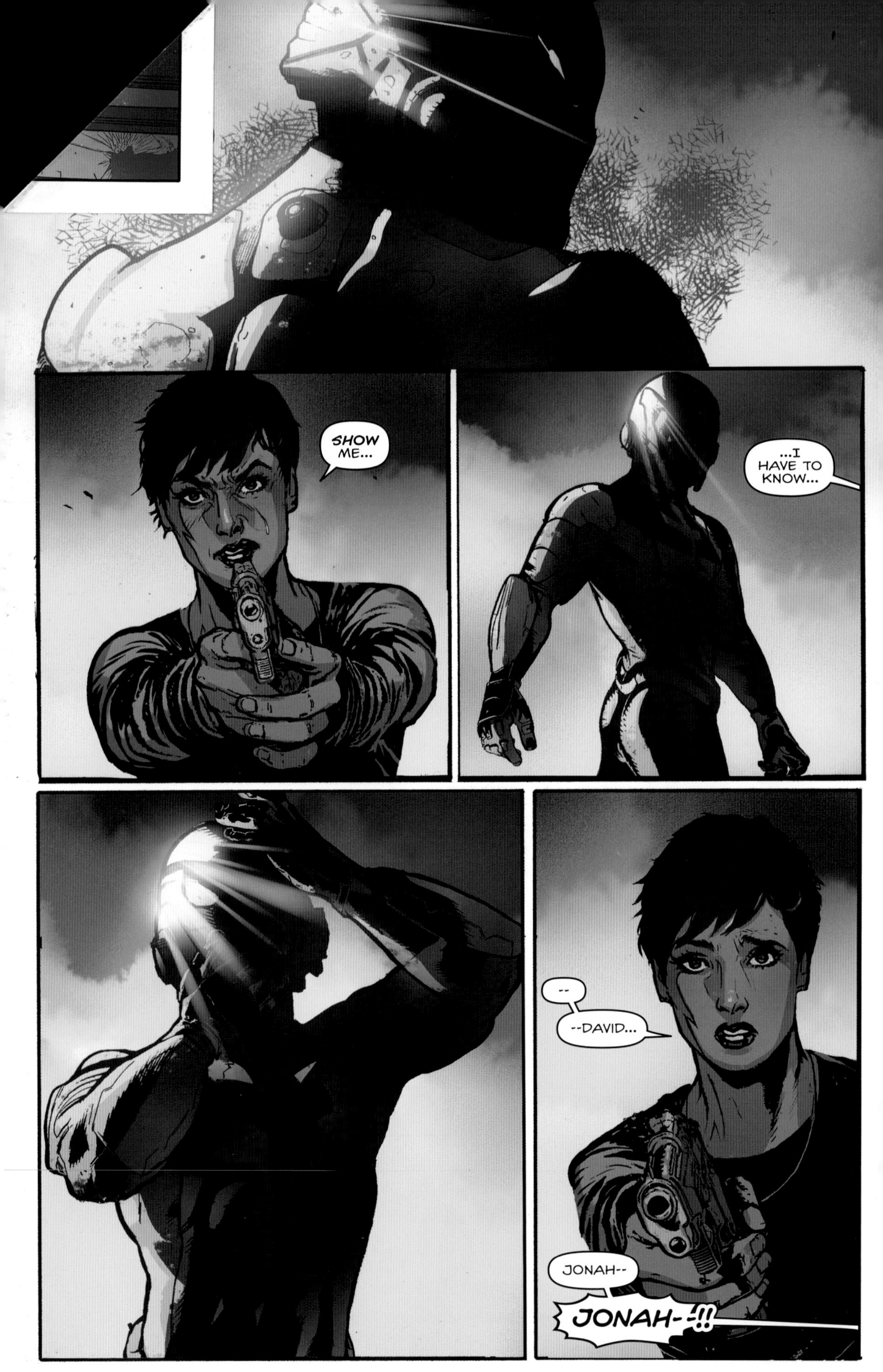
SHOW ME...
...I HAVE TO KNOW...
--
--DAVID...
JONAH--
JONAH--!!

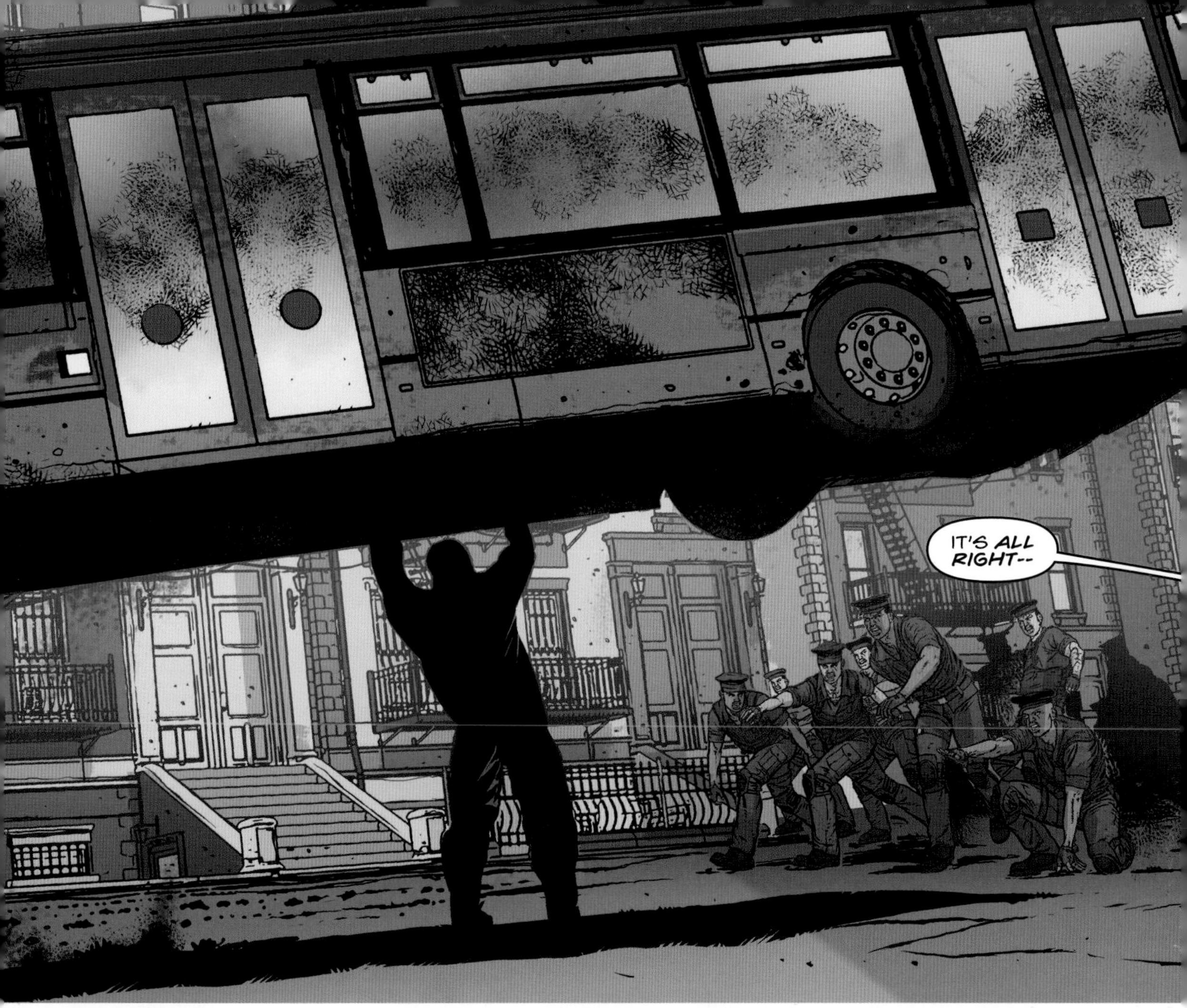
IT'S ALL RIGHT--

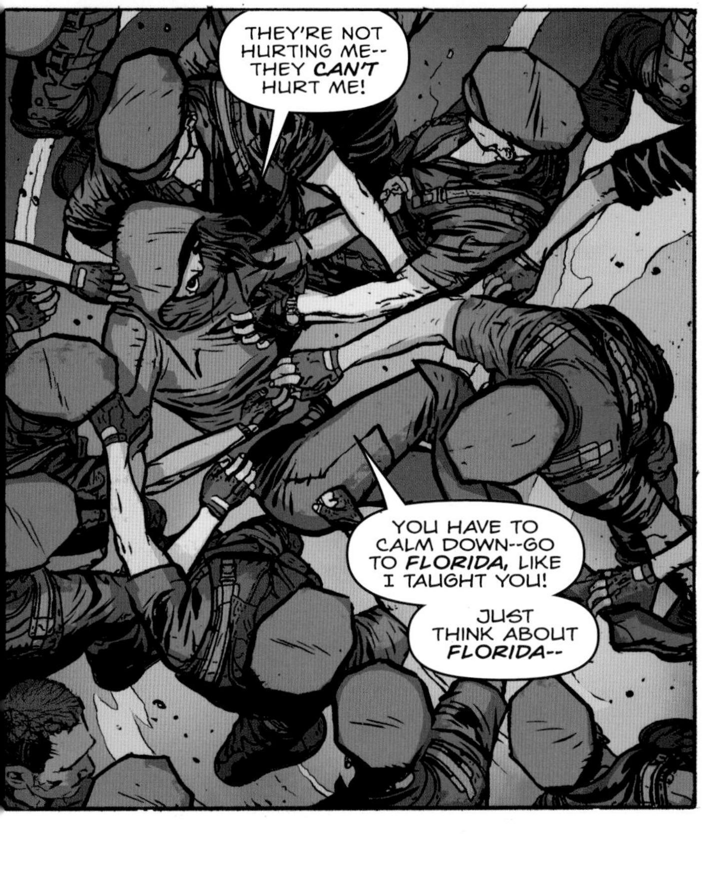
THEY'RE NOT HURTING ME--THEY CAN'T HURT ME!
YOU HAVE TO CALM DOWN--GO TO FLORIDA, LIKE I TAUGHT YOU!
JUST THINK ABOUT FLORIDA--

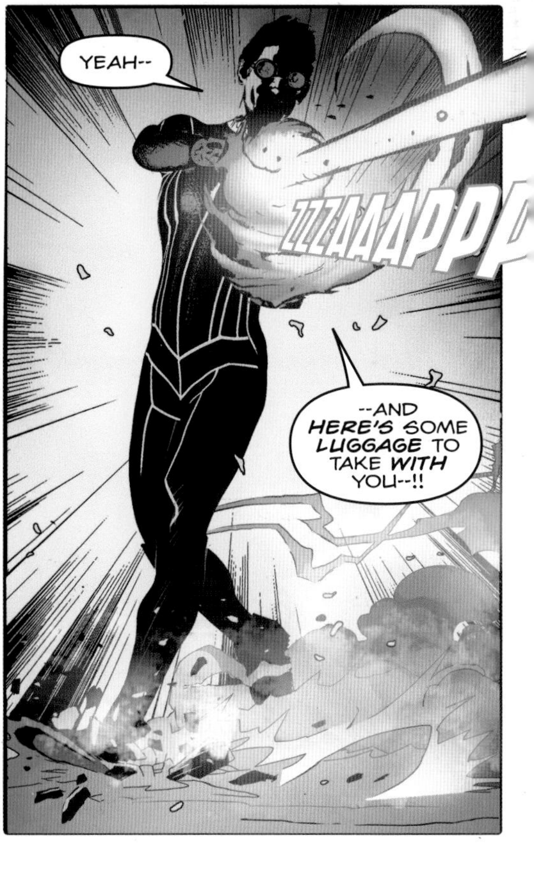
YEAH--
ZZZAAAPPP
--AND HERE'S SOME LUGGAGE TO TAKE WITH YOU--!!

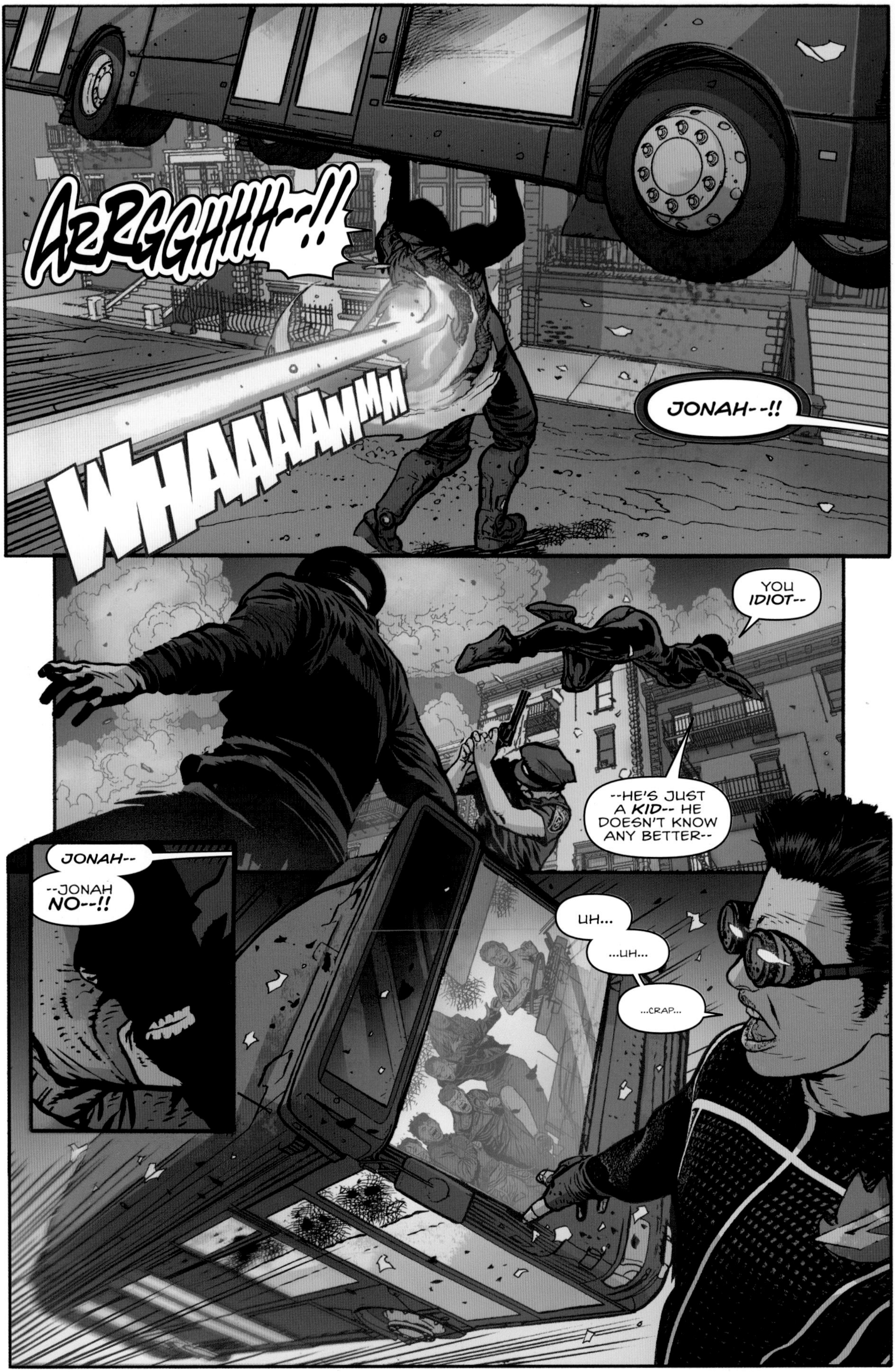
ARRGGHHH--!!
WHAAAAAMMM
JONAH--!!
YOU IDIOT--
--HE'S JUST A KID-- HE DOESN'T KNOW ANY BETTER--
JONAH--
--JONAH NO--!!
UH...
...UH...
...CRAP...

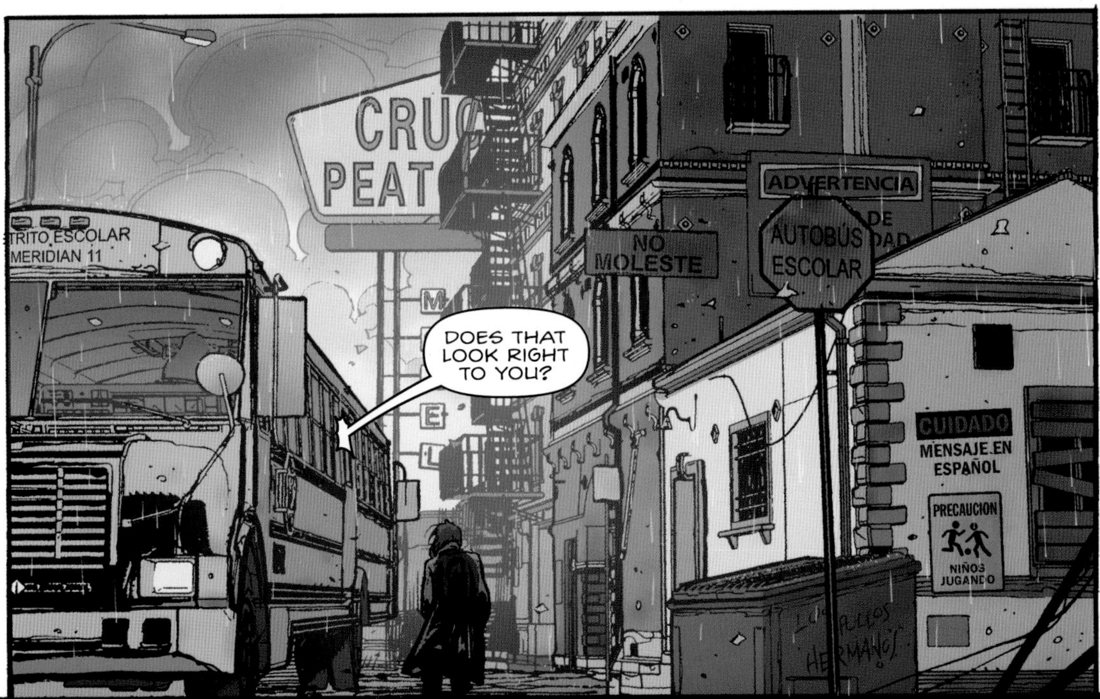
CRU
PEAT
TRITO ESCOLAR
MERIDIAN 11
ADVERTENCIA
NO MOLESTE
AUTOBÚS ESCOLAR
CUIDADO
MENSAJE EN ESPAÑOL
PRECAUCION
NIÑOS JUGANDO
DOES THAT LOOK RIGHT TO YOU?

"La Dama en El Autobús"

ONE WEEK BEFORE THE EVENT

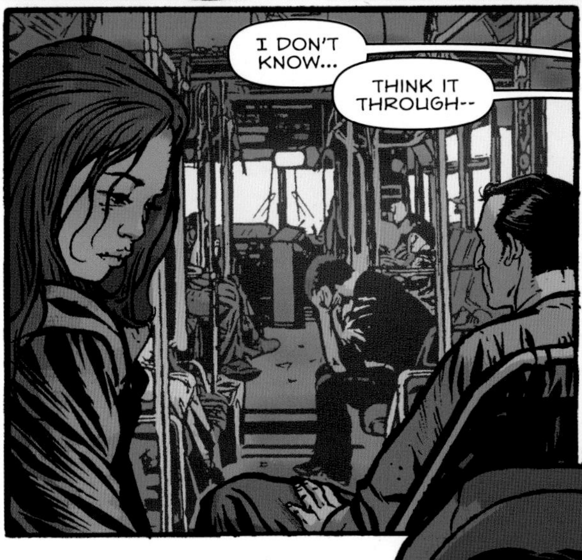
I DON'T KNOW...
THINK IT THROUGH--

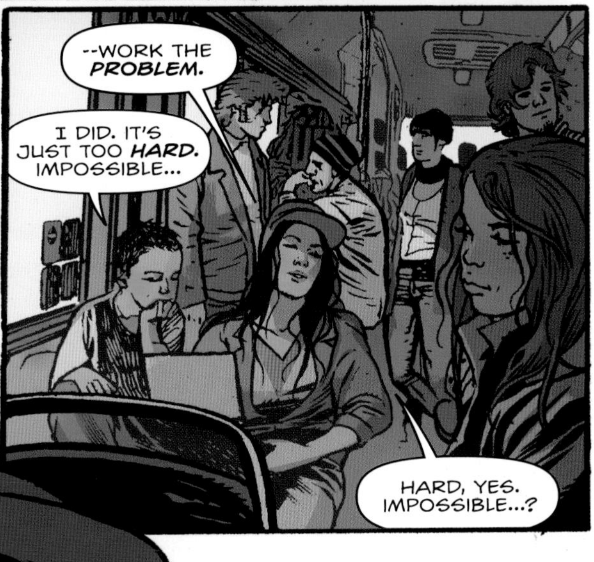
--WORK THE *PROBLEM.*
I DID. IT'S JUST TOO *HARD.* IMPOSSIBLE...
HARD, YES. IMPOSSIBLE...?

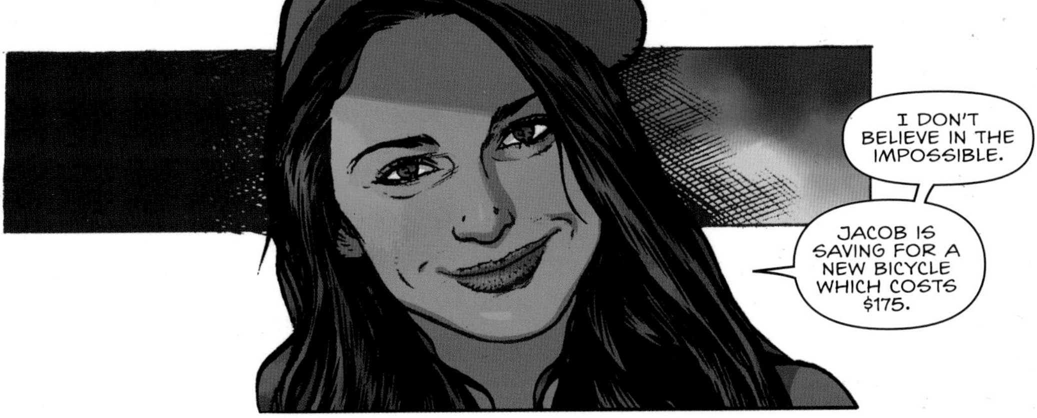
I DON'T BELIEVE IN THE IMPOSSIBLE.
JACOB IS SAVING FOR A NEW BICYCLE WHICH COSTS $175.

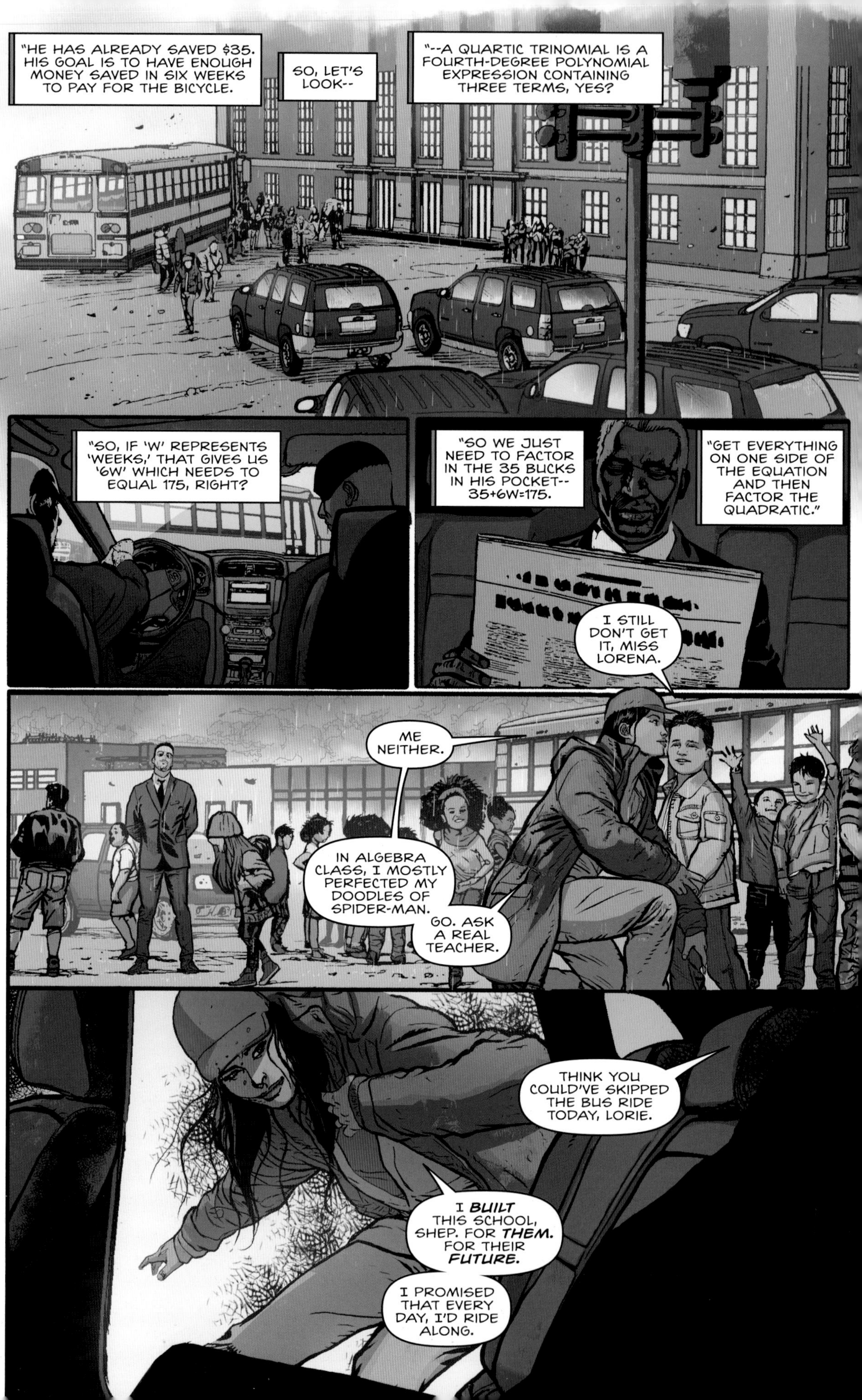
"HE HAS ALREADY SAVED $35. HIS GOAL IS TO HAVE ENOUGH MONEY SAVED IN SIX WEEKS TO PAY FOR THE BICYCLE.
SO, LET'S LOOK--
"--A QUARTIC TRINOMIAL IS A FOURTH-DEGREE POLYNOMIAL EXPRESSION CONTAINING THREE TERMS, YES?
"SO, IF 'W' REPRESENTS 'WEEKS,' THAT GIVES US '6W' WHICH NEEDS TO EQUAL 175, RIGHT?
"SO WE JUST NEED TO FACTOR IN THE 35 BUCKS IN HIS POCKET-- 35+6W=175.
"GET EVERYTHING ON ONE SIDE OF THE EQUATION AND THEN FACTOR THE QUADRATIC."
I STILL DON'T GET IT, MISS LORENA.
ME NEITHER.
IN ALGEBRA CLASS, I MOSTLY PERFECTED MY DOODLES OF SPIDER-MAN.
GO. ASK A REAL TEACHER.
THINK YOU COULD'VE SKIPPED THE BUS RIDE TODAY, LORIE.
I BUILT THIS SCHOOL, SHEP. FOR THEM. FOR THEIR FUTURE.
I PROMISED THAT EVERY DAY, I'D RIDE ALONG.

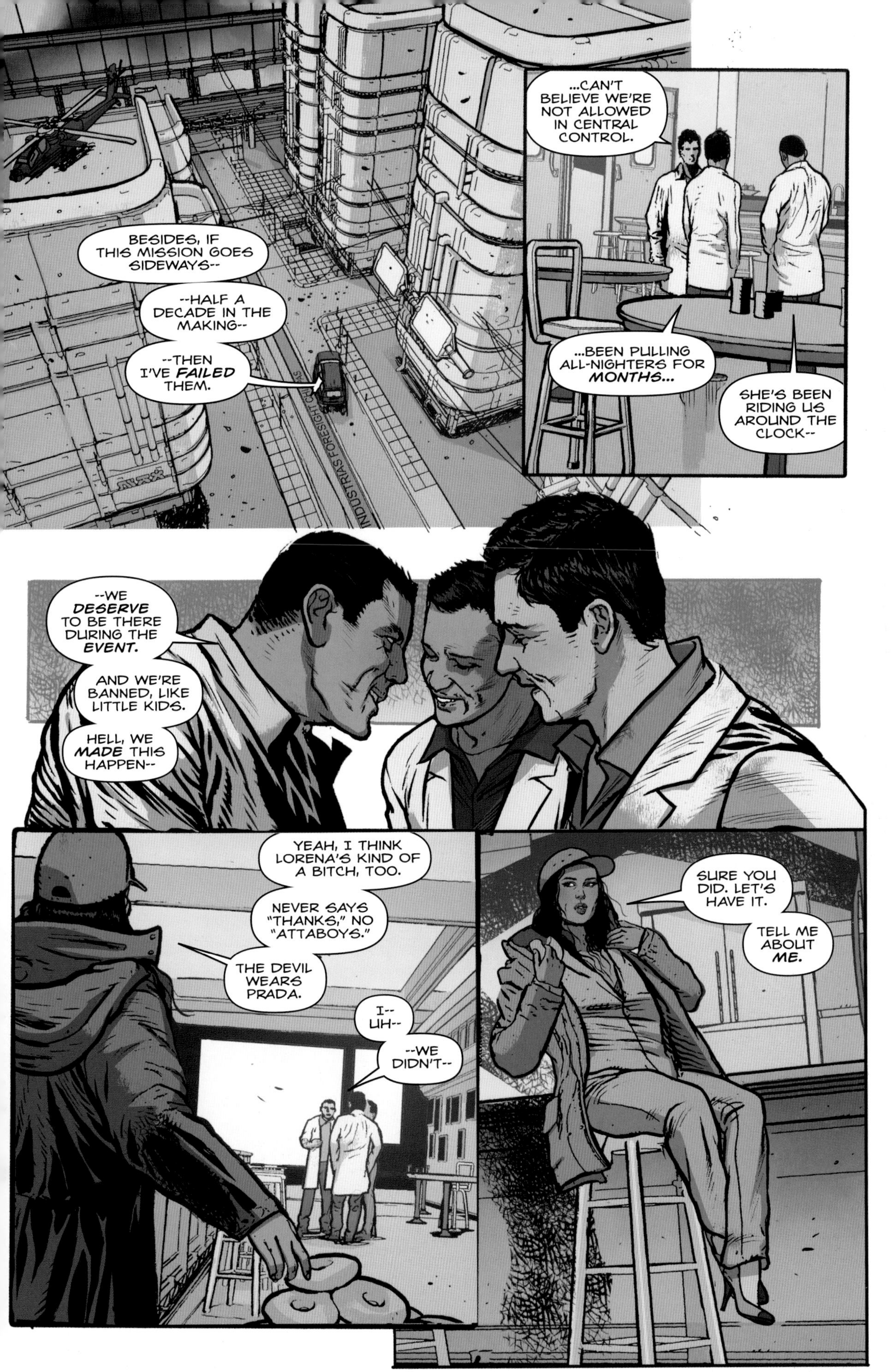
BESIDES, IF THIS MISSION GOES SIDEWAYS--
--HALF A DECADE IN THE MAKING--
--THEN I'VE *FAILED* THEM.
INDUSTRIAS FORESIGHT
...CAN'T BELIEVE WE'RE NOT ALLOWED IN CENTRAL CONTROL.
...BEEN PULLING ALL-NIGHTERS FOR *MONTHS...*
SHE'S BEEN RIDING US AROUND THE CLOCK--
--WE *DESERVE* TO BE THERE DURING THE *EVENT.*
AND WE'RE BANNED, LIKE LITTLE KIDS.
HELL, WE *MADE* THIS HAPPEN--
YEAH, I THINK LORENA'S KIND OF A BITCH, TOO.
NEVER SAYS "THANKS," NO "ATTABOYS."
THE DEVIL WEARS PRADA.
I-- UH--
--WE DIDN'T--
SURE YOU DID. LET'S HAVE IT.
TELL ME ABOUT *ME.*

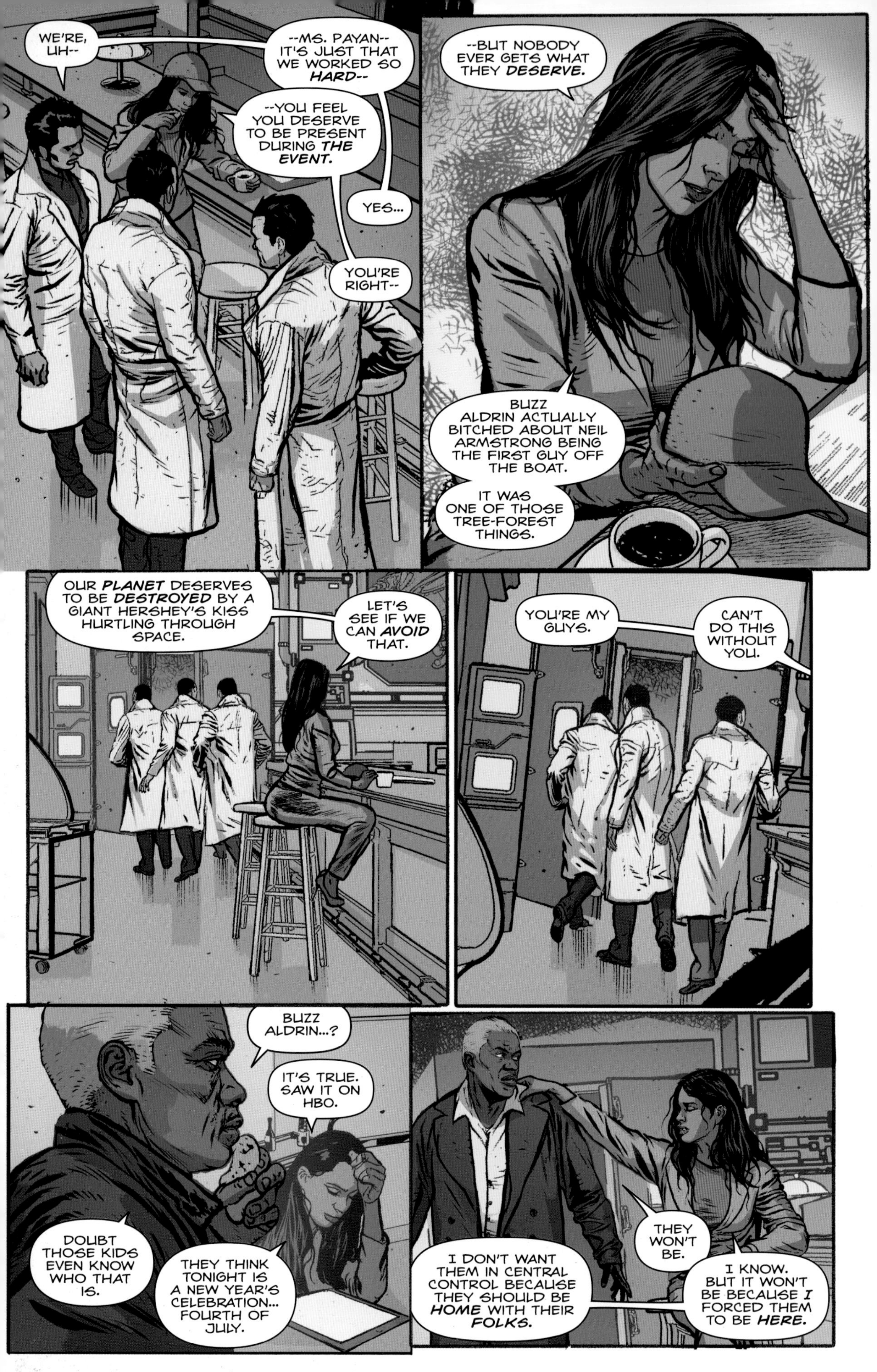
WE'RE, UH--
--MS. PAYAN-- IT'S JUST THAT WE WORKED SO HARD--
--YOU FEEL YOU DESERVE TO BE PRESENT DURING THE EVENT.
YES...
YOU'RE RIGHT--
--BUT NOBODY EVER GETS WHAT THEY DESERVE.
BUZZ ALDRIN ACTUALLY BITCHED ABOUT NEIL ARMSTRONG BEING THE FIRST GUY OFF THE BOAT.
IT WAS ONE OF THOSE TREE-FOREST THINGS.
OUR PLANET DESERVES TO BE DESTROYED BY A GIANT HERSHEY'S KISS HURTLING THROUGH SPACE.
LET'S SEE IF WE CAN AVOID THAT.
YOU'RE MY GUYS.
CAN'T DO THIS WITHOUT YOU.
BUZZ ALDRIN...?
IT'S TRUE. SAW IT ON HBO.
DOUBT THOSE KIDS EVEN KNOW WHO THAT IS.
THEY THINK TONIGHT IS A NEW YEAR'S CELEBRATION... FOURTH OF JULY.
I DON'T WANT THEM IN CENTRAL CONTROL BECAUSE THEY SHOULD BE HOME WITH THEIR FOLKS.
THEY WON'T BE.
I KNOW. BUT IT WON'T BE BECAUSE I FORCED THEM TO BE HERE.

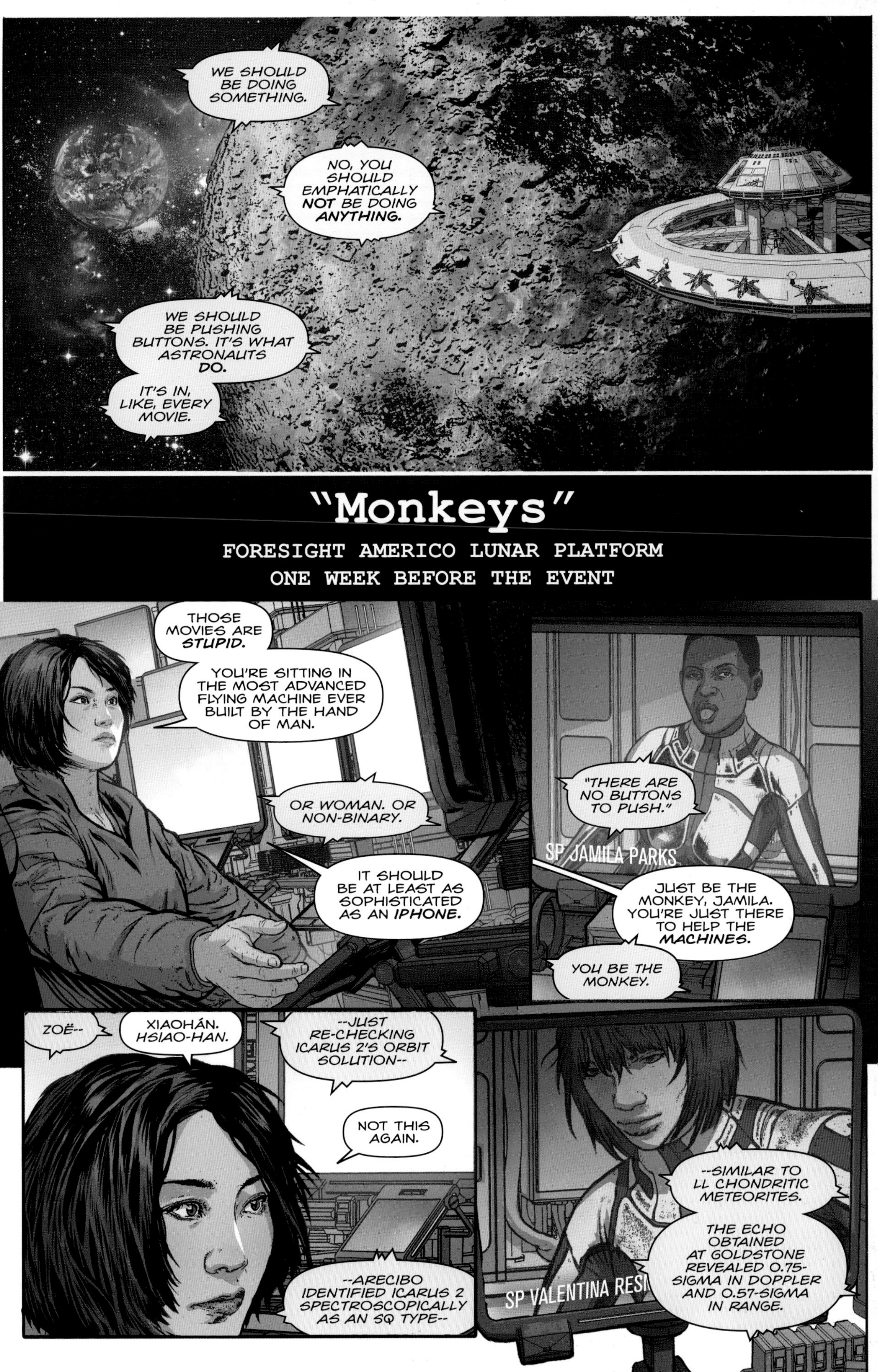
WE SHOULD BE DOING SOMETHING.
NO, YOU SHOULD EMPHATICALLY **NOT** BE DOING **ANYTHING.**
WE SHOULD BE PUSHING BUTTONS. IT'S WHAT ASTRONAUTS **DO.**
IT'S IN, LIKE, EVERY MOVIE.
"Monkeys"
FORESIGHT AMERICO LUNAR PLATFORM
ONE WEEK BEFORE THE EVENT
THOSE MOVIES ARE ***STUPID.***
YOU'RE SITTING IN THE MOST ADVANCED FLYING MACHINE EVER BUILT BY THE HAND OF MAN.
OR WOMAN. OR NON-BINARY.
IT SHOULD BE AT LEAST AS SOPHISTICATED AS AN ***IPHONE.***
"THERE ARE NO BUTTONS TO PUSH."
SP JAMILA PARKS
JUST BE THE MONKEY, JAMILA. YOU'RE JUST THERE TO HELP THE ***MACHINES.***
YOU BE THE MONKEY.
ZOË--
XIAOHÁN. HSIAO-HAN.
--JUST RE-CHECKING ICARUS 2'S ORBIT SOLUTION--
NOT THIS AGAIN.
--ARECIBO IDENTIFIED ICARUS 2 SPECTROSCOPICALLY AS AN SQ TYPE--
SP VALENTINA RES
--SIMILAR TO LL CHONDRITIC METEORITES.
THE ECHO OBTAINED AT GOLDSTONE REVEALED 0.75-SIGMA IN DOPPLER AND 0.57-SIGMA IN RANGE.

THOSE ARE STATISTICALLY SMALL VARIANCES, DR. BAKER.
DOES IT BOTHER ANYBODY ELSE THAT WE'RE LAUNCHING FROM AN ORBITAL PLATFORM--
--NAMED AFTER AN EXPLORER WHO CIRCLED THE NEW WORLD A DOZEN TIMES BUT NEVER FOUND IT--?
VESPUCCI WAS UNDERRATED...
THAT'S MY POINT, ZOË--
VESPUCCI--?
I MEAN, WHAT IF WE BUMP A CURB OUT THERE.
THEN I GUESS YOU'LL HAVE TO WING IT.
EXCUSE ME--?
GUESS, DR. BAKER. JUST KNOW THAT GOING MANUAL MIGHT KILL ELEVEN BILLION PEOPLE.
ZOË--
FOR CRYING OUT LOUD...
--THERE'S NO SPRITE UP HERE.
THERE'S SOMETHING CALLED "SIERRA MIST" BUT, YOU KNOW, WHAT THE HELL, ZOË?
SP DAVID POWELL
I SAY WE ABORT.
HOW ABOUT YOU, AL--?
AL--? AL--?!
SP MAJ ALISTAIR MEATH
COMING UP ON EVENT HORIZON, FOLKS--
MISSION CMDR EVAN CHESS
--HATE TO SPOIL THE FUN, BUT IF DR. BAKER CAN TOLERATE OUR BEING A FEW CENTIMETERS OFF--
--AND IF THE GOOD MAJOR IS THROUGH REVIEWING HIS LUNCH--
--LET'S GO TO MARS.
ICARUS 2 IS ONLY 216,924 MILES FROM LUNA, COMMANDER--
LET'S GO TO MARS ANYWAY.
MIGHT WANT TO WORK ON DEVELOPING A SENSE OF HUMOR, DR. BAKER.
WE'RE GOING TO BE FLYING TOGETHER FOR A WEEK BEFORE WE FIND THAT ROCK OUT THERE.
Who is Lorena Payan--?

GLOBAL **NOW**

LORENA

HOW THE FATE OF THE WORLD CAME TO REST IN HER HANDS

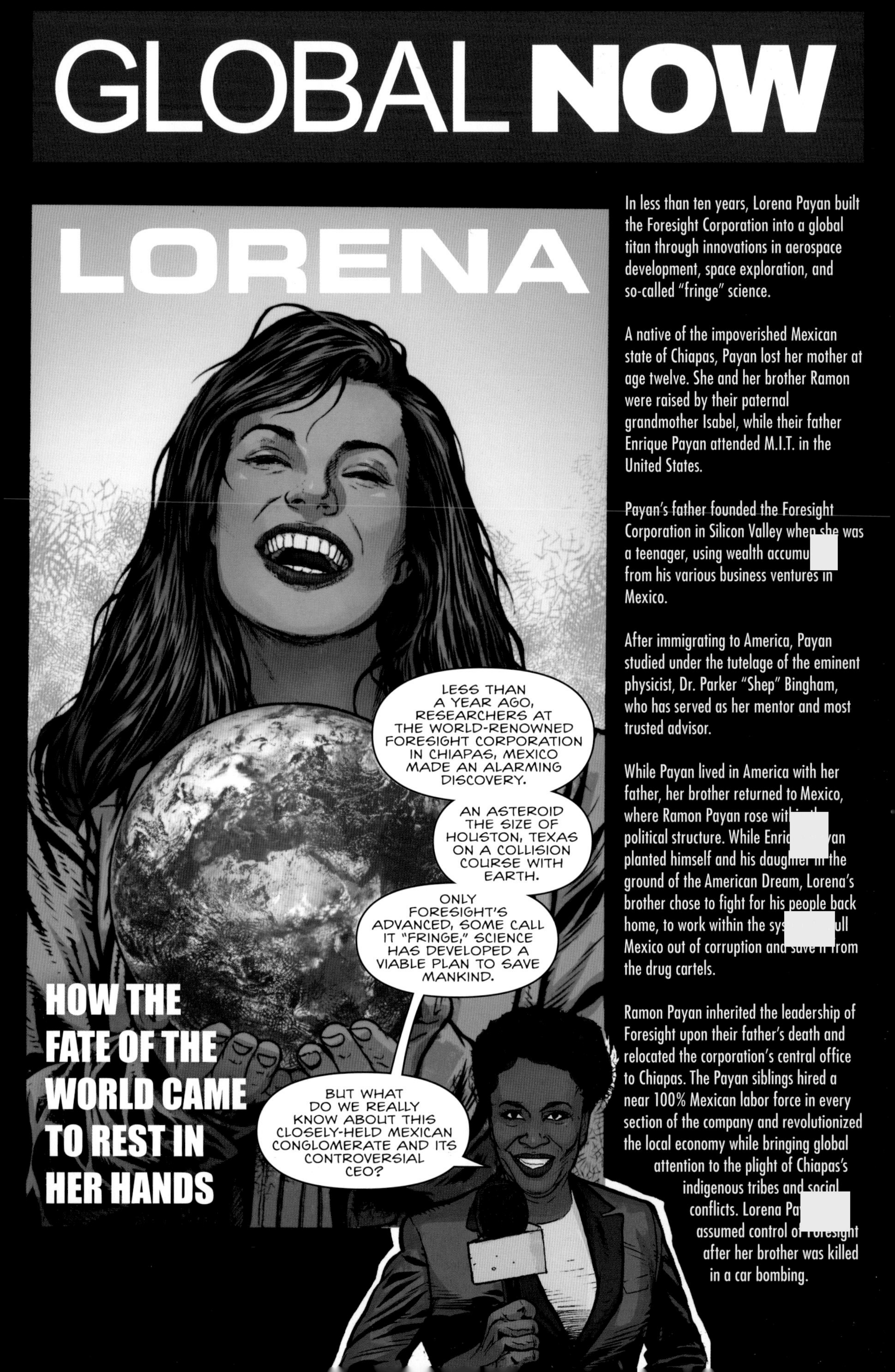
LESS THAN A YEAR AGO, RESEARCHERS AT THE WORLD-RENOWNED FORESIGHT CORPORATION IN CHIAPAS, MEXICO MADE AN ALARMING DISCOVERY.
AN ASTEROID THE SIZE OF HOUSTON, TEXAS ON A COLLISION COURSE WITH EARTH.
ONLY FORESIGHT'S ADVANCED, SOME CALL IT "FRINGE," SCIENCE HAS DEVELOPED A VIABLE PLAN TO SAVE MANKIND.
BUT WHAT DO WE REALLY KNOW ABOUT THIS CLOSELY-HELD MEXICAN CONGLOMERATE AND ITS CONTROVERSIAL CEO?

In less than ten years, Lorena Payan built the Foresight Corporation into a global titan through innovations in aerospace development, space exploration, and so-called "fringe" science.

A native of the impoverished Mexican state of Chiapas, Payan lost her mother at age twelve. She and her brother Ramon were raised by their paternal grandmother Isabel, while their father Enrique Payan attended M.I.T. in the United States.

Payan's father founded the Foresight Corporation in Silicon Valley when she was a teenager, using wealth accumu[illegible] from his various business ventures in Mexico.

After immigrating to America, Payan studied under the tutelage of the eminent physicist, Dr. Parker "Shep" Bingham, who has served as her mentor and most trusted advisor.

While Payan lived in America with her father, her brother returned to Mexico, where Ramon Payan rose wit[illegible] political structure. While Enriq[illegible]yan planted himself and his daughter in the ground of the American Dream, Lorena's brother chose to fight for his people back home, to work within the sys[illegible]ull Mexico out of corruption and save it from the drug cartels.

Ramon Payan inherited the leadership of Foresight upon their father's death and relocated the corporation's central office to Chiapas. The Payan siblings hired a near 100% Mexican labor force in every section of the company and revolutionized the local economy while bringing global attention to the plight of Chiapas's indigenous tribes and social conflicts. Lorena Pa[illegible] assumed control of Foresight after her brother was killed in a car bombing.

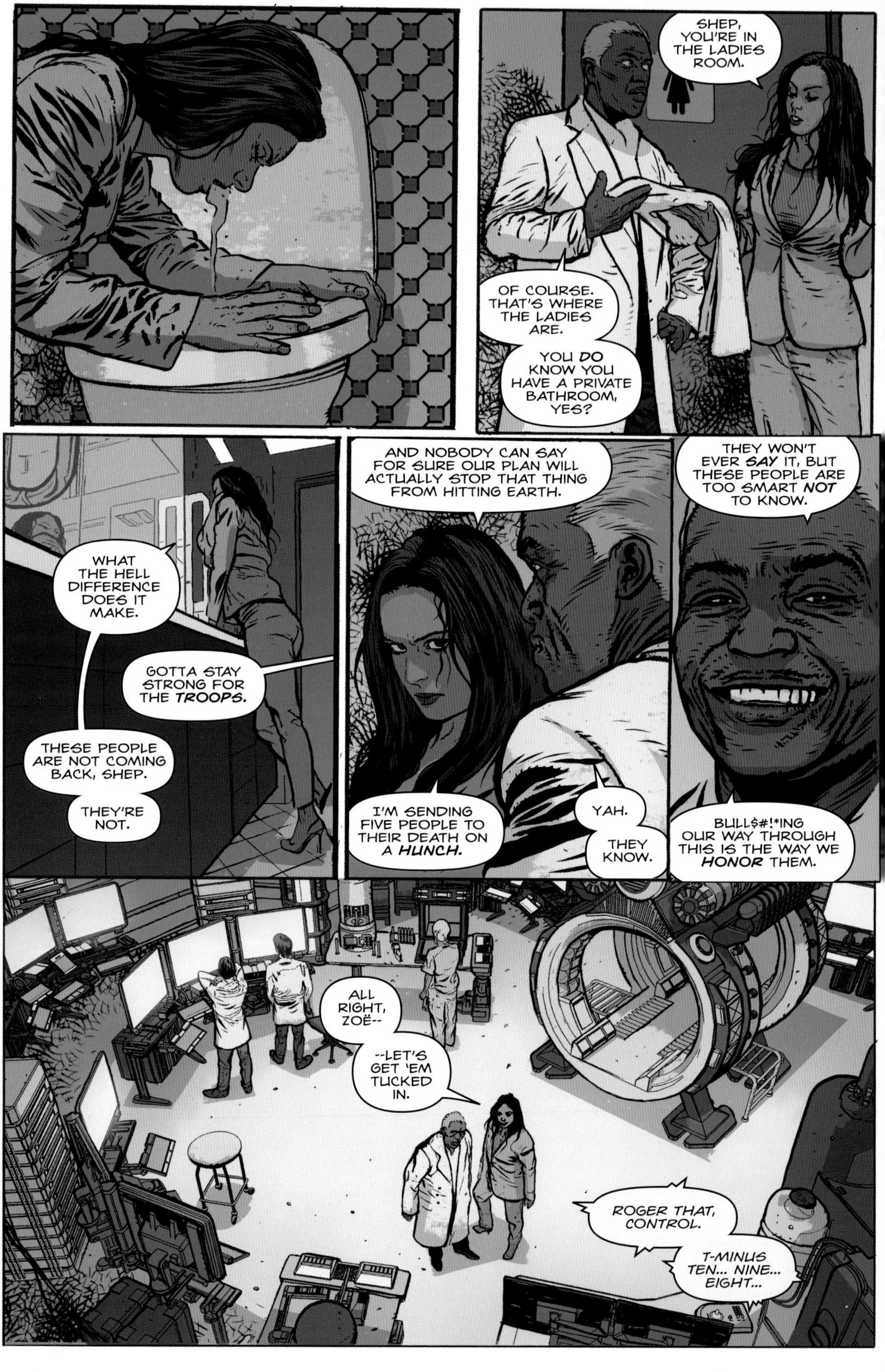

SHEP, YOU'RE IN THE LADIES ROOM.
OF COURSE. THAT'S WHERE THE LADIES ARE.
YOU DO KNOW YOU HAVE A PRIVATE BATHROOM, YES?
WHAT THE HELL DIFFERENCE DOES IT MAKE.
GOTTA STAY STRONG FOR THE TROOPS.
THESE PEOPLE ARE NOT COMING BACK, SHEP.
THEY'RE NOT.
AND NOBODY CAN SAY FOR SURE OUR PLAN WILL ACTUALLY STOP THAT THING FROM HITTING EARTH.
I'M SENDING FIVE PEOPLE TO THEIR DEATH ON A HUNCH.
YAH.
THEY KNOW.
THEY WON'T EVER SAY IT, BUT THESE PEOPLE ARE TOO SMART NOT TO KNOW.
BULL$#!*ING OUR WAY THROUGH THIS IS THE WAY WE HONOR THEM.
ALL RIGHT, ZOË--
--LET'S GET 'EM TUCKED IN.
ROGER THAT, CONTROL.
T-MINUS TEN... NINE... EIGHT...

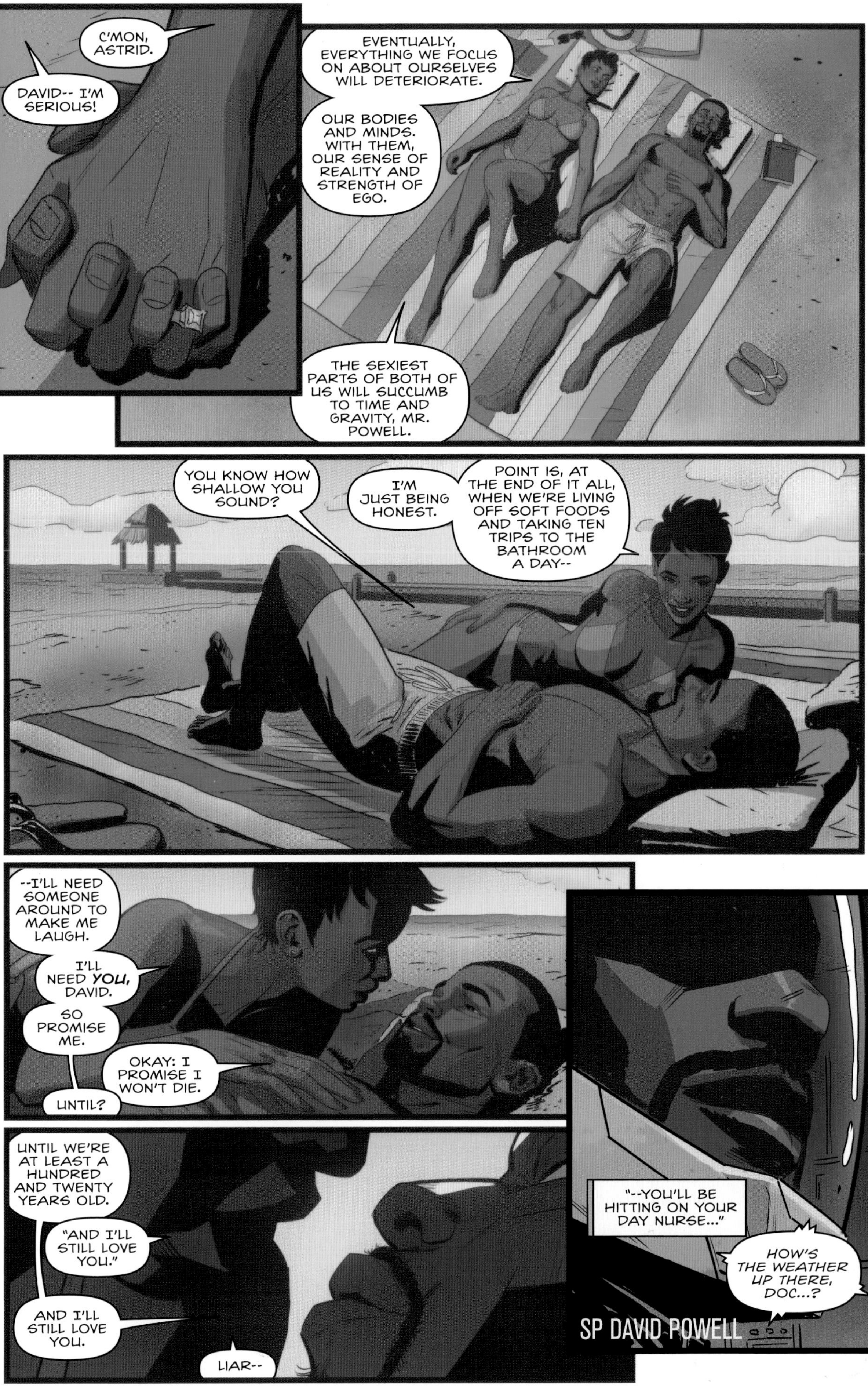
C'MON, ASTRID.
DAVID-- I'M SERIOUS!
EVENTUALLY, EVERYTHING WE FOCUS ON ABOUT OURSELVES WILL DETERIORATE.
OUR BODIES AND MINDS. WITH THEM, OUR SENSE OF REALITY AND STRENGTH OF EGO.
THE SEXIEST PARTS OF BOTH OF US WILL SUCCUMB TO TIME AND GRAVITY, MR. POWELL.
YOU KNOW HOW SHALLOW YOU SOUND?
I'M JUST BEING HONEST.
POINT IS, AT THE END OF IT ALL, WHEN WE'RE LIVING OFF SOFT FOODS AND TAKING TEN TRIPS TO THE BATHROOM A DAY--
--I'LL NEED SOMEONE AROUND TO MAKE ME LAUGH.
I'LL NEED ***YOU,*** DAVID.
SO PROMISE ME.
OKAY: I PROMISE I WON'T DIE.
UNTIL?
UNTIL WE'RE AT LEAST A HUNDRED AND TWENTY YEARS OLD.
"AND I'LL STILL LOVE YOU."
AND I'LL STILL LOVE YOU.
LIAR--
"--YOU'LL BE HITTING ON YOUR DAY NURSE..."
HOW'S THE WEATHER UP THERE, DOC...?
SP DAVID POWELL

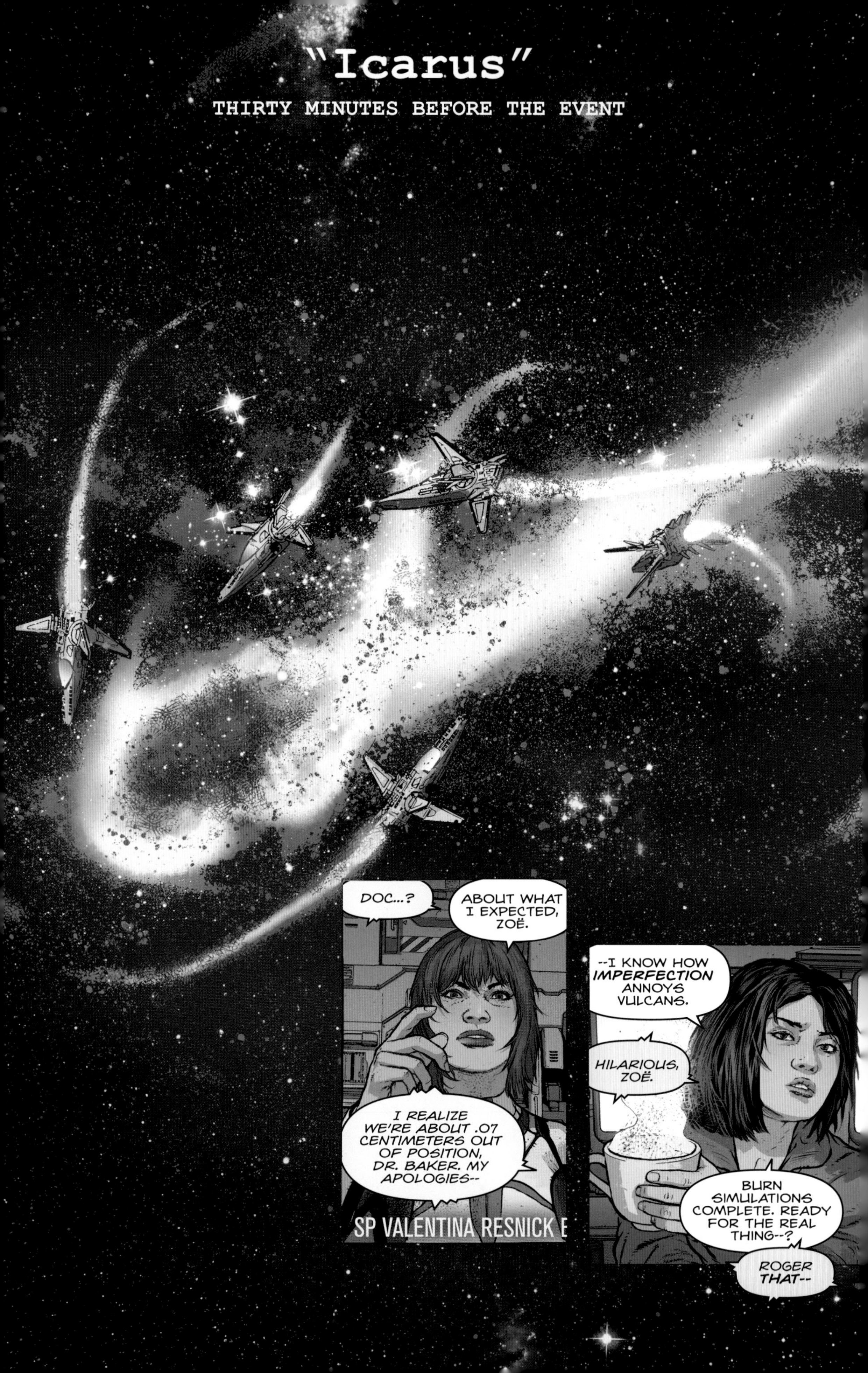
"Icarus"
THIRTY MINUTES BEFORE THE EVENT
DOC...?
ABOUT WHAT I EXPECTED, ZOË.
I REALIZE WE'RE ABOUT .07 CENTIMETERS OUT OF POSITION, DR. BAKER. MY APOLOGIES--
SP VALENTINA RESNICK E
--I KNOW HOW IMPERFECTION ANNOYS VULCANS.
HILARIOUS, ZOË.
BURN SIMULATIONS COMPLETE. READY FOR THE REAL THING--?
ROGER THAT--

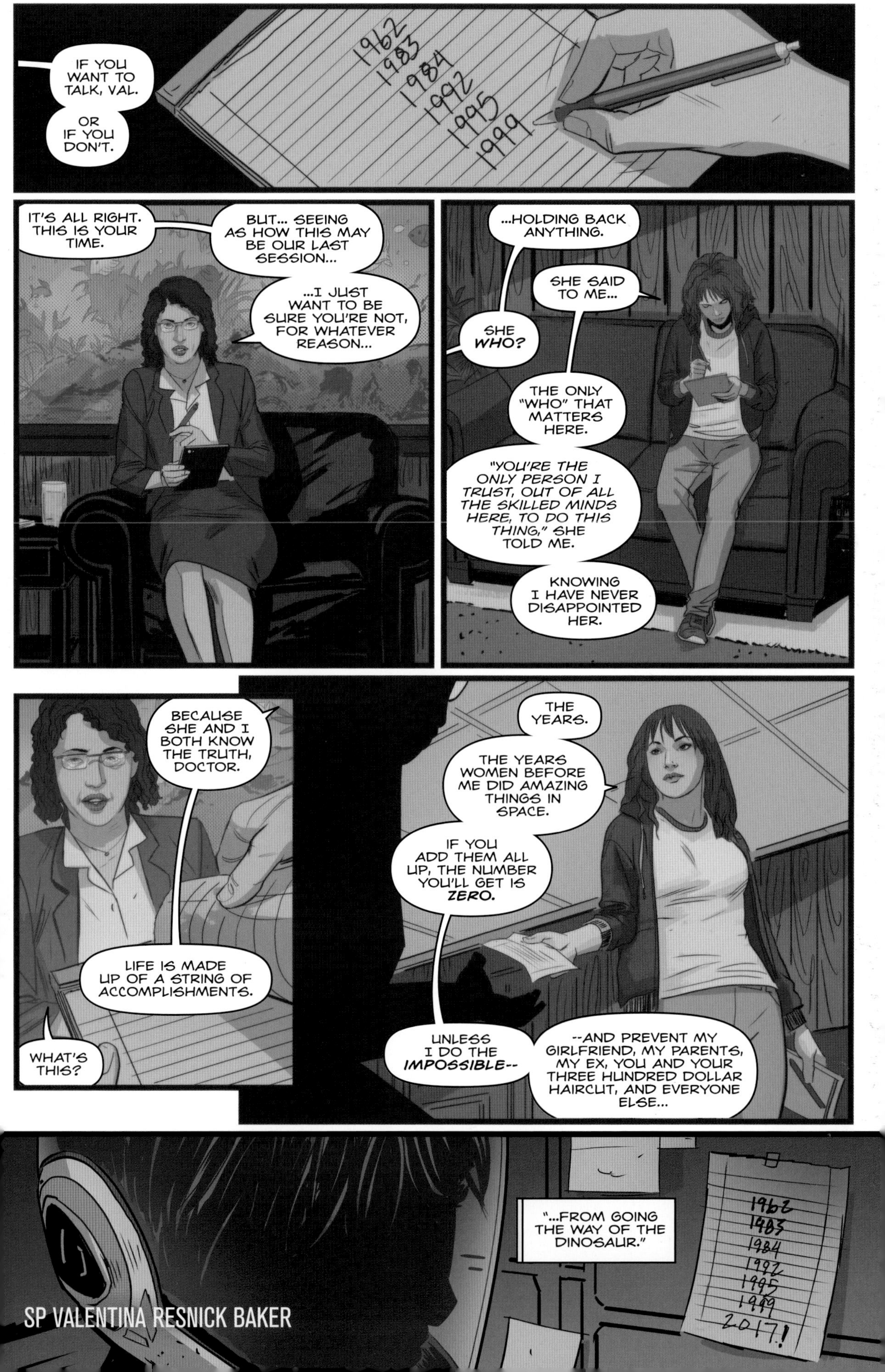
IF YOU WANT TO TALK, VAL.
OR IF YOU DON'T.
1962
1983
1984
1992
1995
1999
IT'S ALL RIGHT. THIS IS YOUR TIME.
BUT... SEEING AS HOW THIS MAY BE OUR LAST SESSION...
...I JUST WANT TO BE SURE YOU'RE NOT, FOR WHATEVER REASON...
...HOLDING BACK ANYTHING.
SHE SAID TO ME...
SHE *WHO?*
THE ONLY "WHO" THAT MATTERS HERE.
"YOU'RE THE ONLY PERSON I TRUST, OUT OF ALL THE SKILLED MINDS HERE, TO DO THIS THING," SHE TOLD ME.
KNOWING I HAVE NEVER DISAPPOINTED HER.
BECAUSE SHE AND I BOTH KNOW THE TRUTH, DOCTOR.
LIFE IS MADE UP OF A STRING OF ACCOMPLISHMENTS.
WHAT'S THIS?
THE YEARS.
THE YEARS WOMEN BEFORE ME DID AMAZING THINGS IN SPACE.
IF YOU ADD THEM ALL UP, THE NUMBER YOU'LL GET IS **ZERO.**
UNLESS I DO THE ***IMPOSSIBLE--***
--AND PREVENT MY GIRLFRIEND, MY PARENTS, MY EX, YOU AND YOUR THREE HUNDRED DOLLAR HAIRCUT, AND EVERYONE ELSE...
"...FROM GOING THE WAY OF THE DINOSAUR."
1962
1983
1984
1992
1995
1999
2017!
SP VALENTINA RESNICK BAKER

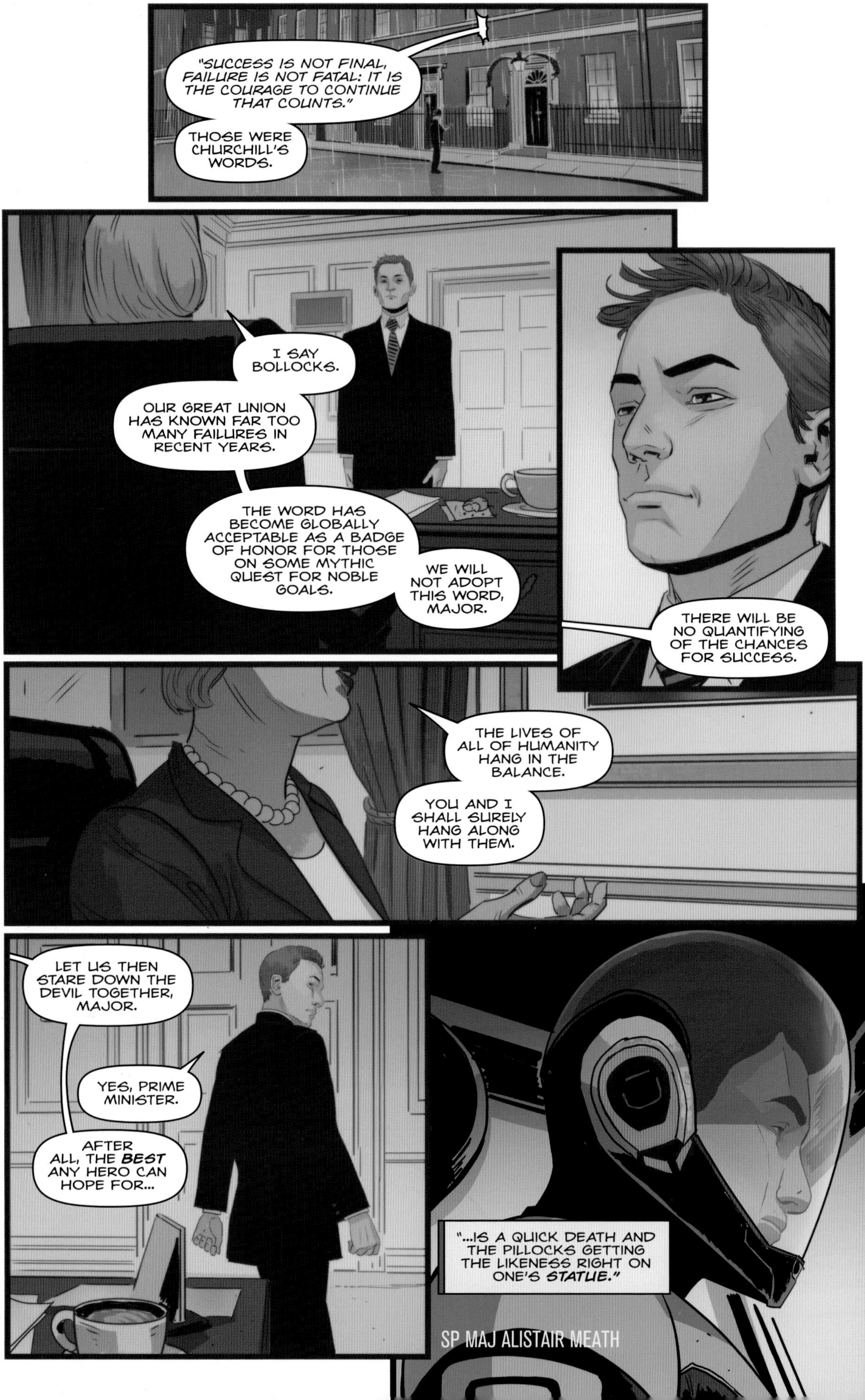

"SUCCESS IS NOT FINAL, FAILURE IS NOT FATAL: IT IS THE COURAGE TO CONTINUE THAT COUNTS."
THOSE WERE CHURCHILL'S WORDS.
I SAY BOLLOCKS.
OUR GREAT UNION HAS KNOWN FAR TOO MANY FAILURES IN RECENT YEARS.
THE WORD HAS BECOME GLOBALLY ACCEPTABLE AS A BADGE OF HONOR FOR THOSE ON SOME MYTHIC QUEST FOR NOBLE GOALS.
WE WILL NOT ADOPT THIS WORD, MAJOR.
THERE WILL BE NO QUANTIFYING OF THE CHANCES FOR SUCCESS.
THE LIVES OF ALL OF HUMANITY HANG IN THE BALANCE.
YOU AND I SHALL SURELY HANG ALONG WITH THEM.
LET US THEN STARE DOWN THE DEVIL TOGETHER, MAJOR.
YES, PRIME MINISTER.
AFTER ALL, THE *BEST* ANY HERO CAN HOPE FOR...
"...IS A QUICK DEATH AND THE PILLOCKS GETTING THE LIKENESS RIGHT ON ONE'S *STATUE*."
SP MAJ ALISTAIR MEATH

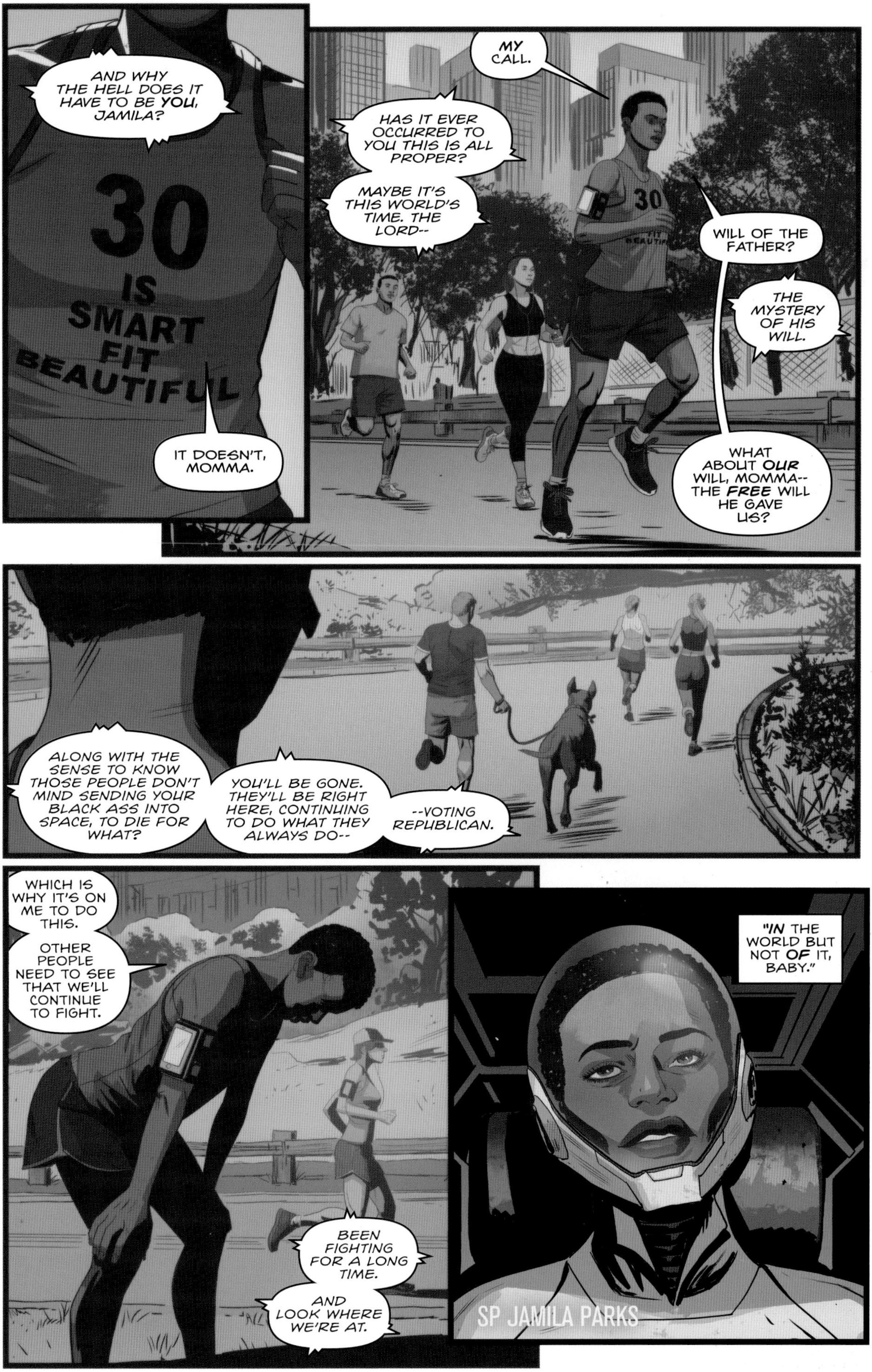
30 IS SMART FIT BEAUTIFUL
AND WHY THE HELL DOES IT HAVE TO BE **YOU**, JAMILA?
IT DOESN'T, MOMMA.
MY CALL.
HAS IT EVER OCCURRED TO YOU THIS IS ALL PROPER?
MAYBE IT'S THIS WORLD'S TIME. THE LORD--
WILL OF THE FATHER?
THE MYSTERY OF HIS WILL.
WHAT ABOUT **OUR** WILL, MOMMA-- THE **FREE** WILL HE GAVE US?
ALONG WITH THE SENSE TO KNOW THOSE PEOPLE DON'T MIND SENDING YOUR BLACK ASS INTO SPACE, TO DIE FOR WHAT?
YOU'LL BE GONE. THEY'LL BE RIGHT HERE, CONTINUING TO DO WHAT THEY ALWAYS DO--
--VOTING REPUBLICAN.
WHICH IS WHY IT'S ON ME TO DO THIS.
OTHER PEOPLE NEED TO SEE THAT WE'LL CONTINUE TO FIGHT.
BEEN FIGHTING FOR A LONG TIME.
AND LOOK WHERE WE'RE AT.
"**IN** THE WORLD BUT NOT **OF** IT, BABY."
SP JAMILA PARKS

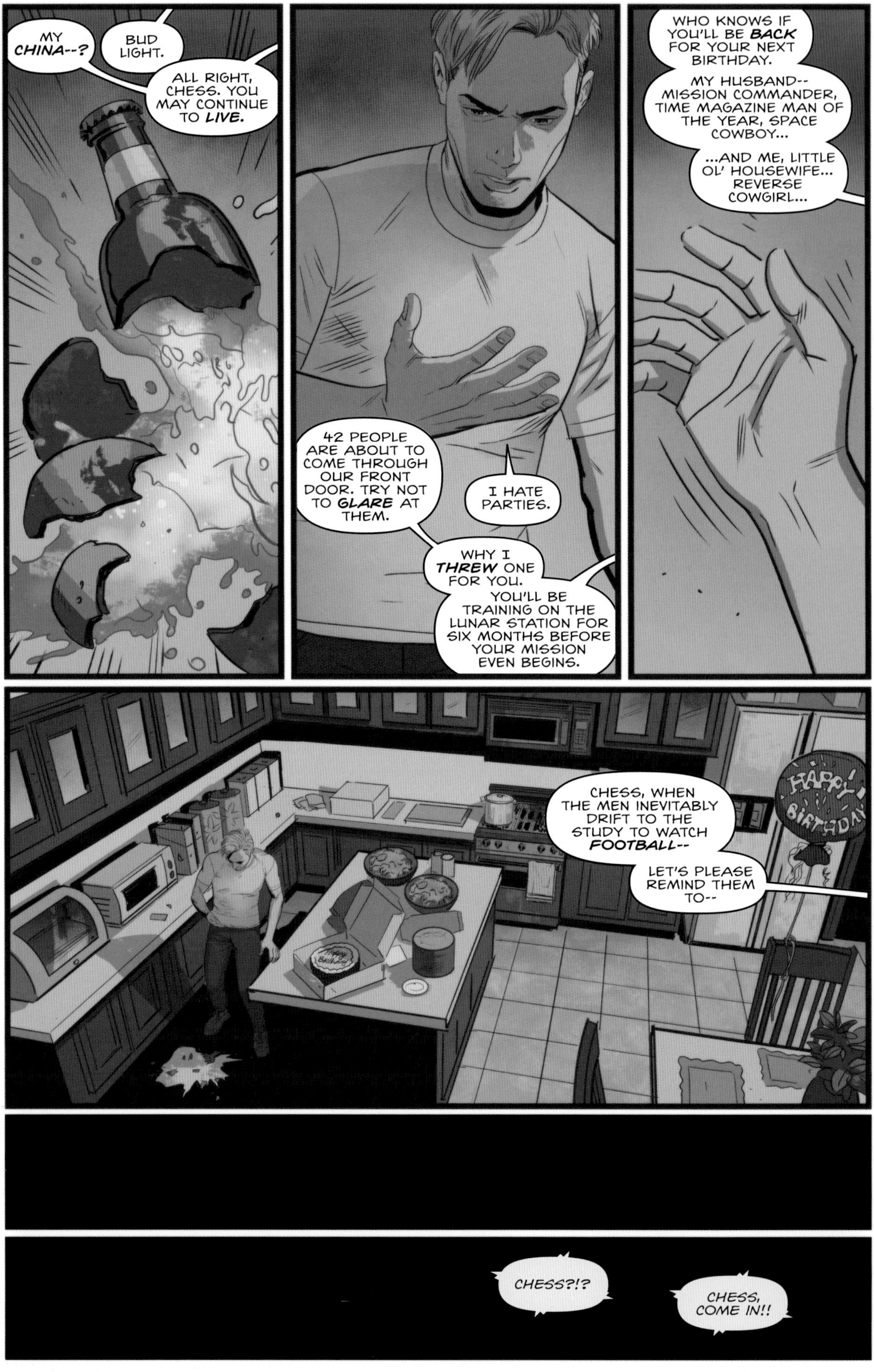
MY CHINA--?
BUD LIGHT.
ALL RIGHT, CHESS. YOU MAY CONTINUE TO LIVE.
42 PEOPLE ARE ABOUT TO COME THROUGH OUR FRONT DOOR. TRY NOT TO GLARE AT THEM.
I HATE PARTIES.
WHY I THREW ONE FOR YOU.
YOU'LL BE TRAINING ON THE LUNAR STATION FOR SIX MONTHS BEFORE YOUR MISSION EVEN BEGINS.
WHO KNOWS IF YOU'LL BE BACK FOR YOUR NEXT BIRTHDAY.
MY HUSBAND-- MISSION COMMANDER, TIME MAGAZINE MAN OF THE YEAR, SPACE COWBOY...
...AND ME, LITTLE OL' HOUSEWIFE... REVERSE COWGIRL...
HAPPY BIRTHDAY
CHESS, WHEN THE MEN INEVITABLY DRIFT TO THE STUDY TO WATCH FOOTBALL--
LET'S PLEASE REMIND THEM TO--
CHESS?!?
CHESS, COME IN!!

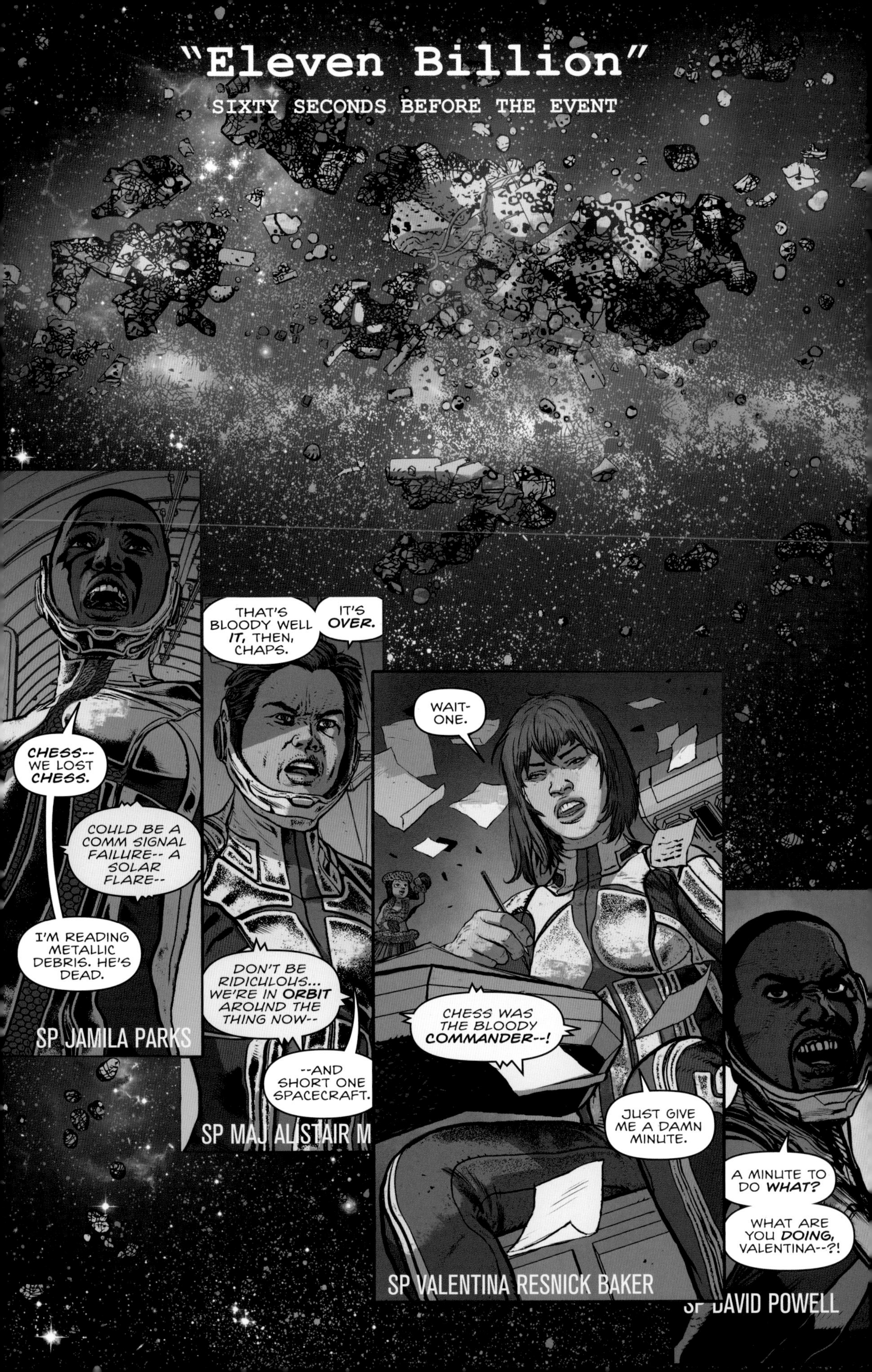
"Eleven Billion"
SIXTY SECONDS BEFORE THE EVENT
CHESS-- WE LOST CHESS.
COULD BE A COMM SIGNAL FAILURE-- A SOLAR FLARE--
I'M READING METALLIC DEBRIS. HE'S DEAD.
SP JAMILA PARKS
THAT'S BLOODY WELL IT, THEN, CHAPS.
IT'S OVER.
DON'T BE RIDICULOUS... WE'RE IN ORBIT AROUND THE THING NOW--
--AND SHORT ONE SPACECRAFT.
SP MAJ ALISTAIR M
WAIT-ONE.
CHESS WAS THE BLOODY COMMANDER--!
JUST GIVE ME A DAMN MINUTE.
SP VALENTINA RESNICK BAKER
A MINUTE TO DO WHAT?
WHAT ARE YOU DOING, VALENTINA--?!
SP DAVID POWELL

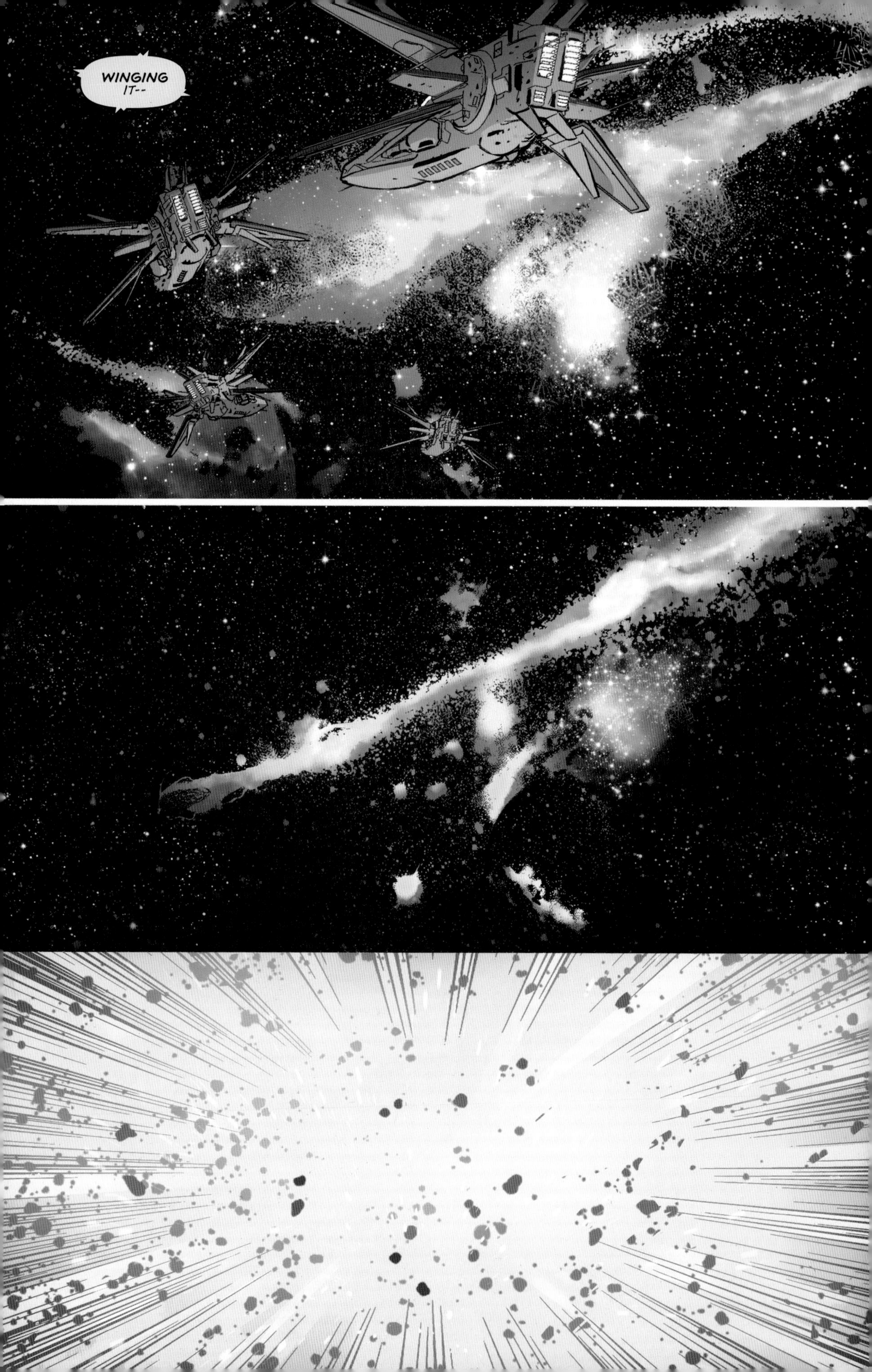
WINGING IT--

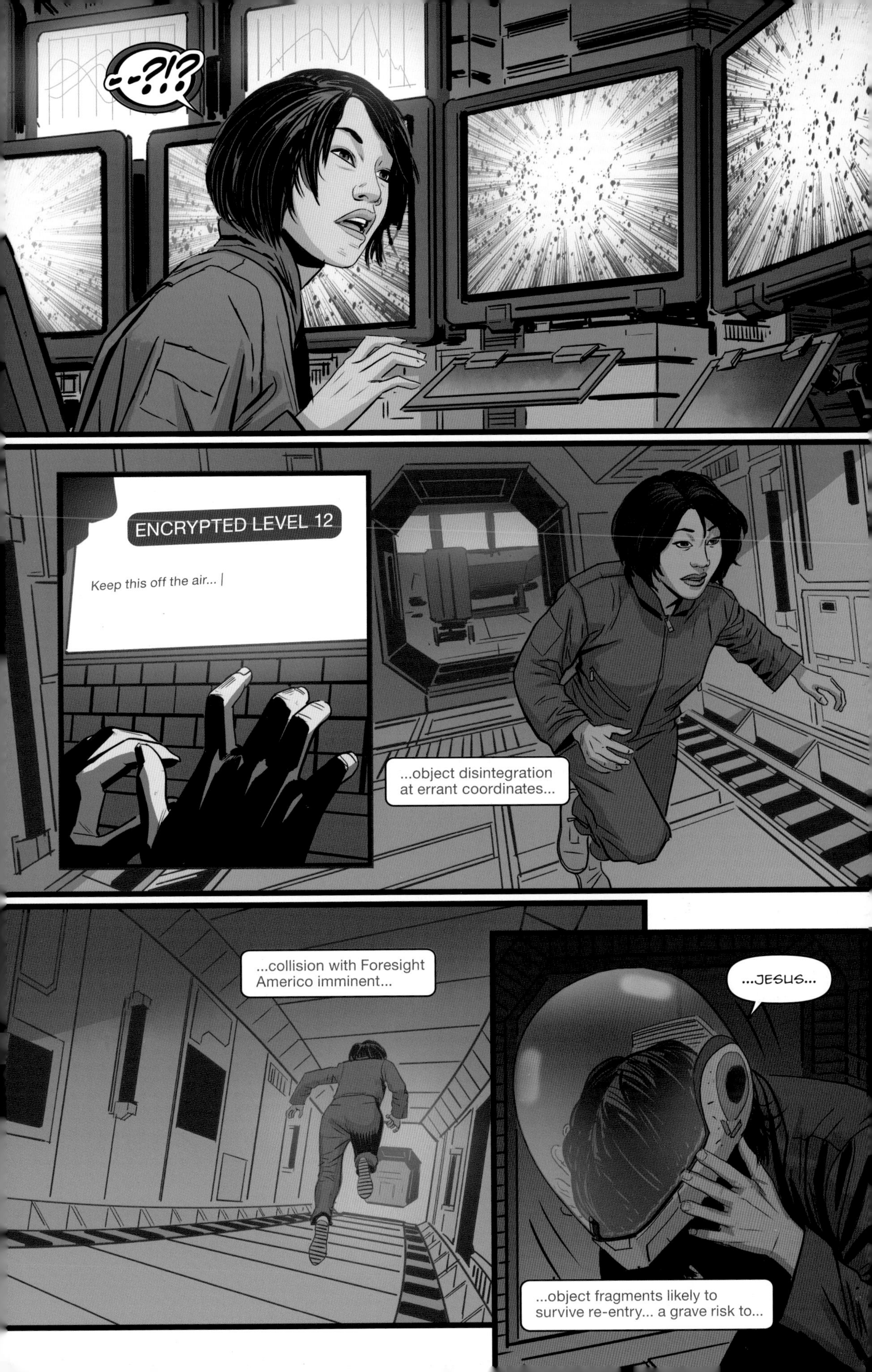
--?!?
ENCRYPTED LEVEL 12
Keep this off the air... |
...object disintegration at errant coordinates...
...collision with Foresight Americo imminent...
...JESUS...
...object fragments likely to survive re-entry... a grave risk to...

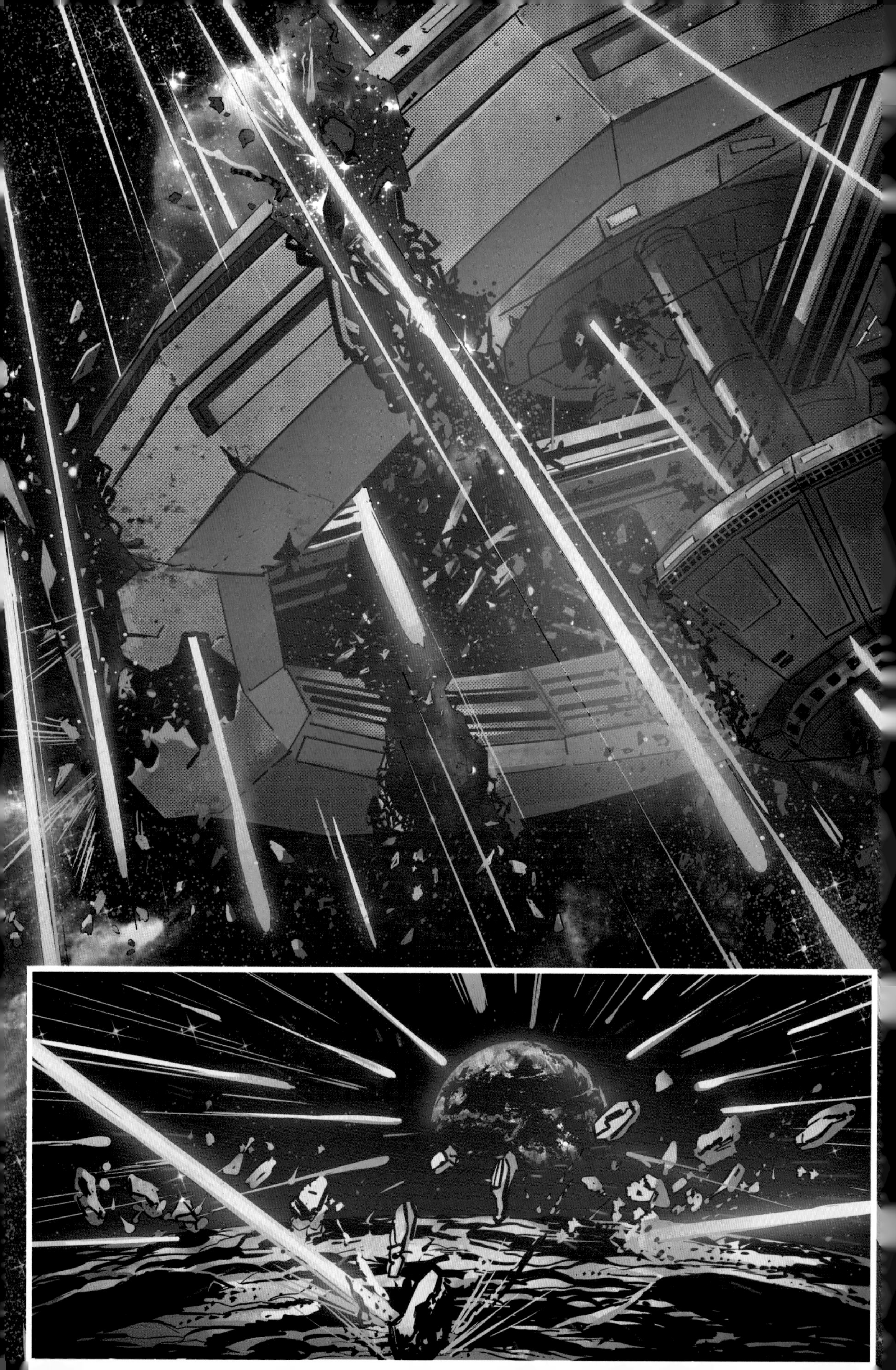

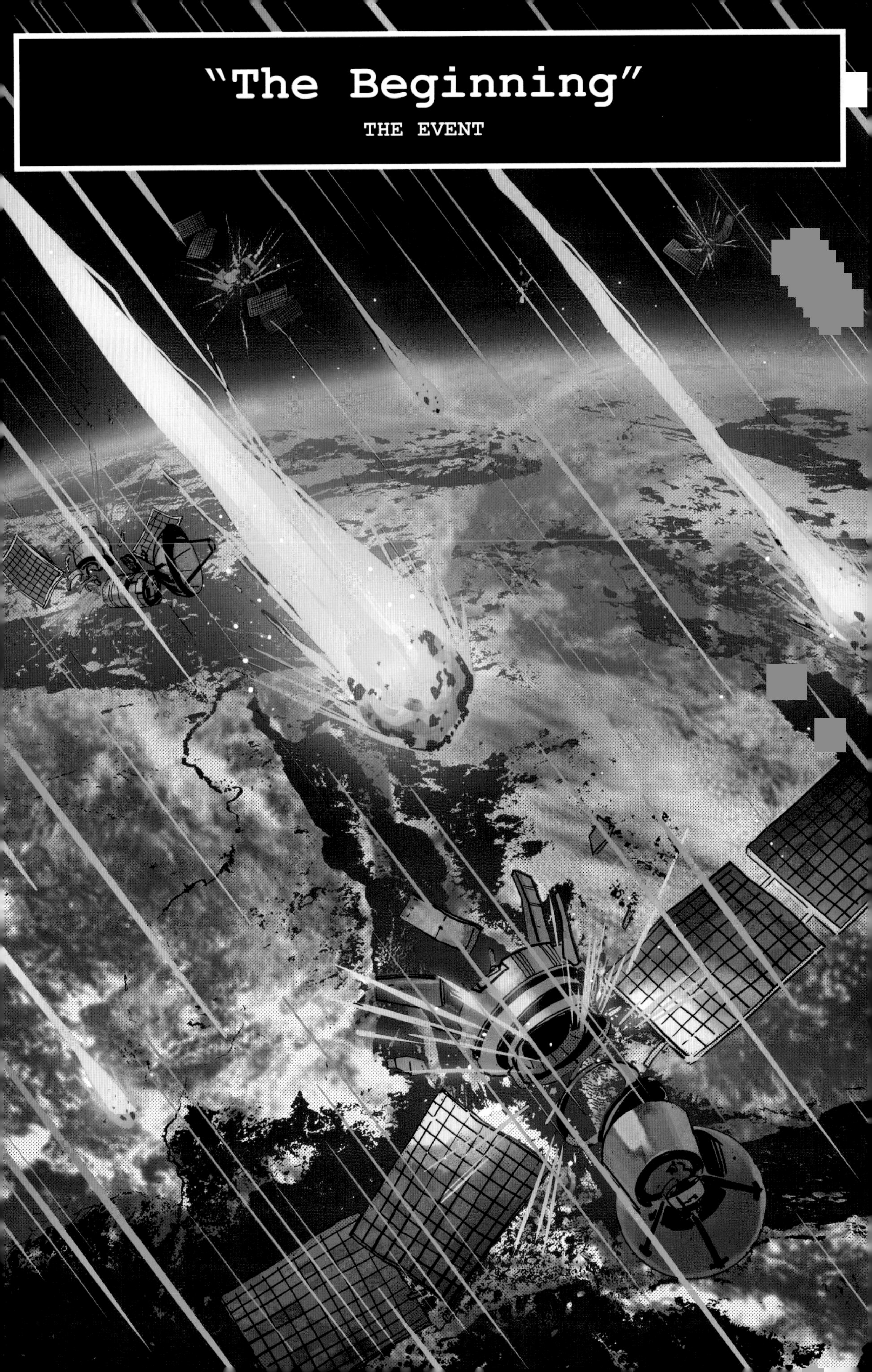
"The Beginning"
THE EVENT

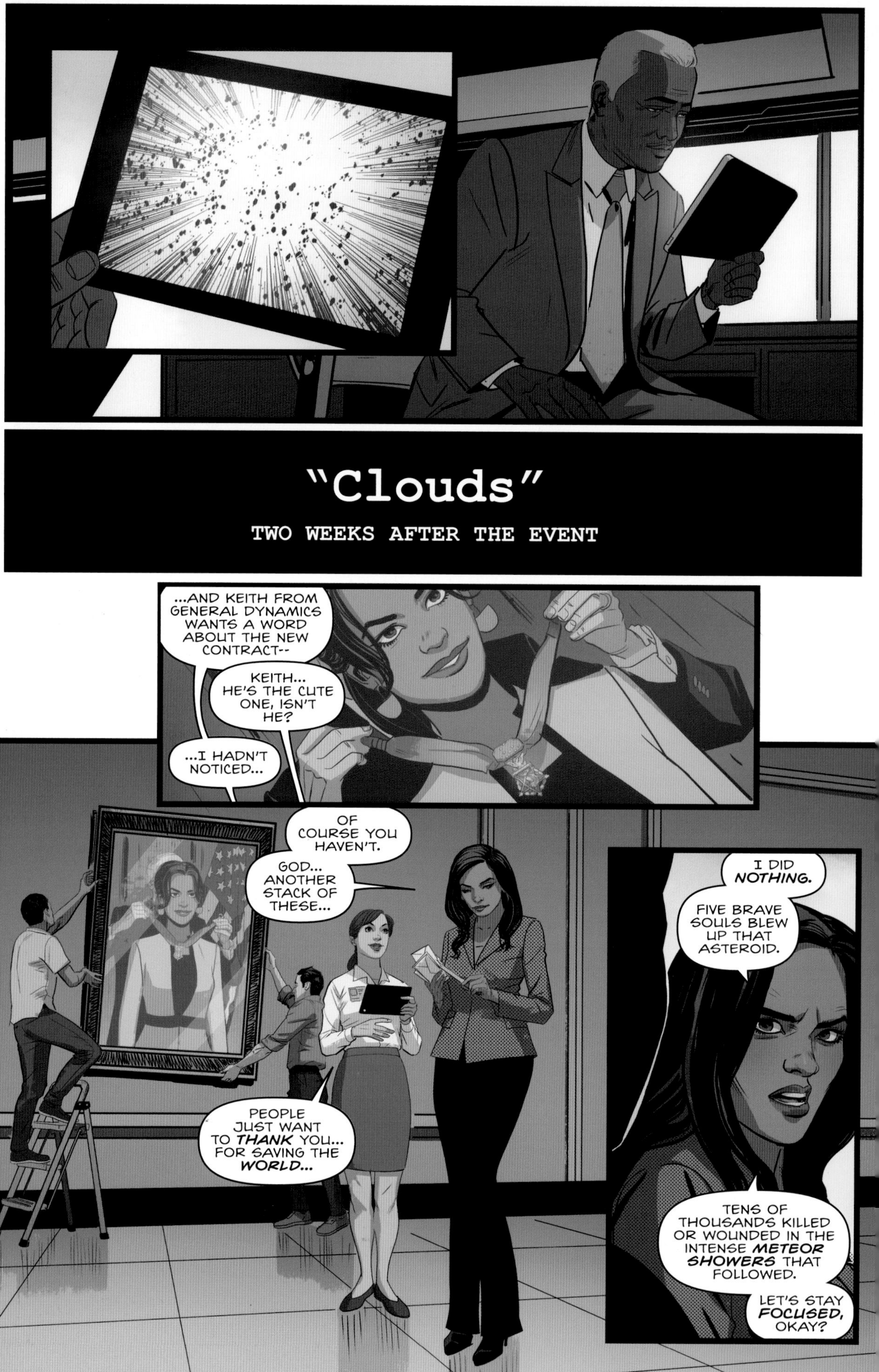
"Clouds"
TWO WEEKS AFTER THE EVENT
...AND KEITH FROM GENERAL DYNAMICS WANTS A WORD ABOUT THE NEW CONTRACT--
KEITH... HE'S THE CUTE ONE, ISN'T HE?
...I HADN'T NOTICED...
OF COURSE YOU HAVEN'T.
GOD... ANOTHER STACK OF THESE...
PEOPLE JUST WANT TO THANK YOU... FOR SAVING THE WORLD...
I DID NOTHING.
FIVE BRAVE SOULS BLEW UP THAT ASTEROID.
TENS OF THOUSANDS KILLED OR WOUNDED IN THE INTENSE METEOR SHOWERS THAT FOLLOWED.
LET'S STAY FOCUSED, OKAY?

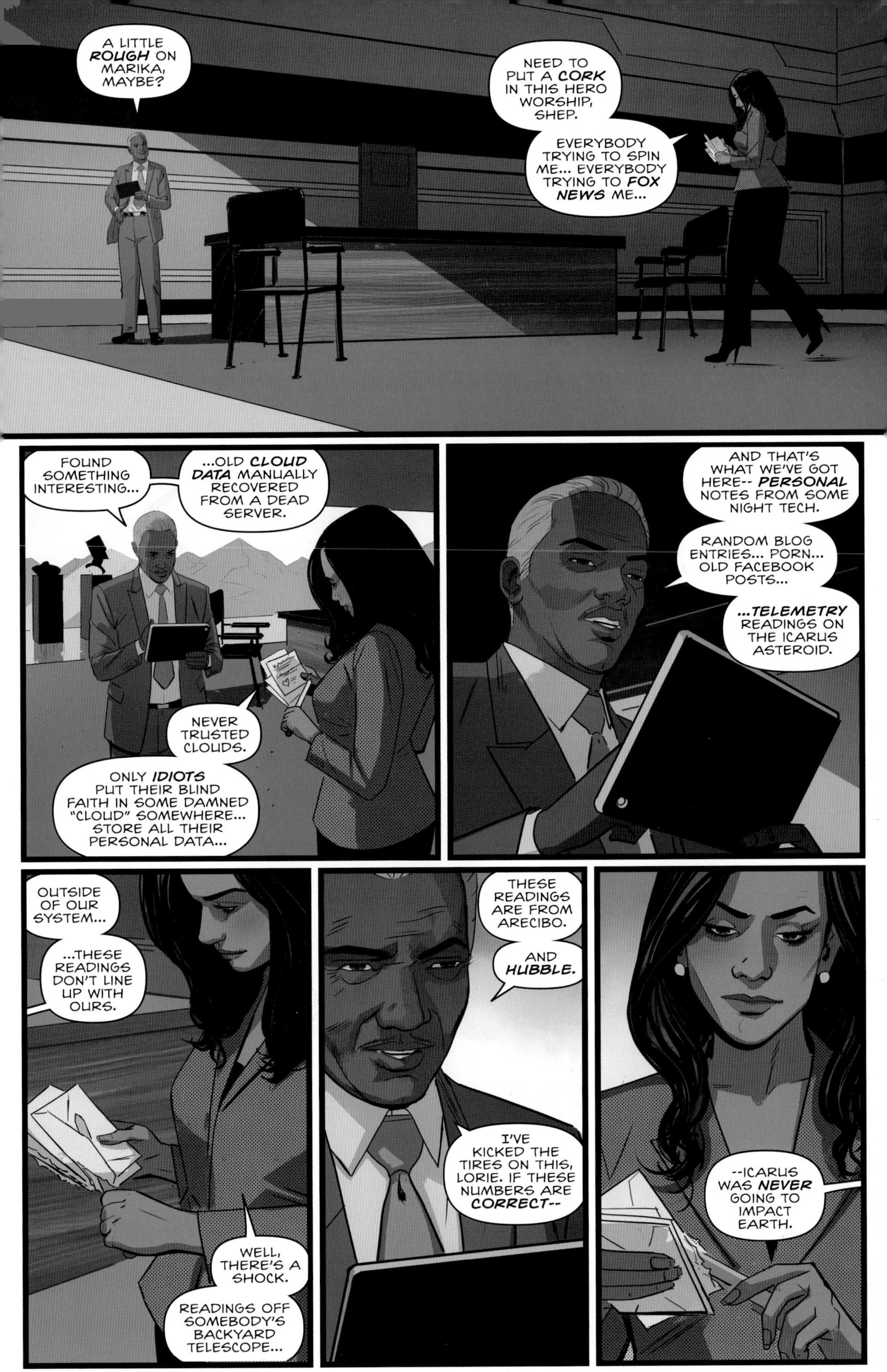
A LITTLE ROUGH ON MARIKA, MAYBE?
NEED TO PUT A CORK IN THIS HERO WORSHIP, SHEP.
EVERYBODY TRYING TO SPIN ME... EVERYBODY TRYING TO FOX NEWS ME...
FOUND SOMETHING INTERESTING...
...OLD CLOUD DATA MANUALLY RECOVERED FROM A DEAD SERVER.
NEVER TRUSTED CLOUDS.
ONLY IDIOTS PUT THEIR BLIND FAITH IN SOME DAMNED "CLOUD" SOMEWHERE... STORE ALL THEIR PERSONAL DATA...
AND THAT'S WHAT WE'VE GOT HERE-- PERSONAL NOTES FROM SOME NIGHT TECH.
RANDOM BLOG ENTRIES... PORN... OLD FACEBOOK POSTS...
...TELEMETRY READINGS ON THE ICARUS ASTEROID.
OUTSIDE OF OUR SYSTEM...
...THESE READINGS DON'T LINE UP WITH OURS.
WELL, THERE'S A SHOCK.
READINGS OFF SOMEBODY'S BACKYARD TELESCOPE...
THESE READINGS ARE FROM ARECIBO.
AND HUBBLE.
I'VE KICKED THE TIRES ON THIS, LORIE. IF THESE NUMBERS ARE CORRECT--
--ICARUS WAS NEVER GOING TO IMPACT EARTH.

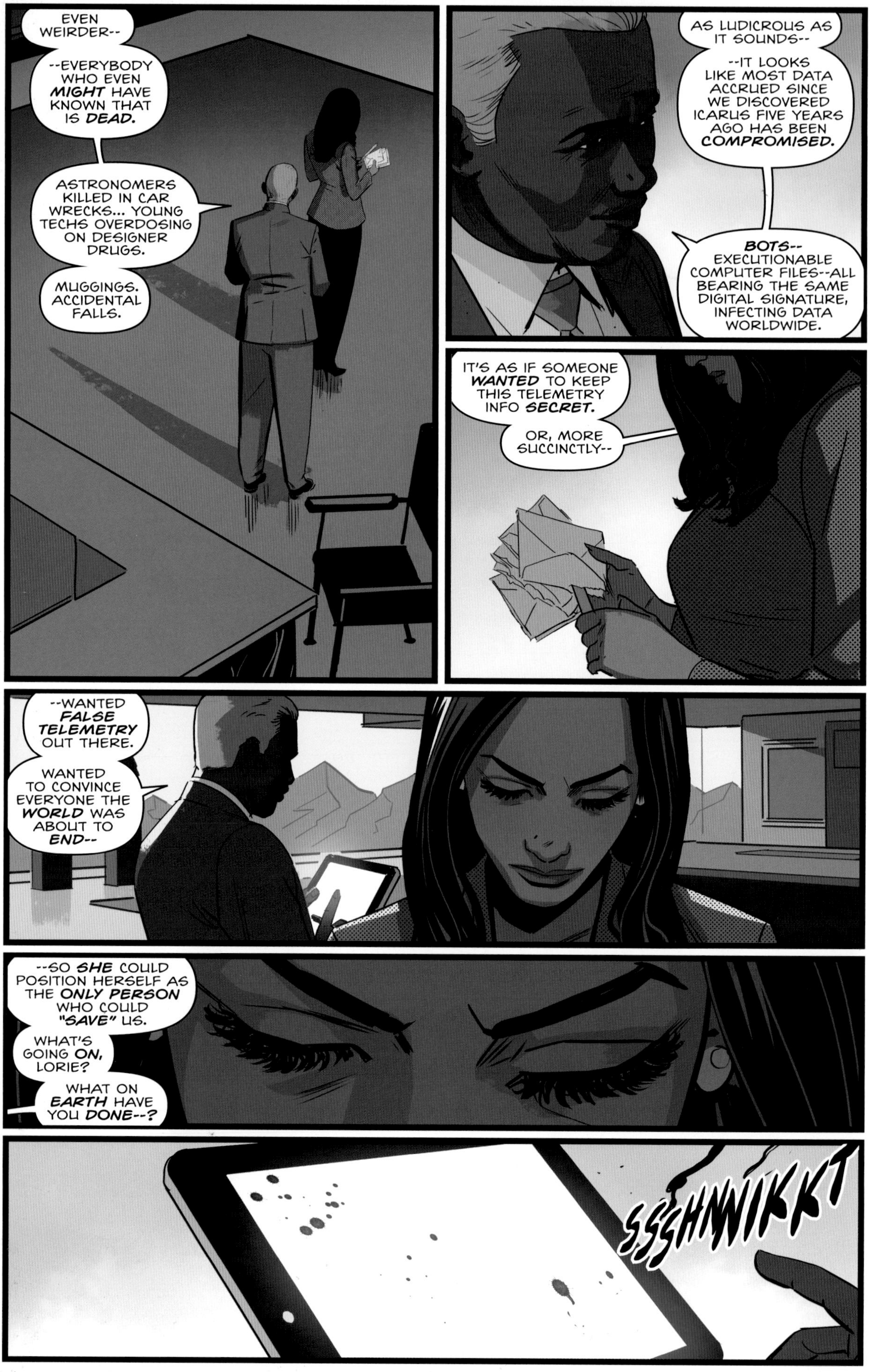
EVEN WEIRDER--
--EVERYBODY WHO EVEN MIGHT HAVE KNOWN THAT IS DEAD.
ASTRONOMERS KILLED IN CAR WRECKS... YOUNG TECHS OVERDOSING ON DESIGNER DRUGS.
MUGGINGS. ACCIDENTAL FALLS.
AS LUDICROUS AS IT SOUNDS--
--IT LOOKS LIKE MOST DATA ACCRUED SINCE WE DISCOVERED ICARUS FIVE YEARS AGO HAS BEEN COMPROMISED.
BOTS-- EXECUTIONABLE COMPUTER FILES--ALL BEARING THE SAME DIGITAL SIGNATURE, INFECTING DATA WORLDWIDE.
IT'S AS IF SOMEONE WANTED TO KEEP THIS TELEMETRY INFO SECRET.
OR, MORE SUCCINCTLY--
--WANTED FALSE TELEMETRY OUT THERE.
WANTED TO CONVINCE EVERYONE THE WORLD WAS ABOUT TO END--
--SO SHE COULD POSITION HERSELF AS THE ONLY PERSON WHO COULD "SAVE" US.
WHAT'S GOING ON, LORIE?
WHAT ON EARTH HAVE YOU DONE--?
SSSHNIKKT

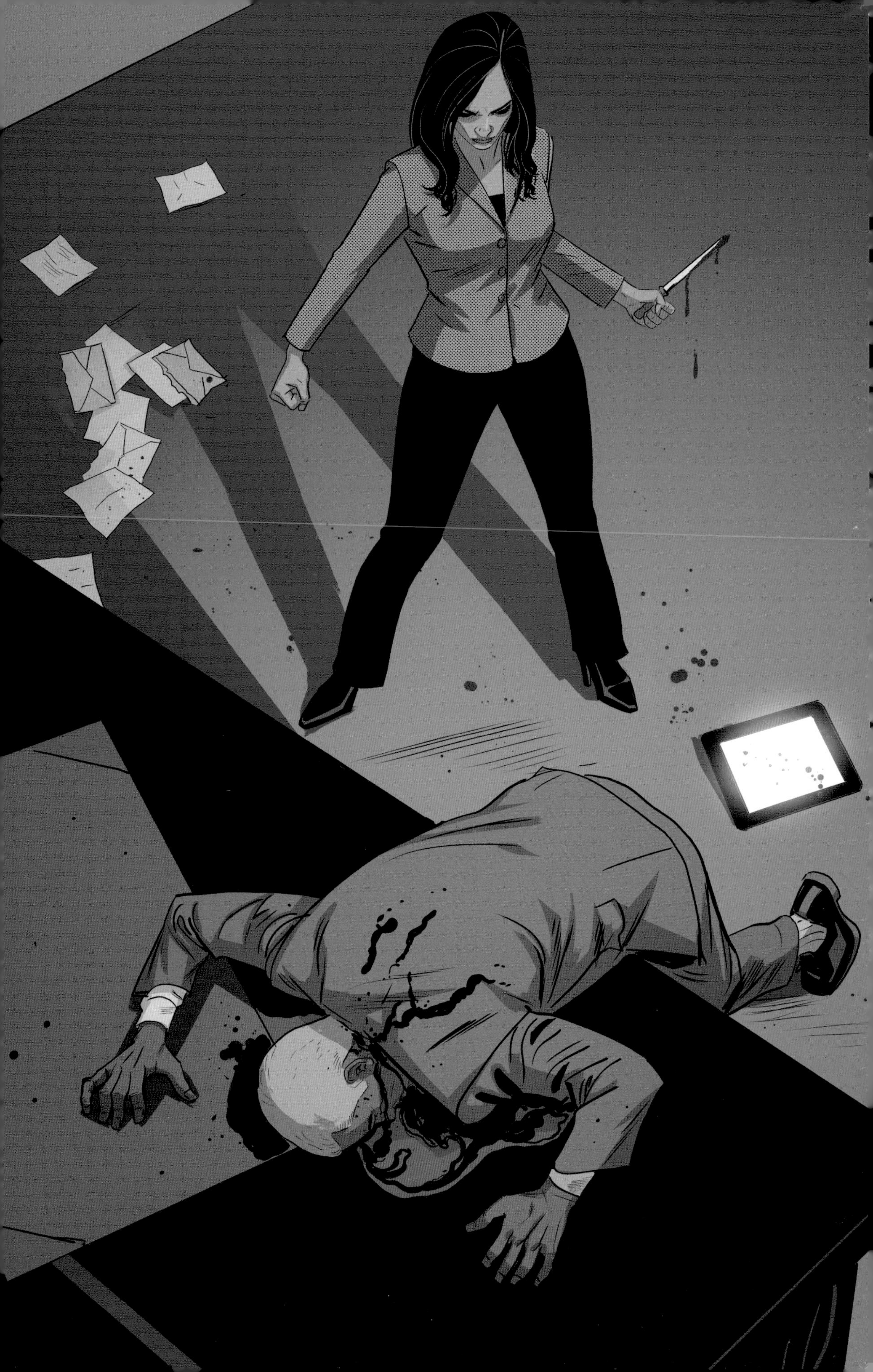

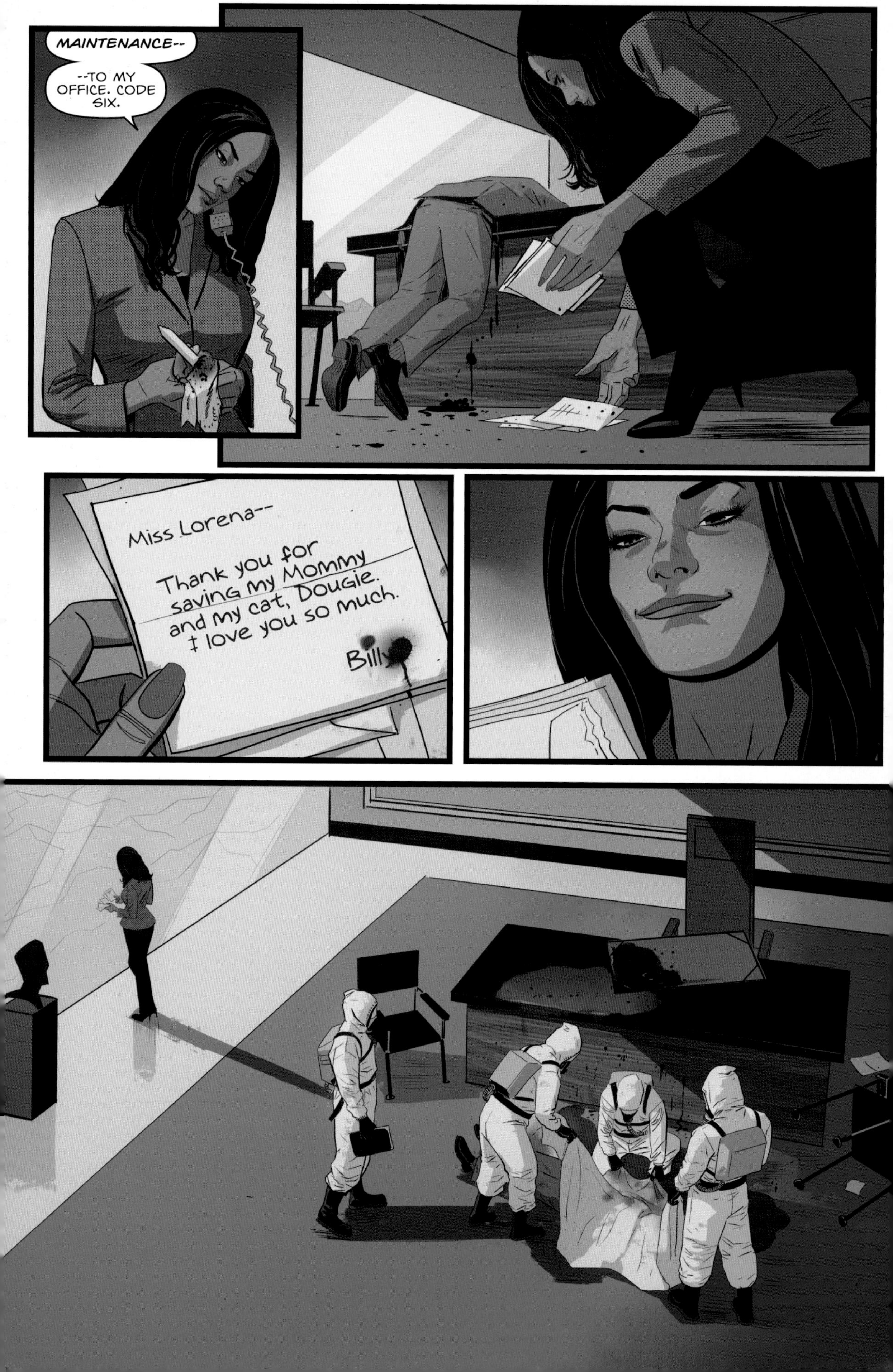

MAINTENANCE--
--TO MY OFFICE. CODE SIX.
Miss Lorena--
Thank you for saving my Mommy and my cat, Dougie. I love you so much.
Billy

COVER GALLERY

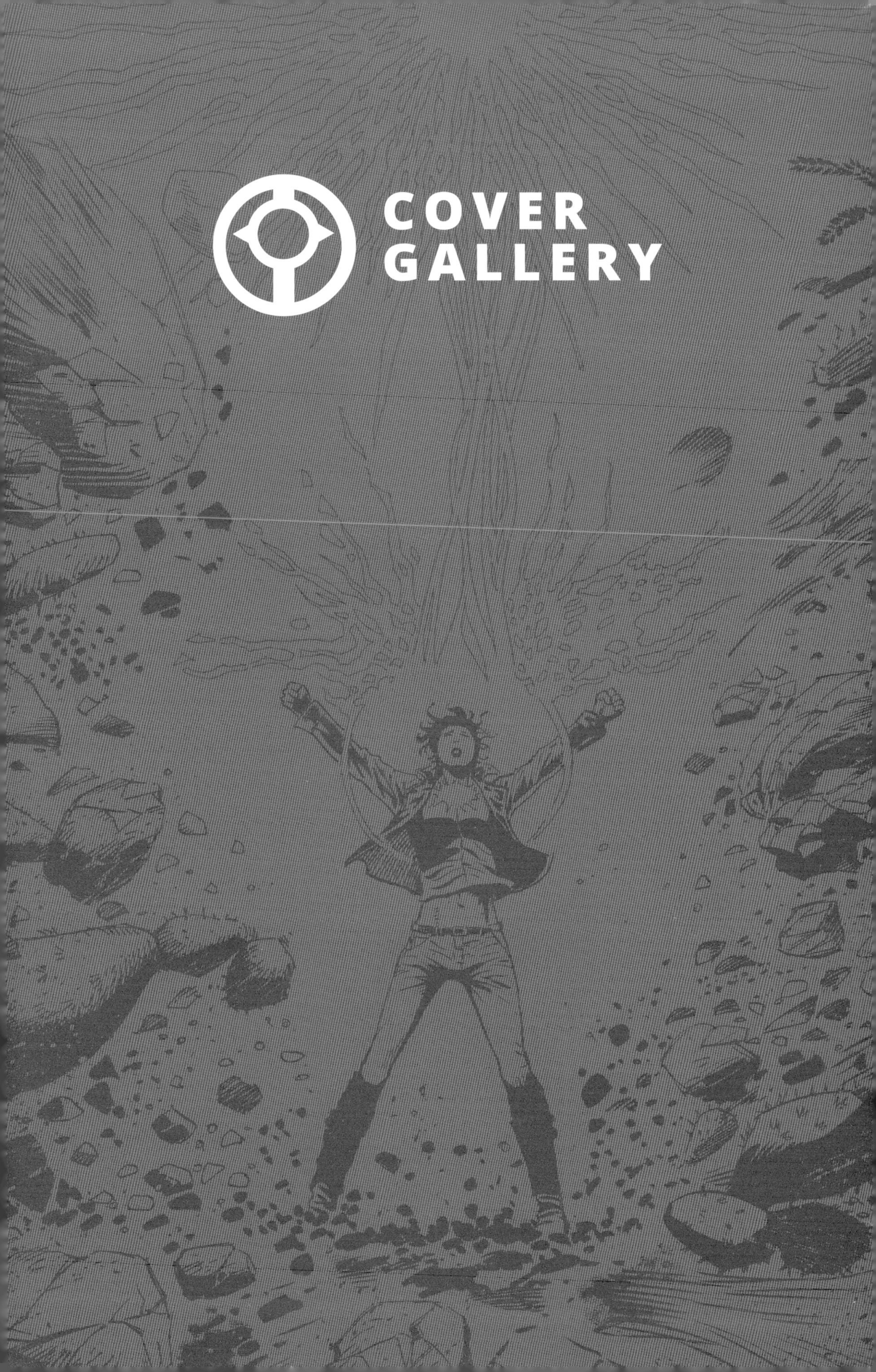

Art by **JAN DUURSEMA**
and **KELLY FITZPATRICK**

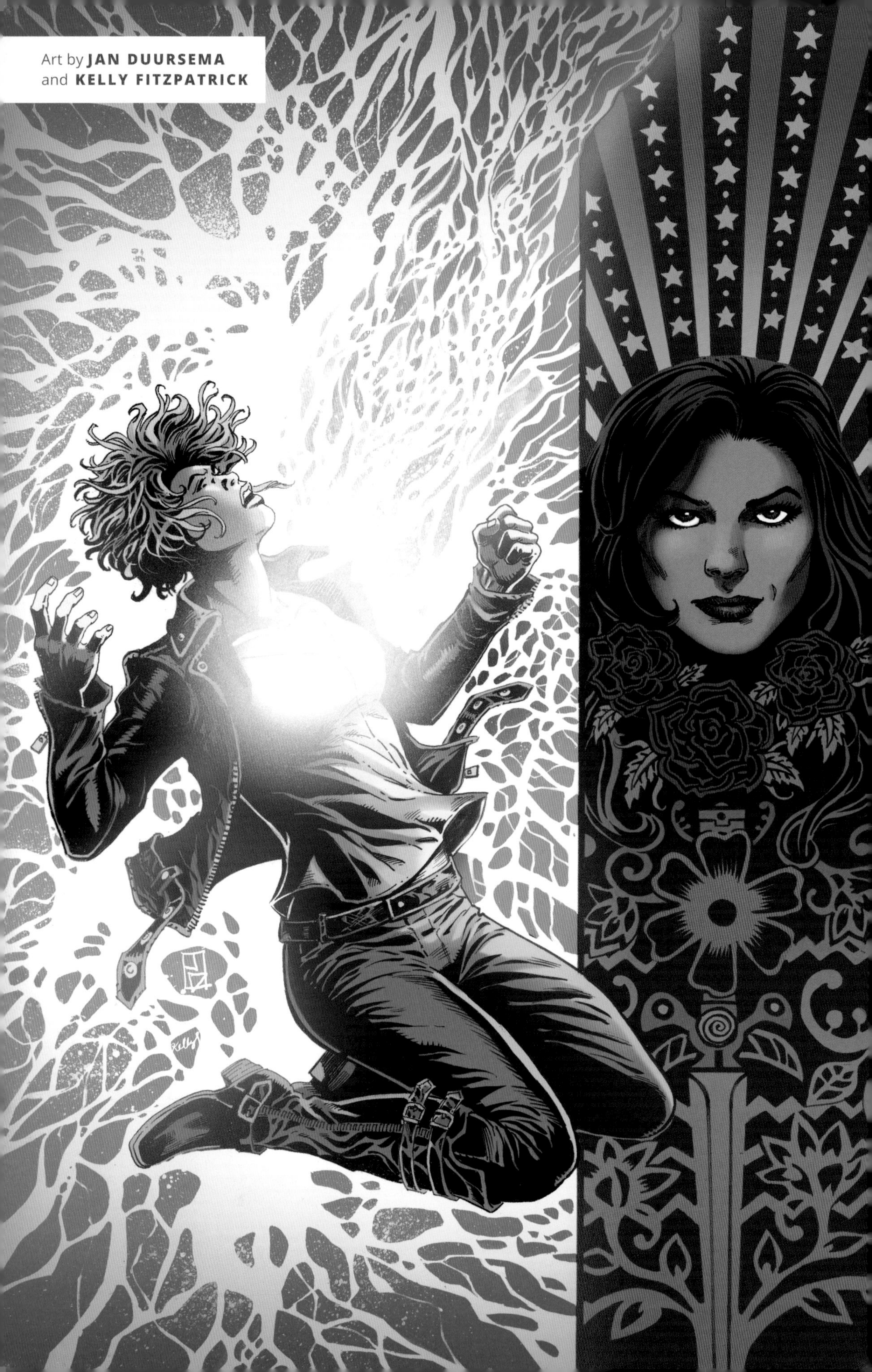

Art by **KHARY RANDOLPH**
and **EMILIO LOPEZ**

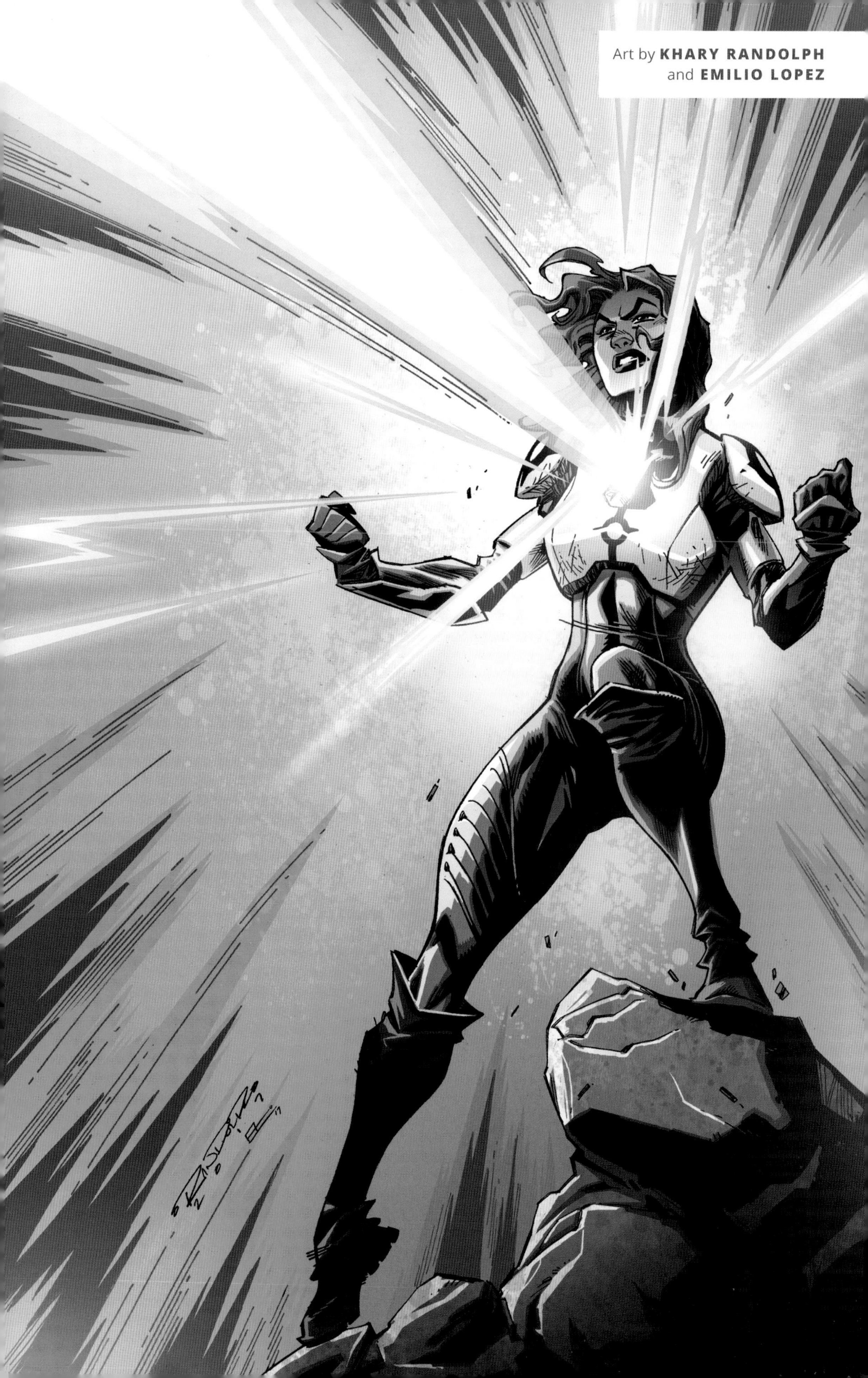

Art by **JOHN CASSADAY**
and **LAURA MARTIN**

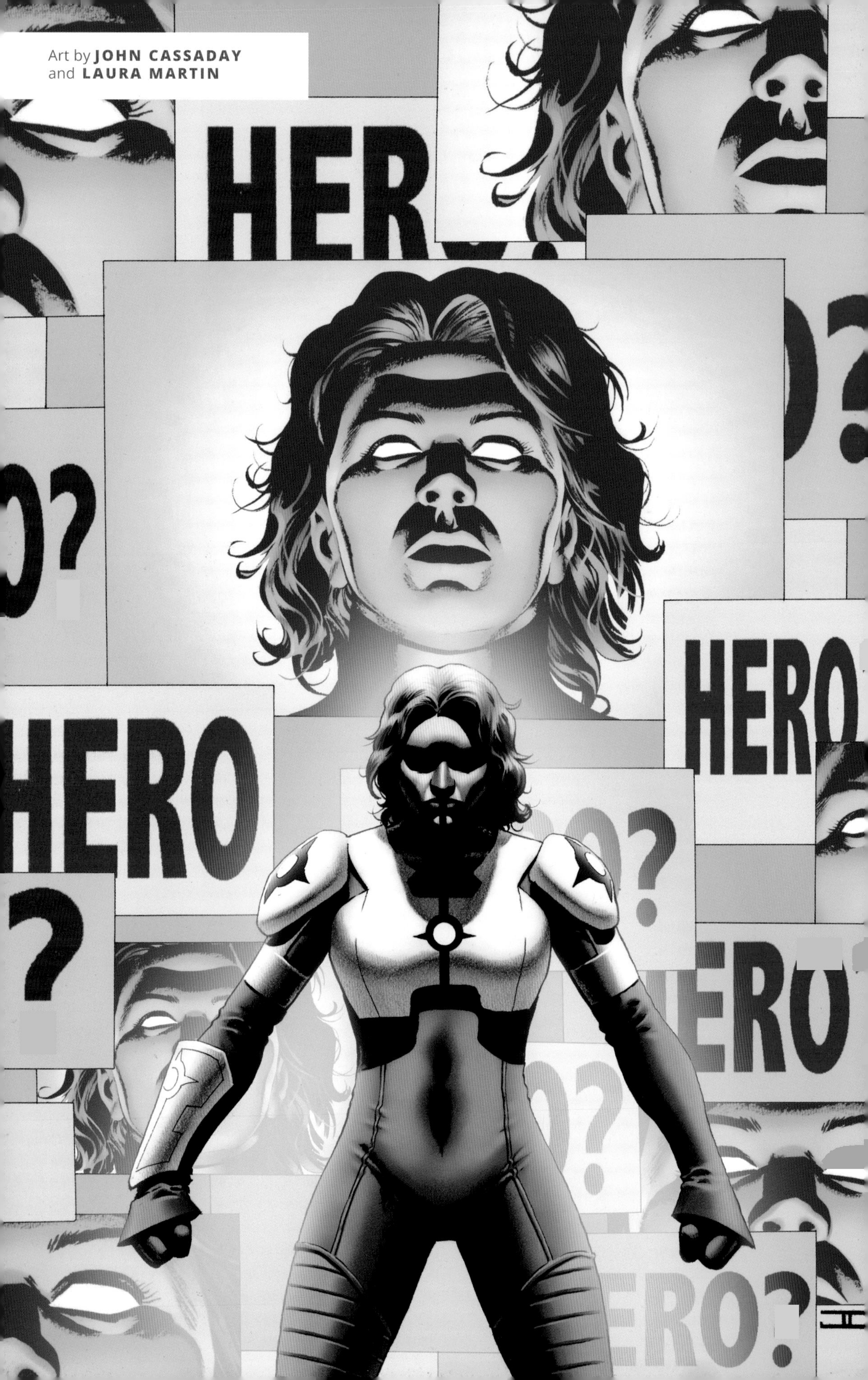
HERO
HERO

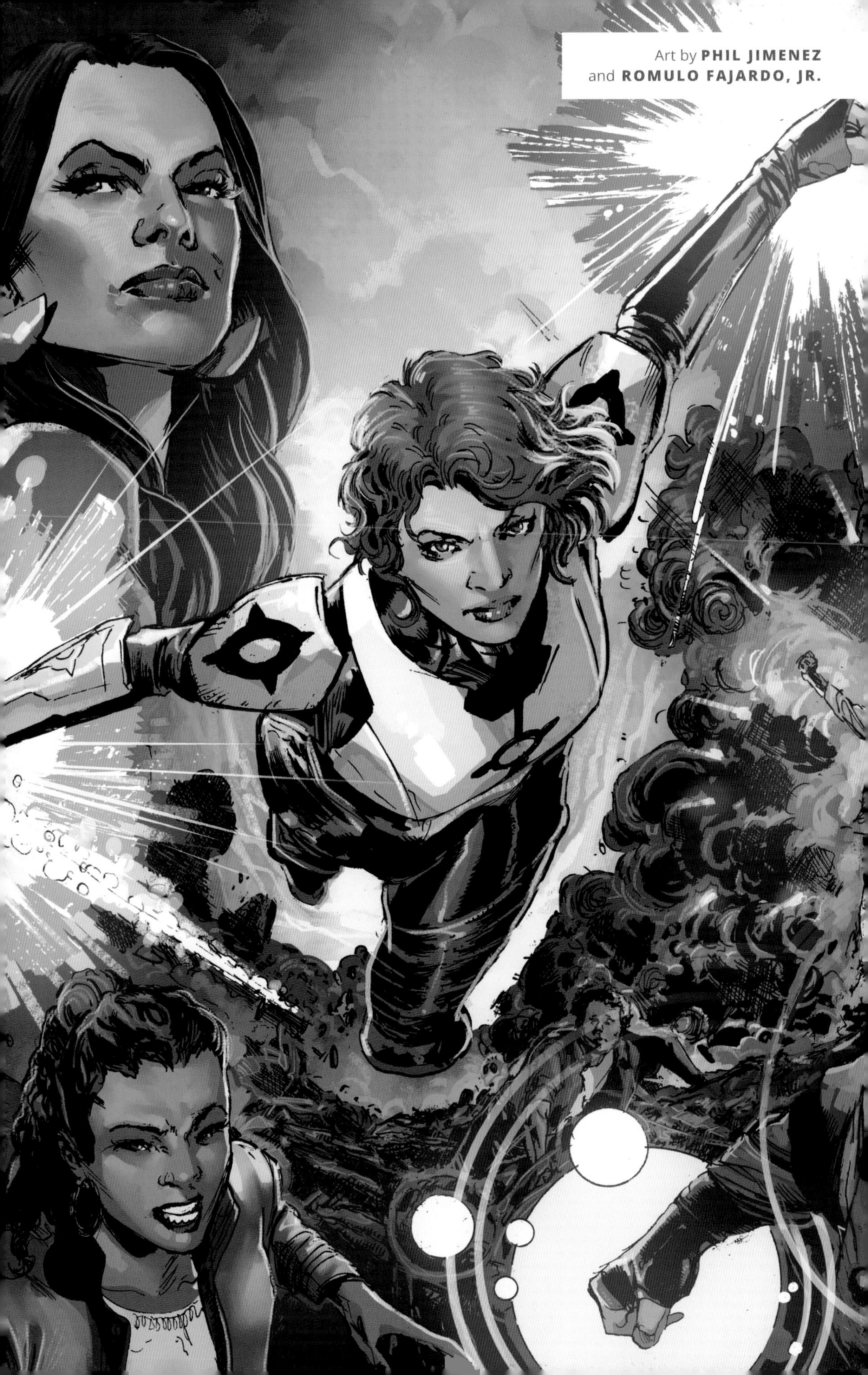

Art by **PHIL JIMENEZ**
and **ROMULO FAJARDO, JR.**

Art by **JAN DUURSEMA**
and **PAUL MOUNTS**

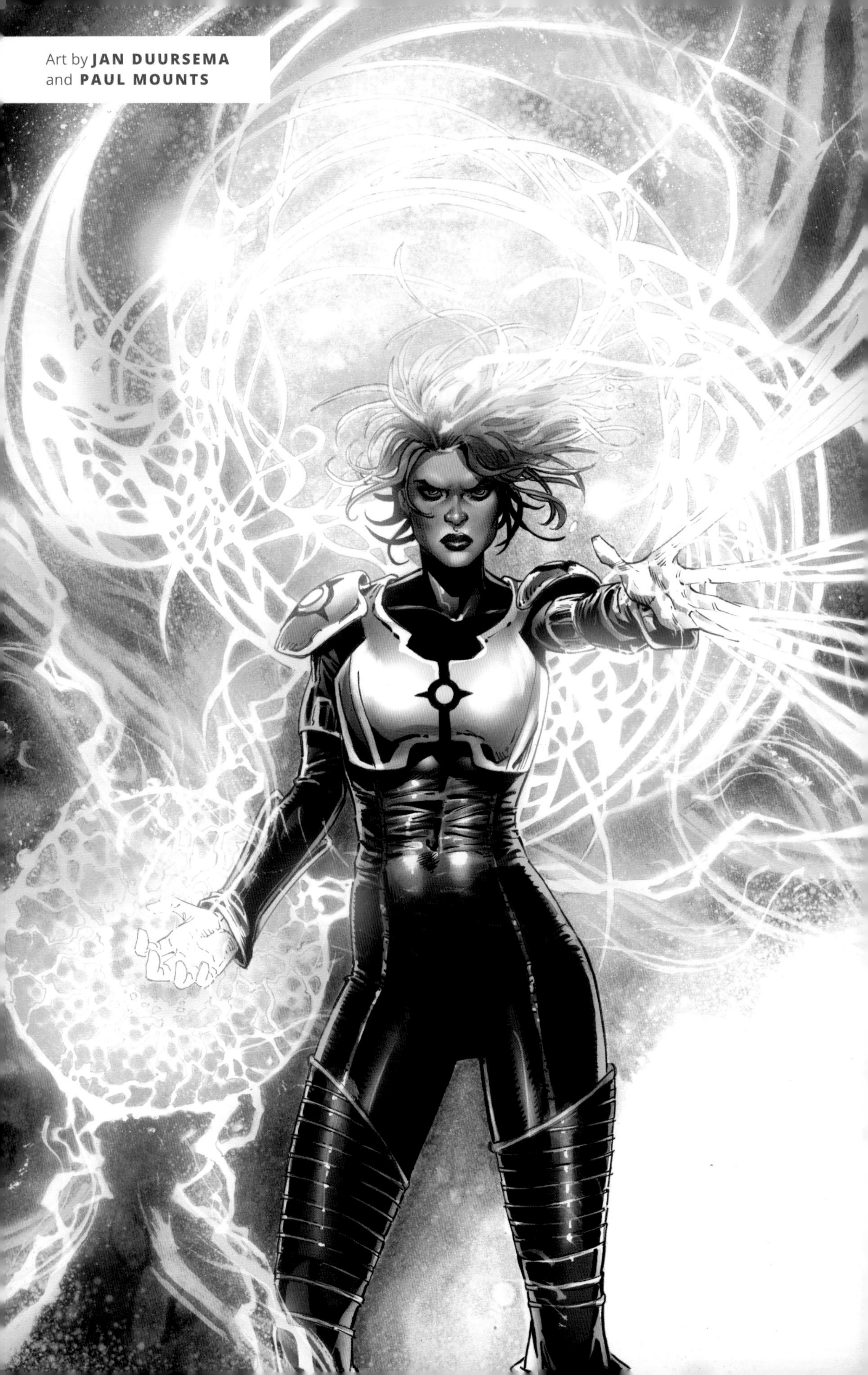

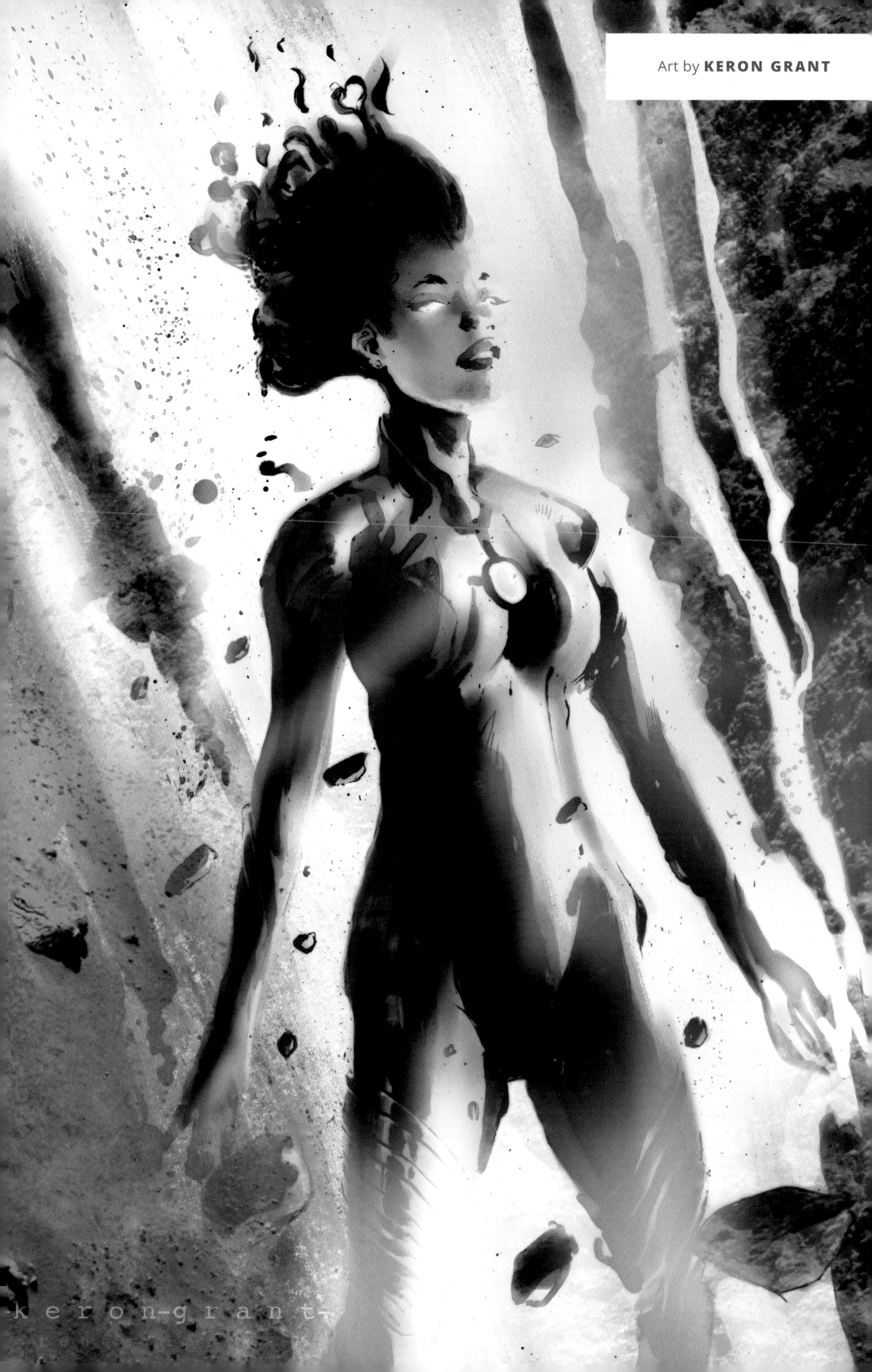
keron-grant

Art by **KERON GRANT**

Art by **PATRICK ZIRCHER**
and **PAUL MOUNTS**

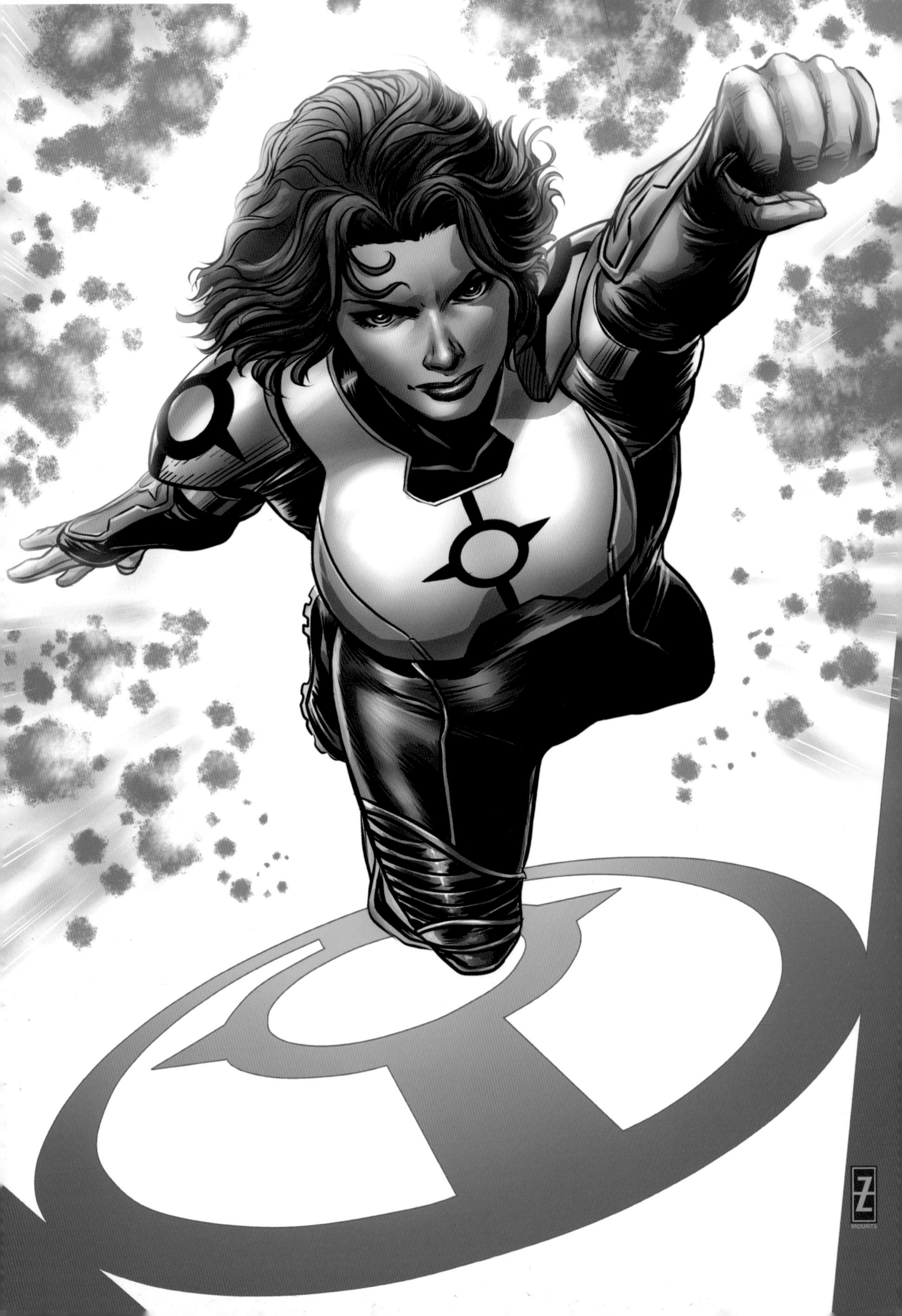
MOUNTS

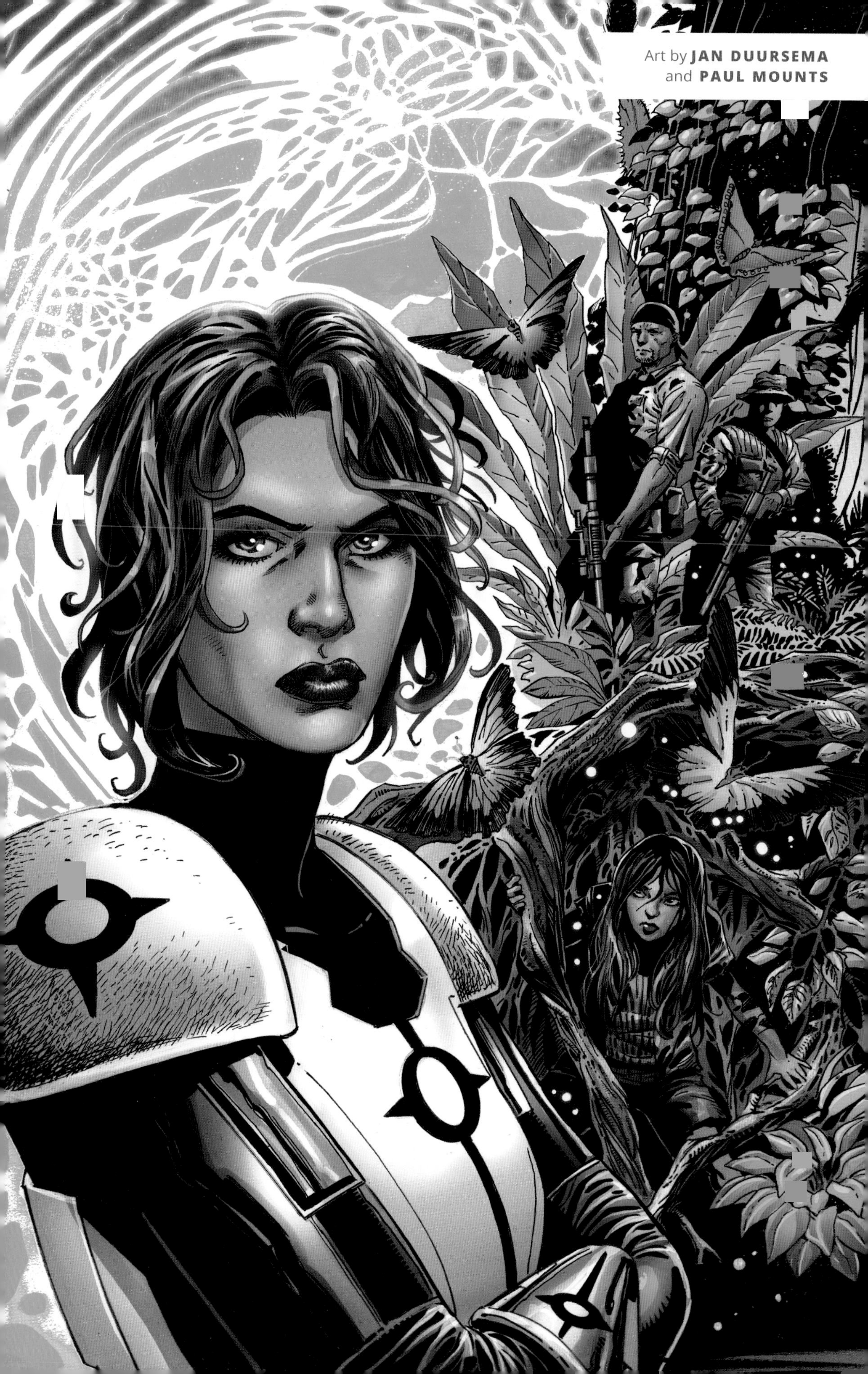

Art by **JAN DUURSEMA**
and **PAUL MOUNTS**

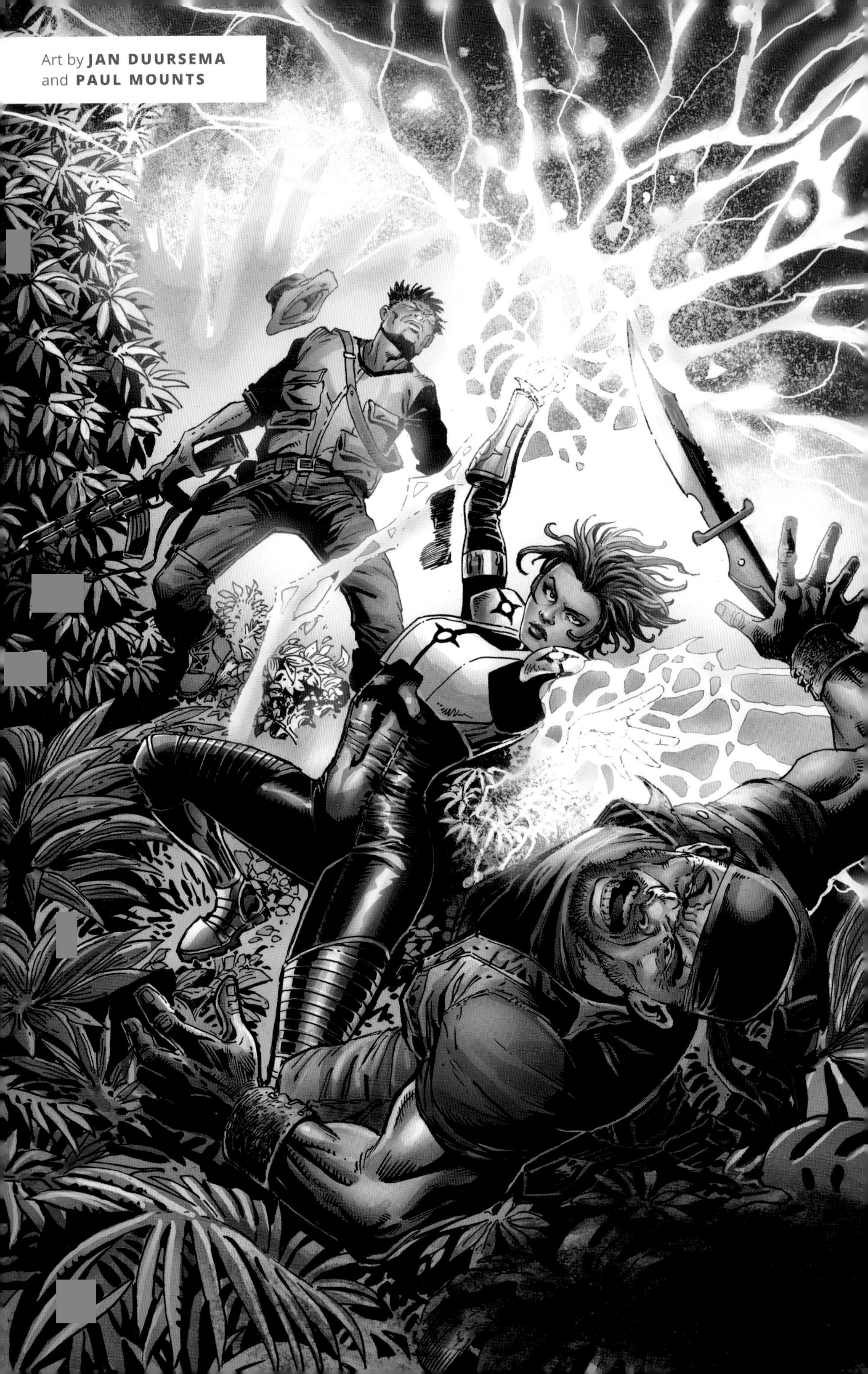

Art by **JAN DUURSEMA**
and **PAUL MOUNTS**

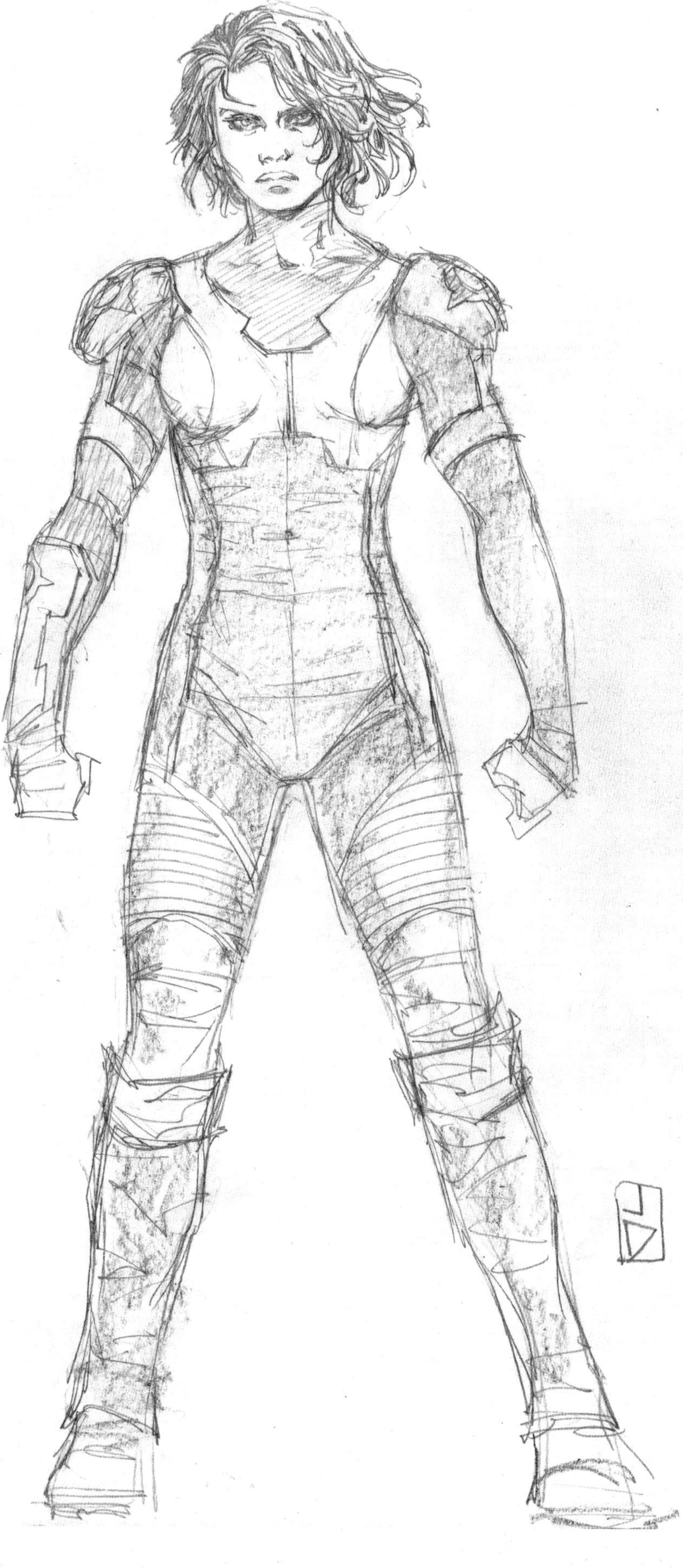

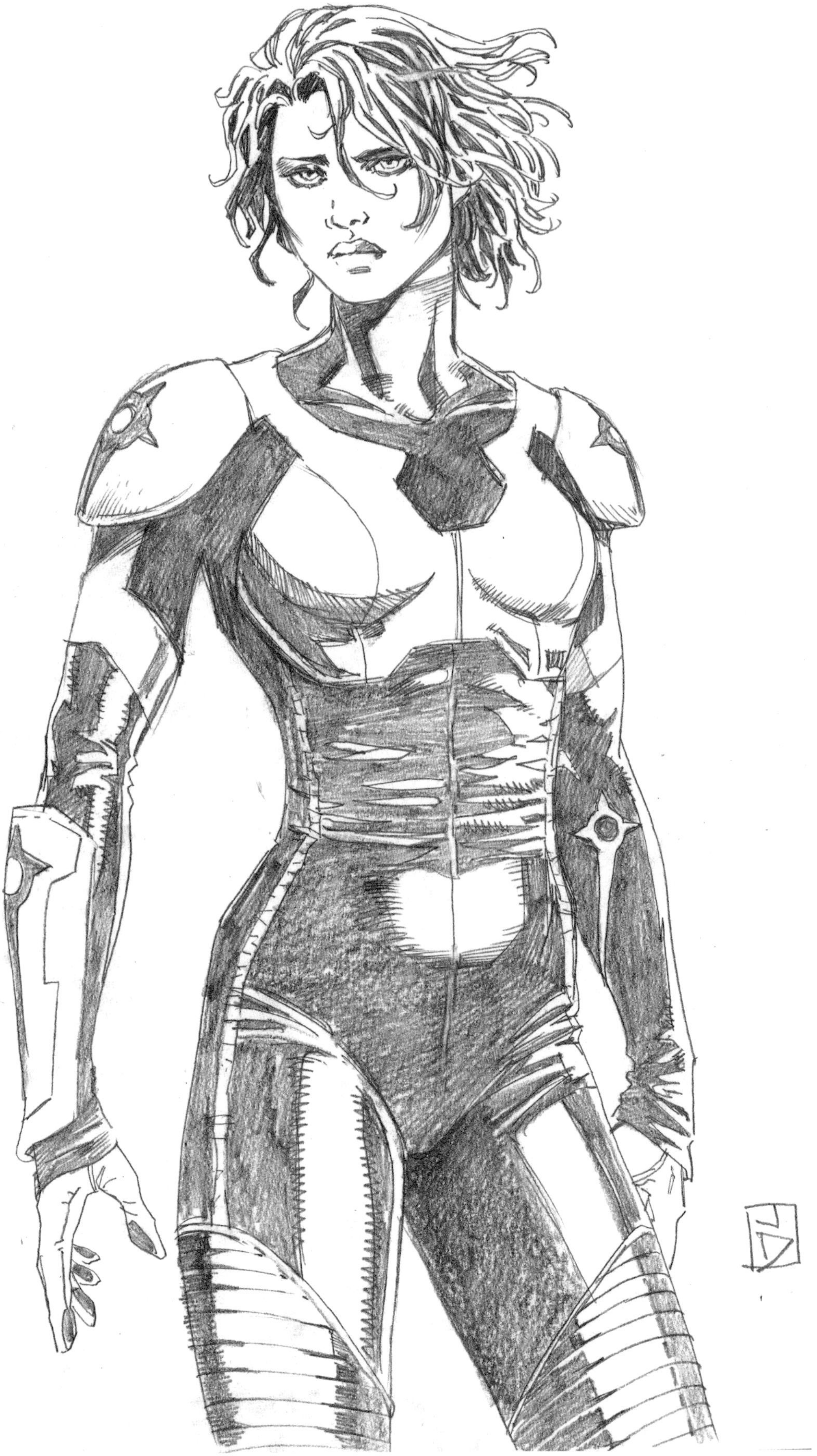

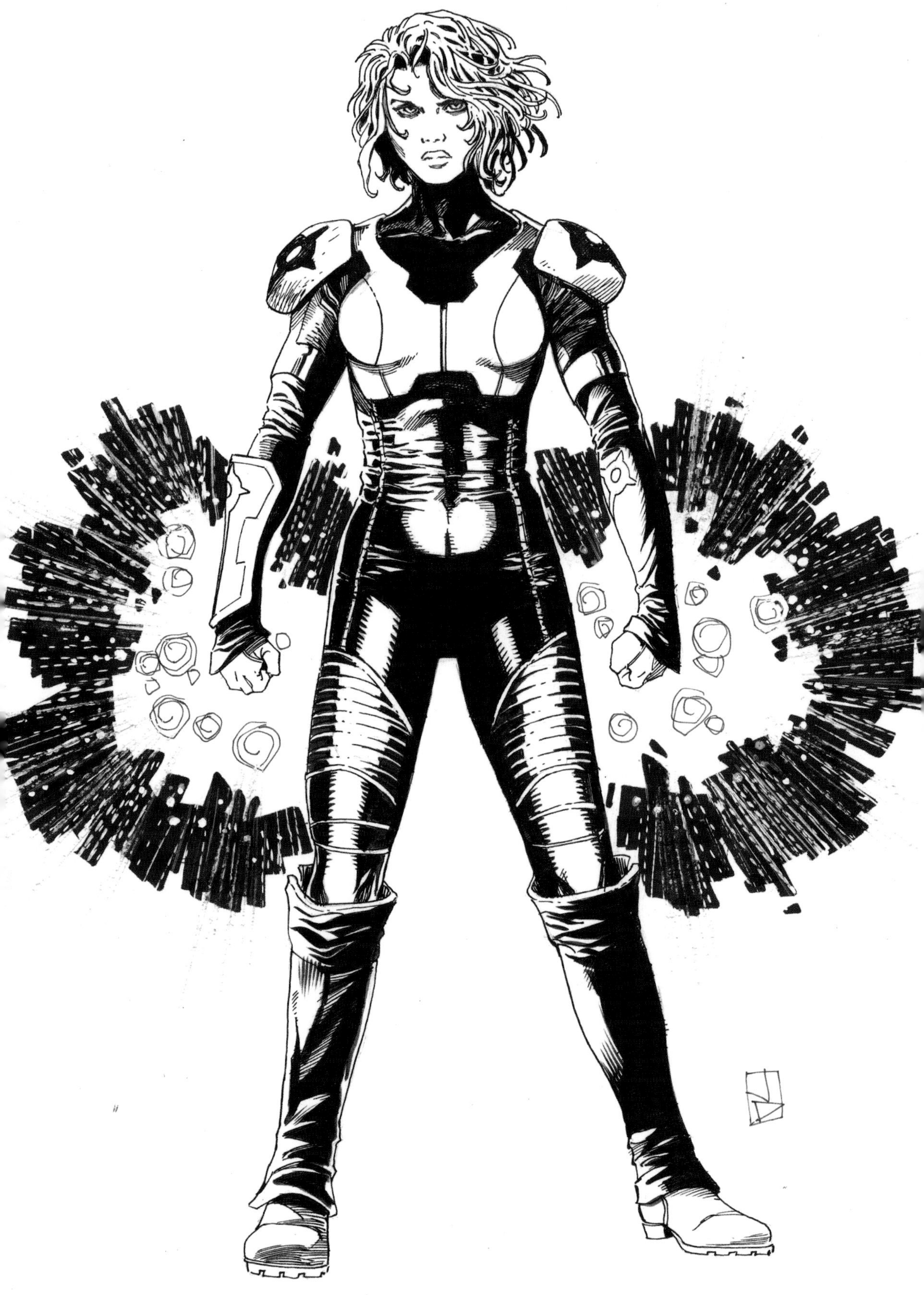

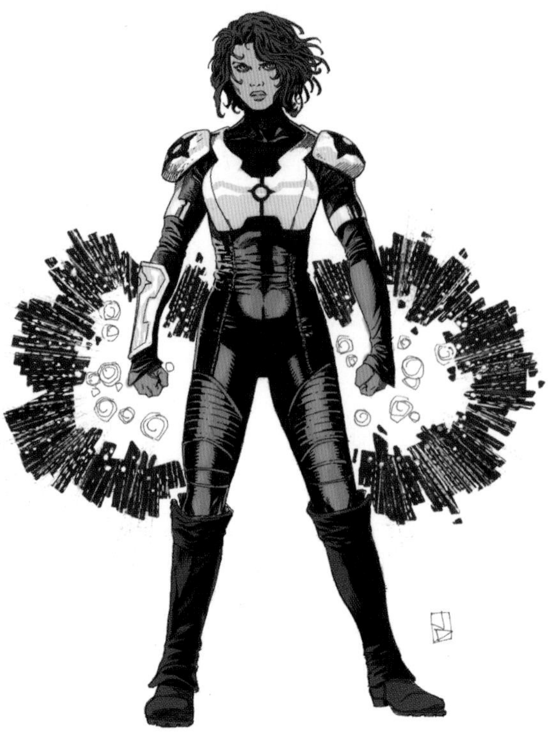

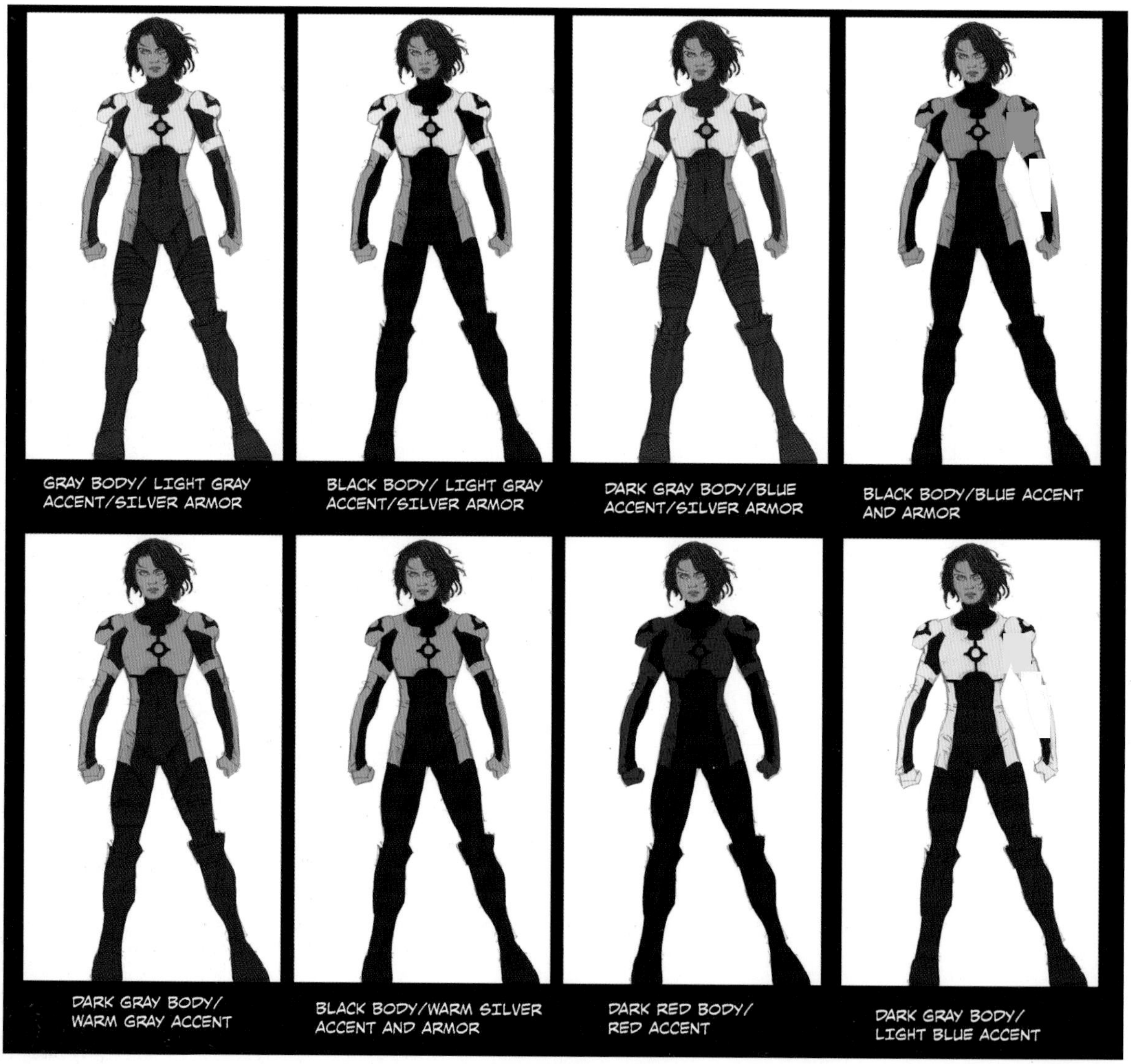
GRAY BODY/ LIGHT GRAY ACCENT/SILVER ARMOR
BLACK BODY/ LIGHT GRAY ACCENT/SILVER ARMOR
DARK GRAY BODY/BLUE ACCENT/SILVER ARMOR
BLACK BODY/BLUE ACCENT AND ARMOR
DARK GRAY BODY/ WARM GRAY ACCENT
BLACK BODY/WARM SILVER ACCENT AND ARMOR
DARK RED BODY/ RED ACCENT
DARK GRAY BODY/ LIGHT BLUE ACCENT